Product Management in India

Product Management in India

Third Edition

Ramanuj Majumdar

Former Professor, Faculty of Marketing
Indian Institute of Management Calcutta

PHI Learning Private Limited

Delhi-110092
2026

In fond memory of ***Shri Asoke K. Ghosh*** *(October 1942 – February 2024), Founder Chairman and Managing Director of PHI Learning, whose vision endlessly inspires.*

The Legacy Continues....

Published by Pushpita Ghosh, PHI Learning Private Limited, Rimjhim House, 111, Patparganj Industrial Estate, Delhi-110092 and Printed by Star Print-O-Bind, F-31, Okhla Industrial Area Phase 1, New Delhi-110020

₹995.00

PRODUCT MANAGEMENT IN INDIA, THIRD EDITION
Ramanuj Majumdar

ISBN-978-81-203-3383-3 (Print Book)
ISBN-978-93-5443-284-2 (e-Book)

The export rights of the book are vested solely with the publisher.

To

the memory of my Beloved Mother

Gita Majumdar,

my role model of a Teacher,

Dr. Sisir Kumar Das

Former Professor, Calcutta University,
and, in particular, to the entire marketing student community
who have been my inspiration and hope that throughout
their professional careers they will find this
book to be their guiding force.

Contents

Part II: Product Management— The Conceptual Issues

Part III: Product Market Analysis

widely acceptedand adopted. I have tried to assess what makes this book different from other books on the subject. I have found a mixture of responses. For instance, some people liked it because of its clear presentation, others seemed to find the examples and cases very illuminating, yet others found it a ready reckoner. I do hope that the new edition would be equally useful to the student community to gather new tools and techniques for understanding product management. I am sure, my marketing colleagues will continue to patronage the book and give me their critical comments from time to time. May I express my sincere appreciations to all of them for their professional support?

I wish to express my sincere thanks to the editorial and production team of Prentice-Hall of India for their professional handling and speedy processing of the Third Edition of the book.

Finally, my heartfelt thanks go to my family members for their support and encouragement.

IIM Calcutta **Ramanuj Majumdar**

Preface to the First Edition

In the eighties, the Indian market offered a large number of options in many product fields. Consequently, marketers adopted many systematic approaches, commonly referred to as *marketing strategies*, instead of relying on instinct or intuition to cope with the new situations. Although there are a few books available today on Product Management written from the perspective of the western markets, they are not appropriate to the Indian conditions. Therefore, it was felt that marketing students and managers required a book that covers concepts and paradigms suitable to the Indian market. This book was written to fulfill this objective. It deals with the various aspects of Product Management, drawing copious examples from the marketing scene in India. The book will be useful for both the students of marketing management and the marketing professionals so that they can have a feel of how products are being managed in India.

The book offers the nuances of Product Management in general and tries to harmonise the conceptual or strategic aspects by presenting varied and real-world problems from the Indian market. In the process, on the one hand it facilitates students of marketing and corporate functionaries to sharpen their analytical and conceptual skills and, on the other, to apply this methodological elegance in setting and achieving marketing goals. For better understanding, examples have been cited from a wide variety of products, and various marketing strategies adopted by leading companies have been mentioned.

The book is organised into two parts: Part I gives an analytical discussion interspersed with vivid illustrations on conceptual issues like branding, segmentation, positioning, new products and planning, and other key elements relating to product management. Part II presents the overall marketing scenario and key strategies adopted in managing twenty selected products. The book begins with an overview of the *emerging panorama of the Indian market* (Chapter 1), highlighting, in the process, recent developments and complexities of marketing operations in India. It then dwells on the topics of *branding* (Chapter 2) as a basic tool for distinguishing one's products from others, and outlines the framework of *segmentation* (Chapter 3) in a macro sense. The text also highlights the different notions of *positioning* (Chapter 4) with the help of examples of some successful brands in India. The discussion on *new products planning* (Chapter 5) deals with the concept of product life cycle and new product launches, and analyses the underlying strategies of some new product successes, and the reasons for some of the failures.

Sufficient attention is devoted to bring to fore the prevailing *changing environment and new opportunities* (Chapter 6) available in the country. The chapter on *distribution channels: structure and strategy* (Chapter 7) explains the various marketing functions of intermediaries and issues affecting selection of distribution channels. An in-depth discussion on *advertising planning* (Chapter 8) highlights the trends in Indian advertising and media planning, which is interspersed with some classic examples of creative Indian advertising campaigns. Issues relating to *pricing concepts and strategies* (Chapter 9) are also analysed. With the help of numerous examples, various pricing programmes, different internal and external factors affecting the pricing decisions, and Government regulations in protecting the interest of consumers are illustrated. Besides, the various aspects of *sales management*, including personal selling and sales promotion, are fully covered (Chapter 10). Also, here the various methods of estimating market potential of a product, and forecasting techniques for predicting future levels of sales are skillfully dealt with. Finally, a brief coverage is given about the utility of *marketing research* (Chapter 11) in Product Management.

Part II (Chapters 12–13) presents the overall marketing scenario and key strategies adopted in managing twenty selected products, namely, tea, soft drinks, cigarettes, toilet soaps, detergents, toothpaste, wristwatches, television, two-wheelers, audio systems, refrigerators, automobiles, commercial vehicles, tyres, paints, paper, cement, air-conditioners, photocopiers and personal computers.

I fervently hope that this book would be of considerable help to the teachers, who will adopt this text, the students of management course, and marketing executives. Any constructive comments for improving the contents of this book will be greatly appreciated.

Ramanuj Majumdar

Acknowledgements

Writing a book of this nature is an arduous task. I was fortunate enough to get help and guidance from a large number of persons and organizations. It is my pleasure to acknowledge them though it is still an inadequate appreciation of their contributions. Though it is not in any sequential order, I acknowledge here the names of those people and organisations to whom I shall always remain grateful.

At the outset I express my profound gratitude to Late Narendranath Brahmachary who has been a constant source of inspiration to me. I am grateful to Srimat Saumyendranath Brahmachary, the present Acharya of Dev Sangha, Deoghar and my spiritual master, who inspired me to take up this assignment of book-writing. From the very beginning, he offered incisive and valuable suggestions which significantly influenced my thinking process.

Thanks are spcially due to my past students of Indian Institute of Management Calcutta whose sharp intellectual power and analytical frame of mind made me to think a lot to answer their queries. In particular, I wish to thank the 32nd batch PGP students such as Arnab Sen, N. Rukmini, Shruti Sardeshmukh, Uma Iyer, Krithika, Tulika Khunnah, Malini Parmer, Rini Dutta, Nilesh, Ramana, Venkata Swami, R. Madhusudan, N.A. Keshav, V. Sriram, Rana Das, Rajesh Jiaswal, Brajesh Kumar of the 32nd batch PGDM and Vishal Bhave, Gouri Thyagarajan, Rohan Prabhu, Anatu Roy, K. Prabhakar, Subhasis Paul, Vinay Bansal of the second batch PGDCM for their significant support extended in the preparation of the various product analyses incorporated in Part III of the book.

It has been my good fortune to meet Professor Russel S. Winer when I visited University of California, Berkeley in 1991. His insights into this subject helped me to revise this edition in many places. Also, my association with the senior-level managers of Unilever Group of Companies in India while teaching the "Marketing in Practice Course" at IIM-C has been especially rewarding. Among them I must mention Harish Manwani, M.S. Banga, Hasit Joshipura, Adhiraj Sarin, who freely shared their practical wisdom which helped me to understand the product manager's job in the changing Indian market scenario. I have assimilated many of their ideas or examples about the Indian market in this book.

To offer a glimpse of the marketing reality, I have deliberately used the names of actual companies, their brand names, and strategies adopted. Those companies whose names appear here should find it a privilege and honour for sharing their data. I take this opportunity to express my deep appreciation for their support. Similarly, acknowledgement is due to many economic journals like the *Economic Times, Financial Express, Strategist*, and others as I have made extensive use of their many articles and reports published. I made generous use of this book in numerous management development programmes. Indeed, the patience of those unsung participants, and their willingness to share market reality has been very useful. I thank this community of practising managers for sharing their thoughts and experience.

The marketing success of this book lies more on the imaginative skills and drive of Asoke K. Ghosh, Chairman and Managing Director of Prentice-Hall of India, and his dedicated team. My special thanks are due to them.

My deep appreciation goes to Rajan of LOGS, and my secretary, Gopinath Banerjee who did an outstanding job to put the manuscript on the word processor. Finally, I thank my wife, Sriya, and son, Rwitajit for their encouragement and patience while I was preparing this edition.

IIM Calcutta **Ramanuj Majumdar**

Part I

THE MACRO PERSPECTIVE

CHAPTER 1

The Indian Market: Emerging Panorama

Till the early eighties, the Indian market was known to have a "license regime", when consumer products market was operated mostly by a large number of Indian companies and subsidiaries of some Multinational Companies (MNCs). In those days leading players used to command a virtual monopoly. Managing any product involved only production planning, at best it required some distribution and logistics planning. As such, marketing of any product was primarily done by intuition or "gut feeling".

In the mid-eighties, the Indian market experienced the first taste of competition when the government allowed capacity expansion and entry of new players in certain product fields (e.g. Maruti Udyog Ltd. in passenger car). It offered some amount of choice to the consumers. To market the added volume and those newly introduced products, marketers felt the necessity to formulate new strategies, commonly referred as "selling approach".

The new economic policies that were initiated in July 1991 changed the entire perspective of the Indian market. It ushered in a new era in the history of Indian market. The magic of liberalization, apart from withdrawing restrictions or the pledge to remove trade barriers, slowly created an atmosphere of free market economy. This change in the national policy led to a paradigm shift in the means and ways of managing any product in India. Consumers soon found a variety of choice in terms of price and quality and hence, they were allured by the variety of promotion and advertising programmes. Like in any free market economy, marketers in India realized the importance of the "consumer" as they started getting a taste of intense competition to retain or expand their business.

Indian Market—A Goldmine of Untapped Opportunities

India with its one billion population size is the second largest market in the world. The Indian economy in the 21st century has seen a transformation (e.g. consistent GDP growth rate over 7.5%, higher per capita income and the government's decision to build a better infrastructure etc.). It naturally drew the attention of the entire world. But the flip side is that India is known as a country with enormous economic, social and cultural diversity. To be successful in India, a marketer has to develop many consumer insights, arising from changing demographics, psychological dispositions, many customs and habits. It is a large market, primarily commodity driven, that is waiting to be tapped. This chapter makes an in-depth analysis of some of the emerging panorama of the Indian market.

RECENT DEMOGRAPHIC PICTURE OF INDIA

Population Size

Exhibit 1.1 shows the population of India as per the Census 2001. The population figure of India is sufficient to attract any marketer to operate here. However, for managing a product, it is necessary to make a proper segmentation of the total market using bases such as age, sex, geographic territory, urban/rural etc. (as shown in Exhibit 1.2 and 1.3)

EXHIBIT 1.1

Indian Market: A Demographic Picture as on 2001

Sl. no.	States/ Union Territories*	Population			Population variation 1991–2001	Sex ratio (females per thousand males)
		Total	*Males* (in thousands)	*Females*		
	India[1,2]	1,027,015	531,277	495,738	21.34	933
1.	Andaman & Nicobar*	356	193	163	26.94	846
2.	Andhra Pradesh	75,728	38,287	37,441	13.86	978
3.	Arunachal Pradesh	1,091	574	517	26.21	901
4.	Assam	26,638	13,788	12,851	18.85	932
5.	Bihar	82,879	43,154	39,725	28.43	921

(Contd.)...

Exhibit 1.1: Indian Market: A Demographic Picture as on 2001 *(Contd.)*

Sl. no.	States/ Union Territories*	Population *Total*	*Males* (in thousands)	*Females*	Population variation (1991–2001)	Sex ratio (females per thousand males)
6.	Chandigarh*	901	508	393	40.33	773
7.	Chhatisgarh	20,796	10,452	10,344	18.06	990
8.	Dadra & Nagar Haveli*	220	122	99	59.20	811
9.	Daman & Diu*	158	92	66	55.59	709
10.	Delhi*	13,783	7,571	6,212	46.31	821
11.	Goa	1,344	686	658	14.89	960
12.	Gujarat 1	50,597	26,344	24,253	22.48	921
13.	Haryana	21,083	11,328	9,755	28.06	861
14.	Himachal Pradesh 1	6,077	3,085	2,992	17.53	970
15.	Jammu & Kashmir 2	10,070	5,301	4,769	29.04	900
16.	Jharkhand	26,909	13,861	13,048	23.19	941
17.	Karnataka	52,734	26,856	25,878	17.25	964
18.	Kerala	31,839	15,469	16,370	9.42	1,058
19.	Lakshadweep*	61	31	29	17.19	947
20.	Madhya Pradesh	60,385	31,457	28,928	24.34	920
21.	Maharashtra	96,752	50,334	46,418	22.57	922
22.	Manipur	2,389	1,207	1,181	30.02	978
23.	Meghalaya	2,306	1,168	1,138	29.94	975
24.	Mizoram	891	460	431	29.18	938
25.	Nagaland	1,989	1,042	947	64.41	909
26.	Orissa	36,707	18,612	18,095	15.94	972
27.	Pondicherry*	974	486	487	20.56	1,001
28.	Punjab	24,289	12,963	11,326	19.76	874
29.	Rajasthan	56,473	29,381	27,091	28.33	922
30.	Sikkim	540	288	252	32.98	875
31.	Tamil Nadu	62,111	31,269	30,842	11.19	986
32.	Tripura	3,191	1,636	1,555	15.74	950
33.	Uttar Pradesh	166,053	87,466	78,587	25.80	989
34.	Uttaranchal	8,480	4,316	4,163	19.20	964
35.	West Bengal	80,221	41,488	38,733	17.84	934

Notes:

[1]The population of India includes the estimated population of entire Kachchh district, Morvi, Maliya-Miyana and Wankaner talukas of Rajkot district, Jodiya taluka of Jamanagar district of Gujarat State and entire Kinnaur district of Himachal Pradesh where population enumeration of Census of India 2001 could not be conducted due to natural calamity.

[2]Based on geographic areas where census could be conducted.

Source: Census of India 2001.

EXHIBIT 1.2

Segmentation

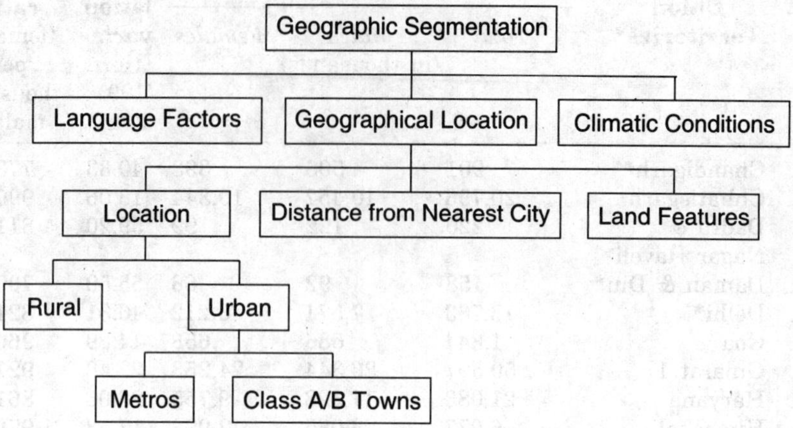

EXHIBIT 1.3

Consumers: Demographic Segmentation

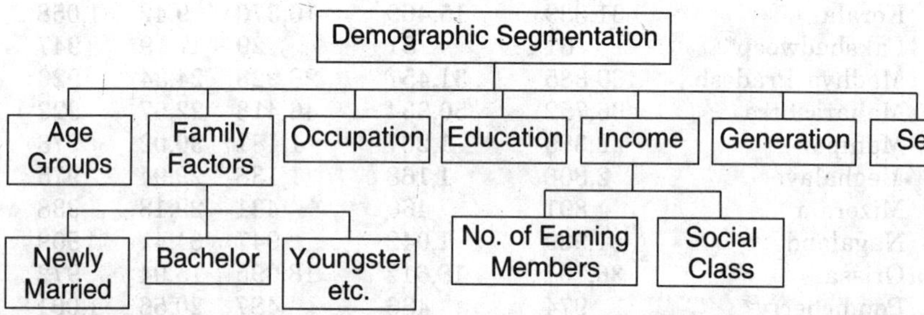

Urban Market

The urban market has always been a prime target of any marketing action because of higher purchasing power and ease of access as compared to the rural market. The Census figures show a massive level of urbanization is happening in India.

Literacy Level

The past few decades have experienced a considerable increase in the literacy level of both the male and female population. The Exhibit 1.4 below shows the total literacy rate and its break-up within male, female population across different States/ Union Territories. It has increased by 13.75% in total and in one state, namely Chattisgarh, the growth is nearly 22%. Refer to Exhibit 1.4 for more details. The rise in literacy level has many implications for marketing, specially for advertising and packaging decisions.

EXHIBIT 1.4

India's Literacy Rate: Across States/Union Territories

Sl. no.	States/ Union Territories*	Literacy rate (2001 census) (%)			Literacy rate (1991 census)	Change in literacy rate (1991–2001)
		Total	*Males*	*Females*		
	India[1,2]	65.38	75.96	54.28	51.63	13.75
1.	Andaman & Nicobar Is.*	81.18	86.07	75.29	73.02	8.17
2.	Andhra Pradesh	61.11	70.85	51.17	44.09	17.02
3.	Arunachal Pradesh	54.74	64.07	44.24	41.59	13.15
4.	Assam	64.28	71.93	56.03	52.89	11.52
5.	Bihar	47.53	60.32	33.57	37.49	10.04
6.	Chandigarh*	81.76	85.65	76.65	77.81	3.94
7.	Chatisgarh	65.18	77.86	52.40	42.91	22.27
8.	Dadra & Nagar Haveli*	60.03	73.32	42.99	40.71	19.33
9.	Daman & Diu*	81.09	88.40	70.37	71.20	9.89
10.	Delhi*	81.82	87.37	75.00	75.29	6.53
11.	Goa	82.32	88.88	75.51	75.51	6.81
12.	Gujarat	69.97	80.50	58.60	61.29	8.68
13.	Haryana	68.59	79.25	56.31	55.85	12.74
14.	Himachal Pradesh	77.13	86.02	68.08	63.86	13.27
15.	Jammu & Kashmir	54.46	65.75	41.82	NA	NA
16.	Jharkhand	54.13	67.94	39.38	41.39	12.74
17.	Karnataka	67.04	76.29	57.45	56.04	11.00
18.	Kerala	90.92	94.20	87.86	89.81	1.11
19.	Lakshadweep*	87.52	93.15	81.56	81.78	5.74
20.	Madhya Pradesh	64.11	76.80	50.28	44.67	19.41
21.	Maharashtra	77.27	86.27	67.51	64.87	12.39
22.	Manipur	68.87	77.87	59.70	59.89	8.97
23.	Meghalaya	63.31	66.14	60.41	49.10	14.21
24.	Mizoram	88.49	90.69	86.13	82.27	6.22
25.	Nagaland	67.11	71.77	61.92	61.65	5.45
26.	Orissa	63.61	75.95	50.97	49.09	14.52
27.	Pondicherry*	81.49	88.89	74.13	74.74	6.74
28.	Punjab	69.95	75.63	63.55	58.51	11.45

(Contd.)...

Exhibit 1.4: India's Literacy Rate: Across States/Union Territories *(Contd.)*

Sl. no.	States/ Union Territories*	Literacy rate (2001 census) (%)			Literacy rate (1991 census)	Change in literacy rate (1991–2001)
		Total	*Males*	*Females*		
29.	Rajasthan	61.03	76.46	44.34	38.55	22.48
30.	Sikkim	69.68	76.73	61.46	56.94	12.61
31.	Tamil Nadu	73.47	82.33	64.55	62.66	10.81
32.	Tripura	73.66	81.47	65.41	60.44	13.22
33.	Uttar Pradesh	57.36	70.23	42.98	40.71	16.65
34.	Uttaranchal	72.28	84.01	60.26	57.75	14.53
35.	West Bengal	69.22	77.58	60.22	57.70	11.52

Notes:

[1]The population of India includes the estimated population of entire Kachchh district, Morvi, Maliya-Miyana and Wankaner talukas of Rajkot district, Jodiya taluka of Jamanagar district of Gujarat State and entire Kinnaur district of Himachal Pradesh where population enumeration of Census of India 2001 could not be conducted due to natural calamity.

[2]Figures shown against Gujarat and Himachal Pradesh have been arrived at after including the estimated figures where the population enumeration of Census of India 2001 could not be conducted due to natural calamity.

Source: Census of India 2001.

RISING INCOME ACROSS ECONOMIC CLASS

Exhibit 1.5 contains the income levels of India, classified into five segments of consumers, since 1995–96, 2002–03, 2006–07 and projection in 2009–10. It indicates a growing prosperity. It also shows that there is rapid increase in the number of middle class population.

EXHIBIT 1.5

India's Consuming Segment

Consumer Segment	Annual Household Income ('000)	No. of Households (in million)			
		1995–96	2002–03	2006–07	2009–10 (P)
Affluent	>Rs. 1,000	0.3	0.5	0.8	1.4
The Aspirers	Rs. 500–1000	3.4	5.2	10.7	15.1
The Middle Class	Rs. 200–500	25.4	27.6	37.5	50.2
The Climbers	Rs. 90–200	44.5	52.8	56.3	63.1
The Deprived*	<Rs. 90	90.2	88.9	82.9	93.4
Total		**163.8**	**175.0**	**188.2**	**223.2**

*Excluding population below poverty line. (P): Projected.

Marketing Implications of Rising Income

While absolute income level of any Indian household is on the rise, more important points to notice are: growing purchasing power of women, participation of children and youth in buying decisions of the family etc. These factors affect the macro-structure of the marketing decisions.

Larger number of affluent people means there will be a huge market opportunity for many premium products ranging from automobiles, electronic gadgets, home appliances, cosmetics, garments to host of branded fast moving consumer goods. Similarly, rising affluence among the aspirers (i.e upper middle) will lead to lots of upgradation in consumer choice. Similarly, middle income consumers generally look for thresh-hold or minimum quality. It would naturally create larger opportunity for many mid priced brands.

CONSUMER TRENDS

With the rise in the disposable income, consumers are found to spend more on personal needs and indulgences. Globally, it has been observed that as the income levels rise, the share of food and grocery in the total household income goes down and the proportion of income spent on lifestyle-related activities goes up. Here too, consumers are found to spend more on apparel, entertainment, eating out, vacations and lifestyle-related activities. Consumer studies show that aspirations of the Indian consumers are converging across Socio-Economic Classes (SEC) and also, coming closer to global trends. Between Socio-Economic Class (SEC) A & B the gap between spending on lifestyle-related activities is declining.

Consumer expectations and lifestyles of people in urban areas are undergoing major transformations. More and more Indians are getting exposed to the western way of living through media and direct visit. With ease of credit facility, the urban market is witnessing a massive upsurge in the level of consumption.

Earlier, consumers used to assess worthiness of acquiring a product by judging its price and affordability. Today, they value a product through a complex equation of judging many new parameters like,

- Quality
- Image
- Convenience in use etc.
- Service
- Payment terms

Consumers are today buying more and more branded products instead of generic commodities. They are buying expensive items as a way of self-expression. For example, improvement in mobile connectivity and reduction in price of cell phones have led to massive adoption of cell phones across urban India. The same phenomenon is likely to happen in case of digital camera, personal computers, laptops and many electronic goods.

Working population among women in metropolitan and larger towns is on the rise. Such people find less time to buy or procure various products for their households. Working women generally tend to prefer a modern trade outlet where they can purchase their household requirements under a single roof.

"Shopping is a pleasure rather than boring experience of standing in a crowded retail market." This statement is most appropriate for a large number of urban people. This is another reason why the housewives are increasingly stepping into the modern retail outlets. In other words, the traditional '*kirana*' stores will have to find some newer elements of attraction to retain their existence.

With increased literacy levels and media explosion, today's consumers are exposed to a whole host of new products. Their expectations have undergone a sea change, moving from purely cost-centric products through value-for-money propositions to higher value offerings. They are willing to experiment and adapt new product experiences. They are able to articulate their aspirations and seek solutions even by paying a higher price. Quality and reliability are the new buzzwords even though prices remain very important. A lot of impulse buying and upgradation in choice is happening and this is not restricted to the young and rich, but across all segments of the market.

Home Shopping

Ease of shopping has become an important factor to reckon with. Shopping through the Internet is the newest trend among urban youth and elite class and is likely to pick up with time.

Credit Purchase

Credit purchase was, once upon a time, confined to very affluent or the poor section of the society. The rapid growth in the use of credit cards has proved this to be a myth. Nowadays, purchasing through credit has become very common. The popularity of credit buying can be attributed to lower interest rate and the ease of getting loan or credit. Also, it is due to convenience of the transactions and the flexibility available to the users.

Explore Opportunities in Children's Market

Earlier, marketers used to give scant attention to the children's market, primarily due to limited direct purchasing powers of the customers. However, the growing size of children segment (see Exhibit 1.6) and recent developments of young India have raised as eye openers.

Today marketers of many products have realized the importance of the children's market segment (i.e. catch them early). The increasing influencing power of the young people, coupled with creation of exclusive communication channels for children, have made this market very lucrative. The marketers are targeting even many household durables at this group of population. As young lots are capable of remembering the advertisements of products, there is a widespread awareness of branded goods. In fact, purchase decisions of many durables are often decided by these groups and hence, communications are developed based on the psyche of young and children in mind.

EXHIBIT 1.6

Future of India: Children Population (below 6 years) as on 2001

Sl. no.	States/Union Territories*	Children Population			Sex ratio (Number of female children per 1000 male children)
		Total	*Males*	*Females*	
	India[1,2]	157,863,145	81,911,041	75,952,104	927
1.	Andaman & Nicobar*	44,674	22,733	21,941	965
2.	Andhra Pradesh	9,673,274	4,926,200	4,747,074	964
3.	Arunachal Pradesh	200,055	102,010	98,045	961
4.	Assam	4,350,248	2,215,104	2,135,144	964
5.	Bihar	16,234,539	8,375,532	7,859,007	938
6.	Chandigarh*	109,293	59,238	50,055	845
7.	Chatisgarh	3,469,774	1,756,441	1,713,333	975
8.	Dadra & Nagar Haveli*	39,173	19,856	19,317	973
9.	Daman & Diu*	20,012	10,394	9,618	925
10.	Delhi*	1,923,995	1,031,584	892,411	865
11.	Goa	142,152	73,547	68,605	933
12.	Gujarat 4	6,867,958	3,656,956	3,211,002	878
13.	Haryana	3,259,080	1,790,758	1,468,322	820
14.	Himachal Pradesh 3	769,424	405,618	363,806	897
15.	Jammu & Kashmir	1,431,182	738,839	692,343	937
16.	Jharkhand	4,796,188	2,440,025	2,356,163	966
17.	Karnataka	6,826,168	3,501,499	3,324,669	949
18.	Kerala	3,653,578	1,861,669	1,791,909	963
19.	Lakshadweep*	8,860	4,488	4,372	974
20.	Madhya Pradesh	10,618,323	5,504,422	5,113,901	929
21.	Maharashtra	13,187,087	6,878,579	6,308,508	917
22.	Manipur	312,691	159,448	153,243	961
23.	Meghalaya	457,442	231,571	225,871	975

(Contd.)...

Exhibit 1.6: Future of India: Children Population (below 6 years) as on 2001 *(Contd.)*

Sl. no.	States/Union Territories*	Children Population			Sex ratio (Number of female children per 1000 male children)
		Total	*Males*	*Females*	
24.	Mizoram	141,537	71,817	69,720	971
25.	Nagaland	280,172	141,852	138,320	975
26.	Orissa	5,180,551	2,656,046	2,524,505	950
27.	Pondicherry*	113,010	57,722	55,288	958
28.	Punjab	3,055,492	1,704,142	1,351,350	793
29.	Rajasthan	10,451,103	5,474,965	4,976,138	909
30.	Sikkim	77,170	38,856	38,314	986
31.	Tamil Nadu	6,817,669	3,515,562	3,302,107	939
32.	Tripura	427,012	216,244	210,768	975
33.	Uttar Pradesh	30,472,042	15,903,900	14,568,142	916
34.	Uttaranchal	1,319,393	692,272	627,121	906
35.	West Bengal	11,132,824	5,671,152	5,461,672	963

Notes:

[1]The population of India includes the estimated population of entire Kachchh district, Morvi, Maliya-Miyana and Wankaner talukas of Rajkot district, Jodiya taluka of Jamanagar district of Gujarat State and entire Kinnaur district of Himachal Pradesh where population enumeration of Census of India 2001 could not be conducted due to natural calamity.

[2]The areas of Gujarat and Himachal Pradesh affected by natural calamities have been excluded.

Source: Census of India 2001.

Growing Focus on the Women Segment

With increase in the number of working women and their disposable incomes, changing lifestyles, women segment has become important for any product manager. Today Indian woman plays a dominant role in purchasing everything for her family. So they have assumed a new focus of attention. One may recall the ad of Asian Paints which showed that a women are making purchase decisions, for products hitherto considered a male domination.

Women as consumers have undergone a transition in purchasing behaviour as well. Today, urban women want to purchase everything under one roof. No longer are they looking for just VFM (Value For Money) in products. With 'time pressure', many of them are looking for VFT (Value For Time). Women by nature are 'bargain-seekers'. (e.g. "*ek pe ek free*"). Be it India or anywhere, she has a great sense of pleasure in bargaining because she feels that the amount of money she has saved is what she has earned.

NEW FOCUS IN MARKETING

Packaging

Along with the improvement in the quality of the product, nowadays, companies are paying a lot of attention to the packaging of the product, because it has come to convey a lot about the quality and the status of the product. Products aimed at the premium segment of the market today come with elaborate packaging. Also, packaging is so designed to increase the utility of the product and ease in handling.

Retail Boom and Emergence of Modern Trade

The opening up of the economy initially brought out a wide range of new household appliances, stylish apparel, and a host of consumer goods. But what the Indian consumer still lacked was a world-class shopping experience: a pleasant, open, relaxing, air-conditioned place to make many family and personal used shopping where one could compare prices, quality and styles without other customers trying to squeeze through the shop doorway or shout over one's head to the shopkeeper or his man.

With the development of infrastructure in the metropolitan and urban areas, a number of modern retail outlets are increasingly noticed across the country. All over India, such retail outlets have already captured 6% of the market. Also in cities, apart from considerable, increase in the number of retail outlets, there is a lot of facelifts given to suit consumers' lifestyle.

The elegant looks of shops, and in general, growth of modern shopping centers have led to significant change in merchandising methods. Special promotion offers have become increasingly important tool to encourage impulsive purchase by many urban customers.

Implications: Various implications of this new class of outlets and payment mechanism are as follows.

- There can be better tracking of product movement and hence, more accurate data leading to better targeting and positioning.
- Impulse purchase of even high value items because of the availability of payment facility through credit cards.
- Consumers get wider choice.
- Standardised quality.
- Convenience for the consumers.
- More comfortable shopping and viewing environment.
- In some cases, one is also getting lower prices, which result from economies of scale, sourcing from the cheapest suppliers and cutting out middlemen from the supply chain.

- Entry of more branded products affects the commodity form of mass produced goods.
- To the extent the big retailers establish a direct linkage with the farmers by cutting out many layers of middlemen, develop the processing facilities and export the products to meet their global requirements, farmers would get better prices and bigger markets while the consumers would benefit in terms of lower prices, better quality, greater variety, superior shopping ambience.
- Consumerism will increase.
- More intense competition among players as well as trading channels.
- Easier for customers to do all their shopping in one place.
- Real estate for retail space are getting more and more costly.
- The consumer may have visited the mall only for fun but the marketer has the opportunity to attract the consumer by proper merchandising, display and POP promotions.
- With increase in scope of organized retail, more new categories of products are like to come into this fold. Until recently food was not a full-fledged category in the organized retail, but there are endless opportunities.
- Kids retailing is growing by leaps and bounds in India and those in the industry say it is likely to see 30–35 percent growth per annum. From clothes to stationary, sportswear, outerwear, tailored clothing, eyewear, watches, fragrance, footwear and accessories, the list is endless. Apparel, however, remains the key revenue driver accounting for almost 80 percent of the total sales of modern retail.

Event Sponsorship

Event sponsorship is fast picking up. It is mainly due to the huge viewership of popular sports, entertainment and television events. This results in direct marketing of the product as well as association of the product with the event leading to increased cognition.

Media

Media explosion has resulted in an unprecedented cluttering of the conventional means of advertising. This has resulted in many marketers trying to exploit different methods of advertising and differentiating their products from the rest available in the market. The most significant and dramatic change that has taken place in recent times is the tremendous growth and expansion of both the electronic and print media in India. Even radio is fast shedding its old image. Thus, mass media like radio has become the most lucrative, effective and far-reaching means of advertising for any company.

Credit Purchase

Buying durable goods in credit has become a regular practice among a section of urban population. It is reported that credit cards and ATM have now made dent into the purse of many youth and middle income segment. Credit cards are being appreciated for the convenience they offer and also, it has assumed a sign of status. Thus, marketers have enhanced his/her appetite for acquisition by making available different forms of buy now pay later offers or deferred payment schemes.

e-Commerce

e-commerce is the process by which an order is placed or accepted via the Internet, i.e. a buyer clicks an order button on the Internet, thereby representing a commitment for a transfer of funds in exchange for goods or service. e-commerce in India is in its infancy. There are some categories of products like rail or airline reservations, books, music, gift purchases which are attracting online sales.

Who Buys Online? Research shows e-commerce has become popular among

- 21–35 years age group; mostly male;
- Students, professionals and executives;
- Owns a PC and accesses the net at least once daily, not just for mail but for other information-related activities as well;
- Purchases out of desire to experiment rather than habit;
- Contrary to belief, most online buyers are moderate net users.

Although sophisticated online payment mechanism will take some time to popularize, they will form an important facilitator of e-Commerce. In future, there will be convergence of media, Internet, cable and satellite networks with mobile telephony. The ease of access to and use of these media will bring about an increase in the size of the market. Such shopping or buying practice will require companies to plan more effectively their nature of offerings and delivery mechanism appropriate to their target market/audiences.

RURAL MARKETING

Rural market contains different nature of diversity. With the growing awareness and spreading media, the rural customers are no longer a homogeneous lot; their needs and expectations are fast changing. However, the most difficult task of a marketer is to understand this change and operate accordingly. Exhibits 1.7, 1.8, 1.9 give some picture of rural market in India. Let us also discuss some of the challenges faced in operating in rural India.

EXHIBIT 1.7

Prospects in Rural India by Income

Consumer Class	Annual Income	1995–96	2006–07
Very Rich	Above Rs 215,000	1.6	5.6
Consuming Class	Rs 45,001–215,000	2.7	5.8
Climbers	Rs 22,001–45,000	8.3	22.4
Aspirants	Rs 16,001–22,000	26.0	44.6
Destitute	Rs 16,000 & below	51.4	20.2
Total		**100.0**	**100.0**

NCAER Projection Based on 7.12% GDP Growth.

Vast population and distribution task: With large population spread across the length and breadth of a country like India, managing a rural distribution network is a big challenge. In today's world an efficient distribution channel is absolutely essential for successful marketing. The sheer volume of the rural market is simply an unparallel attraction to any marketer. But tapping such an opportunity poses an enormous distribution task.

EXHIBIT 1.8

Low Penetration Rates in Rural (per 1000 Households)

Durable	Urban	Rural	Total
• Motor Cycle	77	28	42
• CTV	304	48	121
• Pressure Cooker	635	178	309
• Refrigerator	335	35	120
FMCG	**Urban**	**Rural**	**Total**
• Shampoo	663	352	442
• Tooth Paste	822	449	556
• Health Beverage	324	67	140
• Packaged Biscuits	579	315	390
• Face Cream	429	185	254

Illiteracy: Due to illiteracy or low level of exposure, the communication methods and messages should be properly chosen for the rural consumers than those followed in the urban India. The messages should be simple and yet attractive. Brand creation process should keep in view this aspect of consumer characteristics. Use of colours, jingle and image can help the marketers.

EXHIBIT 1.9

Number of Literates and Literacy Rates (excluding J & K)

	Persons	Males (in thousand)	Females
Total	359,284	229,532	129,752
%	52.21%	64.13%	39.29%
Rural	226,144	151,217	74,927
%	44.69%	57.87%	30.62%
Urban	133,140	78,315	54,825
%	73.08%	81.09%	64.05%

Periodic market: Weekly *hats* are still the prevalent practice of bringing different produce at a common spot in a major part of rural India. The periodicity of such market and lack of developed market place increases the cost of distribution and takes away some of the key strengths of the product. This offers immense opportunity for modern trade to enter the rural India.

Poverty: With low disposable income, the rural customers naturally can afford only the low cost products or may choose to consume a smaller quantity of a product. Marketers need to create products that will deliver value for money to the rural consumers. Advanced technology that will reduce the cost of packaging and manufacturing can be very useful to meet this challenge.

Infrastructure: Lack of infrastructure in rural India hampers the distribution and storage of the product, so it becomes difficult to create a regular market in many of the villages.

Media: The coverage of conventional print media in rural India is still very low. Assuming future penetration of electronic media and print media in the form of bill boards, the design of advertisements meant for the rural customers is a real challenge to any marketer.

Unbranded local made products: With the fragmented market and need for low price product, local small manufacturers are able to attract a large part of customers. A closer understanding of the customer and accordingly adding proper value shall enable marketers to defeat such shoddy products.

UNIQUE ASPECTS OF RURAL MARKET IN INDIA

The unique features of rural India which call for special attention and thus, subsequent changes in the application of marketing concepts are as follows:

(a) **Traditional outlook:** Basic **cultural values** have not yet faded in rural India. The rural consumers still maintain many old customs, values and traditions. Buying decisions of rural folks are influenced by many such social customs, traditions and beliefs.

(b) **Levels of literacy:** As observed earlier, the literacy rate is low in rural areas as compared to urban areas. This comes in the way of the marketer in **promoting the product.** Advertising is very expensive and thus making it difficult to communicate with the target audience.

(c) **Lack of proper communication and infrastructure facilities:** Nearly fifty percent of the villages in the country do not have all-weather roads. The infrastructure facilities like roads, warehouses, communication system, financial facilities are inadequate in rural areas and thereby making physical **distribution more costly.**

(d) **Many languages and dialects:** The number of languages spoken. In particular, rural dialects **vary** widely from state to state, region to region and at times even from one district to another district. Although the number of recognized languages is only 16, the dialects are estimated to be around 850.

(e) **Low per capita income:** Even though about 33–35% of gross domestic product is generated in the rural areas, it is shared by 70% of the population. Hence, the per capita incomes is low compared to the urban areas. Normally, the rural consumers spent a majority of their income in basic necessities, which make them very **price sensitive.**

Marketing Challenges in Rural India

- How to tap the growing rural market with appropriate products
- Rural consuming systems: evolving and emerging
- Storage conditions are not apt
- Problem of dealing with fake/look alike products
- Difficult to reach. Distribution is a major problem as infrastructure is not so much developed
- Totally different set of perceptions and beliefs about consumption of many items. Hence, a different perspective is called for when marketers try to choose their advertising message and promotion schemes for rural consumers
- Segmentation of the rural market has to be done based on age, sex, literacy, earnings, class and caste, occupation of the principal earner of the family, economic prosperity of the region etc. A proper and focused segmentation is required before entry into the rural market.

The vast rural market is witnessing a rapid change. But the marketers here face many unique problems and challenges when they try to penetrate into the Indian rural market.

EMERGING MARKETING ISSUES

The dimensions of marketing are changing and so new issues are to be faced.

- Consumer are becoming more demanding.
- Consumer awareness is increasing and posing new challenges.
- Quality and after-sales service are likely to be given more emphasis by the marketers.
- The rural market is going through transition and has become the latest find of the marketers.
- Powerful retailers, savvy consumers, all challenge **consumer goods** companies.
- Retailing boom in India.
    - Supply chain management issues are going to dominate the Indian market as well.
    - With the entry of international players, there will be greater pressure to perform and be efficient
    - How to increase margins without compromising on the brand value and footfalls? Private label brands or national brands
    - Challenges for the traditional wholesalers and *kirana* shop-owners, how to survive?
    - The bargaining powers of the modern retailer is going to increase which would be a challenge for the marketers
    - Depth and width of the assortments is going to increase
- Increasing media clutter.
    - How to cut through media clutter
    - Developing effective consumer insights and making a communication theme would be a difficult
- Increasing consumerism.
    - There will be problems in differentiating any product and communicating it clearly to the target group
    - Price wars: How to deal with it?
    - Difficult to keep the consumer loyal to one's brand
- Changing consumer behaviour in different segments in India.
- There are fast changing demographic and psychographic patterns. It is difficult for marketers to adapt to these numerous changes. They have to be dynamic to survive.
- The changing aspects of consumer information.
    - *Profile*
        - Demographic/Socio economic characteristics
        - Psychological/Lifestyle characteristics

— *Behavioural*
  – Awareness/Knowledge
  – Behavioural intentions
— *Perceptual*
  – Attitudes and preferences, beliefs, values and opinions
  – Motivation

Hence, it is becoming difficult for the market researchers to find out, compile and infer the data like buyer profile, their preference at each stage of the product development.

- Another problem for marketers is that consumers have become harder to reach. They are busy, more distracted and lead more complicated lives.
- The traditional patterns of family life are also getting sharply eroded with rise in dual income families. It is common to see husband and wife spending a lot of time outside home. Communicating with them and building a community of brand loyalists have become much more difficult.
- New catchments are coming up and hence, the old business centers are shifting to new places making it difficult for the mall owners and retailers to compete. For example, in Delhi lot of new business activity has shifted to Gurgaon, Noida etc. because of which the big retailers and mall owners are facing problems.
- Advertising is becoming less effective due to the advertisement clutter.
- Newer methods of advertisement coming up like bluetooth marketing, mobile marketing, web centric marketing, interactive marketing (e.g. *'pay per click'*). Technologies such as WAP push, TXT triggers, short codes, SMS, MMS and WAP sites will all play a key role in mobile marketing initiatives. Designing for a tiny screen is also a challenge.
- As manufacturing standards increase it will become more tougher for marketers to differentiate their products on quality alone. This is particularly true for any packaged consumer goods such as food, beverage etc.
- Consumers are becoming more environment conscious. Hence, marketers are compelled to give emphasis on the environment friendliness of their products. For example, Nike had to revamp its whole supply chain after being accused of running sweatshops.

Managing any product in today's marketing environment in India is indeed tough. To understand the impact of growing economy, let us consider the cell phone market. Initially any typical service provider of cell phone used to offer only pre and post paid connections. Nowadays, they manage more than twenty need and value-based offerings. Rather than viewing prepaid connection as a single product, the industry has created a number of sub-segments and differentiated each one by the

2. **Credit cards:** As the Indian economy develops, deferred payment mechanisms is gradually gaining popularity with the advent of credit cards. The shift is primarily revolving around changing consumer needs and the evolution of financial markets in the payment service area. As more people are being convinced about the value of credit cards, there is already an explosion of credit cards in India. The real growth of the cards market has happened in the late eighties. Much is owed to Citibank for carefully implanting the concept of marketing which led to acceptance of credit throughout the country. This has helped popularise the card concept enormously. Now the payment services have become more complex and technology driven. As a result this market is at the cutting edge of technology in implementing changes. As people in this country accept the culture of enjoy now and pay out of future expected income, the credit card companies will come up with more innotions. The challenge for those marketing credit cards is to change its image from being just a status symbol to a secure, convenient means and a necessity in daily life for making all kind of payments.

STRATEGIES FOR DEFENDING MARKET POSITION

With entry of new players, whether in the name of new domestic companies or MNCs, the market dynamics in the various product categories is undergoing a sea change.

Any company has only two options—either withdraw or fight. Three warriors do not surrender before a war. Therefore, companies are making new strategies to face the competition. Sharper and focused competitive strategies will have to be adopted. And this would come from honing existing strength and leveraging the first-mover advantage to gain a competitive advantage. Let us enumerate some of the strategies adopted by the erstwhile marketers to defend their market positions.

Strategic Response

Diverse strategies used, (see Exhibit 2.3) are briefly explained below.

EXHIBIT 2.3

Strategic Responses to Defend Market Position

- Pre-empting the competition
- Filling in the gaps
- Strengthening the brand equity
- Synergistic communication

(Contd)...

Exhibit 2.3: Strategic Responses to Defend Market Position *(Contd)...*

- Increasing usage and market expansion
- Becoming futuristic
- Mergers and acquisitions
- Strengthening the distribution network
- Creating hurdles
- Creating price gaps
- Being the leader in a segment
- Selling the brand name
- Quiting the premium segment
- Offering a gamut of services
- Innovation in packaging
- Multibranding
- Exclusive retailing
- Rejuvenating old brands

1. **Pre-empt competition:** Companies are at times strategically re-focusing their marketing programmes with a view to pre-empt competition. Take the example of Philips India. They have attempted to rejuvenate their international image by communicating their international parentage. They have launched a series of international brands in both audio and colour television. Further, they have moved up-market through introducing some domestic appliances and personal care products for higher lifestyle clientele. At the trade level Philips is improving service and trying to penetrate into new outlets. The company is trying to develop its business in India anew using a combination of marketing strategies. The idea is to introduce top of the line models and ranges (to combat possible launches in top end quality) without losing sight of the mass market.

2. **Fill-in the gaps:** Some companies have resorted to plugging possible niches in the market through product innovations and increasing penetration levels as for market leaders the future lies in achieving numbers.

Take, for example, Videocon, which has sought to improve its penetration levels by entering new territories and filling gaps in product quality. Its range is very exhaustive, and covers every possible niche in the television industry. It includes: the 14 inch private for the yuppies, *Bazooka* for the top end consumer, *Turbo Tough* for the middle price segment and *Budgetline* for the economy segment. It launched 25 inch and 29 inch models to compete with the more expensive top end Sony ranges, leaving its other ranges to cope with the value for money segment of CTV targeted by Goldstar.

3. **Strengthening the brand equity:** There has been a spurt in the advertising of old brands to strengthen the brand equity that matters. This is done on the principle that increasing the brand equity of long nurtured successful brands are effective means to defend the flanks when new products pour in. The UB Group, for example, has positioned several brands in every price segment. Though the brands in each segment compete with each other, they aim at defending new competition. The UB Group is adding new brands at a faster pace, in the premium liquor segment.

Titan is another company which used this sort of strategy. After redefining the watch market from the functional to a lifestyle platform, Titan has taken on the challenges posed by the imminent entry of foreign companies by creating watches for every consumer and income segment. It has introduced *Royale* for the upmarket buyer, *Raaga* for women and *Classiques* for executives. Similarly, *Timex* is positioned at the popular segment and *Tanishq* at the super premium end. The company also launched its international watch range, *Insignia* (priced at Rs. 10,000), and silver jewellery watches in the *Raaga* series. Titan's strategy has not only expanded the market but has also fragmented it, making it more difficult for new entrants. They have created barriers to competition by product innovation, keeping prices low, developing a strong brand identity and retailing presence.

4. **Synergistic communication:** The companies are found to devise dual, even multiple, communication themes in order to address specific segments. For instance, Videocon used to stress the Toshiba connection for the double window model and a common man approach for the *Budgetline* and *Turbo Tough* ranges. The company has overcome its value for money image by successfully introducing specific ranges of CTVs and using the name *Sansui,* thereby accentuating its foreign collaboration.

5. **Increasing usage and market expansion:** The companies are trying to increase the product usage by growing the consumer base, offering a better value for money product and evolving new parameters for use.

Cadbury has done just this kind of thing. While repositioning *Five Star,* the company has gone low on "self indulgence" and high on suggesting it as an in-between meals snack substitute. Similarly, the company expanded chocolate consumption by bringing adults into the habit of eating chocolates through the launch of *Perk.*

6. **Becoming futuristic:** Take, for example, the strategy adopted by HUL which test marketed two detergent powders like *Radion* and *Omo* in the early 90s. According to the industry, these brands were not launched as a deliberate strategy. They were likely to be introduced when the time is right and specially to face possible newer entrants.

Johnson & Johnson also has test marketed a baby soap with a similar motive.

7. **Mergers and acquisitions:** Consolidating one's position through acquisition of another company or by merging with them can give a company a substantial competitive edge with respect to manufacturing, distribution and/or encashing on the old brand's name. This is used for both strengthening the current position of the company and for pre-empting the new competition from entering through the same route.

In a similar move Brooke Bond India bought over Pepsi's tomato processing plant in Punjab in anticipation of a possible threat by the international Ketchup giant Heinz. The purchase of Kothari General Foods' instant coffee plant, *Dollops, Kissan* and *Milkfood,* etc. can be seen as a well planned strategy of creating barriers to any new players to enter into this business. Likewise, Hindustan Unilevers (HUL) took over TOMCO as a planned strategy to make sure that their brand equity could be accumulated along with HUL's own brands in the toilet soaps and detergents business. In anticipation of foreign companies entry, Colgate acquired Ciba-Geigy's *Cibaca* brands.

8. **Strengthening the distribution network:** After liberalization and the consequent brand proliferation, distribution equity has provided valuable "extension and reach" to brand equity. Companies like Titan, Ceat, etc are strengthening the distribution channel outlets which bring about the biggest advantage of shelf space. Some companies like Akbarallys, Benzer, Shoppers' Stop in Bombay and Nilgiris in Tamil Nadu are building exclusive retailer outlets which enjoy a good image. This gives them a positive image and rub off their old image.

As fast moving consumer companies try to reach more and more diverse markets, the access to use an established channel of another company offer a lot of advantages, e.g. Birla 3M uses the channels of TTK to distribute its Scotch Brite and Coca-Cola is using some petrol pumps as distribution outlets. Liquor manufacturers have identified pubs to create brand association and position their specific brands.

One could hope to gain credibility and consumer loyalty by naming one's distribution channels. Wipro's channel for Apple's Macintosh is branded *Maxima* whereas PCL's channel is called *Access.*

Having an established distribution system is the major strength of some Indian companies and, therefore, all new comers are trying hard to get quick access to them as they are aware that it will take years to develop an effective distribution network.

9. **Creating hurdles or indirect entry barriers:** As in any game, at times companies create structural hurdles to shut out elbow space to new competition. Blocking off a new brand's access to retail shelf space is one way to keep it out of the market. The Gujarat Cooperative Milk Marketing Federation (GCMF)—the makers of *Amul* butter and *Sagar* brand—have had in the past unleased a promotional blitz for *Amul*

whenever some new company tried to enter the butter market They hike the butter production of the cheaper brand, and start flooding the retail outlets with excess stock. The newcomer thus had to fight for shelf space with two established brands. Typically when the newcomer failed to gain foothold, GCMF used to withdraw *Sagar* and left the shelf space empty for the high-priced *Amul.*

Similarly, media channels is another blocking tactic used by some big advertisers.

10. **Creating substantial price gaps:** The strategy which Bajaj Auto has been following over the years is to keep rivals away by creating a huge price gap that makes competitive products appear overpriced. Bajaj is able to offer the two-wheeler models at lower prices because of its technology. Generally market leaders could earn sufficient profits by following the low-margin, high-volume strategy.

11. **Being the leader in a segment:** Another strategy to prevent rivals away from creating some niche is to simply be the leader in that segment. Colgate Palmolive stayed with its *Colgate Dental Cream* till the market share dropped from 65% to 50% when HUL and other competitors launched gel varieties of toothpastes. The company realised the problem of not being the first in the market and subsequently introduced *Colgate Fluoride, Colgate Tartar Control, Colgate Gel* with red and blue variants and *Colgate Total* This move helped the market leader to regain its stronghold.

12. **Selling the brand name:** The communication strategy of Eveready battery and Bajaj Electricals is based on selling the brand name rather than any specific product benefits. For example, Bajaj Electricals, its *'Jab main chhota bacha tha'* campaign, combines the heritage and the technology value of the brand.

13. **Quit the premium segment:** Moving out of the premium segment which MNCs are most likely to enter is another viable strategy to face competition. Onida decided to do just that. They tied up with JVC and agreed to leave the upper segment to the foreign company.

14. **Offering a range of services:** Of late companies are realising the importance of service. Which is why they augment their offerings by extending a combination of service facilities. SAIL, for example, is a case in part—this giant public sector company has changed its marketing process after the competition came in.

15. **Innovation in packaging:** Earlier the role of packaging was nearly to protect the product. With the proliferation of brands in consumer goods, packaging no longer takes a backseat in the marketing mix. Today with so many parity brands trying to vie for consumers attention and shelf space, attractive packaging has become a necessity. Also because brand loyalty is fast eroding in case of fast moving consumer goods, consumers are resorting to more of impulse buying and are eager to try

new brands. In the light of this tendency, attractive packaging has gained importance. Hence, the companies today are just not catering specific benefits according to their buyer specifications, but are trying to add value by innovative packaging.

16. **Multi-branding:** Companies have adopted a strategy of multi-branding to keep the competition at bay. The idea behind multi-branding is to arrest brand switches away from the company. Besides this, the other resultant benefits are that it gives the company a greater leverage at the retailer end for precious shelf space and at the same time results in economics of scale in terms of warehousing, stocking, etc. The new brand creates excitement and efficiency within the company itself and forces the older brand into action, and the most obvious benefit is that it saturates the market, thereby making it difficult for others to enter. This strategy was used successfully by Hindustan Lever, Procter & Gamble, Cadbury's, Lakme, Brooke Bond Lipton and a host of others.

17. **Exclusive retailing:** Some companies, especially premium products, have switched to exclusive retailing. ITC, for instance, has opened exclusive outlets in key locations in the metros, known as the *Classic Shop* or *Wills Shop*. This is being done more to increase exclusivity of those premium brands.

18. **Rejuvenating old brands:** With the onslaught of new brands being launched in Indian market, and the concept of brand loyalty fast eroding, it is difficult for old brands to maintain their leadership position if it continues to follow the same old marketing strategy. Sometimes brands are found to be unable to keep pace with the changing technology while others tend to suffer from their fuddy-duddy image. These brands usually come with baggage from the past—a set of core values from which they draw sustenance and that is why they still enjoy tremendous brand equity and it becomes easier to revive such brands, rather than nurture some new brands. In other words, rejuvenation is a means to attract those brands keeping in view the contemporary consumer needs and competition. For example, *Vicks Vaporub,* a 100-year-old cold remedy, was relaunched with 'stronger formulation for faster relief'. Similarly, *Dabur Chyawanprash* went in for a change in packaging and advertising in 1993 and the result was that its market share rose to 68.5%. Such rejuvenation by improved aesthetic appeal, new formulations or additional ingredients must be done through market research.

Conclusion

The existing players have over time experimented with a bundle of strategies and have arrived at the appropriate mix, a task that newer entrants will take time to work out.

The coming years will see greater efforts by marketers at understanding the diversities of the Indian market place. At present, it is evident that marketers are wasting no time in trying to retain their equities. The inherent strengths of the existing players lie in distribution and old brand equities. An understanding of the consumer's psyche will be a tough act for newcomers to duplicate. But undoubtedly, some shakeout is destined. In time, fragmented companies will get integrated with marketers giving up their shotgun approach in favour of clearly defined marketing strategies. In case of durables, technology and the country of origin will no longer remain strong base of developing one's Unique Selling Proposition (USP).

CHAPTER 3

Product Management—A Preview

WHAT IS A PRODUCT?

A product is any tangible or intangible offering that might satisfy the needs or aspirations of a consumer. At the time of visualising any product, the marketer thinks of it at three levels as shown in Exhibit 3.1. The most fundamental aspect is the core product, which tries to answer the question of why the buyer should have it. That is, every product tries to offer some core benefits or purpose. The marketer's job is to reveal the underlying motives behind buying the same product. That is, to ascertain from the buyer whether he is really satisfied by having the same product or not.

EXHIBIT 3.1

Anatomy of a Product

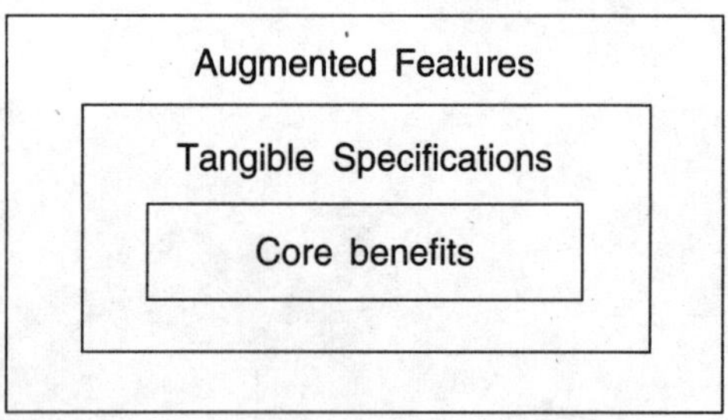

Core benefits: What the product means to the customer? For example, a refrigerator offers the generic benefits of storing, preserving and cooling a food or similar items.
Tangible specifications: Features, colour, design, quality, size, weight, materials used in making the product, durability, operating resource (say, diesel, petrol or electricity) and price.
Augmented features: Company name, brand image, warranty/guarantee for the whole machine or specific parts. It may include dimensions like delivery, easy accessibility, credit, packaging, repair/service facilities.

Alternatively, one may call it the 'generic' requirement. This is what Theodore Levit pointed out when he said: "Purchasing agents do not buy drills, they actually buy its ability to make the same size holes". Similarly, people do not buy shoes to cover their feet. They derive a satisfaction of some feeling—masculine, feminine, rugged, young, glamorous—so the generic need may be excitement rather than sheer feet coverage.

When applying the generic product concept, two key issues should be kept in mind. First, it is the consumer's view of what a given product represents. Thus, a marketer should determine what that product means to the consumer before designing the product. Secondly, aspirations of consumers differ from place to place and time. Thus, the same product (such as a car) may satisfy different generic requirements (such as a means of basic transportation; comfortable in driving and a symbol of success in life, etc.). The marketer should design the product after considering the impact of different possible generic requirements.

At the next level, a marketer usually tries to identify many tangible aspects in the form of features, style, packaging, quality, etc. In the above example of cars, the marketer could offer particular features like fuel economy, elegant design of the machine, driving comfort, external appearance, colour, size, etc., depending on the nature of the buyers.

Finally, consumers are attracted by diverse augmented services—for example, marketers may use their corporate image or brand name, delivery, warranty, credit terms, after sales support programmes etc. The augmented facilities of a computer may be its popular name, the availability of software packages, the services, the warranty, etc. If a company could customize the various types of augmented service in a product, it stands the best chance to succeed in the long run.

CLASSIFICATION OF CONSUMER PRODUCTS

Depending on the tangibility and durability found in an offering, consumer products are typically classified as durable and non-durable are FMCG, fast moving consumer goods (explained later). As the name suggests, service has more of intangibles, whereas durable products offer both tangibility and durability. Non-durable products are normally consumed fast and hence purchased regularly. Here, consumers tend to spend the minimum of effort in comparisons and buying the item.

Consumer products used for personal, family or household use were classified as three types, namely, convenience, shopping and speciality categories by Melvin T. Copeland[1] way back in 1923. See Exhibit 3.2 to have a glance at the various conditions and characteristics of each of these product categories.

---

[1]Melvin T. Copeland, Relation of Consumers' Buying Habits to Marketing Methods, *Harvard Business Review,* Vol. 1, April 1923.

WHAT IS A FMCG?

Fast Moving Consumer Goods usually refer to non-durable products. Examples include soft drinks, toiletries, grocery items, etc. A customer usually spends a minimum of effort to procure them. However, much of astute marketing activities have evolved from this class of products, where consumers show low involvement, get wider choice and allured by a host of inducements.

Based on the prime factor behind their buying, fast moving consumer goods (henceforth called FMCGs) can be further subdivided into three classes:

EXHIBIT 3.2

Classification of Consumer Product

Characteristics	Type of Product		
	Convenience	*Shopping*	*Speciality*
Example	Grocery items	Clothing, fashion items	Fancy goods, applliances
Major motive	Easy availability	Spend effort to choose the item of personal taste	Make long delibe-rations before making the final selection
Knowledge prior to purchase	High	Medium	Low
Effort spent to acquire a product	Minimal	Moderate	As much as necessary
Frequency of purchase	Regular	Season/occasion	Varies
Willingness to accept substitutes	High	Moderate	Low
Buyer behaviour	Little information search	Comparing options to acquire best within budget	Intensive consultation before actual purchase

1. **Staples:** Goods that consumers purchase on a regular basis. For example, a buyer purchases a toilet soap, detergent, sauce, toothpaste and biscuits as and when stocks reach a critical level.

2. **Impulse goods:** Goods that are purchased without any planning or search effort. These goods are usually procured due to external stimulus. Thus chocolates soft drink, and potato chips are displayed in the *Kirana* store because shoppers may not have thought of buying them until spotting them.

3. **Emergency goods:** Emergency goods are purchased when that particular need arises. The requirement for umbrellas arises during the rainy season or pullovers with the advent of winter. Manufacturers of emergency goods will place them in specific outlets so as to capture the sale when the customer requires these goods.

Characteristics of an FMCG from Consumers' Perspective

An FMCG is characterised by a few distinct factors. By its very name one is able to make out the fact that an FMCG has a low shelf life. There are a host of other characteristics which have considerable implications for any marketer. These are now briefly described.

1. **Frequent purchase:** As is obvious from the name itself, these goods lend themselves to frequent purchases by the consumers. A product like salt is bought very frequently. It is an inexpensive product, costing anywhere between Rs 2.00 to Rs 5.00 a kg and is also available in almost all the corner shops which cater to their respective neighbourhoods. It is never stocked at home beyond a level as it is easily available thus making it all the more attractive to buy at all times and even at odd hours!

2. **Low involvement:** FMCGs are by their very nature low involvement purchase decision. When a consumer walks into a shop to purchase a packet of salt or a bottle of tomato ketchup, the consumer rarely makes an effort to choose the item. Even if the consumer is aware of the various brands, of that particular product, should the brand he or she ask for not be available, the consumer will, in most cases, take what ever is offered in its place. Another factor which works in this direction is that there is usually a very large variety of options available in these product classes. So if the brand asked for is not available, the consumer still has a large choice.

There are a few exceptions to this rule. Products like cigarettes, personal hygiene products, although satisfying all the other criteria of FMCGs, are found to command a high level of brand loyalty. Once a consumer gets used to a particular brand of shampoo, consumers do not easily accept any other brand. In the case of personal hygiene products, like shampoos or sanitary towels, consumers do not like to change brands because it is a matter of prior habit or personal liking and as such those group of users form a very brand loyal market. They even go to different shops if the preferred brand is not found at the first shop.

3. **Low price:** FMCGs are usually low priced. However, a consumer may perceive an option to be high priced when tacitly compared to popular brands. For example, the most expensive toilet soap may cost Rs 50. Goods like soaps, detergents, tea, potato wafers etc., are high volume products with a wide potential market base. This feature of low price paid per transaction places these products in the low involvement category. This is another reason why consumers show a limited interest in selecting these.

Characteristics of the FMCG from Marketers' Angle

1. **High volumes:** The market for FMCGs is characterised by high volumes. A medium sized family, for example, may use two to three cakes of soap in a month. If that number is multiplied by the number of such families throughout the country, one arrives at a very large number. The phenomenon is noticed for toothpastes, flakes, biscuits, soaps, chewing gums and so on. These goods are, therefore, manufactured in millions of tonnes. As a result, if a marketer cannot ensure large volume sales, the operation may not be viable.

2. **Low margins:** Because of the high volume and as a consequence of intense competition, these products are usually sold at prices which are very close to their production costs and the margins offered to dealers/distributors on these products are rather low. So, a marketer sets prices as low as possible and ensures turnover through large volumes. Similarly, distributors and dealers operate in low margins which they manage with high volume sales and quick disposal of stock.

3. **Extensive distribution networks:** Consumer preferences in the FMCG products are not rigid. A consumer may ask for a brand whose advertisement he or she has seen recently, thanks to easy recall. Usually a buyer will ask for a product and accept whatever brand is given by the shopkeeper. Even in the unlikely event that the consumer does ask for a specific brand-name, in case the brand is not available, he or she will settle for some other one. In other words, the notion of brand loyalty is not very prevalent among a large section of market. In the case of impulse good consumers will generally require the product only on sight. The consumer allows the shopkeeper to decide for him. In view of such customer behaviour and low loyalty on the part of the dealers, it becomes necessary for companies to make sure that their product is well distributed. With this in mind, most FMCG companies have built up highly extensive distribution networks all over the country. It is because of this reason that a foreign company initially tries to acquire another Indian company to have access to its distribution network. HUL, ITC, Colgate-Palmolive, Britannia, Eveready etc. today have developed extensive distribution networks in India. Moreover, HUL has a very far reaching network in the rural markets. Little wonder then, that *Lifebuoy* is the largest selling soap in the world!

4. **High stock turnover:** A characteristic feature of FMCGs is that they have a very high stock turnover. This is a consequence of the fact that these products are bought frequently and at regular intervals. In other words, these goods have a short shelf life. Shopkeepers, therefore, are willing to trade in these goods more readily because they find a high stock turnover, which consequently allows them to rotate his capital a number of times in a month or so. A pouch retailer, for example, can turn his capital over almost daily. He buys his stocks in the morning and by the time he shuts shop at night, he has regained his investment and more. The next day, the same money is reinvested.

PRODUCT MIX AND LINE DECISIONS

Product Mix

It is the set of all product lines and items that a particular company offers to buyers. The **width** of a product mix refers to how many different product lines a company carries. For example, P & G's product mix in India consists of four lines such as detergents, bar soaps, personal hygiene products and disposable diapers.

The **depth** of a product mix refers to how many variants of each product are offered in the line, e.g. Colgate-Palmolive's Halo shampoo comes in three formulations and three sizes and hence has a product mix depth of nine. This kind of assortment is popularly referred as stock keeping units (SKUs).

The **consistency** of a product mix refers to how closely related the various product lines are in end use. Hence, Nestle's product lines are consistent in the sense that they are all food category products, P&G has an unrelated product mix.

The width, depth and consistency of product mix enables a company to define its product portfolio, appeal to different consumer needs/segments and encourage one-stop buying. A broad width or deep mix goes to satisfy the needs of several consumer groups and maximise shelf-space and sustain dealer support.

A consistent mix is generally easier to manage than diversified mix. It allows the marketer to concentrate on its core competence, build or create a strong image among consumers and trade channels. However, excessive consistency may leave the marketer to a narrow range of business. Example, ITC being in the tobacco business, is vulnerable to environmental threats, the vagaries of business or sales fluctuations if consumer groups are too sharply defined. On the other extreme, companies like Philips, Videocon, BPL, etc. may enjoy the benefit of a diversified product mix. The following discussion will highlight the various considerations taken in deciding the product line.

Product Line

It is a group of products that is closely related because they perform a similar function, targeted at the same customer groups, and marketed through the same channels.

1. **Line stretching:** Decisions pertaining to line stretching are taken whenever the marketer feels he can increase his profits by either adding or dropping items from the line. It can be upwards, downwards or both ways.

Downward stretch takes place when the company finds that its offerings are at the high price end of the market and then stretch their line downwards. For example, P&G's *Ariel* detergent began at premium end and then the downmarket *Ariel bar* was introduced to tap the lower segment.

Conversely, **upward stretch** occurs when a company enters the upper end through a line extension. The reasons for this may be a higher growth rate, better margins or simply a wish to be a full line marketer. An example of a successful upward stretch would be that of *Lifebuoy,* which started from a hygienic bath soap for the masses to a premium quality liquid hand wash for the higher strata of society. Throughout this stretch the brand had used hygiene as its core benefit, so that there was no dissonance in the minds of consumers.

2. **Line filling:** A product line can also be lengthened by adding more items within the present product range. There are several reasons for line filling.

- Reaching for incremental profits.
- Trying to satisfy dealers who complain about lost sales because of missing items on the line.
- Trying to utilise excess capacity.
- Trying to offer a full line of the product.
- Trying to plug holes in the positioning map.

The launch of *Cinthol,* in different variants is an example of line filling. Today *Cinthol* is a lime soap with yellow packaging and a cologne variation with blue wrapping apart from the initial Cinthol fresh. There is also a *Cinthol International,* packed in a red pack with a picture of mountains depicting freshness.

The company needs to differentiate each item in the consumer's mind. For this, each item must possess a difference which sets it apart from the others. We have later on discussed various significant dimensions relating to product positioning and differentiation.

3. **Line modernization:** Even when the product line length is adequate, the line might need to be modernized. The issue is whether to overhaul the line completely or one at a time. A piecemeal approach allows the company to see how customers and dealers react to the new

style. Piecemeal modernization is less of a drain on the company's cash flow. A major disadvantage of piecemeal modernization is that it allows competitors to see changes and start re-designing their own line.

In the rapidly changing market, product modernization is carried out continuously. Because competitors are constantly upgrading their options, each company must redesign their own offering. A company would like to upgrade customers to higher-valued, higher-priced items. A major issue is the timing of the product line improvements so that they do not happen too early and damage the sales of their current product line, or come out too late so that the competition can establish a strong foothold.

4. **Line featuring:** In the case of durable products, marketers at times select one or a few items to "feature". The idea is to attract consumers into the showrooms and then try to get them exposed to other models. At times, the marketer will feature a high end item to lend prestige to the product line. These products act as "flagships" to enhance the whole line.

Sometimes a company finds one end of its line selling well and the other poorly. The company may try to boost the demand for the slow-moving items, especially if they are produced in a factory that is lying idle due to the lack of demand.

GROWTH STRATEGIES FOR FMCG

Keeping in mind various fundamental characteristics of fast moving consumer goods and their markets, let us now discuss the various growth strategies followed by FMCG companies.

Generally, the success of an FMCG depends greatly on its marketing strategy. Typically, a marketer pursues a wide combination of strategies. For instance, when prices are competitive the company would use an extensive distribution network, design suitable advertising and sales promotion schemes from time to time. However, what is it that can make an FMCG brand sell more than its competitor? What makes some outstanding brands? How does a marketer convert a customer from buying a generic washing powder to buying a particular brand, say Surf? Or what makes Lifebuoy a symbol of health for over a century? Let us now discuss various methods employed by the companies in an FMCG market.

1. **Multibrand strategy:** A company often nurtures a number of brands in the same category. There are various motives for doing this. The main rationale behind this strategy is to capture as much of the market share as possible by trying to cover as many segments as possible, as it is not possible for one brand to cater to the entire market. This also enables the company to lock up more shelf space.

Take, for example, the strategy adopted by Hindustan Lever. They have introduced many brands in the personal wash and detergents category so that no segment is left untouched. It has *Dove* in the ultra-premium segment, *Lifebuoy* for the economy segment and brands like *Liril, Lux* and *Le Sancy* for the intervening segments. In the detergents market also, *Surf* itself is available in different forms—*Surf Ultra, Surf Easywash,* apart from the generic product. It has the *Surf* range in the premium segment, and *Wheel* for the economy segment. It has thus covered itself against any form of attack and captured market shares in every possible segment.

Cadbury's has also done something similar to their range of chocolates. It has *Eclairs,* which is positioned in the economy segment, *Break* and *Five Star,* which cost less than Rs. 10 each for popular categories and then it has chocolates with fruits and nuts, crispies and other exotic combinations which are slightly more expensive than the plain milk chocolates. At the premium end, Cadbury offers bigger sizes of its "dry fruit filled" range and it also manufactures gift boxes containing big sized chocolates. *Perk* was positioned as a snack-food. In this way, they are covering wide variety or usages of chocolates.

Another reason to adopt multiple brand strategy is to protect its major brand by setting up flanked brands. Sometimes the company inherits different brand names in the process of acquiring other companies and each brand name has a loyal following. An example of this strategy in the Indian context would be that of *Coca Cola* which acquired *Thums Up,* prior to its entry into the market. Today they have a portfolio of soft drinks, each with a substantial market share.

2. **Product flanking:** Product flanking refers to the introduction of different combinations of products at different prices, to cover as many market segments as possible. It is basically offering the same product in different sizes and price combinations to tap diverse market opportunities. The introduction of shampoos in small sachet has, for example, made them affordable to the lower segment of consumers who previously could not afford to spend anywhere between Rs. 30 and Rs. 40 for a standard bottle of a good shampoo. Although the sachets were initially launched to guard the main brand, surprisingly they have become a big success among new and small quantity users.

The idea behind this concept is to flank the core product by offering different variations of size and price so that the consumer finds some variety of brand to choose from. Stayfree has introduced so many variations of its product where consumers can now buy *Stayfree* singles, doubles, compacts, *Stayfree Regular,* packets of 10 or 20 sanitary towels. *Vicks,* the cough and cold relieving medicine is offered in small containers and also as inhalers, cough drops and cough syrups. They have come up a whole range of the same product in many sizes and prices to flank their main brand, *Vicks Vaporub.*

3. **Brand extensions:** Marketers like to have a loyal consumer base so that those particular brands enjoy high brand equity in the market.

In such cases, companies make brand extensions in the hope that the extensions will be able to ride on the equity of the successful brands, and that the new brand will stand in its own right in the course of time. However, at times, the idea does not work and the result is that the strong preference for the original brand itself gets diluted in the bargain. If this strategy works, it has been of tremendous value leading to the formation of a number of umbrella brands in a variety of products. Brand extension strategy offers a number of advantages. A well respected brand name gives the new product instant recognition and easier acceptance. It enables the company to enter new product categories more easily. A classic example of this is *Lifebuoy* and its brand extensions. Today this brand has a number of extensions like *Lifebuoy Plus, Lifebuoy Liquid* and *Lifebuoy Gold* apart from the regular Lifebuoy. All these brands have been positioned at different segments.

Another example is that of *Amul.* With the success of its first product, Amul milk powder, the company came out with *Amul butter, Amul chocolates, Amul cheese,* cheese spread, etc. and finally added *ice cream, curd* etc. to its portfolio.

An example of the extreme success of brand extensions is that of *Classic Milds,* a brand extension of the premium cigarette of ITC Ltd. At the time when *Classic Milds* was launched, *Classic* was fully entrenched in the premium cigarettes range and enjoyed tremendous brand equity. Within a few months of the launch, the market share held by *Classic* began to slide down. *Classic Milds* became such a favourite that it cannibalised the sales of its own mother brand! Today *Classic Milds* enjoys a much higher market share than *Classic* which has been relegated to the number two slot.

4. **Building product lines:** Some companies add related new product lines to give the consumer all the products he/she would like to buy under one umbrella. Revlon and Britannia have done precisely this. The former company added related products in the cosmetics range so as to offer their customers a one stop shop for all the cosmetics they could possibly need, ranging from moisturising creams to face scrubs and delicately shaded eye colours. Revlon today is associated not just with nail colours and lipsticks, but also with the entire range of make-up and hair-care.

Britannia has adopted a similar strategy. It has introduced different kinds of biscuits and baked foods in the past few years. By adding a number of flavours in each product line the company grew in the industry. Building related product lines is today the market leader in the biscuits and related baked food products industry.

5. **New product development:** Given the intense competition in most products today, companies that fail to develop new products are exposing themselves to great risk. Their existing products are vulnerable to changing consumer needs and tastes, new technologies, shortened product life cycles and increased domestic and foreign competition.

A company can add new products through the acquisition of other companies or by devoting one's own efforts on new product development. With the help of new products a company can enter a growing market for the first time, and supplement its existing product lines. New products could also mean offering improved performance like black & white TVs to colour sets or greater perceived value and replacing existing products or relaunching old products which are target at new market segments. For instance, transistor sets may be relaunched with a view to attract the rural market or customers who wish to catch FM programmes.

Dove is an example of creating an entirely new premium segment. For the first time in India, a soap with "One-fourth moisturiser" was offered to the consumer. It has been positioned for the super premium segment as a skin care product and not as a soap. Dabur, on the other hand, identified an existing consumer need and developed *Dabur Vatika* Hair Oil. Consumer research revealed that Indian ladies mixed a variety of herbs with their hair oil before application. By adding henna, lime, and other such ingredients to coconut oil, Dabur created Vatika as a solution to the above need.

6. **Innovations in core products:** In the FMCG business, the life of a product is short. Marketers, therefore, continually try to introduce new brands to offer some thing new and meet the changing aspirations of the customer. A consumer is also open to try out new options and, on the other hand, brand loyal segment is persuaded to upgrade their choice. Hence it is prudent for a marketer to innovate from time to time both by technological expertise and/or based on the consumer's or dealers feedback. Such innovations are tried out around the core products of a company.

7. **Long term outlook:** Many companies adopt a long term outlook towards growth in an FMCG market. In the process, short term loss might be absorbed for the long term prospects of the company. The historic example of this was the strategy adopted by Kelloggs' in Mexico. The concept of cornflakes for breakfast promoted by Kelloggs' is entirely American in nature. A country like Mexico, which is culturally and ideologically so different from America, could not accept the Kelloggs' offer. However, Kelloggs' with its long term outlook took 28 years before finally breaking even. Today it is the market leader in the breakfast cereals market, enjoying an unparalleled monopoly.

8. **Extending the PLC:** During a product's life, an FMCG company may have to reformulate its marketing strategy because economic conditions change, competitors make new assaults, and, the product encounters new types of buyers and new requirements. Consequently, an FMCG company try to extend the PLC and plan successive strategies appropriate in each stage in the new environment. In the mature stage of the PLC, some companies abandon their weaker products. They prefer to concentrate their resources on their more profitable products and

quickly develop new products. Yet the main loophole in this is due to ignoring the high potential that many old products still have. For example, existing models in products like automobiles, motorcycles, televisions, watches, and cameras in India have experienced a good demand whenever new options were offered. Here, older models become more attractive in the popular price segment or first time buyers.

Similarly, Forhan's was steadily losing its market share when the company decided to go in for a major repositioning of the product. With *Colgate* and *Close-up* coming up with gel variations of their toothpastes, with a much younger positioning, *Forhan's* was being viewed as fuddy-duddy, a toothpaste which was prescribed by the doctor and meant for the older generation. In order to regain the young consumers which the brand had lost to its competitors, Forhan's came up with a brand extension, *Forhan's Fluoride.* Repositioned for the younger generation, the new brand was given a better and tangier taste than the original, with more foam and packaged stylishly. This process extended the lifecycle and the marketer hope to have a larger lease of life for a one-time successful brand.

9. **Expanding markets by usage:** A company usually expands the market for its brand in two ways. That is, either to increase the number of customers or by encouraging more consumption per intake. Note that Sales volume = number of brand users * usage rate per user.

The usage rate of the consumers can be increased in a number of ways. For instance, it may try to educate or persuade customers to use the product more frequently. Archies did this with cards. The concept of sending cards in India was limited to festivals and birthdays. By aggressively promoting cards more as a medium of communication than as a way to send good wishes, Archies has increased the usage of cards to cover just about every occasion and every kind of message. It is now a booming business with Archies recently going into collaboration with Hallmark cards of the U.S.A. to market its cards in India.

Secondly, a company can try to induce users to consume more of the product on each occasion. Say, a shampoo marketer might convince the users that the shampoo is more effective with two rinses rather than one.

Thirdly, the company can try to discover new product uses and convince customers to use the product in more varied ways. *Fevicol* and *M-Seal* were both industrial products till they decided to enter the consumer market. Fevicol came out with consumer friendly small tubes and jars to suit the individual consumer who would not buy the huge packages which were sold to commercial users. *M-Seal* also positioned itself as an all purpose fixer which could be used in places where even *Fevicol* could not be used. By extending their consumer base to the individual consumers and by convincing them of the product benefits, both the companies have greatly increased their market shares. *Keo-Karpin* was initially introduced as a remedy for falling hair. It was later on extended to cover prevention of falling hair also. Finally, it was repositioned as a cosmetic and not just a hair oil. Different ways of styling hair were shown in its advertisements. The usage has increased from that of a pure hair oil, to that of a part of a lady's total styling kit.

10. **Wide distribution network:** A very simple way of increasing an FMCG company's market share is by developing a strong distribution network, preferably in terms of more locations. Once the reach of the product has been extended, it is likely to gain in market share because of its deep penetration. An extensive distribution system can be developed over time, or the company may acquire another company which has an extensive distribution network. As stated earlier, Brooke Bond, Asian Paints, Hindustan Lever, Union Carbide have developed a good distribution network. This stands as the prime reason behind their market leadership in respective businesses.

11. **Monitoring the pulse of the consumers:** Companies spend considerable effort to find out the whats, wheres, hows and whens of their consumers. They figure out all sorts of things about them that the latter are not even aware of.

Well-known companies frequently undertake marketing research to find out more about their consumers and how to satisfy their needs and wants in a better manner. It helps them to monitor the pulse of their buyers so that they are able to identify and/or anticipate the needs of the consumers and be able to satisfy them in a better manner than the competitors.

We may cite here the famous MR study about instant coffee users. When instant coffee was first introduced, housewives complained that it did not taste like real coffee. Yet in blindfold tests, many housewives could not distinguish between cups of instant and decoction coffee. This indicated that much of their resistance was psychological. Researchers decided to design two almost identical shopping lists, the only difference being that regular coffee was on one list and instant coffee on the other. The instant coffee list was given to a different but comparable group. Both groups were asked to guess the social and personal characteristics of the woman whose shopping list they saw. The comments were pretty much the same with one significant difference: a higher proportion of the housewives whose list contained instant coffee described the subject as "lazy, a spendthrift and failing to plan well for her family." These women obviously were imputing the fictional housewife in to their own anxieties and negative images about the use of instant coffee. The instant coffee company now knew the nature of the resistance and could develop a campaign to change the image of the housewife who serves instant coffee. The lesson seems to be that an FMCG marketer must examine the buyers mind regularly.

12. **Advertising and media coverage:** Advertising is required to build awareness about an FMCG or brand which is available in the market

but not many people might know about it. Informative advertising figures heavily in the pioneering stage of a product category, where the objective is to build primary demand.

Persuasive advertising becomes important in the competitive stage, where the company's objective is to build a selective demand for a particular brand. Most advertising falls into this category. For example, Pantene shampoo attempts to persuade consumers that it delivers more benefits than any other brand of shampoo. Marketers try to establish the superiority of its brand through specific comparisons with one or more brands in the product class.

Reminder advertising is quite common with mature products. Expensive four colour *Coca-Cola* ads in magazines do not have the objectives of informing or persuading buyers. Perhaps it tries to remind people to purchase *Coca-Cola*. A related form of advertising is reinforcement advertising, which seeks to reassure current purchasers that they have made the right choice.

The basic idea about growth through advertising by a company is to increase market share through more share of mind as more information about the company and its products will induce the viewer at the time of actual demand.

13. **Sales promotion:** Sales promotions offer a direct incentive to buy more in the short term. They are designed to stimulate quicker and/or greater purchase of particular products by consumers or the trade. However, a few points have to be kept in mind. They yield faster and more measurable responses in sales than advertising does. They mainly attract the deal prone consumers who switch brands as deals become available. Loyal buyers normally do not change their brand as a result of competitive promotion.

A classic example of sales promotion is that of the Maruti car filled with *Nescafe* coffee packets. The consumers were given forms to fill in and among other things were asked to guess the number of packets of coffee stuffed in the car. The car was finally awarded to the person whose guess was closest to the actual.

Pepsi has been doing a large amount of promotions since the time it entered India. *Pepsi* cassettes and T-shirts have been offered to young people all over the country. The *Pepcard* was the first of its kind in the country. Promotions like "Aishawarya is coming to your home" and "You could be the 13th man" with Sachin Tendulkar have all been a part of the many innovative campaigns carried out by this company.

MANAGING LINE EXTENSIONS—A CLOSER LOOK

There are several factors which can explain why so many companies have pursued line extensions as their marketing strategies. These are now discussed.

1. **Customer segmentation:** *Managers perceive line extensions as a low-cost, low-risk way to meet the needs of various customer segments* and by using more sophisticated and lower-cost market research and direct marketing techniques, they can identify and target finer segments more effectively than ever before. In addition, the quality of audience-profile information for television, radio and print media has improved; managers can now translate complex segmentation schemes into effective advertising plans.

2. **Consumer desires:** Consumers are switching brands and trying products they have never used before. *Line extensions try to satisfy the desire for "something different" by providing a wide variety of products under a single umbrella.* Such extensions, companies hope, fulfill customer desires while keeping them loyal to the brand franchise. The Gujarat Milk Marketing Federation launched a host of milk-based products under the brand name *Amul.* Similarly, Smithkline Beecham made an entry into the faster growing brown beverages segment with its Chocolate *Horlicks* brand to counter the established Cadbury's brand *Bournvita.*

Line extensions can help a brand increase its share of shelf space, thus gaining higher visibility and attracting consumer attention. *When marketers coordinate the packaging and labelling across all items in a brand line, they can achieve an attention-getting billboard effect on the store shelf or the display stand and thus leverage the brand's equity.* However, building enough volumes to offset the additional costs required for such extensions is also necessary.

3. **Pricing breadth:** Marketers often extend the line on superior quality platform and set higher prices for the new offerings than their core items. In markets subject to slow volume growth, marketers can increase unit profitability by attracting current customers move up to the "premium" products. *In this way a marketer also lends "prestige" to its product-line.*

Similarly, some line extensions are priced lower than the lead product. For example, American Express offered its *Optima* card for a lower annual fee than its standard card. *Extensions give marketers the opportunity to offer a broader range of price-points in order to capture a wider audience, and*—thereby serve as "volume builders."

4. **Excess capacity:** On some occasions companies added new product lines to make use of their excess capacity or to improve efficiency and the quality of existing products. In fact, excess capacity encourages the introduction of line extensions that require only minor adaptations to current products.

5. **Short-term gain:** *Line extensions offers the most inexpensive and least imaginative way to increase sales quickly.* The development time and costs of line extensions are far more predictable than they are for altogether new products. In fact, few brand managers are willing to

spend the time or assume the career risk of introducing new products in this crowded market.

6. **Competitive intensity:** Mindful of the link between market share and profitability, managers often see extensions as a short-term competitive device that increases a brand's control over limited retail shelf space and, *if overall demand for the category can be expanded, also increases the space available to the entire category.*

7. **Trade pressure:** The proliferation of retail channels for consumer products compels marketers to offer broad and varied product lines. Retailers object to the proliferation of marginally differentiated and "me too" line extensions *or additional stock-keeping units (SKU). They, instead, demand special package sizes to meet their specific customer demand* (for example, bulk packages or multi-packs of low-price variety). or derivative models that impede comparison shopping by consumers.

8. **Energizing a brand:** *A line extension can be an effective way to make a brand more relevant, interesting, and visible.* In doing so, it can create a basis for differentiation, build the audience for the advertising of an old brand (though the brand may be healthy), and stimulate sales, This would give new as well as old customers sufficient reason to buy the brand.

9. **Exploitation of variety fulfillment:** A brand may be stretched across multiple product categories to take advantage of a common and important consumer benefit existing in both, the products and the consumer perceptions. This is the common benefit of exploitation strategy which ensures that sales in the other categories do not affect the parent brand. Line extensions can also increase a brand's consumer share of requirements within a given product category.

10. **Expanding a brand's core promise to new users:** A brand may have a strong image that promotes loyalty and exclusiveness. A line extension can extend that promise. In fact, line extensions can perform the role of continually improving the core brand. Intelligent line extensions may be used as means to attract users who buy multiple brands.

11. **Managing true innovation:** Line extension is an effective way to foster and manage true innovation, thereby enhancing the value proposition, expanding the usage contexts, and blocking competitive entry.

12. **Blocking or inhibiting competitors:** Although niche markets may represent marginal businesses, they may strategically represent important footholds for competitors. Line extensions have the potential of inhibiting or neutralizing moves by competitor. Failure to see this aspect may result in adverse consequences for market leaders, as can be seen from what happened to companies like Tomco, Calcutta Chemicals, etc. who permitted new companies to gain a toehold in their respective industries.

INTRODUCTION

In order to manage any product, a marketing manager needs to systematically develop the various elements of the marketing programme, such as branding, segmentation, positioning and differentiation, new product development, distribution, advertising planning, pricing, sales management, and marketing research. This constitutes the total marketing programme. We present these concepts one by one in Part II.

CHAPTER 4

Branding

The word "brand" owes its origin to the Norwegian word "brandr" which means to burn. Cowboys used to put some identification mark on the body of their livestocks to distinguish their respective possession. In marketing parlance we say products are what companies make, but customers choose the brands. Therefore, marketers resorted to branding in order to distinguish their offerings from similar products (services) provided by their competitors. Additionally, it makes an inherent assurance to the customers that the quality will be similar in every purchase of the same brand.

Products are made the brand is what gives them meaning and purpose telling us how a product should be viewed. It defines what and how much to expect from the products bearing its name.

WHAT IS BRANDING?

Branding is a process, a tool, a strategy and an orientation.

- Branding is **the process by which a marketer tries to build long term relationship with the customers** by learning their needs and wants so that the offering (brand) could satisfy their mutual aspirations.
- Branding can be viewed as a tool to position a product or a service with a consistent image of quality and value for money to ensure the development of a recurring preference by the consumer. It is common knowledge that the consumer's choice is influenced by many surrogates of which the most simple one is a brand name. Although there may be equally satisfying products, the consumer when satisfied with some brand does not want to spend additional effort to evaluate many other alternative choices. Once he or she has liked a particular brand, he or she tends to stay with it, unless there is a steep rise in the price or a discernible better quality product comes to his/her knowledge which prompts the consumer to switch the brand.

- Branding is used as a differentiation strategy when the product cannot be easily distinguished in terms of tangible dimensions (which invariably happens in case of many non-durables, services and even durables) or in products which are perceived as a commodity (e.g. cement, fertilizer, salt, potato chips etc). In all such situations marketers use branding as a differentiation strategy and try to develop an intimacy with target customer. That is, they try to develop and deliver customized products and auxiliary services with tailor-made communications to match with the customer's self-image. Such differentiation is an on-going process and the initial and on-going actions are depicted in Exhibit 4.1.

EXHIBIT 4.1

Differentiation Mechanism in Brand Building

Means	Initial step	Ongoing actions
Core product or service	• Highlight distinct benefits like contents, design etc.	Use the tangibles or positioning to create an identity
Auxiliary services	• Exceptional handling • Efficient packaging • Innovative promotion, communication • Use channel and ensure push	• Loyalty development programmes • Retain customer interest by repeated communication • Develop customer pull by different marketing mix.

- Brand building is **a conscious customer-satisfaction orientation process.** The brand owner tries to retain customers to its fold by a mix of hardware and software because when a customer feels satisfied he/she develops a kind of loyalty for the same. Therefore, a strong brand, apart from name, symbol or design, ensures quality, stability of assured future market and effective utilisation of an asset. Further, a strong brand which retailers are also keen to stock because of high customer pull. In long run it provides the owner of the brand with a platform for the sale of additional products, called brand extensions.

Benefits from Building a Brand

Brand facilitates consumers to ease decision making and uncertainty because it encapsulates its identity, origin, specificity, guarantee and difference. In turbulent markets where choice is constantly evolving, brand provides a haven of stability, ensures an identity and promises of quality or guarantee. **Though products may change, the spirit of the brand remains the same.** The brand owner is able to earn an easy recognition and image compared to makers of commodities or unbranded products. Thus, the value of creating a brand has been accepted in principle. And it is of late given the status of an intangible asset. Thus, there is not much dispute that a brand has a value, the problem lies in how to create such a brand.

Brand building begins with a consistent, integrated vision. Its central concept is brand identity or the brand image. The identity must be defined and managed. It is the heart of brand management. It calls for innovative thoughts and continuous efforts.

STRATEGIC RELEVANCE OF BRANDING

Brand is thus much more than the name per se or the creation of an external indication that the product or service has received an organisation's imprint or its mark. Exhibit 4.2 outlines the strategic relevance and logic of branding.

EXHIBIT 4.2

Strategic Relevance and Logic of Branding

A brand

- aims to segment the market
- starts with a big idea
- has an enduring value
- tries to protect its innovation
- is a living memory
- shall sustain though the product may die

A Brand Aims to Segment the Market

Brand building is part of a strategy aimed at differentiating the offering and in the process try to fulfill the expectations of specific groups of customers. They do so by consistently and repeatedly providing combination of attributes—both tangible, practical and symbolic, visible and invisible value—under conditions that are economically viable for the company. The company wants to leave its mark on a given field, and sets its imprint on the particular offering.

A Brand Starts with a Big Idea

The first task in branding building: defining just what the brand infuses into the product or service. **Branding, however, is not based on**

what goes on, but what goes **in.** The result is an augmented product or service which must be indicated in one way or the other if it is to be noticed by potential consumers, and if the company is to reap the fruits of its efforts before it is copied by others.

The first task is to define precisely all that the brand injects into the product and how the brand transforms it. So any marketer should questions like;

- What attributes matter to a customer?
- What advantages are created?
- What benefits emerge?
- What obsessions does it represent?

A Brand has an Enduring Value

If a brand is merely a label, then such a product would lose its value as soon as it loses its sign of brand identification. Instead, it continues to incarnate the brand: the brand's passing presence has transformed the product. This explains the value of Lux soap when it carries the HUL label for more than 75 years; similarly, Adidas shoes, stripped of its name, will hardly see much consumer pull. They are worth more than counterfeit imitations because the brand image is present even when it cannot be seen. In contrast, though the brand level may appear on an imitation, it will actually miss the undercurrent of consumer's personal attachment with the offering.

A Brand Tries to Protect Your Innovation

Brands become known through the products they create and bring on to the market. Whenever a brand innovates, it generates 'me-too-ism'. Any progress made quickly becomes the standard to which buyers become accustomed to. Competing brands most often follow through and at times bring out improved versions as they do not want to fall beneath the market expectations. For a short time, an innovative brand enjoys monopoly, but it will be a fragile one unless the innovation is patented or patentable. In other words, the role of brand name is to protect the innovation—it creates a "mental" patent. This is nothing other than the just reward for innovation, making an effort, and taking risks. A snapshot of a given market will often show similar products. A dynamic vision, however, reveals who has innovated and pulled the competition along in the wake of its success.

A Product may Die but the Brand will Sustain

A brand protects the innovator, granting momentary exclusiveness and rewarding the willingness to take risks. Brands cannot be reduced to a symbol or a product or a merely graphic and cosmetic exercise. A brand is the signature on a constantly renewed, creative process. Products are introduced, they live and disappear, but the inner or core value of the original brand endures. This consistency of creative action is what gives the brand its meaning, its contents and its character. Creating a brand requires time to build up that identity.

A Brand is a Living Memory

According to Kapferer[1], "The spirit of the brand can only be inferred through its products and its advertising. The content of the brand grows out of the cumulative memory of various acts, provided they are governed by a set of unifying ideas or guidelines. The importance of memory in encompassing a brand explains why its image can vary structurally between generations. It is precisely because a brand is the memory of the products that it can act as a long lasting and stable reference point."

BRAND NAME SELECTION

The selection of a proper brand name is the first major step in managing a product. The branding of a product is like naming a new-born child. It basically serves to identify the offering. A brand name could be any word, term, sign or symbol that identifies and distinguishes one product from another. For example, it could be

- a word with no meaning related to the product it represents, viz., *Nirma, Titan, Vimal, Surf, Nescafe,* etc.
- the name of the manufacturer of the product, viz., *Bajaj, Godrej. Tata, Levy, Nokia, Sony,* etc.
- a combination of numerals and alphabets, viz., Nokia 1100, *KB 100, LIV 52,* or a word whose meaning suggests some function's or quality of the product. For example, brand names like *Quickfix* (adhesive), *Band-aid* (bandage), *Duroply* (plywood), *Sunflame* (gas stove), etc. indirectly indicate the use of the product. Similarly, brand names for cosmetics should preferably suggest beauty and glamour. Brand names for food products could convey a message of taste or health.

A brand name may manipulate the buyer's perception about the product. Brand names are often useful in establishing an overall product concept. Occasionally, a brand name becomes the generic name of that product (e.g., in the early seventies brand names like Surf and Dalda used to be synonymous with detergents and vegetable oil). A good brand name has a mnemonic quality, something that sticks in the buyers' mind. At times, consumers even derive some recognition and status from using certain brands. In the case of products like textiles, cigarettes or television, the brand names Vimal, India Kings, and Sony may project an aura of

[1]Jean–Noël Kapferer, *Strategic Brand Management* (Kogan Page, 1992), p. 52.

success. Customers here seem to buy the total symbolic meaning or the "image" which the brand conveys.

In a country like India where literacy is still low, branding plays a major role in communication. Apart from identifying the marketer/producer of the product, branding assures the buyer of some uniform quality leading to repeat purchases. Brand names are usually registered under the Indian Trade and Merchandise Act for protection against imitation.

Criterion for a Good Brand Name

The selection of brand names is closely related to the desired positioning and a number of other considerations. As mentioned above, **a good brand name should basically possess qualities of distinctiveness. That is, it should be short, noticeable, impressive, easy-to-remember and should stand out among a host of competing name.** For example, names like Usha, Lux, Rin, Vim, etc., satisfy the condition of being short and easy-to-remember words. Brand names like *Hero Honda, Intel, Amul,* etc., have earned a reputation for good quality. In selecting a brand name, managers should ask themselves what they want to achieve from it. Should it be descriptive, reassuring, evocative or should it convey certain qualities or benefits derived from using these products? Generally, a good brand name should be:

- short, simple and easy to pronounce;
- easy to recognise and remember;
- pleasing when pronounced;
- not offensive, obscene or negative;
- adaptable to packaging, labelling requirements and to any advertising medium; and
- contemporary.

Companies' Perspective on Brand Names

Companies follow different policies in choosing brand names for the wide range of products they market. These are briefly discussed here:

1. **Individual brand names:** Some companies choose distinct names for each of their offerings. For instance, Hindustan Lever, Titan, Bata etc., have been following this method of giving different names to each of their products. There are many reasons why some companies do this. Firstly, products marketed by a company may become diverse and hence, require distinct names. Secondly, they may wish to market their offering to a combination of different market segments. Sometimes they may have multiple brands of a product, which compete with each other. It makes sense to pursue this strategy of individual brand names for each offering. In the footwears business Bata has a large number of brands covering almost all price segments and this enables it to have inter brand competition; in the process a competitor will find it very difficult to carve out a niche.

2. **Family branding:** Some companies prefer to use a common or successful family name, also known as **umbrella branding,** for several products. For instance, *Ponds* is a mother brand name used for shampoos, talcum powder, cold creams and toilet soaps, etc. Family brand strategy is usually pursued to derive the best advantage of the goodwill attached to some erstwhile successful brand name. For example, the name *Amul* has been used to market a large variety of dairy products. Similarly, the success of *North Star* led to Bata using this common name for a host of casual footwear, T-shirts and bags.

The use of the family branding strategy does not always guarantee success. There are many instances where this strategy has failed. Ponds launched its toothpaste, using the distinctive flowered pink packaging which is associated with its talcum powder with the same family brand name. Market survey revealed that this toothpaste had failed despite Pond's name. Similarly, the success of *Maggi* noodles probably prompted Nestle India Ltd., to launch their sauces under the same brand name. But this apparently caused some problems to many consumers. It is even confusing the shopkeepers in making out whether a consumer is asking for *Maggi* noodles or *Maggi* sauces. Though it may be argued that these cases of failure are due to other deficiencies, it is a fact that despite using an established family brand name, these products failed. The lesson one derives from these cases is that it is risky to launch a new product under the brand name of another highly successful product. In fact, if successive products under a family brand name do not perform well, the established goodwill or image may suffer. The strategy of using a common family brand name will be perhaps more effective in marketing new variations of the basic product. For this reason, New *Liril, Cinthol* soap with an improved perfume, and *Cherry Blossom* in liquid form were well accepted in the Indian market.

3. **Corporate name:** Some companies have been found to utilise their corporate name or logo together with some brand names of individual products. For instance, the corporate name of *Godrej, Tata* etc., have been used to market a wide variety of products. Similarly, manufacturers of paints, textiles and several industrial products often resort to this practice.

4. **Alpha-numeric names:** In industrial products, an alpha-numeric name often signifies its physical characteristics, performance and technical specifications. In marketing products like machinery, two-wheelers, personal computers, etc., the use of alpha-numeric names often enables companies to distinguish variations in different models, features, etc. Organisations like, Nokia, Bajaj Auto, markets have resorted to this practice to create some distinctive identity of their products.

Imitation of Brand Names and Consumer Confusion

Every marketer of a successful brand is a potential victim of imitation. The malady of imitation especially afflicts the low unit price, high turnover, low-technology based products. For example, in the antiseptic cream market, *Burnol* is apparently sold in packs of similar shape, size and colour using names like *Bernol* and *Burnil.* Mostly it is the small and regional companies who imitate and survive in the shadow of national brands. Imitated goods are generally marketed by offering higher margins to distributors. Imitation items get an easy entry when the purchase is not very important to the consumers or when they are not very quality/brand conscious, or when they are unable to distinguish between two look-alike brands.

Trademarks

Popular brands are often susceptible to imitation. A trade mark is a legal right to protect a particular name or mark, used by many marketers to assure the customers that they are purchasing an authentic brand at a time when piracy is evidently on the rise. Registration at the patent office confers upon the proprietor a statutory right to exclusive use of that name or mark. It is meant to guard against ditto imitations.

CREATING A BRAND

All brands invariably start life as some up-coming brands. Over the years, they are popularly known as major brands, established brands, powerful brands, etc. Let us pose the question: What established brands have—or what they have done—which the other brands have not? Each has a clear identity and a well determined knowhow. They acquired a brand personality and a system of values—and authentic brand culture—and they establish a relationship, a reflection of a consumer's self image. All these qualities enhanced their position. Every established brand seemed to move in a set direction. These brands were motivated by a precise source of inspiration and by recognition of where they were going in terms of those products or services which they were willing to encompass and set their name on. The best way for a new brand to succeed is to carry the mantle from the old brand, if any.

Brand Launch vs. Product Launch

The confusion between a brand and a product launch arises from situations where a brand is arrived at by chance. Most of the reputed brands, rich in meaning and values, started life as a simple name on an emerging product. The new product is given a name so that it can get public attention. After a period of time, the product becomes obsolete and is replaced by another brand having a better performance. This new product inherits the reputation already attached to the existing name. **Thus a product's form may change, but the brand identity remains.** So at the outset, the firm boasted the merits of the initial product. With the natural waning of the product over a period of time, notice is given to the resurgence, improvement and change in the form of the product with better performance under the same name. This signals the birth of a new offering or a brand launch. While advertising or another marketing mix helps to achieve the bottomline, the brand, however, does the work.

Thus, in launching a new brand one must look upon it from the outset as being truly a brand, and not merely the name of the product which one sees in advertising. One must wait for the name of the product, which in the longer term is a deep symbol, imbued with the meaning which goes far beyond the product itself.

PRINCIPLES OF BRAND CREATION

It is not advertising which speaks of the product—rather, it is the brand. While considering the launch of a new product, the pertinent questions are those making up the classical copy strategy.

Defining brand identity does not simply boil down to a definition of a brand's personality or character. An analysis of all powerful brands shows that they are not entirely restricted. They also have a culture, a system of values, and propose a specific type of relationship, consumer's reflection and self-image. The spirit of a brand grows out of cumulative memory of various acts, provided they are governed by certain unifying ideas or guidelines.

Choosing Products with a Meaning

The more ambitious the brand, and its system of values, the greater the degree of care required in choosing the product or service to launch the brand campaign. This should centre on the product which best represents the brand's intention—the one which best supports brand potential to bring about change. Product features here serve as a potential support for the brand. The whole meaning and direction of a company can be explained by its brand management effort.

Brand Language and Role of Communication

Brand identity is rich in meaning. It cannot be reduced to a mere word or concept. Even if, for the purpose of a campaign, a concept of communication is seized upon, the brand still shines forth through the other facets of its identity prism.

Brand language allows the brand to hold forth more freely. Through a lack of personal language, communications are too often locked into a strangling corset. The code might be artificial but the language is natural. **All communication must express the product's specific attributes—personality, culture and value and allow the brand to be presented in an appealing** way.

Brand language finally serves as a means of decentralizing decisions. Guided by a unified format in which to express themselves, different subsidiaries worldwide can adapt the theme of their message to the local market and product requirements while respecting the singularity and indivisible nature of the brand. As such, brand identity must reconcile freedom and coherence. They must also specify dominant aspects of style, literal and visual.

Brand Equity

The equity of a brand is measured by the awareness and image which it evokes. This is a natural measurement, since the brand is the symbol. Brand awareness relates to the number of persons who recognize the brand's significance and who are conscious of the promise which the symbol expresses. The aim of advertising is to reveal the meaning of the brand and to spread it as far and as wide as possible in order to encourage consumers to try the products offered.

The decision as to which of these different levels of awareness should be pursued depends on the way in which customers are expected to make their choice, and the degree of the personal involvement.

In markets, where the product category is still finding its feet, the first brand to spread its message far and wide benefits from what is called "pioneer advantage". It must be emphasized that the pioneer advantage exists only if an innovating brand gives a satisfying performance. Otherwise, it is better to refrain from any form of communication, in order to avoid becoming the negative stereotype of the market.

HOW TO BUILD A BRAND?

Exhibit 4.3 shows brand building in the form of a flow diagram. The model may be used to illustrate the salient steps of various inputs, assessment and outcome.

Inputs

- Identification of key customer groups or segments.
- Understanding customer expectations, needs and aspirations.
- Assessing competitive offering including substitutes.
- Building customer confidence by
  - — customizing the product,
  - — establishing key image of the brand,
  - — dealer support—easy availability and push,
  - — innovative communication and promotion schemes, and
  - — elegant packaging.
- Total brand management—both hardware and software aspects

EXHIBIT 4.3

Brand Building—A Conceptual Framework

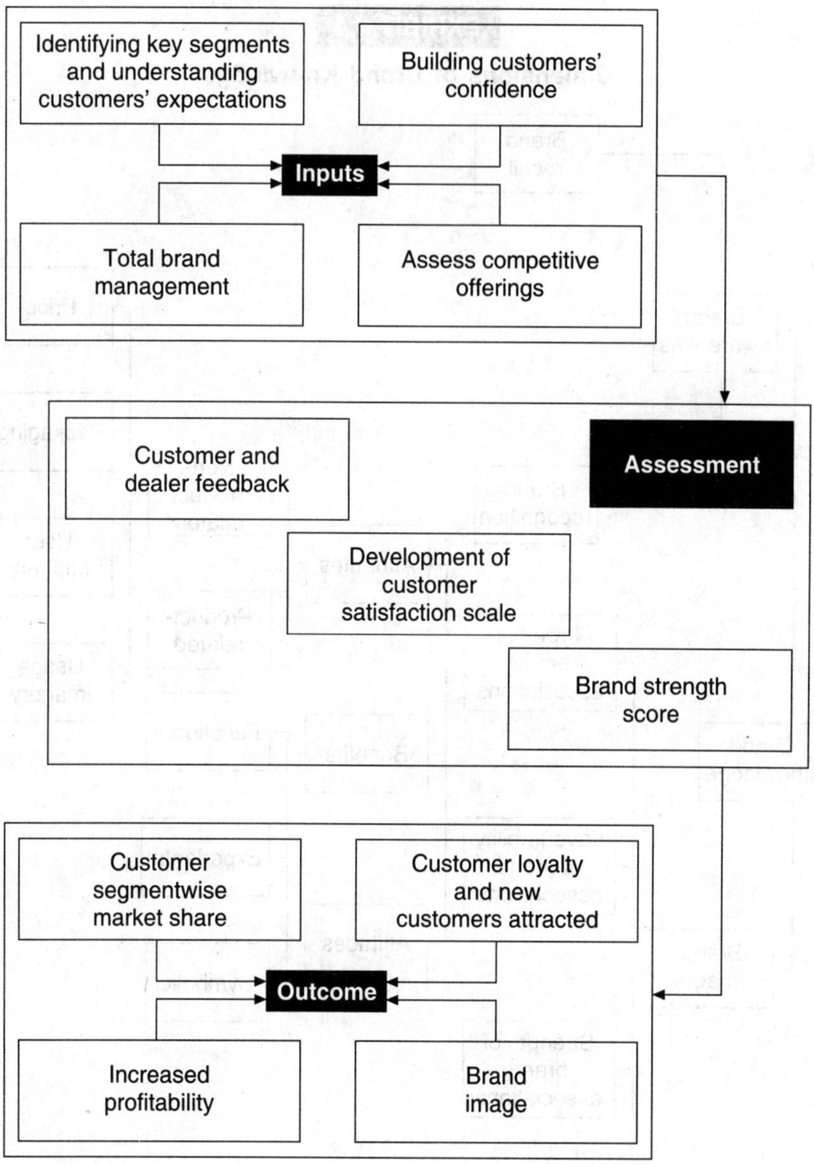

Outcome

- Market share
- New customers attracted
- Customer loyalty index

- Increased profitability
- Brand knowledge (see Exhibits 4.4 and 4.5 for details)

EXHIBIT 4.4

Dimensions of Brand Knowledge

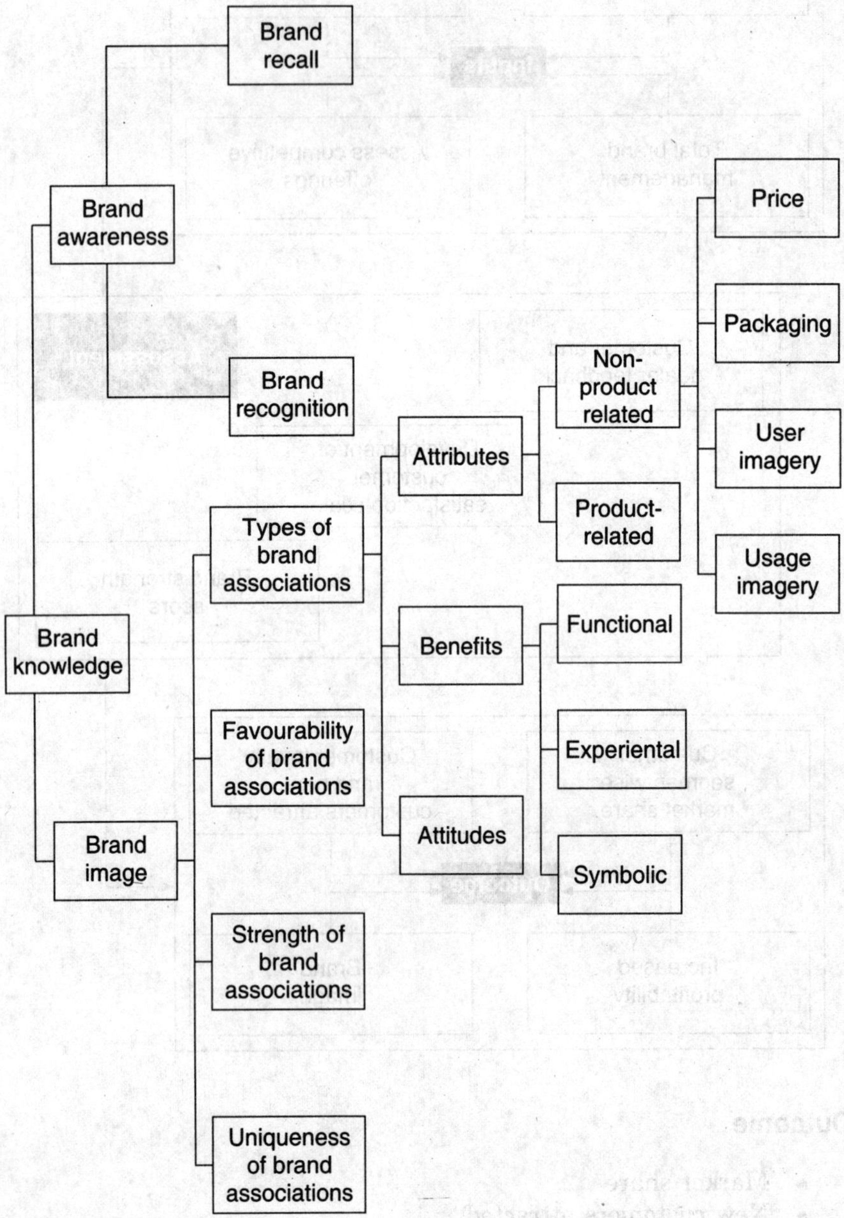

Note: Adapted from David A. Aaker's, *Managing Brand Equity*, The Free Press, New York; 1991.

EXHIBIT 4.5

Measurement of Brand Knowledge Constructs

Construct	Measure(s)	Purpose of measure(s)
Brand Awareness		
Recall	Correct identification of brand given product or some other type of probe as cue.	Capture "top-of-mind" accessibility of brand in memory.
Recognition	Correct discrimination of brand as having been previously seen or heard.	Capture potential retrievability or availability of brand in memory.
Brand Image		
Characteristics of brand associations		
Type	Free association tasks, projective techniques, depth interviews.	Provide insight into nature of brand associations.
Preference	Ratings of evaluations of certain associations.	Assess key dimension(s) producing differential consumer response.
Strength	Ratings of beliefs of association.	Assess key dimension(s) producing differential consumer response.
Relationships among Brand Associations		
Uniqueness	Compare characteristics of associations with those of competitors (indirect measure); ask consumers what they consider to be the unique aspects of the brand (direct measure).	Provide insight into the extent to which brand associations are not shared with other brands; assess key dimension(s) producing differential consumer response.
Congruence	Compare patterns of associations across consumers (indirect measure); Ask consumers conditional expectations about associations (direct measure).	Provide insight into how brand associations are affecting their preference, strength or uniqueness.

Assessment

- Continuous feedback from customers as well as trade channels.
- Scientific inquiry into customer satisfaction level
  - — who is the customer and profile of the target segment,
  - — what constitutes customer satisfaction,
  - — designing the scale to measure customer satisfaction, and
  - — measuring current levels of customer satisfaction,
  - — trend analysis and pointers for management of customer satisfaction,
- Brand strength score (see Exhibit 4.6 for details)

EXHIBIT 4.6

Brand Strength Score

The overall brand strength score is a composite of different weighted factors, each of which can be measured on a suitable scale. The key questions of measurements are as follows:

- **Leadership:** Does the brand lead the market?
- **Stability:** Is there any established status of the brand? Does it have a loyal or definite following?
- **Market position:** What are the prospects for the said brand in the current market? In which areas do the brand excell vis-a-vis competitors?
- **Trend:** Will the brand remain contemporary and relevant to target consumers in the long run? Ascertain the nature of market segment where the said brand has still found its relevance.
- **Support:** Brand which has received consistent investment and focused support is supposed to find much stronger franchise than the one that has no support. Are the consumers aware of the recent marketing support (especially communication) offered to the brand?
- **Image protection:** A brand's image is crucial in retaining its overall strength. If the distinct strength of the brand is suspect it may not be feasible to establish or sustain the brand at all. With time a brand may consolidate or slide down in the perception of consumers. So, one could assess the *image* of the brand in the light of new competition coming up in the market. How do the prospective consumers rate the brand in their preference pattern?

BRAND IMAGE

The term 'brand image' signifies the aura, reputation and the symbolic meaning attached to a brand. In case of many products, consumers are unable to discern the differences among various brands when their labels are removed. But when the brand names are mentioned, they show clear preferences. This is because people tend to define themselves in terms of the *symbolic value* of their possessions. Generally speaking, *brand image* has a more significant role in product situations where the choice is made more on the basis of subjective criteria. In other words, 'brand image' is more prevalent when consumers have difficulty in judging various options on the basis of strictly objective measures. Thus, consumers here seem to buy the total symbolic meaning which the brand conveys. Image is an abstract concept incorporating the influences of past promotion, reputation and peer evaluation of that brand. Generally, the symbolic meaning attached to a brand will depend on various factors.

Dimensions of Brand Image

Each brand has a unique blend of identity in the eyes of its consumers. Broadly speaking, the totality of any brand is made up of three types of appeals.

1. **Appeal to reason (performance factor):** It basically consists of many objective factors of evaluation. For example, what does the brand do? What does it contain? How does it perform? What benefits or functions does it serve?

2. **Appeal to the senses (sensory gratification):** How does the brand look, taste, smell, sound, etc.? Here brands attempt to satisfy the consumer's quest for sensory gratification, convenience, aesthetic pleasure, intellectual satisfaction, etc.

3. **Appeal to emotion (social approval):** It refers to the brand's style, the mood it evokes, and the psychological rewards it gives. Although these are mostly intangible factors, they create significant impressions on the consumer. For instance, a consumer may select a brand of television keeping in view how his/her friends, neighbours, etc., would look upon the choice.

These three appeals collectively form the brand image. However, the image of a brand may vary from one consumer to another. As such, the core of the brand image is created by the advertising function and other marketing programmes initiated by the company. Ultimately, the typical consumer will filter various communications about the brand and will develop an image on the basis of his or her existing beliefs, prejudices and pre-dispositions.

BRANDING OF COMMODITIES

In the past in India most commodities were sold in unbranded form. Today we notice the reverse trend. It all started in the early Nineties when food products, salt, and spices were offered in branded form. This was followed by shoes, trousers etc. Today, more marketers have jumped into the bandwagon. Say, Tata salt has used its corporate name, oranges are stamped with the growers level; tea is sold in special pack designs or names, common nuts and bolts are packaged in cellophane with the distributor's symbol, and automobile components—spark plug, tyres, filters-bear separate brand names from the automakers. This craze for branding, all sorts of commodities is also a result of the changed lifestyle of people, specially working couples who have high disposable incomes and for whom quality and convenience now take priority.

Marketers are entering the commodity markets because of the huge size they offer. For instance, the branded rice market is valued at Rs 1100 crore which constituted just about 10 percent share of the rice market. This goes to show the immense opportunity. Generally speaking, marketers have added value to commodities through branding, be it fertilizer, salt, spices, flour, rice or sugar. For instance, Hindustan Lever has achieved a thundering success when they differentiated its DAP fertilizer under the brand name of "Paras". Similarly, ITC has branded flavour, biscuit with their Ashirvad, Sunfeast brands. DCW Home product had a modest success when it first launched Captain Cook salt and followed it up with Captain Cook Atta. NEPC has offered atta, maida, sooji and spices.

Challenges in Branding Commodities

The commodity market is generally driven by price. Besides, consumers, by and large, show no involvement in the selection of a commodity. Under such conditions, to make them insensitive to price itself is very difficult task. And, afterwards to create a preference for a specific option calls for a more sustained effort on the part of any marketer. Of course, the changes are slowly taking place in the cities and big towns where consumers are able to appreciate the benefits of buying a branded commodity.

Branding a commodity is a great marketing challenge. Unlike in a consumer goods market where the marketer can play around with consumer perception, brand differentiation etc., in a commodity market, branding is about going to the basics or exploring at the grassroot level. To quote, David Aaker, "it involves overturning the rules of the market, establishing new selling propositions in the market which so far has been driven largely by price. And everything from positioning, pricing, brand value and packaging takes on a new sensitivity".

Brand building involves cost, apart from additional cost incurred in packaging, labeling, advertising, legal protection—and a risk that if the brand should prove unsatisfactory to the user, the company's image would suffer and it may even affect market for other products of the company. Thus the challenges involved are formidable. Still any marketer prefers to brand it because of many unique advantages as stated below:

- The brand name makes it easier for the marketer to process orders and track down problems associated with the brand.

- The marketer's brand name and trademark provide legal protection (patent or copyrights) of the unique features, which would otherwise be copied by competitors.
- Branding gives the marketer the opportunity to attract loyal and profitable segment of customers. Loyalty created over time offers the unique advantage of having assured customer base against competition and greater control in their marketing programme.
- It is wrong to assume that any commodity market is a homogeneous mass. Instead, the task lies in skillfully identifying the different segments and understanding their specific needs. Branding helps marketer to form suitable segmentation of the market. Different brands can be aimed at different segments of customers.
- In the long run it helps to build a strong association with the consumers as well as the trade. By highlighting the same name, they could project their quality and image of the company.
- Last, but most important, to derive the first mover's advantage and tap the huge market potential.

Customer's Benefits

From the customer's viewpoint, a branded commodity assures him/her of a standard quality and minimizes the risk associated with choosing from a wide variety of similar product options. Hence the process of branding achieves different things:

- an easy identification process
- highlights special attributes or benefits
- distinct values and personality behind same usage
- connotes some association with type of users.

SPECIAL CONSIDERATION IN BRANDING OF A COMMODITY

As stated earlier, brand is a name, term, sign, symbol, design, or a combination of them, intended to identify the goods or services of one marketer and in particular, to differentiate an option from those of the competitors. The major issues involved in the branding of any commodity are:

- Offering sufficient value to the customer to induce change from a commodity to a branded option.
- Role and degree of consumer involvement in buying decision.
- Segmenting the market, selecting a target segment and positioning of the product to match with the target segment characteristics.
- Communicating the positioning to the target customers expectations.
- Appropriate price-quality position offering sufficient turnover and long term growth.
- Setting and controlling distribution.

- Selecting suitable packaging.
- Channelising marketing investment for brand building.

The following two examples of salt and greeting cards will illustrate how some commodities have been successfully branded in India.

Captain Cook Salt

Product: In May 1991 DCW HPL launched a salt in the name of "Captain Cook" and aimed it at the top end of the market. The product was put in an elegant package.

Target market: Market research revealed that salt was of low importance on the consumer's grocery list. Further, it was found that the consumer associated salt's purity with whiteness, and *Tata Salt* was then perceived as the best. Captain Cook decided to take a shot at the leader from that position, by calling itself the 'purest and whitest' salt in the market.

Pricing and distribution: The company's biggest gamble was pricing. *Captain Cook Salt* was priced at Rs 3 for a 1 kg pack, 50% higher than *Tata Salt,* and thrice the average commodity price. The product expanded its distribution reach gradually to cover outlets in most parts of India except Kerala and areas of the north-eastern states. However, tackling the trade was not easy. Retailers were reluctant to stock the new brand as they were apprehensive about the price. Even after offering a commission above *Tata Salt,* the company had to convince them of their service standards—replacement of spoiled packs and so on.

Advertising: The company launched a high decibel ad campaign to arouse consumer interest in a conceived dull product. The campaign began with teasers warning husbands that their wives were about to fall in love with a mystical man from the high seas. The 'Holy Hygiene' launch commercial showed a ship's captain steering his hungry crew to an island where some food was being cooked, and adding salt to the feast before letting his sailors eat. After that, there was a series of **fun-oriented** commercials, each a take-off on popular themes. The company claims that the brand had a sales of Rs 3.4 crore at 15,970 tonnes in its very first year. In 1992-93, volumes tripled to 48,410 tonnes valued at Rs 10.3 crore.

Competitive reaction and search for new USP: To defend its position, Tata Chemical launched a campaign highlighting its' modern manufacturing process and also made retail commissions at par with Captain Cook. Consequently, Captain Cook's sales began to stagnate and DCW HPL then decided to go in for another round of consumer research in July 1993. The idea was to develop a fresh selling proposition based on what the consumer really desired of high-value salt. According to the study, housewives were looking for a product which would not absorb water, form lumps or stick to her hands. It meant that she would opt for free-flowing salt.

Repositioning Captain Cook: The product was reformulated with additives to keep the salt drier. Its new campaign, while sticking to its spirit of fun, highlighted the salt's free-flow property. The 60-second film showed a housewife gracefully pouring salt from a Captain Cook packet into a jar. Alongside is a packet of 'ordinary' salt (with a pack design which looks remarkably similar to *Tata Salt)* refusing to flow out smoothly. Captain Cook claims to have reached a sales figure of about 90,000 tonnes (valued at Rs 25 crore) in 1994-95, which was 50% more than the previous year's sales. Since the relaunch the prices have been raised to Rs 5 a kg *(Tata Salt:* Rs 4.50 a kg).

Archies Greetings Cards

Archies Gifts and Greetings Pvt. Ltd. dominates the greeting cards market which was traditionally unbranded.

The Market: Archies achieved this position by focussing on two core aspects of product management—**identifying the customer segment and delivering that value by branding.** When Archies started, the cards market was dominated by 30 large, 200 medium and 100 small-time card makers, vying for a somewhat indifferent, small consumer base. The bulk of the market thrived on the more formal, adult or institutional communication. The occasions were largely fixed—season's greetings, birthdays and anniversaries.

At that time both the unorganized sectors and leaders like Tata Press and Vakils targeted the corporate segment, with business centred on festivals. Since the buyer was not concerned with exclusive designs, the same design, could be replicated in bulk and sold to as many clients as possible. Alternatively, companies simply produced a range of cards and then sold them through as many outlets as they could. There was little effort putting in to distinguish the card. Thus, consumers' involvement with the category was low.

Targeting the Segment: Before branding the greeting cards, Archies chose to clearly identify a target group that was amenable to a change in habit. The cards business was seen as a vehicle for personal' expression—an extension of the individual's personality. They targeted young urban consumers between the ages of 15 to 30—a segment that was not only trendy, socially active, high on gifting, but also excitable and emotionally charged. To ensure consistent off-take, it was crucial to make card exchange a regular form of communication. So the company designed what it termed **'cards for every thought'** with messages that were sensitive, humorous, or whacky. The scope of cards for fixed occasions was increased. New 'fixed occasions'—Guru Purav, Bhai Dhuj, Id, Bihu, Parsi New Year etc.—were introduced. Cards with simple messages like 'missing you' or 'sorry' were extended into a large, individualistic, range. In fact, even regular birthday cards saw an increase in depth, with cards for uncles to grandparents.

Distribution

However, branding in itself was not enough. At that time most cards and gifts were sold from stationery shops or general stores. And invariably, cards took low priority when it came to gaining shelf space. **It was felt that only way to trigger store traffic and impulse purchase was to grab the potential buyer through visual displays and a large variety.** It was obvious that unless the cards were placed upfront, the consumer would not be propelled to pick them up. Again, if the product did not move fast, few retailers could be persuaded to specialise in selling cards. So Archies decided to set up its own **exclusive retail chain called Archies Galleries.** The first one was cleverly located near the University of Delhi. The target customer: college goers and teenagers. As investing in exclusive shops is expensive, Archies decided to set up a franchisee network. However, few retailers would be excited at the thought of selling just one brand of cards, despite the 20% to 40% margins. Hence, the initial investment of anything between Rs 3 lakh to Rs 9 lakh was thought to be too high.

Line Extension at Archies

To turn the business into a viable proposition, Archies carefully **expanded the product portfolio by entering into the gift business. The logic:** if cards were a form of gift, the same 'mood' will prompt a consumer to look at a broader display of products—cassettes, mugs, jewellery etc. The customer could glance through the range of items of gift along with the cards and finally decide on a set of gifts to purchases. In many cases, a customer was found to send a card along with a gift, instead of a staid 'best compliments' card only.

The exclusive outlets are classified either as Archies galleries or gift shops depending on the physical size of the outlet. Spread over a minimum of 500 square feet, for each such gallery, in keeping with its focus on the youth, seeks to create a colourful and peppy ambience. And great importance was placed on merchandising. The management and stocking of the outlet was left to the local franchisee, since it was influenced by the location and the profile of its clientele.

Information collected from franchisees also formed a good data base for the company. Ideas that click persist, the rest are dropped. For instance, Friendship Day cards were a huge success; Independence Day cards were not.

Need for Differentiation

Both these examples demonstrate our basic assertion that any commodity can be branded as long as the marketer takes care to position the product or differentiate it from other alternatives, packages and distributes it in a manner to remove the intrinsic price advantages of a commodity, and sets a price which is consonant with the price-value equation.

Conclusion

Here we have introduced the concept of braning as an orientation, a marketing tool, a differentiation strategy and as an on-going process. We also discussed the strategic relevance and logic of building a brand out of a commodity and show how to create a brand and measure the brand equity.

Marketers choose a combination of hardware (product content, design etc.) and software mechanism, e.g. communication, trade push to distinguish its offering. Customers hold a brand in high esteem when they are aware of the brand name and retain some favourable, strong, and unique brand associations in their memory.

A brand is said to have positive (negative) brand equity if consumers react more (less) favourably to an element of the marketing mix for the brand than they do to the same marketing mix when it is attributed to a less known or commodity version of the product or service. Brand knowledge is typically conceptualised as an associative network model in terms of two components, namely, brand awareness and brand image. From the angle of measurement, brand awareness consists of assessing brand recognition and brand recall. Similarly, brand image is measured in terms of their characteristics by type (level of abstraction), preference or strengths, and in terms of their relationship with other associations by congruence, competitive overlap and leverage.

Building a brand means creating a familiar name and a positive image. We have outlined an analytical framework of how a brand is built and its image is measured. Various dimensions of brand knowledge and a scale of brand strength score were also proposed as a measurement of brand value.

Let me end this chapter with a brief discussion on managing brand equity in the following Appendix.

APPENDIX

Managing Brand Equity

Brand equity is the term used to describe the value of a brand's name or symbol. The simplest form of brand equity is familiarity. Choosing a known brand gives the customer a justification for the decision. This justification may also serve as a social approval, indicating that the person has bought something of value.

Brand equity is defined as a set of brand assets and liabilities linked with a particular brand, its name and symbol. Brand equity creates value for both customers and the marketer. Aakar has proposed a structure (see Exhibit 4.7) of five assets underlying brand equity; these are now briefly described.

EXHIBIT 4.7

Managing Brand Equity

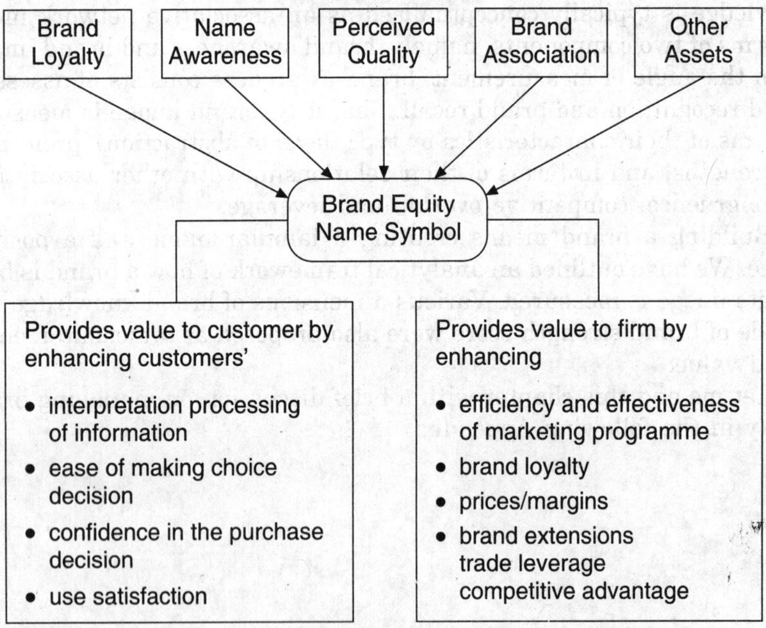

Source: David A. Aaker, *Managing Brand Equity*, The Free Press, New York, 1991.

1. **Brand loyalty.** Higher loyalty to a brand is an important asset. It can be utilised to persuade customers for more purchase or for spreading word of mouth.

2. **Name awareness.** Creating name awareness is a necessary condition for trial. Customers rarely purchase an unknown brand.
3. **Perceived quality.** A known brand often conveys an aura of quality. Customers own judgement about quality induces purchase action.
4. **Brand associations.** Customers attach certain subjective and emotional attachments which form a part of the brand equity. These associations together form a brand "personality", which suggests situations and customers for whom the particular brand is suitable.
5. **Other assets.** Patents, trademarks etc. are valuable other assets of a brand.

CHAPTER 5

Market Segmentation

No country in the world has as much diversity in terms of culture, custom, religion and language as in India. With growing income and changing aspirations of people, the Indian market is getting increasingly fragmented.

Marketers try to identify distinct groups of buyers with similar tastes and preference for their products. In the process, they try to reduce the chance of dissipating their efforts on unproductive activities. A marketer is thus able to develop suitable combinations of marketing mix for the specified 'target segment'. Therefore, any marketer would like to ascertain the differences between market segments so that one may choose appropriate combinations of marketing programmes to appeal to each segment of the market. A good example of a wide diversity of consumer requirements is noticed in the toilet soap market. Here consumers look for attributes such as health, perfume, lather, beauty, skin care, etc. Consumers could be grouped in terms of the degree of importance they attach to combinations of these varied attributes. In this case, we are trying to identify segments by product characteristics. Similarly, segmentation can also be viewed from the angle of consumer characteristics like income, age, sex, marital status, etc. Within a large number of consumers, requirements and preferences may differ even from one segment to another. A meaningful segmentation exercise helps to group them into segments along which a market behaves in a similar manner.

IMPACT ON MARKETING MIX

A segmentation approach has vital implications on decisions relating to the formulation of a marketing mix shown in Exhibit 5.1, for each segment. It may lead to the formation of wide combinations of product designs. For example, desktop and laptop computers today cater to different segments of buyers. The difference between small and large cars is not just a difference of capacity but a substantial difference between the type of customers and usage patterns.

Marketers have utilised their understanding of the differences between consumers in formulating their advertising and sales promotion decisions. For instance, understanding consumers reading and television viewing habits helps greatly in choosing the media mix and message content. Understanding the attitudes, preferences and lifestyle of the target segment has come to be recognized as a prerequisite for formulating the advertising message.

The implications of pricing are obvious. Forming segments on the basis of geographic locations has natural implications on distribution planning. Shopping or purchase behaviour of the target market will also affect decisions on distribution.

EXHIBIT 5.1

Marketing Mix

The marketing mix is the set of marketing decisions that management tries to calibrate to achieve its objectives. These have been popularly termed the four Ps: product, price, promotion and place (i.e. distribution). Now-a-days managers sometimes add two more decisions: service and staff. Each of these decisions is essentially a category under which a number of sub-decisions are made.

- **Product decisions**
  Product variety
  Product sizes
  Product performance
  Product features
  Product design
  Product packaging
  Brand name
- **Promotion**
  Sales force
  Advertising
  Public relations
  Consumer promotion
  Trade promotion
  Direct marketing
- **Service**
  Pre-sale service
  Point-of-sale service
  Post-sale service
- **Pricing decisions**
  List price
  Discounts
  Geographical
  Payment terms
  Credit terms
- **Distribution**
  Channel selection
  Market coverage
  Distribution directness
  Density of distribution
  Dealer support
- **Staff**
  Support staff
  Staff motivation and competence
  Tasks and responsibilities

Consumer motivations vary widely in using a particular product. Operationally, it requires identification of the key benefits sought for. In the case of industrial products, the utility of a product will depend on its specific applications. This exercise will help in formulating the product design as well as in highlighting key product features to buyers and in training of the sales force. Marketers can accordingly appeal to the need of specific consumer segments, and thus meet the diverse demands of the market place.

Conceptually, the rationale for segmentation arises because the market is invariably composed of a heterogeneous type of consumers. One could evolve a set of common strategies to serve a particular segment of the market. From the operational point of view, when we talk of market segmentation, it means grouping a set of consumers into smaller numbers by putting those possessing similar characteristics into the same group. However, a viable market segment must (i) be identifiable (ii) ascribable in some meaningful manner, and (iii) measurable so that the segment's size (potential) can be estimated.

SEGMENTATION CRITERIA

A market can be segmented in many ways (Refer to Exhibit 1.2 and Exhibit 1.3). Some of the popular bases used are again shown in Exhibit 5.2 and are briefly discussed now.

EXHIBIT 5.2

Basis of Market Segmentation

Base	Criteria
Geographic	Region: North, South, East, West, physical location, nature of market, rural, semi-urban, class–1 town, metropolitan city.
Demographic and Economic	Income, age, sex, family size, occupation, stage in family life cycle
Psychological	Life-style—Achievement oriented, Health conscious Family oriented, Innovative, Venturesome, Sociable Personality— Aggressive Complaining Dominant Ambitious Authoritarian Compulsive
Behavioural	Boards/Product category purchased Frequency of purchase Quantity of purchase Degree of credit buying Cash or credit buying Type of purchase (new buy, modified, re-buy) Repeat purchase Domestic or Institutional buying

(Contd.)...

Exhibit 5.2: Basis of Market Segmentation *(Cond.)...*

Price-Value	Economy, popular, premium quality of product used; Amount Re 1 or absolute price-size.
Benefits	Convenience, performance, durability, delivery, quality, service, reputation, image

1. **Geographic:** As the name itself suggests, a market could be partitioned by geographic locations (e.g. by state boundary, region, type or nature of market—rural, semi-urban, metropolitan, climatic conditions, etc.). At times, it may be more meaningful to concentrate the company's marketing efforts in select geographic areas. For example, *Nirma* detergent was initially marketed only in the state of Gujarat.

2. **Demographic:** Traditionally age, sex, marital status, religion, language, etc. have been used to form segments for consumer products. In case of industrial products, demographic variables may include the nature of business activities involved, ownership patterns (public vs private), turnover (size of operation), original equipment manufacturers or replacement buyers and so on. End users of aluminium, for instance, could be segmented by their specific applications such as users of construction materials, household utensils, automobiles etc. Industrial markets can also be segmented according to the type of technologies used by their customers. Users like the aerospace industry, possessing highly sophisticated technology have to be differentiated from small scale manufacturers of utensils.

3. **Economic:** In the case of consumer products, personal/family income, occupation, usage (light or heavy user), purchasing power (saving, credit worthiness, assets owned) are found to be useful means to form segments. In the case of industrial products, quality/performance requirements, servicing required, order size, etc., form good bases for segmentation. In the industrial market, purchasing criteria are a useful basis for segmentation. For instance, some users may look for higher quality whereas others may lay greater stress on servicing arrangements while yet another segment may look for better credit terms.

4. **Social and psychological:** From behavioural sciences, concepts like social class, reference group, personality, stage of family life cycle, etc., have been used to explain consumer behaviour. At times, they provide a meaningful base for constructing market segments. In general, social and psychological variables are easy to identify but difficult to measure. Cigarettes, cosmetics and the fashionable goods market have been segmented on the basis of the consumer's social and psychological (or *status)* needs, (see Exhibit 5.3 for a consumer's social profile) A more detailed discussion on life style segmentation has been provided in the subsequent section.

EXHIBIT 5.3

Factors Determining Consumer's Social Profile and AIO Dimensions

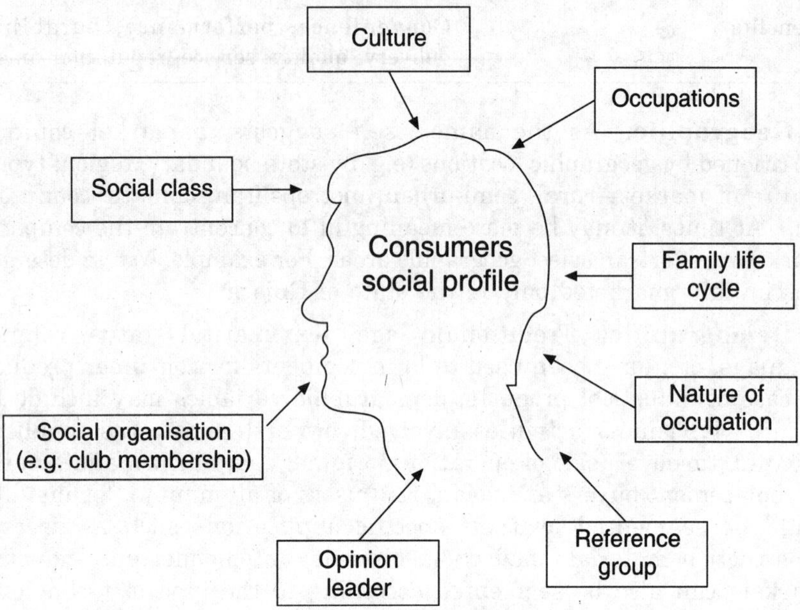

AIO dimensions

Activities	**Interest**	**Opinions**
Work	Home/Family	Social/Issues
Hobbies	Job	Politics/Education
Sports	Community	Culture
Social events	Recreation	Business Economics
Entertainment	Food habit	Past, future, present

5. **Price perception:** Consumers are found to judge the quality of many products by the price. Accordingly, consumers could be divided into many segments vis-a-vis the price of the various brands they consume. For example, in the case of toiletries market, there exist three distinct segments such as *premium, popular* and *economy*. Moreover, for some products, performance and price have been combined, thereby creating a 'value connotation'. The latter phenomenon is specially noticeable in products like cameras, televisions, personal computers, textiles, spare parts, tyres, music systems, etc.

6. **Benefit(s) sought:** In many product fields, the market can be segmented on the basis of benefits sought by the consumers. For example, shampoo brands can be partitioned as conditioners and non-conditioners. *Ponds, Tiara, Halo* and *Clinic* are examples of non-conditioners as against *Sunsilk* or *Lakme* which introduced the concept of conditioners. The

major benefits highlighted by these brands till now are cleaning ability, medicinal (anti-dandruff) property, suitability to hair type (dry, oily, normal hair) and conditioning effects. Today, there are three basic promises or benefits offered, viz., the attributes of *look good, feel good* and *do good.* In the first category consumers seem to perceive that the use of a shampoo would make them look good. This segment will typically include the upper income segment of the urban population. The segment of consumers who wish to *'feel good'* by using a shampoo are looking for certain other qualities like shine and bounce. Finally, the segment which aspires to obtain the *'do good'* property can be called health conscious. Here, medicinal qualities are sought such as an egg shampoo for the nourishment of hair, lemon shampoo for the nourishment of hair, lemon shampoo for oily hair or a herbal shampoo for a balanced/natural feeling. Thus, a product is to be designed and positioned depending on the key benefit sought by the consumers.

Marketing programmes need to be formulated after gaining a thorough understanding about the demographic and psychographic characteristics of the target segment. In general, it is essential to position a brand with specific benefits since sustained success depends on promising and delivering **unique benefit(s)** that are **meaningful** to the consumer. For example, the success of *Maggi, Nirma* and *Rasna* lie in their ability to identify distinct and meaningful benefits. The underlying unique benefits offered here are as follows:

Maggi: Convenient, fast and easy to cook food, appealing to children's tastes.

Barista: New, (though expensive) way of consuming a brand of coffee.

Nokia: Wide range of cell phones, catering to each budget.

LIFESTYLE SEGMENTATION

Lifestyle is viewed as a unique pattern of living which influences and is reflected by one's consumption behaviour. Lifestyle research examines how people spend their time in different activities; what is of the greatest interest or importance in their immediate surroundings; and their opinions about the world around them. Lifestyle segmentation of a market is done in the following manner:

1. **General lifestyle characteristics:** In this approach, the marketer attempts to find out if people can be segmented into distinct groups based on the similarity of their lifestyle. Each group presumably possesses different needs and has a unique consumption pattern. Once these segments are identified, an attempt is made to match the concerned product to one or more segments.

2. **Product-specific lifestyle characteristics:** Here, a marketer attempts to understand consumer behaviour relating to a particular

product. Consumers with similar lifestyles and consumption patterns are grouped together. This process allows the marketers to form a homogeneous group of consumers relevant to a particular product.

Use of Lifestyle Segmentation

The most extensive use of lifestyle information of a market is in the context of developing proper advertising themes. It is often used by advertisers in developing new or changed advertising themes, settings, moods, etc. It also enables one to choose the appropriate media for reaching target markets. Lifestyle information is frequently used for determining creative strategies.

An example: In a study on the shampoo market, a large number of statements of attitudes, interests and opinions were constructed and the data collected from the market was put to cluster analysis. Three distinct forms of lifestyles namely, sociable, health conscious and self-indulgent, emerged from the analysis of the responses. This information about different segments of the shampoo market could be utilized in creating different advertising themes. For the *sociable segment* the campaign could stress on the *look good* benefit that the shampoo provides. It would show people at parties, whereas for the *health conscious* segment, the campaign could possibly stress on the medicinal value of the particular brand, with a brand name as, say, *Doctor*. Finally, targeting the shampoo at self-indulgent people, who want a shampoo to make them *feel good,* the advertising message could show the pleasure of having hair washed with this shampoo; a name like *Comfort* would be more appropriate here. Thus, it can be seen from the above discussion that segmentation by lifestyle patterns and the associated consumer values could prove very useful in formulating an effective advertising strategy.

Conclusion

Given the diversity in consumers' characteristics, by segmentation, a firm is able to determine the most appropriate target market to which to appeal and subsequently choose a combination of marketing programmes to satisfy the aspiration of that specific segment. Operationally it involves a sort of consumer analysis which focuses on consumer demographics and a host of social and psychological factors associated with the final consumer.

CHAPTER 6

Positioning and Differentiation Strategies

The term 'positioning' indicates the place the brand or product occupies in a given market. Operationally, it refers to consumers' mental perception of the offering. For example, one brand of toothpaste may be considered better for its taste. Generally speaking, it is the way consumers perceive various brands that determines their respective positions. By physical constitution, two brands of a product may be identical, yet they could be perceived differently. Conversely, two brands may be dissimilar in terms of their physical characteristics yet they could be perceived as similar if their differentiating characteristics are considered unimportant.

WHY POSITIONING

As competition intensifies and brands proliferate, consumers tend to differentiate between brands in their own way. Positioning is a conscious attempt on the part of the marketer to accentuate this natural tendency and in the process, impart a distinct identity to his own brand to make it stand out among the competitors. The basis on which this differentiation is achieved reflects consumer preferences or attitudes. The marketer, through his diverse and coordinated actions, tries to influence this process.

The concept of positioning is also important to decide the overall marketing strategy. Once a brand manager is clear about the position she/he wants, the other marketing decisions like product design, packaging, pricing, method of distribution, etc., become easier to choose.

FACTORS AFFECTING POSITIONING

Evidence has shown that there are four distinct variables that affect the position of a given product. These are: (i) the product itself, (ii) the company behind it, (iii) the competition, and (iv) the consumers.

1. **The product:** How important the product is or what meaning it has for the consumer and how he relates to it. The fact that a product involves better ingredients or processes is a matter of indifference unless this knowledge offers distinct advantages to the consumer. There may be little point in lavishing sophisticated technology on certain packaging material if the customer throws it to the dustbin as soon as he has unwrapped the product. In other words, one needs to judge the dimensions which are important to the customer. Conversely, packaging may be used to lend an aura of sophistication to a product, but its cost must finally be justified by its intensity of meaning to the customer.

It may also be wrong to assume that the consumer is always in a position to judge the product features and performance. For instance, "the only ceiling fan with double ball bearings" slogan of *Polar Fans* may have imparted an identity to the brand, though the effects of such bearings have never been fully understood.

2. **The company:** A product comes from a company and every company has its own history. Generally, the stronger the company profile the better the image of its products. For instance, consumers may perceive a better image of a product if it comes from a reputed house like Tatas. The company's image also matters to the various channels of distribution involving traders and distributors especially retailers. Even where a company like the Gujarat Cooperative Milk Marketing Federation Ltd., is overshadowed by its popular brand name *Amul,* new product launches like *Dhara* (a non-Amul brand) has been well received by trade channels.

Thus, first the company's own image lends weight to the brand's positioning. Secondly, where a brand is not very strong, as in the case of *Dhara,* the company's name still plays a vital role in successfully launching the product and eventually creates the position in the market.

3. **The competition:** Product positioning is invariably done in relation to various competitive offerings. In most cases, consumers have a tendency to judge a product in comparison to the dominant brand, e.g., all photocopiers are compared with *Xerox,* all PCs with *HP/Compaq,* toothpastes with *Colgate* and so on. It was because of the strong position held by *Modi Xerox* that *HP* had to adopt an aggressive stand to establish its brand, even to the extent of making feature to feature comparisons. This can also be seen as a move to pre-empt the consumers own comparison as well as to educate the consumer. To that extent, leading brand enjoys some edge over others. It is therefore imperative to assess the various competitors while selecting a position. Proper positioning also enables a company to sidestep competitors. In other words, selecting a slot distinctly different from the competitors can avoid a direct confrontation with them. While segmentation serves this purpose by dividing the market into smaller groups, positioning goes a step further to establish a distinct niche in the consumer's mind.

4. **The consumer:** It should be reiterated that positioning is essentially based on consumer perceptions rather than factual evaluations. Hence, it becomes necessary to examine how the consumer views a product. Here the consumer's self-perception comes into play along with his cognitive and connotative factors. If he sees himself as modern and progressive, he will expect a more sophisticated product. If, on the contrary, he sees himself as traditional and possessing a taste for permanence, then he is more likely to view changes as *new fangled.* Thus, it is important to know what kind of person the archetypal consumer is, his lifestyle, and his preferences.

POSITIONING METHODS

The nature of a product is found to have considerable impact on the method of positioning. In this sense, products can be broadly classified as (a) impulse purchase items, (b) daily use items, (c) specialty items, (d) consumer durables, and (e) industrial products.

1. **Impulse purchase items:** Purchase of products like soft drinks and chocolates are generally made with little deliberation, where availability, brand awareness and positioning are the key factors. Therefore, choosing a simple memorable slogan assumes importance for positioning, e.g., *Amul's message "a gift for someone you love"* or both Lays and Kurkure (salty snacks) were positioned on a generic space of irresistibility. Lays tried to emphasis more on the youthful segment, while Kurkure with its focus on tea time, is more family oriented. Both the brands are trying to change habits of Indians and encourage them to consume Potato chips more regularly.

2. **Daily use items:** Daily use items like toothpastes and detergents often command low involvement and are bought by habit. Since elaborate comparisons of performance are rare, positioning efforts are aimed at promoting habitual buying of the brand. Today, there are many options in these types of products. Positioning offers an opportunity to select a specific slot in the consumer's mind so as to influence his or her habit.

3. **Specialty items:** Buying of specialty items like shoes, garments etc. often involves much deliberation as consumers are looking for certain combinations of styles, features and durability. Positioning here attempts to form a favourable pre-purchase disposition by highlighting the product's desirable features. Alternatively, where objective comparisons are not meaningful, positioning attempts to build and emotive appeal by creating an aura around the brand. Such phenomena is often noticed in purchase situation of suitcase, wrist watch, digital camera etc.

4. **Consumer durables:** Products like refrigerators, washing machines, television sets are, by and large, infrequently purchased by most consumers, who invariably gather a fair amount of information prior to the purchase. Positioning tries to win over the consumer by projecting the brand's superiority over others on certain selected dimensions.

5. **Industrial products[1]:** Of late, industrial product manufacturers have also begun to seek positioning slots. Industrial products can be broadly classified into seven categories, viz., raw materials, components, fabricated parts, processed materials, installation, accessory equipment and operating supplies.

The positioning technique to be used will vary with the nature of the industrial product. **Raw materials** are mostly purchased on the basis of their ingredients or composition. Depending on the individual requirements of prospective buyers, positioning involves at best adjusting or matching one's products according to these needs.

Component parts and fabricated material like resistors, screws, motors, etc. are incorporated in the final assembling of the product. Their positioning is mostly done by offering a certain standard quality of components which will in turn determine the quality of the end product.

Process materials like various chemicals, oils and consumables are not part of the end product but they facilitate production process. Positioning here highlights features like ease of handling, productivity, shop-floor efficiency, ease of storage, etc.

Installations are capital items like plant and machinery necessary for the manufacturing process, mostly positioned by the reputation of the manufacturer or superior technology.

Accessory equipments include items like forklifts, copying machines, specialised transport vehicles, etc. These items are generally positioned on the basis of certain specialised features.

Operating supplies include items like paper, inks, lubricants, paints, etc. Since in these product categories there are now a large number of options, they are being positioned similar to consumer products of daily use. Since these items are routinely bought, marketers position them on the basis of brand name, price, delivery schedule or performance guarantee.

Some Examples of Positioning

The Indian marketing experience is replete with instances of successful positioning strategies. While it is not possible to discuss an exhaustive list of such cases, a few distinguished positioning successes are recounted to focus understanding on the above conceptual outlines.

The positioning techniques adopted in these situations can be broadly classified on the basis of their underlying key notions.

1. **Positioning by specific product features:** The most frequently used positioning method has been to highlight certain specific product features or attributes. The Universal Luggage Company positioned its *Aristocrat* brand by highlighting its convenience: Advertisements showed a little girl effortlessly pulling a large suitcase.

---

[1]To explain how positioning methods can be applied in case of industrial products we are making a brief discussion about it here.

2. **Positioning by distinct benefits to users:** Providing specific benefits or problem solution is another effective means of positioning products. The success of *Vicks Vaporub, Ponds Cold Cream* utilised this method of positioning.

3. **Positioning by specific usage:** A finer ramification of benefits is to position a brand by specific usage. *Dettol soap* and *Maggi noodles* are instances of such positioning. The memorable advertising campaign *'Come alive with Nescafe "* is in a class of it's own.

4. **Positioning for a user category or application:** Another emerging positioning strategy is to highlight the product usage for a particular group of users or new applications. Photocopier manufacturers have started directing their machines for special applications or special groups of users such as engineers and architects.

5. **Positioning by product class association:** This is effective especially when introducing a new product. The shortlived success of *Milkfood Yoghurt* was mainly due to this strategy. Its ad headline was "It is not curd, its Milkfood Yoghurt". Similarly *Maruti Omni's* repositioning into the family car category would fall under this method.

6. **Positioning by price/quality:** Marketers have been found to position their offerings in terms of price/quality. The legendary tussle between *Surf* and *Nirma* on these counts is well known.

7. **Positioning by lifestyle of users:** In consumer products marketing especially in the case of items of conspicuous consumption, positioning by lifestyle has become a popular method, e.g., *'Charms—the spirit of freedom': Allwyn Watches—'Time for a new generation'* have capitalised on this concept.

8. **Positioning by reference groups:** The importance of reference groups even in purchase decisions has been accepted as a tool for positioning products. The Indian market has seen extensive use of sports personalities and film stars in the advertisements of many products for personal use. Similarly, when an industrial company mentions its clientele in its promotional material, to derive the advantage of endorsement, it is essentially using the concept of reference groups for positioning itself.

The following section highlights some successful experiences of positioning in the Indian markets.

SUCCESSFUL POSITIONING EXPERIENCES

Promise Toothpaste

The toothpaste market in India had, for a long time, been dominated by a few multinationals. In 1978, however, Balsara Hygiene products launched their *Promise* toothpaste and took an aggressive stand against all multinationals and Colgate Palmolive, in particular.

Promise toothpaste soon commanded the second highest market share. Its success can be traced to positioning. It was not promoted on me-too concepts like fluoride, mouthwash, fragrance or taste. Rather, the slogan *"The unique toothpaste with time-tested clove-oil"*, gave it a very new position hitherto not capitalised on by any other brand. Clove oil in India is a traditional remedy for the prevention of dental ailments and toothaches. This powerful connotation succeeded.

Vicks Vaporub

In the early 50s Richardson Hindustan Ltd. identified the need for a cold remedy in the Indian market. At that time, *Amrutanjan* was the market leader in the balm market. The company had to decide whether to position their product directly against the leader or to carve out a separate niche. It was finally decided to position the brand *Vicks Vaporub* exclusively as a rub for colds. Also, realising that the health of a child was the prime concern of parents, *Vicks Vaporub* was positioned as a rub for a child's cold. This was felt to be the best way of getting it into homes. In addition, this meant further distinguishing it from a balm, because a balm was much stronger and therefore used more often for adults. *Vicks Vaporub's* milder formulation was in contrast more suitable for children.

In a few years, *Vicks Vaporub* became the largest selling brand for cold remedies. The success of *Vicks Vaporub* can undoubtedly be attributed to its proper initial positioning.

Ponds Cold Cream

The cold cream market remains highly urbanised with 70 per cent of the sales taking place in the cooler months, between October and March. Initially, *Ponds* cold cream was positioned as an essential cosmetic item for any urban woman of middle and upper income families. In its advertising campaign, the company projected the theme of discovering one's real complexion in a matter of seven days. Two applications were recommended, the first one for removing the surface dirt and stale make-up, and the second application to reveal natural beauty.

There was a slight shift in the positioning strategy in 1975-76. The new campaign brought out the association of youth with *Ponds* cold cream. An advertising model as well as a mnemonic portrayed the theme. The copy also referred to the utility of creamy natural oil, required for a beautiful complexion and nourishment of the skin, particularly in winter.

Again following some market research, a further shift in the application based positioning strategy took place. The data collected showed that the need for a cold cream was felt (a) by those trying to overcome dryness of skin; (b) by those who recognised the need for softness and smoothness; (c) as protection against the weather. The new. positioning, based on the above, was followed through with a new campaign with the following headline:

"laugh dry winter skin away with cold cream by Ponds"

The advertisement emphasised the extra-rich natural oil content of *Ponds* cold cream which would help provide the required moisture for curbing dryness of skin. The bottom line of the advertisement once again repeated the message. *"extra rich with beauty oils your skin needs in winter"*.

Maruti Van (OMNI)

The *Maruti Van* has demonstrated now the clear positioning strategy of a product can reverse a downward market demand into a rising one. The Maruti van experienced many ups and downs. In 1983, when its launch was announced 13,583 bookings were made. Two years later, there was a demand for as many as 1,22,330 more. But during 1986 and 1987, the scene underwent a radical change. Suddenly, a large scale cancellation of bookings was noticed and the figure dropped, by as many as 90,000 cancellations.

The major problem appears to be a communication gap or unclear positioning in the marketplace. Customers tended to identify the van with a light commercial vehicle rather than a passenger car.

In early 1987, a *brand personification test* was carried out amongst a cross-section of Maruti dealers, van owners and prospective car buyers. Respondents were asked which animal various automobiles reminded them of. The exercise showed that respondents tended to identify the *Ambassador* with an elephant or bullock; and the *Fiat* with a dog or horse. The *Maruti* car was associated with a cat or rabbit, whereas the *Maruti van* was perceived as a larger cat by the majority. The *Maruti* van derived its identity from the Maruti car. The problem was to give the vehicle an independent identity and sort out the problem of unclear positioning.

The van had possessed the distinct quality of space and versatility, and this formed the basis for the positioning strategy. First of all, the van was given a brand name—*'Omni'*. The ad projected *"The most spacious car on the road", as an all-in-one "family car, office car and the knock-about-town car"*. For instance, the trader could use it to transport goods and also to take the family out. Thus, the positioning was based on certain benefits and applications to the user. The sales volume reportedly increased by 15.8 per cent by December 1988.

Rasna

The initial response to the *Rasna* launch was quite poor. In 1982, four years after its launch, sales declined from Rs 2 crore to Rs 80 lakhs. In

1983, an advertising agency was given the task of repositioning *Rasna*. Previously, it had been positioned for the housewife, generally perceived as the decision maker in the purchase of such products. The new positioning strategy incorporated the influencer (the child). While the initial positioning thrust of taste and economy remained, the quality of ease in preparation was added. The ad campaigns showed children asking their mothers to buy *Rasna* for the whole family. Some of the famous slogans were: *"I love you, Rasna"*; *"My daddy loves . . . no, no, not coffee, ... not tea.. . but Rasna"*, *"Serve with love, care and ice"*. The positioning with respect to economy was reinforced by ad campaigns talking of home magic: *"just one under-pack of Rasna makes 32 glasses of delicious soft drink"*. In 1989, *Rasna* was a Rs 25 crore brand with an 85 per cent share of the soft drink concentrate market.

Milkmaid

Milkmaid is another classic example of how accurate positioning can do wonders with an established but dormant brand suffering from static sale level. *Milkmaid,* manufactured and marketed by Nestle India Ltd., used to be perceived by housewives as an expensive, messy, milk substitute. Its premium pricing strategy had possibly resulted in low sales.

An advertising agency was approached to position the brand with respect to its varied use and application. First of all, it was essential to alter housewives' perception of *Milkmaid* as a milk substitute to a necessary culinary ingredient. To demonstrate the multiple usage, the ad campaign carried the message: *"You can-do wonders with Milkmaid"*. A variety of recipes were incorporated on the label, and press advertisements urged housewives to write in for free recipe booklets. Television was added to the media mix to get in-home family exposure and appetite appeal. Following this new positioning strategy, the sales showed an increase of 23 per cent in 1984 and 37 per cent in 1985. Today, *Milkmaid's* prime usage is 93 per cent as a dessert ingredient rather than just as a milk substitute or tea whitener. As such, sales doubled compared to the period when this new positioning strategy was launched.

Charms Cigarette

Any cigarette company has to identify the specific segment it is catering to, the characteristics of that segment, and its major competitive brands. This forms the basis for the positioning of a cigarette brand. An analysis of different cigarette advertisements shows that each brand emphasised distinct quality (i.e. flavour, strength, taste, fineness) or certain lifestyles. Let us take a look at some of the advertising campaigns of leading cigarette brands (see Exhibit 6.1) and note their underlying basis of positioning.

EXHIBIT 6.1

Positioning Strategies for Selected Cigarette Brands

Brands	Campaign	Basis for positioning
Panama	"Good to the last puff"	Value for money
Charminar	"Relax! Have a Charminar"	Economy and satisfaction
Scissors	"For Men of Action—Satisfaction"	
Oxford	"Reserved for those who appreciate the finest"	Social status
Gold Flake Kings	"Worth its length in gold"	Social status
Chancellor	"A cigarette so distinguished, it's by appointment to your majesty" your majesty"	Social status
India Kings	"There is only one original"	Social status
Capstan	"Flavour comes to town"	Trendy lifestyle
Wills Filter	"Made for each other"	Trendy lifestyle
Four Square Kings	"Live life king size"	Trendy lifestyle
Charms	"Charms is the spirit of freedom, Charms is the way you are"	Trendy lifestyle

The success of *Charms* cigarettes is attributed to its positioning based on lifestyle and psycho graphics. In 1982 the key problem of Vazir Sultan Industries Ltd. was declining sales and its image of a one brand company making a cheap, strong cigarette *Charminar.* So the need for developing a new brand was felt. *VST* decided to market a filtered cigarette priced at 20 paise per stick.

Cigarette advertisements in those days portrayed the typical smoker as a socially successful macho male exuding confidence. Brand differentiation could only be achieved by a fresh approach. The positioning had selected an urban non-conformist, with a casual lifestyle. This pedigree was represented by the denim pack and portrayed in the ad.

Within a month of its launch, the *"Charms—the spirit of freedom"* campaign had generated high brand awareness, trial and sales volume. The success of the *"Charms"* positioning strategy was evidenced in VST's increased market share to 25 per cent in the filter segment."

Limca—Soft Drinks

Consumer research revealed that quenching of thirst was an important aspect for consuming soft drinks and even *Coca-cola* was not able to fulfil this desire of Indian consumer. *Limca* was thus perceived as a bottled soft drink with definite superiority over fresh lime juice with respect to convenience, taste, consistency and easy mixability. The "Lime-n-Lemony" slogan reinforced the positioning. The brand was also positioned as a thirst quenching drink. Some of the famous ad campaigns were: 'thirsty minutes to lunch'; 'the groom is twenty but the bride is thirsty'.

Parle also encashed on the fact that Indians, by and large, are attracted to foreign made products: they utilised the name of their collaborator "Signor Bisleri" to boost the brand image. Thus, Parle's clever positioning strategy helped carve out a niche in the Indian soft drinks market.

The Park Avenue Collection

The launching of new products is difficult and often exciting. But the relaunching of an old product is perhaps even more challenging and financially rewarding. *Park Avenue* is a case in point of the revamping of an old product in the history of Indian marketing. The chequered history of the different readymade garments marketed by Raymonds explained below shows the series of positioning strategies adopted in this case.

Raymonds is a famous name in the suiting business. In the early eighties, Raymonds launched some ready-to-wear trousers as Raymond's *Double Barrels.* The product received a lukewarm response and, consequentiy, the company attempted a change in positioning. A new name *Raymond's Legwear* with the advertisement caption "no hassles with tailors" and the promise of a "great fit" was also not very successful.

As a follow-up to this experience, the company decided to make use of formal market research, eliciting response on how Indian consumers viewed the buying of readymade suitings. Consumer feedback revealed that the then available Indian readymade did not fit varying waists, hips and lengths, explaining why the positioning on "great fit" did not work. The feedback also revealed that by and large Indians were attracted to a foreign label. Consequently, the company decided to market their readymade garments under a new brand name, *Park Avenue* which conveyed a 'Western' image. The new positioning also sought to create some sort of total readymade feel, to achieve which the *Park Avenue* range was extended beyond trousers, shirts and suits, to men's accessories, including wallets, belts, kerchiefs and even toiletries. This time round, the product was a success in terms of the sales turnover of Raymonds in comparison to 1983. One may conclude that the product had achieved some brand personality, showing how repositioning with a new image at a critical stage can revive a product faced with being eased out.

Watches

Titan: Titan's range of watches has been positioned towards the design and fashion-conscious customer. As the Titan's ad copy puts it, "those from either the classic elegance of gold with leather; or the glamour and glitter of only gold; or the business-like look of steel; or even trendy casual". The consumer is thus offered a wide range of models to choose from.

In India, when watch smuggling had reached astronomical levels, Titan positioned itself against imported watches. The ad copy said "should you really trust an imported watch when you can get a genuine *Titan quartz?* It went on to describe the Titan's range of collections, widespread after-sales-service and the assurance of years of faultless performance with the backing of the Tata name.

T.S. watch: *T.S. watch* is a product of Indo-French Time Industries. The emphasis of this watch is on the mood and style of the wearer and the occasion. These hi-fashion, trendy and low priced wrist-watches have been positioned to attract youngsters. This is the first time in India a branded watch has been associated with youth. The ad campaign tried to evoke these life-style images. This watch had an adolescent, colourful look, and was priced low to suit this positioning strategy.

Bata Products

Bata provides another classic example of a company undergoing gradual changes in corporate as well as product positioning strategies. Till the mid-1970s, the *Bata* name was synonymous with shoes. Keeping abreast with the changing needs of the market, Bata introduced a wide range of shoes with the *North Star* label, initially positioned for athletics and leisure. Later on, *North Star* shoes were repositioned exclusively as leisure shoes and a range of sports shoes, under the label *Power* were introduced to coincide with the 1982 Asian Games. This positioning was further strengthened by promoting chain stores, selling sportswear and shoes. Bata also positioned shoes and sandals exclusively for women and children under the brand name of *Marie Claire* and *Bubble Glimmers,* respectively. The "Bata *by Choice"* advertising campaign is targeted at all age groups: youngsters, children, adults, women etc., and portrays an image of comfort, exclusivity and style. Subsequently, with the introduction of clothes—track suits, shorts, shirts, teeshirts, jeans, jackets, Bata moved into fashion wear. Bata also launched the *Murjani* collection of fashion wear. This, coupled with the creation of modern looking retail stores, are basically aimed at fashion-conscious youngsters.

Positioning by Packaging

Of late, packaging has been used in the positioning of some products. In particular, the size, shape, type, colour and design of packaging has been carefully chosen to give the product a distinct identity. For instance, fruit juice brands like *Frooti* received a good response from the market partly because of their attractive tetrapacks. This form of packaging also added to the shelf-life of the product and made it easy to store as well as carry. Similarly, the laminate packaging of *Prudent* toothpaste against formidable competitors like *Colgate* gave some distinction. Likewise, *Pond's* cold cream in a handy tube enhanced sales, both through market enlargement and greater consumption. Its new package changed the entire concept of cold cream being used only once (or twice) a day, to one that could be used at any time throughout the day. This positioning by elegant packaging specifically appealed to frequent travellers.

Another frequently applied packaging technique is economy size packaging, e.g. "*Rin* 250 g and *Thums UP* 500 ml". The opposite method, i.e. products in very small sized packets, has also become a popular means of positioning the product for some special group of customers. The Indian market is today replete with cases where success can be attributed to smaller sized packages. Take the case of *Pan Parag* pan masala. Its initial tin package evoked limited consumer response. This was replaced by the concept of fractional packaging, of *Pan Parag* in small sachets which was an instant success. Today, sachets are being used for packaging many items of personal use such as shampoos, meant for a single use.

Another packaging oriented positioning is found in cases of reusable and convenience packaging. This form of packaging has attracted consumers who look for economy and/or convenience, e.g., *Nescafe* in reusable glass jars or disposable sachets. Many other manufacturers of consumer products have resorted to this method of packaging. It has been observed that sometimes particular colours/ shapes of containers have been used to project a certain image. Knowing the preference for certain colours by customers, marketers have, for example, chosen pink for girls, blue for boys, deep colours for rural customers and so on. Likewise, *Amla* hair oil is packed in a transparent glass bottle to reinforce its positioning as a herbal product. *Nirma* detergent's transparent polythene packaging seems to have been one of the factors for its success. Here consumers seemed to have been attracted by the economic packaging.

Market Growth Possibility from Existing Product

Exhibit 6.2 shows possible strategies adopted to achieve market growth after working out a positioning plan for an existing product.

EXHIBIT 6.2

Sources of Market Growth

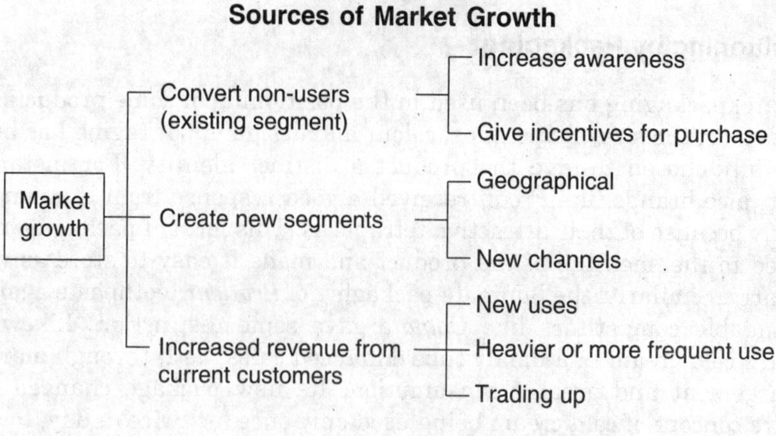

POSITIONING PREMIUM PRODUCTS AND THEIR DIFFERENTIATION STRATEGIES

A company that decides to operate in a heterogenous market recognizes that it normally cannot serve all customers in that market since the customers are too numerous, dispersed, and varied in their buying requirements. In such markets, the company, instead of competing everywhere needs to identify the most attractive market segments that it can serve effectively. One such attractive target market is the premium category.

Of late many companies are increasingly embracing premium markets in view of the rising purchasing power of the Indian customer who constitutes a fairly large size. In this segment, the consumers are willing to pay a higher price in return for the extra value they receive, which could be tangible benefits like performance, quality, superior design or overall better product as well as intangible benefits like status value and image.

In fact, premium products are purchased not only because of what they are or how they work. On the contrary, they connote a sense of exclusivity to the buyer-user. Accordingly, the companies in order to justify their higher prices, select their distribution channels and advertising themes to attract this target market efficiently. At the operational level, instead of scattering their marketing effort, they focus on the buyers who have a taste for quality, exclusivity or personal touch.

The first step in this process is "Target Market Identification"—the act of identifying and profiling distinct groups of buyers who might require premium products. The customers in this niche market have a distinct and somewhat complex set of needs and they will be willing to pay a premium to the firm best satisfying these needs.

The second step is "Differentiation", i.e., to differentiate the offering suitably by designing a set of meaningful differences to justify the premium. Differentiation could be based on product and service qualities or on perceived benefits as communicated to the customer.

The third step is "Positioning" which involves designing the company's offer and image so that it occupies a distinct and valued place in the target customers' minds. The company has to decide which of its differences will appeal most to the target segment and how many of these differences to promote.

I have selected a few premium offerings and have explained their special differentiating strategies. In each case a combination of several interlinked strategies have been highlighted.

EXHIBIT 6.3

Differentiation Strategies Employed by Some Premium Brands

Parameter	Examples
Product features	*Honda City Car, Electrolux* Washing Machines, *Sony Trinitron* TV
Performance quality	*100 Pipers* Whiskey, *Dove* Beauty Soap, *Whisper* Sanitary Napkins
Exclusivity and style	*Titan* Watches, *Vista Levelor* Venetian Blinds, Madura Coats Garments *(Van Heusen, Louis Philippe)*
Product design	VIP *Elanza* Suitcases,VIP *Strolly, Braun* Shaver, *Bentley* Ties, Raymond Suitings
Product range and variety	*Revlon* Cosmetics, *Mescos* Shoes, *Rayban* Sunglasses
Service quality	*Citibank, Shehnaz Beauty Salon, HP-Compaq Laptop* Computers, *Modi Xerox* Copier, *Otis* Elevator, and *Eureka Forbes* Vacuum cleaners.
Packaging	*Sand Piper* Beer, *Planter's Pride* Tea, *Antiquity* Whiskey, *Lays* Potato Chips.

Product Features as a Differentiating Strategy

Features are characteristics that supplement the product's basic functioning. The company can create additional versions by adding extra features or can offer new features to highlight its superiority over the existing product options. This justifies the premium in the minds of the customer. For example, the Honda City Cars offer various features such as automatic transmission, electric windows, central locking and a child proof safety lock (on rear doors). For the first time in India, a car manufacturer has been able to offer these features of international standards. Honda thus secured a position far above any of its present available options in the minds of the consumers.

Another premium brand that has successfully differentiated itself on product features is the **Electrolux** fully automatic washing machines. It has gained a distinct competitive edge by offering features like an in-built geyser for hot water washing required for removal of grease, tumble wash facility, a choice of two speeds for drying, and a front loading facility. Moreover, it has digitalised controls for superior performance.

Similarly, the **Sony Trinitron** Television offers sharper contrast, high resolution and vivid colours, and the picture tubes have very flat screens, which mean edge-to-edge distortion free pictures.

Thus, all these products are able to charge a premium over other brands in their respective categories. Differentiation enables the firm to fetch a price premium based on the extra value perceived by and delivered to the customers.

Performance Quality as a Differentiating Strategy

Basic performance refers to the levels at which the product's primary characteristics operate. Buyers of expensive products normally compare the performance of different alternatives. In fact, customers are willing to pay more for better performance. Experience shows that high quality products tend to earn more profit because their premium quality enabled them to charge a premium price. They are found to have higher repeat purchasing, consumer loyalty, and benefitted by positive word of mouth while their costs of delivering better quality were not much higher than for low quality products.

Again, let us take the example of Honda City Car whose price is slightly higher than its present competitive models, in that category. In terms of performance, it is an extremely fast car with speeds upto 170 km per hour. Servo controlled brakes offer superior braking systems.

Similarly, another brand that has differentiated itself as a premium product on the basis of performance quality is the **100** Pipers brand of Scotch Whiskey. Because of its superior blend, it provides an especially smooth experience to justify its claim that you hear 100 bagpipers playing with each sip.

Dove, a premium complexion soap, has a unique and superior composition of 1/4 moisturizing cream. It has justified the premium price it commands based on the fact that it does not dry skin and helps retain the skin moisture, thus giving superlative performance compared to any of its competitors.

The sanitary towel **Whisper** has obtained a perceptible edge based on superior absorbing powers and dry texture—qualities on the basis of which it claims that it's product performance is much above its competitors. In order to highlight the superior quality and performance, the ad campaign used the caption "Why use half a napkin, when you can have the whole".

Exclusivity and Styie as a Differentiating Strategy

Style describes how well the product looks and feels to the buyer. It has the advantage of creating product distinctiveness which is difficult to copy. Therefore, the companies operating in the premium segment have invested substantially in better styling. Such a strategy attempts to take advantage of the psychological bent of target consumers who associate themselves with such offerings in order to assimilate the style accompanying the brand in their personality.

Titan industries has launched a range of exotic, gold plated jewellery watches under the brand name **Tanishq,** which use style and exclusivity as their instrument of differentiation to justify premium pricing. The name is an adaptation of *Nishka,* a Sanskrit word which means "Necklace of Coins". The prefix "Ta" stands for Tata, while the last letter "q" is added as an element of style. The watches were sold through select Titan's chain of upmarket showrooms, to which special sections have been added to create an aura befitting the upmarket image, style of Tanishq, thus adding to the splendour of the watch. In order to create an image of this brand's exclusivity, the company has limited distribution to exclusive outlets only.

Vista Levolor has created a strong brand in the Venetian blinds market with its wide range of stylish designs and colours by relying on product exclusivity. Its special "view through series", namely *Sheer View,* enables viewing from inside but not the other way round, thus granting both privacy and glare control. *Sheer View* and *Shapella* offer the exclusive convenience of window blinds while trying to maintain the appearance of a pleated curtain. In fact, the company was also the pioneer in the area of branded curtain rods.

Marketers of designer shirts and ties have used style and exclusivity to transform these otherwise unexciting, high use items of daily wear in corporate circles, into instruments of making personality statements. For example, Madura Coats which markets **Louis Phillipe, Van Heusen, and Allen Solly,** also markets ties to complement the personalities of its three shirt brands. The company says that Allen Solly, an "informal" formal brand of shirts, is targeted at *the* young executive and goes well with "Conversational" ties which have friendly and flamboyant designs. *Van Heusen* ties have "Classical" designs, while *Louis Phillipe* targets the older executives with a relatively sober range of ties. These ties are no longer tucked away with socks and handkerchieves, but made visible through exclusive showrooms or exclusive sections in existing showrooms. This helps emphasise the unique style of these products and justify their premium price.

Design as a Differentiating Strategy

As competition has intensified over the years, product design offers one of the most potent ways to differentiate and position a company's products and services. Anecdotal evidence and research study suggest that design investment pays off and hence can be used to justify the price premium. Let us take the following examples.

VIP industries, which has remain market leader in the Indian luggage market, has launched **Elanza,** which is a slick brand of premium moulded luggage, targeted at the Indian travellers going abroad. The product boasts of a unique inner lining fused with the plastic shell and a double-walled shoulder bumper. The lining prevents contact between delicate fabrics and the hard outer shell, besides giving a superior feel. The bumper, on the other hand, is claimed to pack extra strength into the most vulnerable part of the bag. The recessed handle and broad wheels add to the product's aesthetic appeal.

ZTMC, makers of ties for over three decades, introduced **Bentley,** a premium brand of ties, in a vast range of designs in 1985. To keep its brand in the public eye, it maintained product design innovation. It offered a bottle shaped tie, very broad at the base, with a sharp curve at the knot juncture, to enhance the knot's shape. Based on the designs currently in vogue in the fashion centres of the world like New York, Paris, Rome and London, Bentley unveils 250 designs a month on an average in the Indian market.

Braun recently launched dry electric shavers. These exhibit a level of technology and design far superior to any available brands. Hair is fed to the choppers through a sieved "Head" which reduces the danger of nicks. Moreover, the shavers are based on foil technology as opposed to the rotary kind offered by Phillips, which means that the shaving heads are not rounded but rectangular, making it easier to shave the moustache area. **Flex Integral,** the highest priced model in the range, costs much more than *Philishave,* but offers about three weeks of cordless shaving with just an hour required for charging. As opposed to this, *Philishave* takes 8 hours.

Another new segment creator to make waves on the basis of innovative design was VIPs **Strolly,** a small soft material "Cabin" bag equipped with wheels and a long retractable handle to cart it around airports. Because of the first mover advantage it enjoys, *Strolly* has become a generic descriptor for wheeled bags and therefore enjoys a premium.

Product Range and Variety as a Differentiating Strategy

This is one of the crucial parameters on which a producer is able to charge a premium. Despite a number of players existing in the same product category, the marketer can differentiate his products on the basis of the product range and the variety he offers and can hence justify the premium charged. In the premium segment of many products the quality bracket is the same. Only in the event that the buyer gets two equally appealing designs under different labels does he make a brand choice. Thus, the best way to capture market share is to offer a wide range to keep the customer from straying. For example, Revlon, a leading player in cosmetics, offers 24 shades of Super Lustrous Lipstick, 16 of Outrageous Lipstick and 30 shades of Nail Enamel. Other than these, shampoos and hair conditioners (under the brand **Flex**), in variants to suit normal, oily and dry hair have also been introduced in the Indian market as have fragrances and face make-up. Revlon also plans to introduce a wider range of eye and face make-up, skin care products and more fragrances very soon.

The marketing strategy of Mescos was directed towards posing as a prominent brand in premium shoes. It started off with shoes for casual wear for men. Gradually they added shoes of almost all kinds for men, women and children. By high quality intensive advertising, it communicated the availability of this newly introduced wide range of shoes to its target consumers. In fact, the range of women's shoes was so large that it was placed under a separate sub-brand, **Options,** which was so named to indicate the wide variety. This also enabled it to charge premium price.

Rayban, a raving success of Bausch & Lomb's in the optical product segment, charges a substantial premium on the basis of its appeal to the young generation. Scores of sunglass variants were brought out. All these appeal to the quality conscious customer, looking for tangible benefits like quality of the lens, weight of the glasses, the nose bridge fit etc. In addition, various styles have been offered to suit different needs. Wayfarers, a range with plastic frames in unconventional shapes is directed at the modern, young customer. The gold framed range is directed at the upmarket executive and can be worn for formal occasions. The plain, powder coated metal frames are targeted at the more conventional consumer.

Services Quality as a Differentiating Strategy

In addition to differentiating its physical product, the marketer can also differentiate on the basis of the accompanying services and can capitalise on them to charge the premium. When the physical product cannot be easily differentiated, the key to competititve success lies in service augmentation. This is especially true of organisations which render only service such as hotels, banks and beauty parlours. For example, **Citibank** is able to justify the premium it charges by customer friendly and customer facilitating services such as 24 hour banking, speedy clearance of cheques, almost immediate retail financing, etc.

Shehnaz Beauty Salon is another example of an organisation thriving on premium pricing for the services rendered which range from individual beauty sessions with the clients, cosmetic counselling, customer convenience in the selection of hair styles (using on-line display), etc. Shehnaz also has in-house R&D and develops it's own range of herbal skin and hair-care products that cater to the needs of its upmarket clientele.

In the market for computers, after-sales service provides a vital tool for differentiation. This can be classified into the following categories:

(a) **Hardware:** Some computer companies have started making computers that are compatible with their range of fax machines, photocopiers, printers etc. Targeted at senior executives who work at home as well, this facility allows them to set up a "home-office". An example of this is HP-Compaq who has positioned itself as a provider of supports and services which include its range of PC-compatible range of office durables.

(b) **Software:** Providers of hardware often include software packages at discounts to buyers to justify the premium charged. An example of this is **IBM** which offers software by Microsoft to buyers at barely 20% of the actual cost. This allows buyers easy access to patents, licenses etc. which would have otherwise been difficult to obtain.

(c) **Other forms of service:** Providers of hardware for computers have started offering many innovative add-on services with their products to boost sales. This could include facilities like training after installation. Similarly, Tata Telecom has provided buyers access to the Internet as part of the package deal.

Modi Xerox has differentiated itself in photocopiers market by offering excellent after sales service. The market for such photocopiers is small. At the same time the high speed photocopiers are costlier. To this market Xerox offers after sales service on a priority basis and guarantees arrival of a mechanic at the problem site within hours of the receipt of the complaint. Thus Modi-Xerox has bagged large organisations that have a high load of photocopying work to be done at a quick pace and which cannot afford down time of their machine.

The route of excellant service by **Otis** has given leadership to them in the elevator industry. Otis which has set up an on-line system wherein a person stuck in an elevator can call a service centre through a phone installed in the elevator. All service centres are connected by the on-line system and communicate with the service operators at various sites through wireless machines. This ensures speedy communication and ensures the arrival of the mechanic at the problem site within less than 15 minutes. Obviously, this service is available in only a few elevators installed in large office buildings, hotels etc., which can afford this facility.

Eureka Forbes has carved a distinct niche for itself in the market for water purifiers and vacuum cleaners with its prompt, efficient and regular services. This begins with the arrival of the salesman to demonstrate the product (on request), explaining the functioning of the product, finalising the deal at the customers home itself, followed by regular visits for after sales service.

Packaging as a Differentiating Strategy

The package provides the buyer's first encounter with the product and is capable of turning him "on" or "off. Many marketers have called packaging a 5th P along with Price, Product, Place and Promotion. Packaging is treated as an element of the product strategy. Well designed packages can create an image of convenience or quality for the consumer and promotional value for the producer. This could be a useful tool for justifying the premium charged.

Inertia Industries Limited (IIL) launched their premium of **Sand Piper** beer in 1993, but the response was less than encouraging as the customer could not associate the ubiquitous brown bottle with a premium beer and hence the price charged struck a discordant note with the customer. In 1994, to rectify the defect, the company went for a relaunch and the packaging was changed to a green bottle with a golden champagne foil on top. IIL now repositioned Sand Pipers as the "champagne of beers". The effect was startling. It sold out 37,000 cases as compared to a mere 3000 cases a year before.

Planter's Pride, a high quality brand of Darjeeling tea, targeted at the "discerning" consumer of tea was priced at a premium. The brand success is believed to be because of its vacuum packaging.

Antiquity, positioned as the authentic whiskey for the elite, used the base line "the true blue". To help it sink in, the packaging has been done with a rich hue of blue and a better quality embossed label. These sophisticated images and their premium associations helped make the product look classier. The royal colour blue was used as a facet of the brand's personality and therefore enhanced its image of a premium product among the cream of society.

Lays Potato chips seem to command a high premium on its range of packaged potato chips based on its delivery of freshness, crispness and retention of flavour. This is possible by the use of packaging technology wherein the product is packed in air-tight metal foil packets filled with a nitrogen atmosphere to prevent air from leaking in and spoiling the product. Moreover, at a time when potato chips were available only in colourless, transparent, their quality plastic packages, Uncle Chipps' was the first to use packets made of air impermeable metal foil which was brightly coloured for visual differentiation.

VALUE DRIVERS

Positioning is the act of designing the company's offer and image so that the target market appreciates what the offering stands for in relation to its competitors. The company's positioning must be rooted in an understanding of how the market defines value and makes choice among alternative options. The positioning task consists of conveying the superiority of the brand over that of the competitors. Exhibits 6.4 and 6.5 show the different types to values and their strategic linkage.

EXHIBIT 6.4

The Five Value Drivers of Market Choice Behaviour

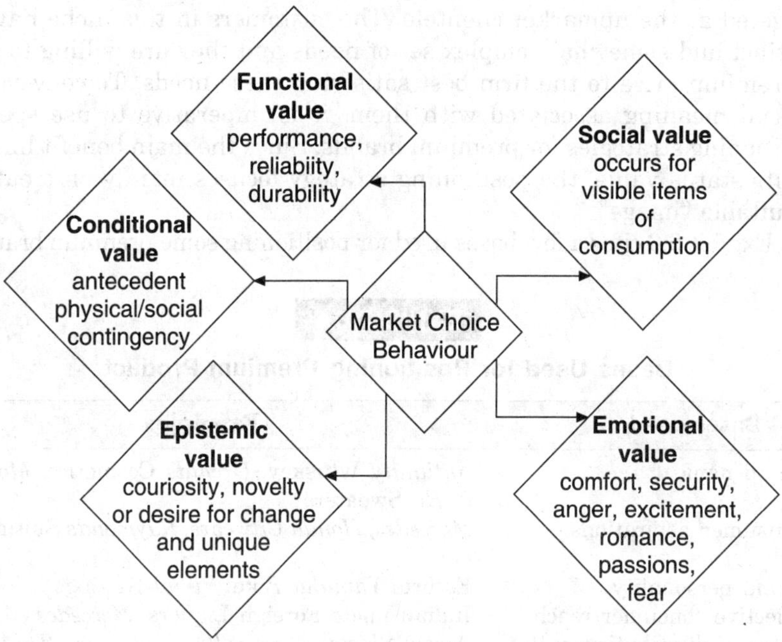

EXHIBIT 6.5

Value-Strategy Key Links

Type of value	Key strategic features for sustained advantage
• Functional	Continuous upgrading required
• Social	Long-term relationship, uncertain in the beginning—stable once established, visible reinforcement required
• Emotional	Periodic reinforcement required because of the need for intimate relationships
• Epistemic	Variety required to take advantage of uncertainty
• Conditional	Niche opportunities to take advantage of happenstance, cross-promotions, possible quick response desired

POSITIONING STRATEGIES OF PREMIUM BRANDS

Every brand tries to provide certain functional and some psychological benefits to its consumers. By following a distinct positioning strategy, the marketer can successfully demarcate the functional benefits provided by the product. In other words, to communicate the functional benefits and the accompanying intangible benefits, a correct positioning strategy must be evolved.

Premium brands generally operate in a niche segment and are targeted at the upmarket clientele. The customers in this niche have a distinct and somewhat complex set of needs and they are willing to pay a premium price to the firm best satisfying these needs. To convey the special meaning associated with them, it is imperative to use special positioning strategies for premium brands. Since the main benefit hinges on its status value, the positioning strategy focuses mainly on creating a suitable "image".

Exhibit 6.6 cites a few bases used for positioning some premium brands.

EXHIBIT 6.6

Bases Used for Positioning Premium Product

Bases used	Examples
Brand name	*Antiquity* Whiskey, *Orchids* Cosmetics, *Monte Carlo* Sweaters
Consumer aspirations	*Mercedes, Honda City* cars, *Raymonds* Suitings, etc.
Brand personality	Escorts *Yamaha* Bike, *Vimal* Suitings
Selective consumer reach	Indian made Foreign Liquors, *Mercedes*
Decor of distribution outlet	*Arrow Shirts, Allen Solly* Menswear, *Tanishq* Watches
Event sponsorship	Archers *Peach Schnappes, Malibu* White Rum

Brand Name as a Positioning Strategy

The name asssigned to a premium brand should conjure up an image of class, quality, exclusivity, and act as a status symbol.

Antiquity was positioned as an authentic whiskey for the upper echelons of society. The task for Shaw Wallace was to evolve a USP to appeal to the connoisseur. With a brand name like "Antiquity" that has connotations of "Old & Precious". especially in the Indian context, the company brought to the fore the quality aspect. It settled on the point of the brand being the only real high quality blended whiskey available in India and therefore could also leverage the premium pricing.

Lakme entered the super premium segment of the cosmetics and skin care market with its "international" range of colour cosmetics, **Orchids.** The selection of the name is of interest to us. The name "Orchids" is indicative of exotic, rare and expensive flowers. Borrowing the idea from English Literature, where the recipients of the orchids were beautiful, sophisticated women (as in classic romances like *Tess of the D'Ubervilles, Gone with the Wind),* the name "Orchids" was intended to capture the vivid imagination of the Indian woman.

Other premium brands that have used this plank of positioning are **Royale** range of watches by Titan, **Monte Carlo** range of sweaters, and **Chivas Regal,** a premium whiskey from Seagram.

Aspirations of the Consumer as a Positioning Strategy

Certain advertising captions used for premium products are symbolic of aspirations of the targeted consumers and hence, these aspirations are used as a positioning platform for the premium products. Let us consider the following examples:

Esteem	What men with drive will drive
Louis Phillipe	The upper crest
Honda/Hyundai	A chosen few will steer Honda/Hyundai
Amex Credit Card	Frankly this card is not for everyone
Wild Orchid	Set the night afire
Camlin Pen	Your handwriting is like nobody else's; What about your pen?
Raymonds suitings	The complete man
Yamaha bike	The rugged personality
Weekender	Wear your attitude

Brand Personality as a Positioning Strategy

The personality of the brand is an amalgam of many things—its name, packaging, price, style of advertising and, above all, the nature of the product itself. The purpose of positioning by brand personality is achieved if the marketer is able to define a desired personality for the brand which is clearly distinct from the personalities of competing offerings.

In many products it is found that there are no real differences among the competitors' options. So marketers begin to explore a more emotional level, and this is where the concept of a brand personality enters the positioning scene.

Raymonds—The complete man: Through its media coverage and advertising, Raymonds has built its personality as a man who has made his mark in both personal and professional circles. This image is very aptly conveyed through the Nawaab of Pataudi, Mansoor Ali Khan. In his professional life he is portrayed as a top business executive, who conducts himself with complete elan and in his personal life he is shown to be full of warmth, love and affection and is therefore a symbol of security. The entire imagery dwells on sophisticated men moving in high class societies.

The **Yamaha** (Escorts) bike was rated as powerful, stylish and speedy. Its brand personality was described as rugged, dominating, youthful, indulgent and vain. Also, it was complex, colourful and exciting. The self concept of the owners was very similar to what they used to describe the personality of the machine.

Selective Consumer Reach as a Positioning Strategy

Through this kind of positioning strategy, the marketer makes the most likely customers aware of the premium brand. For example, a typical up-market consumers of liquor usually frequent clubs, discotheques and hotels of certain class on upmarket standards. Therefore, Indian made foreign liquor brands target at those hotels, clubs, discotheques etc. to make their brand visible to potential customers.

Another kind of positioning strategy employed by premium product marketers, for selective consumer reach, is that of direct database marketing. Examples of this kind are Mercedes wherein direct mailers are sent to the select groups of society.

Exclusive Distribution Outlets as a Positioning Strategy

The outlets for the deliverance of the product to the customer can also be used to enhance the premium of the product. A good example of this strategy of positioning is that of the exclusive showrooms of designer clothing like **Arrow** and **Allen Solly.** Another example is that of Tanishq, the range of exclusive, gold plated jewellery watches by Titan, which is being sold through a limited number of exclusive outlets. Each of these has been designed in keeping with the image projected by the watches, including decor of the shopping centres for the customer, in order to allow them the time and convenience to examine the range and make one's choice.

Event Sponsorship as or Positioning Strategy

Event sponsorships of upmarket cultural activities like fashion shows, sports and musical concerts help increase awareness of the premium brands, the basic assumption being that the audience comprises the higher strata of society.

Another tactic employed by marketers of premium products for building and strengthening of their brand position is that of hyped up product launches. For instance, two brands Archers **Peach Schnappes** and **Malibu White Rum,** both featuring in the super premium range of alcohol, were able to bring about consumer awareness on their premium nature almost instantaneously, through extravagant product launches.

CHAPTER 7

New Products Planning

With advances in technology, consumers' aspirations for change or upgradation of model and intense competition, the creation of new products has become an avenue for growth in India. However, fortunately, India is yet to face a situation of too many brands chase trying to a handful of customers. Perhaps, the sheer size of the Indian market and a consistent economic development have opened up new vistas for launching new brands in variety of products. An analysis of new product developments since early nineties shows that these products have been either off-shoots of technological developments in the West or improvements over the existing products in the areas of their design, style, substance or packaging.

Most products invariably follow a product life cycle in the biological sense. The following discussion is intended to elaborate or the usefulness of the concept of product life cycle (PLC), market characteristis and shape of marketing mix in different stages of PLC.

PRODUCT LIFE CYCLE

A graphic representation of a product's sales history from its inception to final withdrawal from the market is illustrated in Exhibit 7.1.

EXHIBIT 7.1

Different Stages of Product Life Cycle

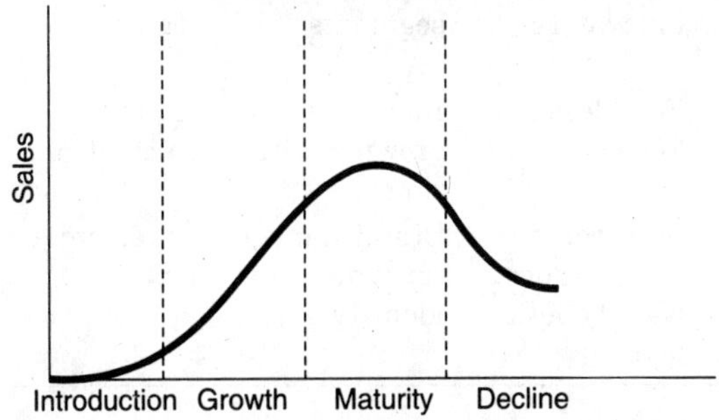

Barring few exceptions most products begin their lives with a low level of sales (defined as the *introductory stage).* The sales gradually pick up; this phase is known as the *growth stage.* Then for some period of time the sales curve remains stagnant of some plateau; this is popularly referred to as the *maturity stage.* Finally, the curve slopes downwards; this is called the *declining stage.* While, in general, this pattern is common, it may vary from product to product. Moreover, a product may jump a stage or two, or remain stagnant in a particular stage, e.g., a fashion may disappear soon after a boom, but a product like salt has come to stay forever.

Traditionally, the product life cycle (PLC) concept has been thought of as appropriate for a product category as a whole. Marketing managers, however, try to use the concept even while evaluating specific brands of a product category, as most brands have a sales history. Similarly, the shape of the product life cycle curve, the slopes of the different stages, and the length of the cycles would vary from product to product. The ultimate utility of the concept lies in its ability to serve as a planning tool for developing marketing strategies at different stages. In general, some of the typical marketing activities and responses during various stages of the PLC are briefly described in Exhibits 7.2 and 7.3.

EXHIBIT 7.2

Marketing Characteristics Seen in Different Stages of Product Life Cycle

Stage	Introduction	Growth	Maturity	Decline
Charateristics				
Sales	Low	Fast growth	Slow growth	Decline
Profit	Marginal or even loss	Rapid rise	Falling margins	Low margin
Strategic thrust	Market development	Penetration	Defend share	Cut cost, reposition or withdraw
Customer targets	Non-users; innovators	Form new segments	Shed segments	Selective; explore new market
Competition	Few, less known	Intensive growing with time	Many efficient ones	Limited
Differential advantage	Superior performance; New benefit; features	Brand name, corporate identity	Price, unique service	Business experience; low cost producer

EXHIBIT 7.3

Shape of Marketing Mix in Different PLC Stages

Stage	Introduction	Growth	Maturity	Decline
Marketing mix				
Product	Unique offering	Improvement on early innovation	Different variety	Rationalise range
Price	Low or premium	Low with, high volume	Maintain margin	Smaller margin
Promotion	Incentive to use	Heavy	Parity, loyalty formation	Threshold level for reminder
Advertising focus	Awareness building	Brand name, performance	Value for money	Rationalise
Distribution	Build network	Fast spread out	Choose specific territory vis-a-vis competition	Limited coverage or enter new market and develop new form of distribution.

Extension of Product Life Cycle

Marketers are naturally keen extend the life cycle of a product. These strategies are usually built around new and improved versions of the existing products that will match the market demands. For instance, the entry of *Maruti* car in the Indian automobile market in mid 80's compelled the existing manufacturers like HM (Hindustan Motors) to improve their "Ambassador" car model.

However, the Indian consumer has shown a tendency of sticking to the use of an existing product and thereby extending its life. In the process, acceptance of even an improved version of a product has been delayed because of this Indian habit of not throwing away an older or inferior item. In general, this tendency has discouraged large scale introduction of new products in India contrary to the trend in developed countries.

Weaknesses of the Product Life Cycle Concept

Undefined concept: Customer needs, demands, technologies, product categories, forms and brands have quite different driving forces.

No uniform shape: The bell-shaped curve described earlier in Exhibit 7.1 may not be an unique PLC curve. Generally it shows the popular perception about market behaviour.

Unpredictable turning points: While most products do peak eventually, there is no specific turning point.

Unclear implications: Growth phase may or may not be associated with high-profit margin. Similarly, rapid growth can be accompanied by low profit (e.g. electronics). By contrast, decline stage can be exceptionally profitable (the foundry business).

Product-oriented: Managers fail to understand those factors that shape the ability of the business to satisfy the needs of the customers in competitive markets. For example:

— Changing requirements of customers
— Strategies of competitors
— Attractiveness of the market to new competitors
— Emergence of new technologies
— Power of companies that supply resources.

Exhibit 7.4 shows the Ansoff's classic model of growth strategies. It also shows the role of new products in present as well as new market in which a company operates.

EXHIBIT 7.4

Ansoff's Classic Model of Growth Strategies

	Current products	New products
Existing market	Market penetration strategies • Increase market share • Increase product usage: — increase frequency of use — increase quantity used — new applications	Product development strategies • Product improvement • Product line extensions • New products for same markets
New market	Marketing innovation and ex-pansion strategies • Expand markets for existing products: — geographic expansion — target new segments	Technological innovation and diversification strategies • Vertical integration: — forward integration — backward integration • Diversification into related business (concentric diver-sification) • Diversification into unrelated businesses (conglomerate diversification)

CLASSIFICATION OF NEW PRODUCTS

The term 'new' is used in a relative sense. New product launches in India can be broadly classified into three categories, as elaborated below.

1. **Marketing innovations:** Companies have made improvements on existing products and have launched these as new products in the market. For instance, *Maggi* noodles, soft drinks in tetrapack, shampoo in pouch, commodities or *Shrikhand, Pan Parag,* etc. are basically slightly alterated versions of existing products. Here, consumers did not require to change their consumption habits drastically to accommodate these new products. These are examples of improvement in the products whose success was derived more from marketing innovations such as packaging, branding, and easy availability, rather than any significant change in the substance of the product itself.

2. **Product improvements:** The launch of detergent powders, 100 cc two-wheelers, radial tyres, instamatic cameras are basically slight innovations on the technology/design of existing products, although the product category as such already existed in some primitive form. Such new products are generally targeted at a new class of buyers. The success of such ventures depends upon the ability of the marketers to convince the consumer about the improvement in the performance over traditional brand(s) as well as over similar new entrants. For example, in the 100 cc motorcycles vehicle market, TVS Suzuki was the first entrant and it captured a sizeable market. Subsequently, *Hero Honda* became the market leader in this category of motorcycles by virtue of superior performance and innovative marketing techniques.

3. **Technological innovations:** The Indian market has experienced a rapid induction of products like personal computers, photocopiers, digital camera, cell phones. Generally, these products require some kind of assembling of imported kits. Although adaptation of such products calls for a substantial change in the consumption pattern, yet these products have succeeded in view of their significant utility to the user. Such ventures require an initial awareness-building and persuasion to install the product. Initial resistance to change may delay any adoption of new technologies. However, a look at the track records of such new products shows that early entrants have reaped the benefits of leadership. Subsequent entrants have faced difficulty in establishing themselves.

ROUTES OF NEW PRODUCTS DEVELOPMENT

- Transfer of technology
- Penetration into new market diversification
- New product lines
- Product line extension

- Cost reduction
- Repositioning or product relaunch

1. **Transfer of technology:** New products have often been launched, based on new technology, either acquired from the parent company or through foreign collaboration. Launch of the personal computer or photocopying machine is a move in this direction.

2. **Diversification:** Sometimes companies have entered into new lines of business(es) and catered to altogether new markets for the first time. DCM's entry into the LCV market fits into this category. Similarly, ITC's decision to enter into hotels, apparels, edible oil, tissue paper is a diversification strategy. Likewise, BPL diversified from pharmaceuticals to consumer electronics business. In general, diversification strategy tries to reduce the dependence of a company on a limited line of products. At times, companies find the new businesses more profitable than their traditional product portfolio.

3. **Additions to existing product lines:** New product lines and brand extensions have sometimes supplemented a company's existing business. Videocon's entry into washing machines and music systems from colour televisions is a case in point. Similarly, as a business group, Godrej's strategy to expand its product range from consumer non-durables like toiletries to durables such as refrigerators, cupboards, and even office equipments is a classic example of product line extension.

4. **Improvements/Revisions in existing products:** New products that offer superior performance and replace existing products are another way of entering the market. For example, the launch of transistor sets and cassette players, though primitive by today's standards, were at one time new to the market. They eventually replaced radios and gramophones. More recently ITC has successfully launched many sportswear, fashion jeans, and apparels.

5. **Cost reductions:** New products that provide similar performance at lower cost (e.g., *Nirma* detergent, *Tata-407* LCV).

6. **Product relaunch:** Sometimes old products have been relaunched with minor improvements and targeted at completely new markets or consumer segments. e.g., the launch of many food products like *Good day* biscuits, *Nes-tea, Pan Parag* etc. fall under this type of new product launches.

NEW PRODUCT DEVELOPMENT PROCESS

How are new products developed? Typically, the product development process consists of the following stages:

1. **Idea generation:** The process of generating new ideas may consist of brainstorming, attribute listing, focus group discussions, or problem

inventory analysis. Broadly speaking, it involves creative thinking and technological developments. But sources of new ideas could be varied, as shown in Exhibit 7.5.

EXHIBIT 7.5

Sources of New Product Ideas

- **Customers:** Customers are sometimes able to discuss their requirements and offer ideas that will meet those problems.
- **Competitors:** Systematic comparison or benchmarking with the competition may offer good source of new product ideas.
- **Distributors:** Suggestions from distributors and their problems in handling present products often throwup new ideas.
- **Creative techniques:** Brainstorming, focussed interviews and technological forecasting enable one to find out the latent capabilities of innovations.
- **External world:** The external world, especially the use of their technology, offers a good source of ideas for implementation in the home market.
- **Research and development:** Create new product ideas through R&D.

2. **Consumer insights and new concepts:** This involves a thorough screening of new ideas from the point of view of the consumers reactions to the new product. Techniques for evaluating new ideas may consist of a series of open discussions with those concerned, where ideas are minutely scrutinised so that market failures can be minimised. Different core concepts are tested among consumers.

The characteristic of a strong product concept would be either to offer entirely new benefits not offered by existing products, or else to offer some secondary benefits in addition to the existing benefits. Some negative aspects of the existing products may be eliminated, or a price reduction over available alternatives may be offered. Finally, the new concept could position the product to fit into the emerging trends in society.

3. **Business analysis:** Product ideas that pass the screening process are subjected to business analysis. Ultimately, more concrete business recommendations are arrived at. This includes specifying product features and information or resources needed in production. The analysis makes an assessment of market demand, cost projections, investment requirements and even of the existing competition.

4. **Prototype development:** During this stage, the new product idea is trans-formed from a concept to a prototype, outlining the physical characteristics of the product, package designs, brand names, etc. while the concept is evaluated from many marketing angles (see Exhibit 7.6, for details), apart from examining production or manufacturing set-up

requirements, cost and other modifications necessary before entering into the test marketing stage. Here, a major activity involves obtaining consumer feedback on different prototype models. Typically, consumers are given a sample to test the proposed new product. This activity is popularly known as **"concept testing"**.

EXHIBIT 7.6

Concept Development

Concept development involves asking questions such as the following:

- **Need:** Do customers find a strong perceived need for the benefit offered?
- **Trust:** Do they believe that the new product has the benefits claimed?
- **Communicability:** Do customers easily understand the key benefits being offered?
- **Usage:** Does it offer easy adoption?
- **Perceived value:** Do customers see it as offering value at the price being considered?

5. **Test marketing:** Test marketing is an experimental procedure that provides an opportunity to examine the prospect of the new product under realistic market conditions to obtain a first hand measure of the potential sales volume in national distribution. The new product is marketed on an experimental basis in a few pockets of the market, choosing some cities and small geographic areas.

Test marketing serves two important functions. It provides an opportunity to assess the outcome of an alternative course of action. Marketers can vary the different marketing mix elements and assess their impact on sales before the optimum course of action is taken. This allows management to identify and correct weaknesses in either the product or its marketing programme before launching the product on a national scale. Thus, if me test market results show any kind of failure or weakness, the product may be reformulated or the marketing mix may be changed in view of the feedback. Therefore, the setting up of test markets can provide valuable information about the nature of the market, marketing strategy changes and product modifications necessary to ensure a successful launch. It is worth remembering that one cannot get a second chance to make the first impression.

6. **Commercialization:** This refers to the decision to market the new product at the full scale of operation, which involves a significant commitment of resources and managerial effort.

Not surprisingly, in spite of extensive preplanning and caution, products still sometimes fail.

THE LATENT FACTORS BEHIND MARKETING SUCCESS OF ANY NEW PRODUCT

Let us take an example to explain the various factors which are apparently responsible for any marketing success.

EXHIBIT 7.7

The Latent Factors behind Any Marketing Success

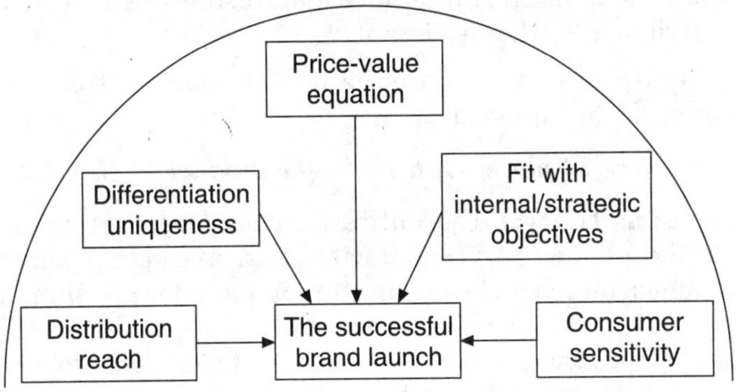

Rexona Deodorants

The market scenario: Before the launch of *Rexona* deodorants (marketed by Pond's (I) Ltd.) the market for Deodorants in India was almost non-existent, with marginal presence for some imported deodorants such as *Impulse, Fa* etc. The biggest problem for any deodorant marketer with regard to the Indian market was the very low levels of awareness amongst the people about the negative aspects of body odour etc. The people, to a large extent, used talcum powder and seemed to be satisfied with the benefits that they got from it.

A preliminary research conducted by Pond's (I) Ltd. revealed that the consumer not only had very little knowledge about deodorants anti-perspirants and perfumes and, more importantly, he/she did not actually feel the need for a deodorant.

Thus, as things stood, there existed the herculean task of actually creating a market for deodorants in India: for which the company had to undertake an intensive consumer awareness campaign to create the need for a deodorant.

The product launch: Entering the deodorants market in India was in line with Unilever's international product portfolio, since the Unilever Group has a major presence in the deodorants market worldwide with brands such as *Axe, Rexona, Impulse,* etc.

After a prolonged spell of consumer research, the company decided to enter the market with three different applicators *(viz., the atomiser spray, the roll-on and the stick).* These were priced in the range Rs 22 to Rs 72 to cover different price ranges in the market. It was felt that a consumers would not hesitate to pay this amount of money for a new and innovative product, thus ensuring trial.

The company spent substantial amounts on R&D in selecting the deodorant's perfume, the product form and mode of application etc. The *Rexona* brand was chosen primarily because, internationally, it is a deodorant *(and not a soap as it is in India).* Additionally, the *Rexona* soap occupies the position of fragrance and freshness which is in keeping with the attributes of the deodorant.

The key to its success: Essentially, the success story of *Rexona* deodorants could be summed up as:

"Being in the right place, with the right product at the right time".

Consumer sensitivity: The entire *Rexona* deodorant as a package deal, be it the product form, characteristics, marketing mix etc., was well researched and had been put through numerous simulated test marketing (STM) tests before the product was finally launched. The decision to launch the product in the three forms *(viz-atomiser spray, stick and roll-on)* was taken following recommendation from market research about the consumer's purchasing behaviour.

Pond's perceived that a latent but unexpressed need existed in the market and were able to effectively gauge the market needs, expectations and sentiments and finally launched a product that not only satisfied the expectations of the consumer but also enthralled him.

- Product match with consumer's needs.
- Prolonged spell of testing before launch to ensure quality.

Consistency with internal/strategic objectives: The entry into the market for deodorants in India made a lot of strategic sense for the Uni Lever Group as it has a big presence in the Deodorants market worldwide.

- Strategic fit with Unilever's international objectives and portfolio.

Pace/Speed of action or reaction: Pond's also scored on this point, since it was the first in India to come up with a deodorant manufactured in India and specifically suited for Indian conditions. Being the first player in the market it has certain advantages but it also comes saddled with its own pitfalls. However, Pond's has been able to manage the situation very effectively with a keen sense of insight into the consumer's psyche. Identifying the consumer's latent and expressed needs, they have managed to fine-tune the marketing-mix for *Rexona* deodorants to a nicety and thus avoided many of the errors that a marketer might commit in such a situation.

- First Mover advantage

Differentiation/Uniqueness of the benefit: The product offered a very strong benefit which not only concluded functional value but also a strong emotional bearing. The benefit and the form in which it was offered was unique in its own sense and the communication of this was handled very effectively so as to make a lasting impact on the consumer.

- Strong functional benefit
- Unique product offering

Price-value equation: The product also managed to score highly on this front. The strategy of the company to offer three different types of applicators at various price levels gave the consumer a strong reason to purchase and use the product.

- Range of deodorants to suit all market segments
- Penetrative pricing at the lower end

Distribution reach: HUL's distribution network, which also handles Ponds' products throughout India gave the *Rexona* deodorant a ready access to a number of retail outlets throughout the nation. This was leveraged very effectively by the company, and with a well knit distributing machinery in place it did not take much effort on the part of the company to ensure a retailer push given the amount of consumer pull that was being ensured by the advertising campaign.

EXHIBIT 7.8

Key Marketing Preparation Before a New Product Launch

- Identification of Consumer needs
- Clear Segment Formation by Effective Market Research
- Choose a Proper Positioning Platform
- Effective Promotion/Advertising
- Ensuring Product Quality
- Effective Sales and Distribution
- Correct Pricing Strategy
- Differentiation of the New Offering
- Leveraging Existing Strengths

Acid Test before Any New Product Launch

A new product must meet the following criteria:

Important: It should be perceived as important by customers. In particular, it must offer a substantial benefit or distinct superiority over the existing options by the consumers.

Unique: The benefits offered should be preferably unique to attract consumer interest.

Sustainability: A company should be able to retain its pioneering position so that it is not quickly imitated by competitors.

Marketable: A company must be capable of offering the product through suitable distribution system.

SUCCESSFUL NEW PRODUCT LAUNCHES IN INDIA

NOKIA 1100 'Mobile Handset Phone'

Nokia's first 'Made for India' model the Nokia 1100 soon became the largest selling model in Indian GSM handset market. The major reasons for the whooping success of this mobile phone set are examined here.

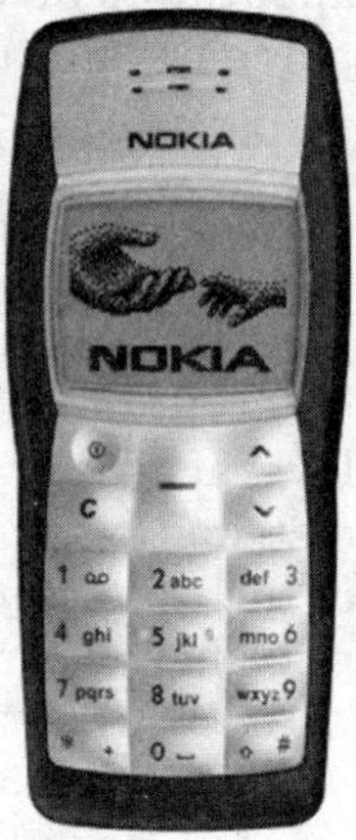

Identification of consumer needs/segments: When Indian cell phone market was really flourishing bulk of the consumers were looking for a basic and low cost and reliable phone. This segment of buyers were not interested to pay the extra money for all the new age sophisticated features like Multimedia Messaging or Java application support etc. because they really wanted a phone for making and receiving calls only. Nokia realised the needs of this market segment and offered the same in this new cell phone model. The market gave an amazing response to this new set called Nokia 1100.

Effective marketing research: Nokia launched 1100 and 1108, after intensive marketing research. The needs of the customers was assessed and this new product was designed to deliver on those needs. For the low budget segment, a rough, sturdy and reliable phone was a necessity. Nokia not only met these needs but also added some useful additional features like anti-slip grip and torch light. These two added features helped them in differentiating the new model.

Effective advertising: Unlike other mobile phone makers, Nokia's advertising compaigns were aimed at the low end consumers only. The advertisement for the Nokia 1100 was targeted at the entry-level phone users. It showed the mobile set in a truck that traverses the length of India. The implicit message is that phone still works at the end of the long, hot, and dusty journey. Nokia's advertisements have dwelt on the human angle of mobile technology, rather than emphasize their technical aspects. Localized communications has helped reinforce the core brand strength of "technology that appeals to ordinary consumers."

Nokia's advertising has also played the role of an educator. During the introductory phase of cell phone when phones in the grey market sold much more than legally approved imported phones, Nokia undertook a campaign to educate people about the advantages of buying original Nokia 1100 model. Through its astute advertising, Nokia has been perceived as the innovator. For instance, it is not the first handset maker to have Hindi text display for SMS, but its hardsell campaign showing the Hindi text on a display has enabled it to usurp that leader's position in the minds of the general consumers.

AIMED AT THE MASS MARKET

Ensuring product quality: Nokia has emphasised upon its image of good product quality in 1100. It has many useful features incorporated in it like silicon keypad, anti-slip phone body, white LED which works as a useful torch.

As for applications, the 1100 has an alarm clock, countdown timer, stopwatch, and reminder functions, which are more or less the basic requirements of any cell phone. The phone's voice clarity and network coverage was pretty good, as it did'nt falter even in low network areas. The battery life stays strong for around 4 days of regular usage.

Correct pricing strategy: Eventually the choice of pricing decides the fate of every low budget product. And that's exactly the area where the Nokia 1100 was more accurate by choosing the launch price at Rs 3,500. The market seems to found some good value for such a new low-budget phone when competitive models were much more expensive.

Leveraging existing strengths: Nokia knew its strengths when it launched 1100 model. The company was known as a reliable phone maker by virtue of its strong access to international technology. In a low budget segment the perception of the brand image and retail presence are very important factors. Nokia has effectively leveraged its strength before introducing the 1100 model.

Differentiation of the new model: In its overall marketing strategy, Nokia ensured that its all 4 P's stand out from the clutter of other existing mobile phones. In particulars, their advertising campaign was aimed at making communication relevant to strengthen consumer-connect with the brand.

The context: ITC entered the branded *Atta* market with the launch of *Aashirvaad Atta* in Jaipur and Chandigarh in May 2002 and gradually expanded its presence across India. At that time, 95% of the *flour* market was captured by loose unbranded *flour*, 2% by local brands and 3% by national brands. *Chakki atta* was the most popular due to two reasons. First, it was the traditional and familiar way of sourcing *atta* and thus the customer felt comfortable with it. Reasonable price was also another key factor.

When ITC launched *Aashirvaad atta*, the other big national players in the segment were Hindustan Lever (Annapurna), Godrej Pillsbury (Pillsbury), Cargill Foods (Nature Fresh). Each of these was making a loss. The players were just seeking to expand their volumes in the market, so that when the business eventually became profitable, they could encash it. Also, all *atta* brands were fighting to capture market share by offering heavy discounts to retailers and freebies to attract the housewife.

Aashirvaad was launched with an aggressive price in order to attract both the retailer and the consumer. ITC entered the wheat handling and trading sector simultaneously.

Factors of Success

1. **Product:** Even before getting into the production of *atta*, ITC did extensive marketing research to find out what are the qualities in *atta* that a consumer looks for. The results found offered nothing less than a challenge as they indicated that the requirements on the fineness of the texture of *atta*, colour etc. differed from region to region across India. Leveraging its internal sourcing through e-Choupals, ITC decided to make customized *atta* for various regions. The wheat that it sourced through e-Choupals was graded as per regional preference of breed of wheat. Initially when ITC had only one plant, it would produce different kinds of *atta* for different regions on certain days and then move on to produce another kind, etc. Subsequently it had several factories in

different parts of India that produced different varieties of *atta*. After making the product, it did extensive consumer preference tests to compare *Aashirvaad atta* to its nearest competitor in various regions. If the consumer likes the competitor's product better, ITC would try to diagnose the issue and improve its product.

Thus, superior quality was a key strategy used by ITC to make *Aashirvaad atta* successful.

2. **Pricing and promotion:** ITC has followed the concept of 'honest pricing'. For this it focused on the cost of production and selling. It sourced the raw material at competitive prices, as it procured directly from the farmers. Then it ensured that it does the major transportation of raw material and finished goods only in off-season so as to keep the prices low.

While the competitors engaged in various schemes like free ketchup, *bhujiya* etc. to attract the customer, ITC decided to go for an "honest price" approach. Retailers welcomed this scheme as they now did'nt have to worry about inventory management of the freebies and also did not lose any sales due to the freebies. Customers also welcomed it, as they would hardly be enticed by the idea of getting a ketchup bottle every time they bought atta.

3. **Packaging:** ITC Foods also aimed at superior and innovative packaging. *Aashirvaad* was packaged in a PET Poly, with the design showcasing the farming process undertaken in the rural heartland of India in the form of a Madhubani painting. [Incidentally, 'Aashirvaad Select' Atta pack has been awarded the World Star Award for Excellence in Packaging in the Consumer Pack Category. This is one of the most prestigious awards in the world for Packaging.] ITC has also created a first in packaging in the branded atta category by introducing its premium offering in carton packaging and offering vacuum sealing in the 5 kg premium pack. Both these innovations maintained the freshness of the product.

4. **Communication:** ITC realized that since *atta* is something that the consumer consumes internally into the body. So there is always much concerns on quality, hygiene and nutrition in customer's mind. Also, the customer (often the mother or the wife) is often emotional about what she feeds to her family. Keeping this in mind, ITC zeroed down on the tag line *chun chun ke* which translates into "the best pick". Ads showed how the family that consumed *Aashirvaad atta* was a healthy and happy family. And the kids in the family performed well and were applauded by other—thus touching an emotional chord with the mothers women at home.

Thus it was mainly the superior product, supported by the right package, proper choice of price and right communication that led to the success of *Aashirvaad atta*. ITC was able to carve out an attractive value proposition of best quality at honest price; and also communicate it well to its customer.

Maruti Swift

Maruti Swift has been a tremendous success in Indian market. Car of the Year 2006, Swift has seen absolute commercial success.

Background: When Japan's Suzuki Motor Corporation decided on a car like Swift, it sent a team of around 50 designers and engineers to Europe, a booming market for the small car segment. Importantly, for the first time, 25 members of the team were Indian engineers from Maruti Udyog Limited (MUL). The result was the Swift, was first showcased as a concept car at the 2002 Paris Motor Show and the 2004 Auto Expo in India. Given that a concept car is a prototype made to showcase a new vehicle's styling and technology, to gauge customer reaction to new and radical ideas, the car was brought into commercial production pretty quickly.

Factors behind success: Swift's success is really due to a combination of carefully thought-out elements in its creation: the product design, marketing strategy and—given the sensitivity of Indian buyers—price.

Product design: The Swift was not merely loaded with all that Maruti was always known for. But it offered elegant style, classy interiors and compelling performance. The Suzuki Swift was vastly different from Maruti's other product designs. No wonder it has stirred up passions in the car industry and kicked up an unprecedented level of hype in favour of Maruti. Its international and likeable looks appeal Swiftly; this may take the fight in the premium hatch category to a new high. The Swift looks radical. Its overall design theme appears to be a brilliant fusion of opposites that appeals from the first look. The rounded, jellybean-like lower half and the almost 'boxy' top-half have drawn comparisons to the BMW Mini (a model that is not available in India). Like the Mini, the Swift's A-pillar arms and midline have also been blacked out to give the car a floating roof look—an ocular illusion. The Swift's design gives it a squat profile, just like the Getz's of Hyundai.

It is a combination of Italian flair and French quirkiness. And although the car was designed for the European markets, MUL realised that it would need to adapt it to Indian conditions. Suitable modifications were made to the original design: the aesthetics were essentially untouched (the raised bonnet line that matches the new European pedestrian safety norms, for instance, stays), but changes were made where they were felt most critical. The suspensions were strengthened, a suitable spruced-up Esteem engine and gearbox was brought in, tyres with extra traction were used and even the paint quality changed, keeping harsher Indian conditions in mind.

Price: Perhaps the Swift's biggest plus print is its price. Introduced at Rs 387 lakh for the base model, it was close to about Rs 50,000 less than its competitors. Even the top-end version was Rs 70,000 cheaper than the Hyundai Getz GLS, its main competitior.

Promotion: The buzz around Swift began in December 2004—five months before its launch. All new WagonRs and Maruti Omnis came with stickers and sunshields that proclaimed "My next car is a Swift". Unlike most car launches, where the look of the vehicle is kept under wraps until the last possible moment, photos and specs were made available at showrooms several months earlier. Models of the car were placed on high platforms at busy intersections at different places; while cars were on display in malls. It works well for those who do'nt have the inclination to really go to a dealer and check out the car. The launch was staggered over three to four days in 15 cities across the country, coinciding with the worldwide launch of the car. Swift appeared in the Bollywood hit *Bunty Aur Babli*, which was released on the same day as the car launch. And it trained 1,000 salespeople—called "energisers"—to exclusively sell the Swift.

Swift is a perfect example of a success story where a product is launched with due care of its design, price and promotion.

NEW PRODUCT FAILURE EXPERIENCES

Maggi Pickles

Nestle, upbeat with their success with Maggi Noodles, went to brand extension Maggi pickle. However, they failed to impress Indian customers with this new launch.

Pickle being a typical Indian ethnic food supplement, has a distinct place in Indian consumers' mind. But it was difficult, if not impossible, for somebody sitting in Switzerland to decide what kind of pickle will attract Indian consumers. A typical Indian customer will ask to herself,

"My *dadima* (grand mom) used to make the best *achaar* (pickles) in the world. Who is this foreign company selling pickles to us? What do they know about pickles?" There was an inert reluctance to taste the new brand. The positioning was completely wrong.

The product choice itself was essentially wrong. There was a distinct gap between the perceived application of Noodles and pickles in consumers' mind. Also, pickles are taken during a full meal and Maggi was positioned as a snack. Nestle probably thought that the brand extension will work as both these things come under "food" category, but they overlooked the fact that the usage occasions were different.

Vanilla Coke

Introduction: In April 2004, Coca-Cola India launched Vanilla Coke, the company's first flavour extension in India, with much fanfare. Vanilla Coke was expected to boost Coca-Cola's sales in India, which had taken a plunge following the pesticide contamination controversy in 2003.

Coca-Cola: Blind tests done before launching Vanilla Coke revealed that consumers liked the taste. The concept of ice-cream floats in cola was quite common in urban restaurants in India. Vanilla Coke targeted urban teens and young adults in the high and middle income groups.

It carried the tag line Ice Creamy Thanda. The India campaign took a cue from the "hip-hop" commercial used in Hong Kong, where it had been successfully launched earlier. The jingle in the commercial stressed: "No more conventions" and started with the word "Wakaw" meaning cool and different. The 60-second ad was played on youth-centric channels like MTV, Channel [V], HBO and AXN and even regional channels like Sun TV. With a retro-Bollywood theme, the ad urged consumers to "try something new and different".

A relatively new celebrity, Vivek Oberoi was chosen as the protagonist in the ad.

To promote the product, Coke activated key accounts, started promotional activities in colleges, shopping malls and launched a retrospective music album.

Consumer response: Vanilla Coke failed to excite the Indian palate.

Retailers reported slow offtake of Vanilla Coke. According to a retailer in south Bombay, the product's sales were rapidly dropping. 'Irrelevant' advertising was cited as one of the reasons for Vanilla Coke's failure. The other issues pointed out by the respondents included "wrong positioning", "no connect with Coke as a brand" and "bad product". Respondents believed that "no proper research was done on Indian palate" and that there was a "mismatch of target group and communication".

"Not too many people could remain hooked to a drink that tasted like an ice-cream. There is an initial craze for everything new. But then people get bored. And this is the exact fate of Vanilla Coke."

The television commercial and outdoor promotions seemed to have been successful in generating hype and awareness for the brand. But, Vanilla Coke's target market, the younger consumers felt that the commercial itself was out of context and had no connection with Coke as a brand.

With young, aspirational and tech savvy youth as the target audience, the consumer felt that the commercial was a clear mismatch. Consumers also did not like the taste of Vanilla Coke. The retailers believed that the taste—sweeter cola with a hint of vanilla—was not accepted.

Slice Fruit

The juice drinks market is estimated at Rs 600 crore, of which glass bottles account for roughly Rs 300 crore. Of the glass bottles market, Pepsi's Slice and Mangola together have a 48 per cent share. According to industry estimates, traditionally in the juice drinks market, mango has always been the most popular flavour, followed by orange. Other juice drink brands in the market are Coca-Cola's Maaza and Parle's Frooti. In the 100 per cent juice market, in contrast, orange remains the preferred flavour. Coca-Cola's Maaza is leading in this market, followed closely by Slice and then Parle's Frooti. Among pure fruit juices, PepsiCo's Tropicana and Dabur Real together control a 75 per cent share of the Rs 100-crore market. Tropicana is available in orange, sweet orange, pineapple, black grape, apple, tomato and mixed fruit variants.

The context: PEPSI Foods rolled out a series of fruit cocktail variants under its Slice brand. The fruit cocktail variants, priced at Rs 10 each, included flavours such as Slice litchi, guava, strawberry, tropical orange, pineapple orange and strawberry orange. But the entire brand extension was withdrawn very soon. The prime reasons behind the failure of the brand seem to be the following;

1. **Supply chain problems led to difficulties in production:** PepsiCo was sourcing lichis from Muzaffarpur, guavas from Karnataka and Allahabad, and mangoes from Ratnagiri. Just when the product offtake was on the upswing, the soft drinks major ran out of fruit pulp for some of its cocktail variants. According to Pepsi Foods Ltd., the company could not ensure steady supply for some of its Slice fruit cocktails. The supply chain for niche products such as these is complex. Take Slice litchi. The variant was a hit in all cities when they launched the product in, but the peak litchi season is limited to only about four weeks.

2. **Unattractive advertisement with a confusing message did not appeal to audiences:** The message they tried to convey was that Slice fruit cocktails are:

- Fresh
- Fortified with calcium (therefore beneficial)
- Thirst quenching, and
- Stimulating.

But the message that reached the consumers confused them. The central character "Rasik Bihari", who was portrayed as one of the typical target consumers, failed to convey the intended message. The ad was termed silly and background was considered weird. The fresh appeal of fruit drink was missing and the thought that calcium fortified drink provides one with required courage was ridiculed.

Lack of a touching advertisement to launch a product failed to create trial purchases.

Maintaining a costly supply chain for such a small amount of market demand did not make sense in the long run and thus the product was withdrawn.

Godrej Powerwash

Godrej powerwash was launched as the first brand after the formation of Godrej-GE alliance. However, unfortunately it was not able to make dent in the washing machine's market. It turned out to be a failure. It was a big blow to both partners. For GE, it marked the entry into Indian white goods market and for Godrej it was the first attempt to extend its franchise from refrigerators to another white good. Following are the key reasons for its failure.

Lack of differential advantage: At the time of the launch of Godrej powerwash, Videocon was the market leader in the washing machines market. So when Godrej powerwash entered into the market, consumers started comparing it with Videocon. But unfortunately, there was little perceptible difference between the Videocon and Godrej machines, except a few additional frills like a separate wash basket with Godrej machines.

Improper positioning: Godrej positioned its washing machines as a reliable and durable product with new technology. But unfortunately, the claim about technology was not accepted by consumers as both Godrej and Videocon machines appear similar. Consumers, by and large, preferred product superiority of Videocon over the reliability and durability promised by Godrej.

Work of product superiority: Godrej powerwash arrival was preceded by the announcement of a number of dealer conferences in metros, and 1200 direct dealers and 400 retailers were roped in for the launch. Despite the dealer's involvement in the launch of the product from the very start, the dealers found nothing unique in the new machine.

Advertising focused on the existing Godrej values of reliability and durability which were not able to attract the consumers, as they were looking for tangible superior product features.

Tanishq 18 Carat Jewellary

Among the branded jewellery, Tanishq is considered a trendsetter in the Indian market. When it was launched in 1995, Tanishq began with 18-carat jewellery. But it did not perform well in the domestic market. The reason for the failure was inadequate prior marketing research before the launch of the product. Given below are some of the other aspects which were overlooked while deciding the marketing mix of the product.

Improper target market choice: Titan Tanishq 18 carat jewellery was targetted at elite segment. But there was a contradiction as to why the elite segment should go in for a low carat gold because the usual norm for gold in India at that time was 22 carat. The product failed to attract the consumers who were supposed to be their best target.

Distribution related problems: When Tanishq was launched, titan used to market most of its products through multi-brand stores. But it soon realized that selling jewellery was actually a more retail-intensive activity. The real value addition and competitive challenge was to establish itself at the front end. Perhaps this also had detrimental effects on sales of its 18 carat jewellery.

CHAPTER 8

Distribution Channels: Structure and Strategy

The Indian market[1] is very vast, both in terms of the physical size of the territories involved and the diversity of consumers. The need for an effective distribution channel assumes importance because the product has to move to the customer in the **right quantity,** at a **specific time,** and at the **particular place.** In general, distribution channels consist of huge number of interdependent organisations who are involved in the task of reaching the product or service from the point of production to the user, preferably at the point of consumption. The need for intermediaries in the delivery of goods is sometimes questioned, particularly because the profits they earn are viewed as adding to the cost of the item. However, this argument is fallacious, since it should be recognised that the functions these intermediaries perform are understood to be more efficient and cheaper than what the manufacturer can manage. This notion of efficiency is crucial when a distribution channel is set up. Thus, the rationale for having a distribution channel is to create value for the consumer through the generation of form, possession, time and availability utility. In other words, the major objective of distribution management is to ensure delivery at a minimum cost so that the consumer's interest is served.

CLASSIFICATION OF INTERMEDIARIES

Many types of intermediaries are operating in India. It is important to have an idea about the marketing functions performed by the channel members and major types of intermediaries. Exhibits 8.1 and 8.2 provide a list of the various distribution functions performed by the intermediaries.

---

[1]India has a total area of 3,287,000 square kilometres with a population size of 1027 million, of which 24% live in 3250 towns, and the balance 76% stays in 5.75 lakh villages.

The use of channel intermediaries with their specialisation in marketing activities streamlines activities for manufacturers and retailers. Various types of channel members exist, all of them contributing in their own way. Exhibit 8.3 shows a possible classification of the various types of intermediaries by the distinct activities they are primarily engaged in.

In addition, there are other special types of intermediaries, referred to as the **dealer, distributor, stockist, "clearing and forwarding agent"**, etc., who act as manufacturers agents. These people also specialise in one or more distribution tasks and work on a commission basis.

EXHIBIT 8.1

Functions Performed by the Marketing Channel Members

Selling	:	Promoting a product to potential customers.
Buying and assorting	:	Purchasing a variety of products from various sellers, usually for resale.
Physical possession	:	Taking possession of goods, maintaining storage facilities, maintaining stocks of goods sufficient in both variety and quantity to supply customers on regular basis.
Grading	:	Taking legal title from the manufacturer, labelling the products with content specification or breaking bulk items into smaller amounts desired by customers.
Financing	:	Extending credit to customers (thereby financing the customers inventory). Also, maintaining inventories for manufacturers, thus reducing their working capital requirements.
Transportation	:	Physically moving the product between the manufacturer and the end user.
Negotiation	:	Making contact and negotiating over quality, price, quantity, terms of sale, etc. with both supplier(s) and customers. In effect, they ensure matching of end products with consumers' requirements.
Risk-taking	:	Absorbing all business risks, especially the risk of failure to sell goods, product obsolescence, or changes in the prices of the goods.
Payment	:	Payment from the customers is routed through various intermediaries who in turn forward the money to the manufacturer after deduction of expenses and commission.
Market information	:	Communicating information about market conditions including expected sales potential, fashion trends, competitors' activities, etc.

EXHIBIT 8.2

Marketing Functions Performed for Manufacturers/Customers by Intermediaries

Marketing functions	Manufacturers	Customers
Physical distribution	Storage; transportation; breaking bulk into desired assortments.	Storage; delivery; assorting items.
Communication	Gathering market information and dissemination.	Assessment of consumer needs and levels of satisfaction with existing products.
Facilitating	Risk taking; providing service; financing projects or other activities.	Credit financing; repair and maintenance assistance.

EXHIBIT 8.3

Major Types of Intermediaries

Retailer	: A middleman who sells to ultimate customers.
Wholesaler	: A middleman who sells to retailers, commonly found in consumer product marketing.
Agent	: Any middleman with legal authority to act on behalf of the manufacturer.
Broker	: A middleman who performs limited selling functions like seeking orders for a principal. Usually, brokers have neither title to, nor possession of, the merchandise.
Jobber	: Normally used in an industrial marketing context as a limited function wholesaler.

MODERN TRADE

Traditionally in India retail business used to be run by shopkeepers, popularly known as grocers or *kirana* stores. This types of retail shops usually sell many family fast moving consumer goods or used items. Similar kind of stores are used to deal with durable products, clothing etc. In this kind of stores, there was often lots of familiarity between the shoppers and shopkeeper; and in some cases sales were even permitted under an informal credit system.

In contrast, under modern trade, large size retail stores are fast coming up in the metropolitan and large cities or towns. It is typically a multi-outlet chain of stores or distribution outlets, running under the banner of some corporate organization and therefore, they are having lots of professional back-up. In other words, modern trade is a paradigm shift away from the conventional small retail shops.

Formats and Category

Retail stores are using a number of formats. Some such existing stores and their categories are described in Exhibit 8.4, Exhibit 8.5 and Exhibit 8.6. Within these broad formats, there are sub-formats too.

EXHIBIT 8.4

Formats and some of the existing stores under Modern Trade in India

Formats	Category	Examples
Supermarket chains	Food and groceries FMCG, convenience goods	Nilgiris, Foodworld, Food Bazaar, Apna Bazaar, Trinethra
Department stores	Apparel, accessories, lifestyle products	Shopper's stop, Ebony, Globus
Seamless mall	Apparel, accessories, lifestyle products, entertainment services	Central
Speciality stores	Product focus: Durables/ Books and Music/ Entertainment	Vijay Sales, Viveks, Planet M, Musicworld, Crossword, The Home Store
Hypermarkets	Apparel, Food and Groceries, Household Items	Big Bazaar; Spencer's (earlier called Giant, from RPG)
Wholesale/Cash and Carry	Apparel, Food and Groceries, Household Items	Metro Cash and Carry GmbH, Radhakrishna Foodland
Convenience Stores	Food and Groceries	Convenio; In and Out.

Depending on the nature of operation these modern retail stores can be classified as in-store retailers (who operate from fixed location where customers visit these stores) and direct delivery retailers (who reach out to the customers at their homes or offices). Again based on the specific nature of formats, these in-store or direct delivery retailers are known by a variety of names as described below.

EXHIBIT 8.5

In-Store Retailing Formats

Sl. No.	Formats	Description	Distinct Characteristics
1.	Branded stores	Exclusive showrooms either owned or franchised out by a manufacturer	Complete range available for a given product, certified product quality
2.	Specialty stores	Focus on a specific consumer need; carry most of the brands within a category	Greater choice to the consumer, comparison among brands possible
3.	Department stores	Large stores having a wide variety of products, organized into different departments, such as clothing, house wares, furniture, appliances, toys, etc.	One stop shop catering to varied consumer needs
4.	Supermarkets	Extremely large self-services retail outlets	One stop shop catering to varied consumer needs
5.	Hyper-marts	Larger than a supermarket, sometimes with a warehouse appearance	Low prices, vast choice available including services as cafeterias, food plaza etc.
6.	Shopping malls	An enclosure having different formats of in-store retailers, all under one roof	Variety of shops located close to each other
7.	Convenience stores	Small self-service formats located in crowded urban areas	Convenient location and extended operating hours
8.	Category killers	Focus on a specific nature of consumer behaviour i.e. deal proneness. Offer a variety of promotion packages discounts on retail prices	Complete range available for a given category, Famous for offering low prices
9.	Discount stores	Stores offering discounts on the retail price through selling high volumes and reaping the economies of scale	Low prices

EXHIBIT 8.6

Non-Store Retailing Formats

Format	Description
e-tailing	Communication through internet, e.g. Ebay.com
Stalls	Communications in trade fairs etc., e.g. Comdex
Door-to-door	Giving demonstration and then making a sale, e.g. Eureka Forbes
Infomercials	Showing the product, price and method of purchase on television and radios, e.g. Teleshopping network
Catalogues	Sending catalogues to people and making a sale when they show or communicate their interest, e.g. Books
Telephones	Making a sales pitch through a telephone, e.g. Credit cards

Key value propositions: This new form of retail stores offers many key features, such as

- Greater range of products in terms of variety or SKUs;
- It offers a family's requirement of most food and non-food items under a single roof;
- It offers a self-service, as opposed to counter-based service, at the taditional retail stores. In some cases professional assistance is offered, if shoppers asked for. Typical size of such stores varies from 5,000 sq. ft. to 50,000 sq. ft.; it makes a lively ambience and permits shopping at one's own pace;
- They procure most items directly from the manufacturers, i.e. cutting out the existence of traditional multiple layers of middleman;
- Unlike traditional shops, they generally apply inventory management techniques to bring in efficiency or reduce storage cost; It makes best use of information system to manage inventory, track of stocks and adopt supply chain concepts.
- It generally markets the goods at a somewhat lower price to attract price-conscious customers in India and designs innovative discount or promotion schemes at its target consumers.

KEY DRIVERS OF GROWTH OF MODERN TRADE

Consumers Perspective

With growth in the economy and moreover, as regulatory environment is getting more liberal, modern retail stores are naturally witnessing a boom. From the consumer's point of view, the key drivers of growth are:

- More affordability;

- Rising income levels;
- Easy accessibility;
- Better infrastructure;
- Convenience factor.

Companies' Perspective

From the point of view of the companies who have entered the modern trade, factors such as the following influenced their decision.

Regulatory changes: There have been some favourable regulatory changes in the recent years. The Government of India now allows FDI to the extent of 51% for single-brand name retailing. FDI in multi-brand retailing is yet to be allowed. In that case, many global trading giants (e.g. Wal-Mart, Tesco, and Target) are likely to setup their operations in India. Another favourable change has been the introduction of the VAT regime that has made seamless trade possible for organized retailers. This has made organized retail activity attractive to large Indian players.

Meet changing aspirations of the consumers: The cumulative effect of economic growth, higher discretionary spending power has created tremendous amount of opportunities. Generally speaking, it meets consumers' changing aspirations. In fact, under the present urban life (time pressure, small or nuclear family, access to personal transport facilities etc.), consumers liked the idea of making choice under a single roof. Moreover, the facility of exercising one's own choice in the selection at the retail counter is an added attraction for many customers. Lastly, modern trade delivered greater efficiency and a superior shopping experience.

LIMITATIONS IN THE GROWTH OF MODERN TRADE

Though modern trade in India is growing rapidly at this point of time, there are some factors that might limit its success in the long run. Some of these limiting factors are:

- **Absence of proper location:** Finding retail space is proving to be a problem in India. Locations in central part of many large cities are difficult to come by. Low density of personal vehicles and poor public transport facility make the idea of establishing such stores outside the city—as seen in case of may Western countries—less meaningful.
- Property regulations that specify high stamp-duties and fix land-use, as either commercial or residential for instance, too might slow the growth of the modern trade format.
- The system of having a uniform Value Added Tax (VAT) across the country has been introduced all over India. However, many small retailers are still able to evade this VAT. Till such time provisions

of VAT is followed by entire distribution channel, small retail store shall continue to offer goods at a somewhat cheaper price.

- **Convenience:** Because of many unique services (e.g., getting emergency purchases, at times credit facilities, and home delivery etc.) and proximity to one's residence which the modern trade will possibly never be able to provide, traditional retail stores will continue to get the patronage from a section of the consumers.

LONG RUN IMPACT

Let us also look at the impact of modern trade.

Cut out inefficiency in existing trade channel: Modern trade with its emphasis on inventory management, information systems, and tight operational control will try to deliver value to the consumer in the form of lower prices, greater choice, and fulfillment of new aspirations. In order to deliver this value to the customer, modern trade relies on efficient supply-chain management. For example, organized food retail business is among the least developed in India. The Indian food chain involves multiple intermediaries, and cumulative wastage during transportation and storage usually varies from 24% to 40%. The development and growth of modern trade, with its emphasis on low costs and an efficient supply chain, will lead to cutting out of the middle-men and sourcing directly from the farmers themselves. In fact, contact farming is being spoken of already. The modern grade, in turn, will demand higher quality and better prices (resulting in higher productivity) from the farmers. In this way, modern trade has the potential to establish a new era of distribution.

Reduced role of manufacturers, even MNCs: The modern trade model delivers value to the consumers in the form of lower prices, greater product choices, and fulfillment. All these value propositions are attained due to the altered sourcing model used by the modern trade. Instead of the "indirect wholesale led service" model, as is prevalent in India today, modern trade uses the "relationship based direct service" model. This will possibly have an impact even on the established large players such as HUL and P&G. They will require to directly negotiate with the modern format retailers. In the process the balance of power is likely to shift from the manufacturer (HUL say) to the retailer (Reliance Retail, say). The modern trade in the long run will possibly acquire greater bargaining power and may demand larger margins even from large MNCs. Thus large manufacturers are likely to face challenging task to maintain their superior control on the trade.

Impact on employment: The growth of modern trade is yet to threaten the existence of the traditional *kirana* stores. Till now, modern trade has generate employment to urban youth of 21 million. Retail sector being largely labour-intensive, it is predicted to generate an additional 8 million jobs in the near future.

IMPEDIMENTS TO ACHIEVE FULL POTENTIAL OF MODERN TRADE

Retail industry in India have to learn both the art and science of retailing by closely following how retailers in the advanced countries are organizing, managing, and coping up with new challenges in an ever-changing world. Indian retailers must use innovative retail formats to enhance shopping experience, and try to understand the regional variations in consumer note. Improving retail efforts through advertising, promotions, and campaigns; building loyalty by offering benefits to regular shoppers; efficiently managing high-value customers; and monitoring customer needs constantly, are some of the aspects which Indian retailers need to focus upon on a pro-active basis. One of the key impediments is the lack of full industry status granted to the retail business. This has largely limited capital investments in supply chain infrastructure, which is a key for development and growth of retailing and has also constrained access to world-class retail practices. Multiplicity and complex tax system, lack of proper infrastructure and relatively high cost of real estate etc. are the major impediments to the growth of retailing. While retailers give the necessary ambience to customers, little effort is put to introduce world-class customer care practices and improve operating efficiencies. Experiences gathered from similar large retail outlets in the developed countries show that performance of organized retail is strongly linked to the performance of the economy as a whole. Exhibit 8.7 shows various factors that inhibit growth of modern trade.

EXHIBIT 8.7

Factors Limiting Growth of Modern Trade

Factors	Description	Implications
Barriers to FDI	• FDI not permitted in pure retailing • Franchisee system allowed	• Absence of global players • Limited exposure to best practices
Lack of industry status	• Government is yet to recognize retail as an industry	• Restricted availability of finance • Restricts growth and scaling up
Structural impediments	• Lack of urbanization • Poor transportation facility • Consumer habit of buying fresh foods from traditional markets • Administered pricing	• Lack of awareness among Indian consumers • Restricted retail growth • Growth of small, one-store formats, with unmatchable cost structure • Wastage of almost 20%–25% of farm produce

(Contd.)

Exhibit 8.7: Factors Limiting Growth of Modern Trade *(Contd.)*

Factors	Description	Implications
High cost of real estate	• Pro-tenant rent laws • Non-availability of land, zoning restrictions • Lack of clear ownership titles, high stamp duty	• Difficult to find good real estate in terms of location and size etc. • High land price leading to huge initial setup cost • Disorganized nature of transactions investment
Supply chain bottlenecks	• Several segments like food and apparel reserved for SSIs • Distribution and logistics constraints—restrictions of purchase and movement of food grains, absence of cold chain infrastructure	• Limited product range • Makes scaling up difficult • High cost and complexity of sourcing and planning • Lack of value addition and increase in costs
Complex taxation system	• Uniform VAT introduced only recently across an states • Sales tax avoidance by smaller stores	• High amount of distribution cost • Cost advantage for smaller stores
Multiple legislations	• Stringent labour laws governing hours of work, minimum wage payments • Multiple licenses required	• Limits flexibility in operations • Irritant value in establishing chain operations; adds to overall costs
Customer preferences	• Local consumption habits • Need for variety • Cultural issues • Small shops offer more personal touch	• Leads to product proliferation • Need to stock larger number of SKUs at store level • Increases complexity in sourcing and planning • Increases the cost of store management
Non-availability of proper trained men power	• Highly educated class does not consider retailing as a career profession of choice • Lack of proper training	• Lack of trained personnel • Higher trial and error in managing retail operations • Increase in personnel costs

EMERGING ISSUES FROM GROWTH OF MODERN TRADE

While megasize retail stores is a relatively new discipline in India; it is not marketing by another name. The most important difference is that where marketing has the classic 4 Ps, in retailing a fifth P, "People" is added, which becomes more critical because in a service business like retailing it is the employees who execute the business through proper interaction with the customers. The following steps are to be taken to be a successful retailer in the new context:

- **Focus on the consumer:** Understanding customers' evolving aspirations and lifestyles is the underlying key to success for any new form of retail. The primary emphasis should be on access, experience and service and the secondary emphasis shall be on product and price. Better trained staff, better availability of products (both variety and assortments) and conveniences like free home delivery etc. will contribute to early success.
- **Branding the store:** It enhances customer loyalty. If it does not do so it will not develop a strong preference, which is critical, in maintaining a competitive advantage.
- **Knowledge about private label:** Private labels act as margin generators, for trade increasing sales volume by positioning the label as providing higher perceived value to consumers. In the long run, they also increase the retailers' bargaining powers with national brand suppliers. Private labels generate customer loyalty by providing exclusive products, which assumes an important differentiation tool.

The opportunities in the retail sector are galore. But it calls for concerted efforts on the part of both the retailers and the regulators to ensure that the consumer is finally benefited.

To become a truly flourishing industry, modern trade retailing needs to cross the following hurdles:

- Automatic approval is not allowed for foreign investment in retail.
- Regulations restricting real estate purchases, and cumbersome local laws.
- Taxation, which favours small retail businesses.
- Absence of developed supply chain and integrated IT management.
- Lack of trained work force.
- Low level of knowledge about what today's consumers expect from retailing management.
- Intrinsic complexity of retailing—rapid price changes, constant threat of product obsolescence and low margins.
- Come up with innovative forms of service to the customers (not just price reduction or promotion schemes).

ALTERNATIVE CHANNELS OF DISTRIBUTION

A channel of distribution is the combination of intermediaries used to move the product to the ultimate consumer. The typical channel of distribution for consumer products is:

Manufacturer → Agent → Wholesaler → Retailer → Consumer

However, some manufacturers, may avoid some of the intermediate links or utilise other agencies to deliver their goods to customers. In contrast, the industrial goods manufacturers prefer to sell directly to the ultimate consumer if their products are more engineering oriented. Industrial distributors market products and services like maintenance, repair, and operating supplies. Of late, many industrial goods manufacturers have started using agents or distributors, as in the case of the consumer market, for a variety of reasons. In fact, on the one hand, the market has grown in size, and on the other, a number of industrial products have become commodities. For example, much of the equipment and machinery used in the operation of a business, such as fasteners, bearings, power tools, electrical motors and conveyors, have experienced this tendency. In the process, the industrial good companies are increasingly making use of intermediaries and are gradually specialising their operations.

SELECTING THE DISTRIBUTION CHANNEL

Given the numerous types of functions and channel members that are found, the task of designing a channel would depend on various factors. However, it is also true that in many industries the distribution channels have evolved over the years. In such cases, the producer may not have any flexibility to change the structure. In general, however, there are six basic considerations that influence the choice of channels. These are briefly outlined in Exhibit 8.8.

Service Level Concept

In addition to the above-mentioned factors, ultimately the channel design will depend upon the nature of the target market the company wants to serve. It calls for an understanding of end-users' behaviour, particularly the knowledge about what the end-users need, where they buy, when they buy, and how they buy. In other words, it is essential to ascertain what the end-users in the target market look for in terms of service.

EXHIBIT 8.8

Important Factors for Channel Selection

Product characteristics
- Nature—perishable, convenience, shopping or specialty item
- Degree of standardisation
- Unit value
- Installation and maintenance support required

Customer characteristics
- Number
- Geographical dispersion or concentration
- Purchasing patterns

Middleman characteristics
- Availability
- Willingness to accept the product
- Financial strength and technical competence
- Past performance in reaching target markets

Competitive characteristics
- Nature of the key competitors, product lines
- Geographic proximity, market coverage (outlets per market area)
- Method of distribution followed

Company characteristics
- Financial strength/Company policy
- Product mix and assortments
- Past channel experience

Environmental characteristics
- Economic conditions
- Legal regulations and controls

The decision of Asian Paints to sell decorative paints through small size retail outlets in the semi-urban areas provides an excellent illustration of how high service levels to customer enable a company to enhance its business. Such markets are geographically dispersed and do not require a large amount of paints at a time. The company decided to pack paints into small quantities, disperse the distribution outlets and ensure quick delivery.

In the case of industrial products, consideration of delivery time, lot size, technical advice, provisions of warranty or guarantee, flexible financing, product demonstration, availability of spares and repair facilities, etc. form important service output levels. In general, any distribution channel should be constructed by evaluating the various service levels desired by the customers and the type of channel members that would be most suitable to provide these services to the consumers. In particular, for a durable product, service level may assume different nature, as shown in Exhibit 8.9.

EXHIBIT 8.9

Possible Ways of Delivering Service in Any Durable Product

- Pre-sale education
- Delivery on time
- Installation and on-the-spot service
- Produce spares and create maintenance support facility
- Easier terms of payment and establishing linkage with financial companies
- Single window service option
- Constant improvement of service facility
- Technical competence of the service team
- Prompt in correspondence/Responsiveness
- Prepare guarantee scheme in customer's language

DISTRIBUTION COVERAGE AND CHANNEL CONTROL

After stating the channel objectives in service output terms, two strategic issues of distribution management remain. These are: the amount of market coverage and control on the channel required to achieve a company's objectives. The first issue, discussed here, examines the number of sales outlets necessary in a given geographic location. Generally, three types of distribution coverage are noticed:

1. **Intensive distribution:** Here the company chooses to place the product in as many outlets as possible. Hence, when the consumers prefer to buy the most readily available brand of product at the nearest accessible retail store, or the product is frequently purchased or where the unit value is low, an intensive distribution strategy is preferable. Among industrial products, maintenance and operating items may also adopt intensive distribution.

2. **Selective distribution:** Here the product is made available in a selected number of outlets. Generally, appliances, clothing, speciality goods and industrial supplies are distributed in this manner.

3. **Exclusive distribution:** When a product requires aggressive personal selling, repair service, investment in unique facilities, or other special efforts, a company usually chooses an exclusive distribution strategy. For example, the manufacturers of *Bata* shoes, *Maruti* cars, personal computers, air conditioning equipment, and industrial machinery adopt this policy.

Channel Control

The other crucial issue pertains to the degree of control desired over the distribution channel. With the selection of distribution coverage strategy, a company automatically makes a trade-off with the channel members over the issue of control. That is, if a company decides to adopt an intensive distribution strategy, it gives up some amount of control over the channel. Generally, the degree of control achieved by a manufacturer also depends on the size of the firm, size of the average order, technical skill required for the product's success, the stage in the product's life cycle etc. Thus, as a firm grows larger or average order size decreases, or the technical knowledge/service required is more, or, the more mature the product becomes, the producer is found to exert a higher amount of control over the distribution channel. However, to achieve a higher amount of control over the channel, a company uses many indirect means, such as sharing promotional materials, imparting sales training, creating sales potential through advertising, and other marketing strategies.

EXHIBIT 8.10

Organising Distribution System

An effective distribution system adds to the value of its offering in different ways. For example:

- Selecting a wide product variety to enable choice.
- A combination of lot size (minimum to maximum), quantity depending on the nature of consumption
- Speed of delivery
- Ease of storage/Convenience in carrying
- Guarantee and return option facility

Channel Conflict

Channel conflict arises when one channel member finds another member of the channel to be engaged in a way that prevents him from achieving his goals. For example, consider the following instances of channel conflict:

1. The manufacturer forces the dealers to buy more than they require.
2. The manufacturer demands that the dealers concentrate only on their brands.
3. The company allocates insufficient share of choice items to a dealer.
4. The dealers are forced to adjust their inventories as per the directive of the manufacturer. For example, the company may insist on a high inventory level during the off season.
5. The company wants its products to be given more shelf/showroom space.
6. A wholesaler is frustrated because the manufacturer sells directly to the larger accounts.

7. Responsibility for the payment of damaged merchandise/unsold goods is not clearly defined at the initial stage.
8. Delays in processing orders by the manufacturer.
9. Inadequacy of sales support (i.e. advertising, salesman training etc.) service extended by the manufacturer.
10. The channel member varies the price set by the manufacturer. On many occasions, it has been found that the channel members exploit their customers by charging more during the peak season..
11. One distributor transgressing into another distributor's territory. This occurs especially when the wholesale distributors supply to areas of company-appointed distributors.

In general, channel conflict seems to develop from the absence of clearly defined policies about the channel's common purpose. Nevertheless, when some conflicts arise regularly, channel members must discuss and/or negotiate the issues and arrive at some amicable solution before they lead to major confrontations.

DISTRIBUTION CHALLENGE

Distribution management has always been a crucial element of marketing. In fact, the poor performance of a number of international brands in India is mainly due to their inadequate distribution arrangements and lack of understanding of the ethos of the trade channel behaviour.

Growing pockets of high purchasing power in semi-urban, some smaller towns and metropolitan areas and the emergence of the rural markets, clamour for shelf-space from retailers among ever increasing number of brands. Customers growing service expectations, the importance of visibility at the point of purchase, logistic support necessary to reach even longer distances, high working capital, costs of locked-up inventory in the distribution pipelines—all these have made distribution management a high priority area for any marketer.

Contractual channels like franchises are slowly gaining popularity in product categories like shopping goods, soft drinks and services. Traditional stockist or primary level wholesalers are asked to provide additional sales, coverage, promotion and merchandising functions in addition to normal inventory holding and financial functions.

The trade channel behaviour, the power relationship between different members in that channel, the presence of large number of intermediaries and emergence of modern trade in different urban centres are important issues of learning for any marketer. In fact, the growing power of retailers, the increasing cost of reaching goods to distant markets, specially, upcountry, the North-Eastern states and vast rural markets, order cycle management—all these have to be carefully understood. It is therefore no exaggeration to say that distribution channel setting, which is a key competitive weapon for establishing market leadership, is indeed a difficult task.

CHAPTER 9

Advertising Planning

Advertising is a form of direct persuasive communication to the target market which attempts to stimulate demand for the generic product category, highlights the key benefits, promotes uses of specific brands. Any ad tries to influence the consumers psychologically go as to lead to sales at some future point of time. Advertising not only projects the brand into the perspective vision of the consumer but is, more importantly, the instrument that imparts a distinct **personality and image** of a brand. Exhibit 9.1 shows the role of various communication tools for product adoption process.

EXHIBIT 9.1

Product Adoption Process and Communication Tools

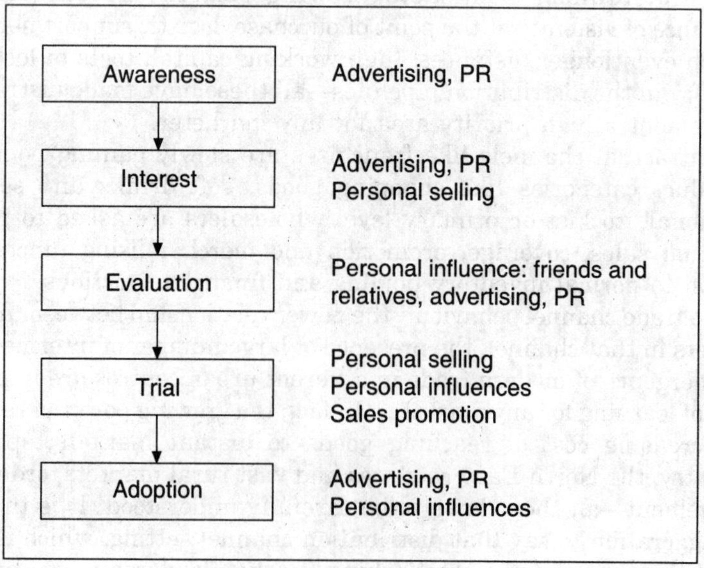

ADVERTISING AND MARKETING MIX

Frank Jefkins[1] proposed that advertising is related to the different elements of marketing mix as follows:

(a) The volume, emphasis and timing of an advertisement will depend on the product cycle situation. For instance, at the introductory level the amount of advertising will be higher than at the decline or maturity stage.

(b) Marketing research will provide evidence of motives, preferences and attitudes which will influence not only the theme but the media in which to advertise.

(c) Branding, initiated by the product management team, advertising department or agency, shall play an important part in advertisement design.

(d) The desired product image will be projected by the advertisement.

(e) The market segment will decide the tone or style of advertisement and the choice of media.

(f) Pricing usually plays an important role in the formulation of the copy.

(g) Packaging will be a vital aspect of the advertisement, as when pack recognition is sought. It is by itself a form of advertisement to identify the product at the point of sale.

(h) Distribution will influence trade advertising format such as direct mail or participation in exhibitions.

(i) Test marketing requires a miniature advertisement campaign and simulates the future campaign decision.

(j) The maintenance of customer interest and loyalty is achieved by the repeated advertisement which promotes additional uses and accessories or simply works as a reminder.

TRENDS IN INDIAN ADVERTISING

The consumer boom, coupled with the expansion of the print media and increased television coverage caused an advertising explosion in the country. A host of advertising agencies, were set up to cater to the new demands of companies all over India. The advertising industry became one of the fastest growing industries in India. The sales-oriented advertising of the late seventies gradually gave way to more sophisticated advertising. The presentation became slicker and the sales pitch less strident, more subtle and sophisticated. Indian advertising had at last come of age.

[1]Frank Jefkins, Advertising Management.

In recent years, Indian advertising has also become more professional. Formal marketing research studies are used in a big way to arrive at advertising appeals or themes; at the same time media planning has assumed greater importance due to the explosion in number of media channels or vehicles now available to an advertiser. Advertising is now accepted as a necessity part of the marketing mix. This has given birth to the concept of a 'Total Plan', where advertising combines harmoniously with other elements of the marketing mix in order to successfully market a product. Thus advertising is no longer looked at in isolation from other elements of the marketing mix. It is increasingly being realised that advertising must be coordinated with other aspects of a marketing strategy.

Advertising, which used to rely mainly on 'creativity' element, has now increasingly begun to take cognizance of research to make the advertisements more appealing and hence, effective. At the same time, Indian advertising has to some extent shaken off the western influence in recent years. Advertisements are now more 'Indian' than ever before. Indian words and phrases are being increasingly used in advertisements: Even when the advertisement is in English, there are instances of Indian phrases, slogans or expressions being used. For example, Hindi advertising of *Khich-Khich Dur Kare (Vicks), Thanda Matlab Coke (Coca Cola), Palmolive ka Jawaab Nahin (Palmolive* shaving cream), etc. have become legendry advertisement. This trend of creativity in Indian languages continue as it enables marketers to reach customers in a more effective manner.

To summarise, advertising has assumed special significance for product management. Indian advertising has undergone many changes since Independence which can be classified into four distinct periods:

1. **The period of artistic advertisements:** This phase of Indian advertising continued till the mid-Sixties. This was the period of the sellers' market in the country—competition was almost non-existent during this period. Advertising was mostly very artistic and aesthetic, and took on the form of corporate advertising as companies seldom produced many brands and therefore, the company's names were more or less synonymous with their products. Also, the advertisements focussed mainly on certain product features only. Advertising in the period was placid and non-aggressive.

2. **The period of sales-oriented advertising:** The period of mid-Sixties, to mid-eighties is characterised as more aggressive, sales-oriented advertising era. There was marginal shift in advertising tone and presentation style. The Indian market, hitherto a seller's market, slowly felt the pinch of Increasing competition which led advertising to build up distinct images for various brands. Companies also realised that advertising was a long term investment for future growth of their portfolio of products.

3. **The period of sophisticated advertising:** This phase began sometime from mid eighties. The consumer boom in the country, together with the spread of television coverage, revolutionised Indian advertising. As such advertising became more sophisticated and professional; emotional values and appeals were increasingly used; advertisements became more entertaining and pleasing. The sales pitch was made more subtle and visuals were used more than words to draw the consumers' attention and to pitch the sales message. Also, advertising campaigns were increasingly coordinated with other facets of the promotional mix. Thus, in the period of sophisticated advertising, each product tries to create a position in the prospect's mind, and takes into consideration not only the product's features, consumer benefits, company's strengths and weaknesses, but those of the competitors as well.

4. **The period of relationship building and nature in advertising:** In 21st century, there has been a phenomenal growth in advertising spending. In fact, the growth of advertising has come primarily from the growth in the consumer goods sector. In the past it was common to look upon advertising as a **fashion** which could, at best, cater to the upper strata of society. Today, it is no longer, a necessary means of informing huge market and it has become a means to development a relationship.

The reasons for this change in attitudes are not difficult to find: The greater choice of brands in many products—whether toiletries, personal use fashion or beauty products, household used food items and durables—all jostling with each other in the market to inform the vast number of buyers. And it is not just the higher income strata of the Indian market that is important now. Advertisements are being designed keeping in view varied segments of consumers such as children, teenagers, working adults, young married couples, working women, housewives, the 40 plus age groups, the rural rich, etc. A rise in awareness, literacy levels and expanding reach of the new media, in particular, the television network, has not only reached distant corners of the country, but has also provided a means of taking a brand into the living rooms of the people. All these changes, combined with the changing social and cultural values, have made the task of advertising to look for more personal touch.

MEDIA SCENE

During the last decade or so the Indian Media Industry has shown explosive growth both in numbers and in reach. Exhibit 9.2 shows the spectrum of different media channels in India.

EXHIBIT 9.2

Indian's Changing Media Spectrum

Medium	No. of	1993	2006
TV	channels	17	300+
Press	publications	303	400+
Radio/FM	stations	90	275+
Cinema	theatres	7692	9650+

Newspapers are still most popular media for advertising to the urban educated population in India who still have an habit to glance through at least one newspaper daily. Similarly, televisions have widest possible reach. Cinema and FM channels are most effective vehicles to reach the rural India, urban youths and blue colour workers. Lots of new media such as Internet, Mobile SMS etc. has also evolved in India. According to current estimates, there are around 16 million PC homes of which around 14 million have Internet facility and mobile phones have already crossed 100 million connections. Internet, mobile SMS are not only low in cost, but they deliver messages to the target consumers more precisely. All these new media hold immense potential to reach urban youth and working executives.

Types of Media

Media may be classified into three classes:

Static: Static media comprises newspapers, magazines, posters, billboards, wall paintings, direct mailers.

Broadcast: This form of media is very popular because of its reach advantages. It consists mainly of television, radio, events and word of mouth.

New media: The various forms of new media that are coming up in big way are the gaming, internet, mobile phones etc.

Exhibit 9.3 below depicts different nature of media and the merits/ demerits of each type of medium.

EXHIBIT 9.3

Types of Media

Static	Broadcast	New Media
Newspapers Magazines Posters Billboards Direct mailer	Television Radio Events (sports/film festivals, and other events) Word of mouth	Gaming Internet Mobile Buzz marketing

Exhibit 9.3: Advantages and Disadvantages of Key Medias *(Contd.)*

Medium	Advantages	Disadvantages
Television	Reaches extremely large audience; uses picture, print, sound, and motion for effect; can target specific audiences.	High cost to prepare and run ads; short exposure time and perishable message; difficult to convey complex information.
Radio	Low cost; can target specific local audiences; ads can be placed quickly; can use sound, humour, and intimacy effectively.	No visual element; short exposure time and perishable message; difficult to convey complex information.
Magazines	Can target specific audiences; high-quality colour; long life of ad; ads can be clipped and saved; can convey complex information.	Long time needed to place ad; relatively high cost; competes for attention with other magazine features.
Newspapers	Excellent coverage of local markets; ads can be placed and changed quickly; ads can be saved; quick consumer response; low cost.	Ads compete for attention with other newspaper features; short life span; poor colour.
Internet	Video and audio capabilities; animation can capture attention; ads can be interactive and link to advertiser.	Animation and interactivity require large files and more time to "load". Effectiveness is still uncertain.
Outdoor (OH)	Low cost; local market focus; high visibility; opportunity for repeat exposures.	Message must be short and simple, low selectivity of audience; criticized as a traffic hazard.
Direct mail	High selectivity of audience; can contain complex information and personalized messages; high-quality graphcis.	High cost per contact; poor image (junk mail).

Exhibit 9.4 depicts some of the typical mediums in a two-dimensional space with engagement and reach being the two coordinates. TV has got good reach and moderate engagement features. Similarly, Internet has got high engagement levels though its reach is still at low level. Newspaper, and outdoor hordings (OOH) have decent reach levels though they suffer on the engagement criteria.

EXHIBIT 9.4

Graph Showing the Position of Some Medium: on Reach vs Nature of Engagement Axis

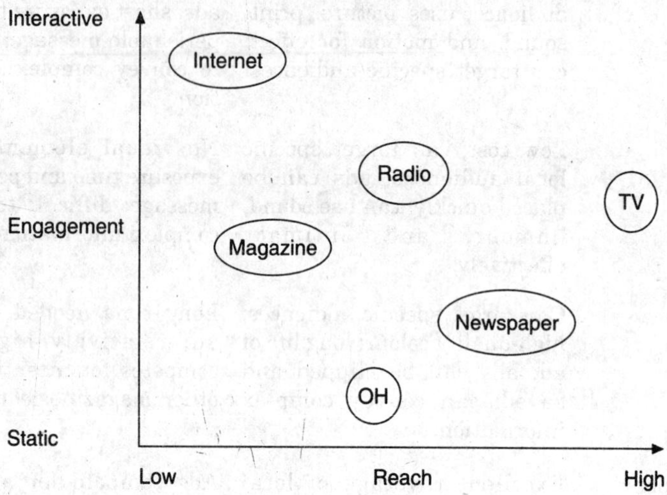

The Challenge of the Media Landscape

Everything is changing, everything is evolving, and everything is growing. This whole new dynamic structure has given rise to new challenges for the media managers. With such a tremendous growth seen in almost all types of the media, it has become increasingly difficult to decide which combination of medium to choose and what kind of communication to undertake.

Drivers of media choices: The choice of exact media hinges on trade-off between reach and frequency. They are defined as follows:

Reach: It is a measure of how many prospective customers the typical advertisement is able to reach. That means, it is the number of distinct target market members who are exposed at least once to a media vehicle in a given period of time.

Frequency: The average number of times the target audience was exposed to a message in any medium.

Generally, it is observed that as frequency increases, effective reach decreases. Thus, reach measures the total number of distinct consumers who are exposed to a message. Frequency measures the number of times the target audience is exposed to a message in any medium. Thus, a marketer may choose media with smaller audience and insert the advertisement more frequently. Or it may select such media which have large audience and use them less frequently.

EXHIBIT 9.5

Relationship between Reach and Frequency

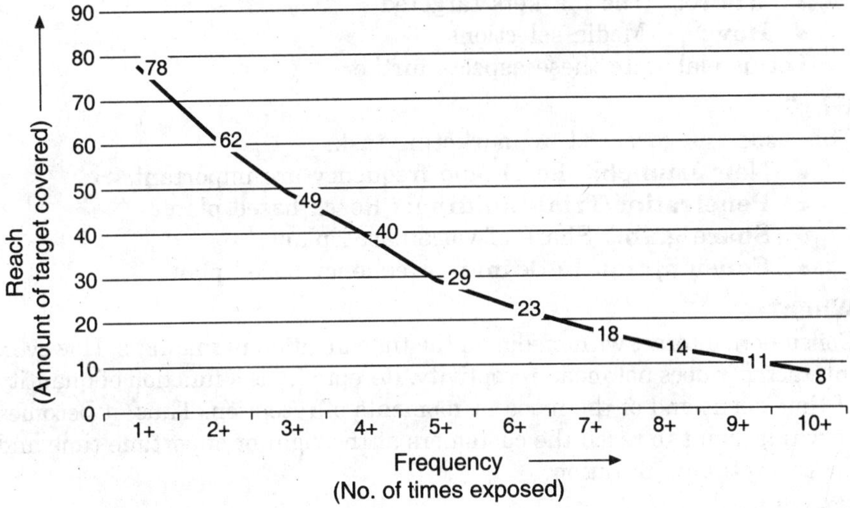

- **Relevance:** Given the target audience how effective it is to reach that particular audience. That is, how relevant is the media choice and how it augments the customer's beliefs.
- **Cost effectiveness:** How the returns compare to the cost among the various mediums. It is basically a kind of cost-benefit analysis.

MEDIA PLANNING

Exhibit 9.6 shows various issues involved in Media planning. Basically it means specification of 4Ws and 1H, as explained below.

EXHIBIT 9.6

Media Planning Issues

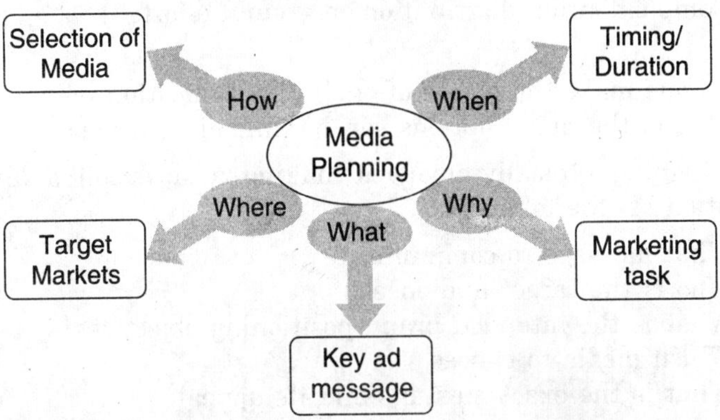

- **Why:** The marketing task
- **When:** The timing and duration
- **What:** The key ad message to be used
- **Where:** The markets targeted
- **How:** Media selections

Let us elaborate these aspects further.

Why?

This aspect is governed by marketing task.

- **New Launch:** Reach and frequency are important
- **Penetration/Trial building:** Reach based plan
- **Share gain:** Share of voice based plan
- **Consumption building:** Frequency based plan

When?

Consumers interact with media all the time in different manners. However, interactivity does not mean receptivity. Receptivity is a function of quantity of time spent and of the mood at moments of reception. Thus, it becomes very important to reach the customers at the right or opportune time and for the optimum duration.

What?

The advertising message will dictate the choice of media. It depends on what kind of image or picture the brand wants to portray about itself. The key ad message gives a fair bit of idea about what the company stands for and what is its offering. The various options are Music cds, TV ads, Posters, Banners, Interactive multimedia.

Where?

In today's world of information and media clutter, it has become a very important aspect of media planning. How does one choose where to communicate to and whom to communicate? Does one become a niche player or a mass player? Does one look at priority markets or mass markets? There are various ways of segmenting the target market and it differs from company to company. Based on specific requirement, one could choose its media communication for its

- Priority markets/clusters
- Complementing distribution/on-ground efforts

How?

How does one make the choice of one's communication medium? Media selection from the many options can be difficult at times.

Media planning typically involves making a situation analysis and specification of the following:

- What message to communicate
- Who is the target audience
- What is the intended brand positioning objectives
- Which media to choose
- What is the exact message and its appeal

An Assessment of Media Options

Evolution of new media—Internet & SMS: Digital revolution has opened up various new avenues for advertisers. The Internet, SMS based advertising have various advantages over traditional media channels. It is low cost, easy to monitor and analyse. These channels can be made interactive wherein customers can communicate back to the advertiser which help in understanding customers better. In India Internet and mobile coverage are exploding and have shown double, and in some places even triple digit growth in number of users. Although ad expenditure on these non-traditional and new medium is still very small, they are ready to take off in a big way in the near future.

Radio: Just a few years back, the radio as a medium was almost written off. However, rationalization of license fees and allocation of FM radio frequency to private players have made radio to become a hot favourite choice for many advertisers. Radio covers 90% of the country, available in 24 languages and 146 dialects from 236 AIR channels and 22 FM channels. It is great as a reminder medium, using advertising and topical sponsorships. Also, flexibility of the radio allows for leveraging branded contents. It has better penetration in rural areas which itself is poised for strong growth, given the increase in income in these areas. This all, along with lower cost, makes it an attractive medium.

Print Media: The evolution of digital media has not affected and Indians still prefer to read newspapers and magazines. Print market is dominated by market leaders and there is a fair amount of consolidation in the market, and hence some players enjoy monopoly in few markets. Print media has still not grown to its fullest as there is a significant gap between literacy and reach of print media.

Print media do provide access to correct segment of population by offering different content based print media. For instance, different nature magazines may be used to advertise about different types of Automobiles, Lifestyle, Parenting etc.

Television: TV is the most popular medium in India for entertainment, it has recently taken over non-TV media in terms of level of penetration.

The number of channels has grown exponentially with increasing localization. So, advertisers can communicate with local consumers in their own language. However, this growth is not uniform and clustered in north and western parts of the country. Prime Time at top 3 channels attracts most of the Ad spend, but over the years it has become very cluttered and costly. It has been observed that the channel providing **Exclusive** content gains for a short period (one week) and drops in subsequent years. However, **Non Exclusive** content means gains for the entire genre and longer sustained growth.

EXHIBIT 9.7

Level of TV Penetration in India

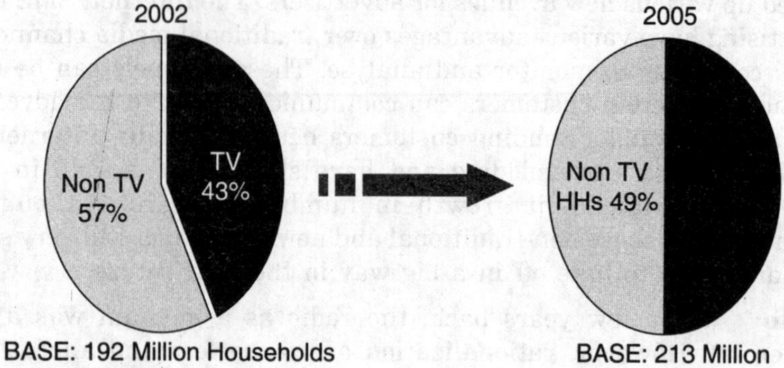

News channels attract viewership mostly during some significant news or event, for example Budget, Election, Terrorist attack etc.

Media to Choose From

SMS: The most lethal missile of recent times: The mobile penetration is growing rapidly and SMS's exchanged growing even faster. Over 15 million SMSs are exchanged every day. India is standing on the threshold of the new age. The penetration levels of mobiles are increasing by leaps and bounds every day. Mobile telephony has made it possible even for the common man to own a phone. At this present rate of growth, SMS provides an excellent opportunity for marketers to explore newer avenues for communicating to the consumers.

Internet: The ubiquitous Internet has been a new story for India. But since the 90's, it has seen tremendous rise in use with plummeting PC prices and today internet is one of the leading media in India and worldwide.

- Over the last 2 years
  - Number of PC households has grown by 40%
  - Internet usage has gone up 181%
  - Broadband penetration has gone up 5 times
- Internet has grown over 10 times since 1999

Internet also provides growing opportunity in terms of 16 million PC homes; 14 million Internet; 2.5 million Broadband

Gaming the new craze: This is another one of the new media avenues. Gaming as such is still at a nascent stage in India. However, worldwide it is already pretty big. With increase in the PC usage per household, this is one industry in India which is poised for tremendous growth in the future.

Radio: This has been out of vogue for long. However, it has made recent inroads by means of popularization of the FM channels with increased penetration and enhanced sound quality. This age-old medium

- Already covers 90% of the country
- 24 languages, 146 dialects
- AIR 236 channels, FM 22 channels

Radio advertising has the scope for increased media usage as it can reach rural India very easily compared to the other means.

- Great as a reminder medium, using advertising and topical sponsorships
- Flexibility of radio allows for leveraging branded content
- Allows for medium to be interactive

Out of Home (OOH) advertising is another medium for communication. It can include anything from simple posters on the wall to big hoarding at cross roads and important junctions. Conventional formats are already spreading to smaller towns. Already wall paintings and signages are omnipresent in rural India.

Conventional formats include bus shelters, public utilities, hoardings, bus backs, Metro stations, mobile hoardings. The new and emerging formats include malls and multiplexes, cinema hall branding, historic buildings being branded.

Print Media: In the present age of digital media, the print continues to grow. Though its relative importance in advertising may have diminished, it is still one of the cheaper mediums used to reach to a large group of target customers.

It is an industry which is chiefly dominated by a few players. These market leaders and media monopolies are able to enforce pricing and policies for the industry. There are some second round publications which usually sell on relationships and some unique offering. There are also some marginal/niche players which survive on discounts and value adds.

Five crore newspaper copies are sold every day in India out of which only 50 lakh odd copies are in English. This means that the vernacular press is still fairly strong and well entrenched in the industry. However, with increasing literacy rate and proliferation of weeklies and dailies, this is bound for improvement. About 18 crore people read at least one newspaper daily. The total print advertising market is Rs 7500 crore of which 67% is brand related advertising while the rest includes classifieds, tenders etc. Though over 22,000 advertisers utilize print in their plans, the top 200 among them account for more than 50% of the total spends.

The main issue with print medium is that though it is growing but not at the rate at which the other media forms are growing.

Audience tastes have also evolved over the years and have become more discerning. This has led to the

- — Emergence of niche publications
- — One publication for each target group—Upper class men, modern housewives, brides to be, teen magazines

TV: It is the ultimate source of brand awareness creation and promotion. With the rise in economic outlook and the resultant rise in disposable income, more and more people can now afford to have a TV. Its penetration figure has risen tremendously over the years. In fact, in the last 3 years it has risen from a measly 43% to a respectable 52% now. Over 100 million homes have TV now, out of which about 65% is colour TV. Cable and satellite (C&S) penetration which stood at around 41% at the start of the century has risen well above 56%. The number of channels which stood at around 5 in 1990 has risen to over 250 today.

But not everything that is shown is seen by the people. More than 60% of the contribution comes from the top 5 channels. The cable explosion also has not been uniform. High C&S penetration in South and West is driven by local languages in South and affluence levels in West. Though Punjab and Kerala have high TV penetration, they suffer from low C&S penetration because of undeveloped local language options. Because of the high diversity in the TV watching public and the difference in their viewing tastes, a single, mass marketing communication effort targeted towards everyone is not equally relevant or effective to all subgroups of the population across the country.

In TV, it is the serials and the daily soaps which attract the most viewers. However, newer concepts like game shows and talent shows are also catching up and giving the former a run for their money. Hindi mass, cable, music and English movies are losing the interest levels among the viewers while news, kids, regional news, hindi movies have shown significant jump in viewership numbers.

Issues that matter for television industry

- The power shortage and the resultant power cuts.
- Connectivity—Limited frequencies/bandwidth through cable 300+ channels vie for 70 total slots. The big ones dominate the Prime band—6/8 slots carriage fees have become the norm in many markets. Earlier, operators used to pay channels a share of subscription, now many channels pay operators to get on air.
- DTH—The skies are opening up with the arrival of Direct To Home service. It will provide more bandwidth and digital quality—better signals and improved quality. This will lead to pay per view system where one pays for what he wants and also freedom from the operators both for the viewers and broadcasters.

Innovative Ways

Advertisers have started using media in more innovative ways to break through the clutters such as:

- Integrating into the theme
  - — Lux *Kahin to Hoga*
  - — Fair and Lovely *Kumkum*

- Sponsorships linked to brand themes
  — Fair and Lovely *Fourth Umpire*
- Co-branded tie ups
  — Timex watches with movie *Kaal.*
  — LG mobile with movie *Ek Ajnabee*

360° requirement for communications: The conventional use of communication involves using one or two media but changing competitive landscape and increasing clutter has paralysed this model. Now advertisers are creating a complete experience for consumers to know about their products. They are trying to be present at every touchpoints of media. This mindset is also known as 360° communication. For example, Mountain Dew has used this approach to attract its target group of adventure loving consumer by using both above the line and below the line (conventional and non-conventional media) as shown in Exhibit 9.8.

EXHIBIT 9.8

A Possible Communication Spectrum

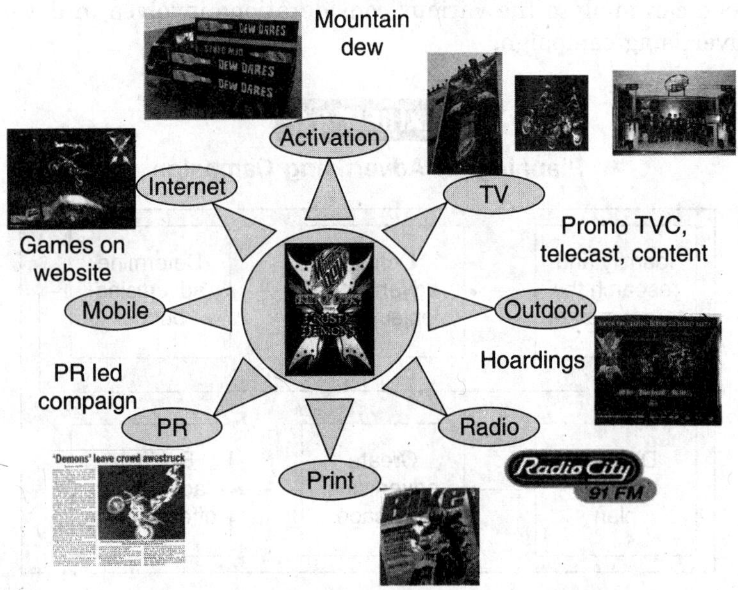

The core of all marketing initiatives lies in its communication and the effectiveness of the communication lies on the media chosen and its receptivity. Brands have to go beyond advertising and they should become a form of entertainment. The clutter in advertising is omnipresent. Over 13000 brands advertise on TV. Over 1,00,000 unique brands advertise in Print while 400+ TV ads watched on an average in a week. Too much advertising can be annoying at times and can put off the prospective consumer or create confusion in his mind. This makes the brand integration into content more important. What is required is a 360°

requirement for communications with content as its core and includes experience, interaction, engagement and response as its key elements. An integrated 360° marketing communication would include all forms of medium from print to internet, depending on the marketing task at hand and the corresponding requirements.

ADVERTISING CAMPAIGN DEVELOPMENT

Having fixed a budget for advertising and having chosen the type of media, one needs to carefully develop the actual advertising message and decide on the manner of executing the campaign. The entire gamut of such activities is shown in Exhibit 9.9, called the **creative process.** In general, this involves answering two questions: What to say, referred as the **advertising theme,** and how to say it, known as the **execution format.** Answering these two questions involves a lot of planning, market research and creativity by the company and the advertising agency. It is true that creativity is an art and one cannot exactly describe how creative sparks are generated. Nevertheless, it is reasonable to assume that one can analyse the various considerations involved in developing an advertising campaign.

EXHIBIT 9.9

Planning an Advertising Campaign

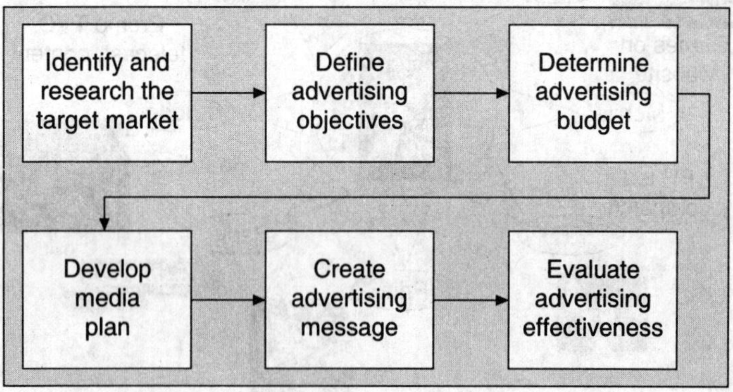

What to Say—The Advertising Theme

The central idea of an advertising message is referred to as the **advertising appeal.** When the same advertising appeal is emphasized upon in different advertisements to provide some continuity to the central idea, it becomes the **advertising theme.** However, creation of advertising theme shall depend upon the nature of audiences as shown in Exhibit 9.10.

EXHIBIT 9.10

The Multiple Decision-making Units in Many Purchase Decision

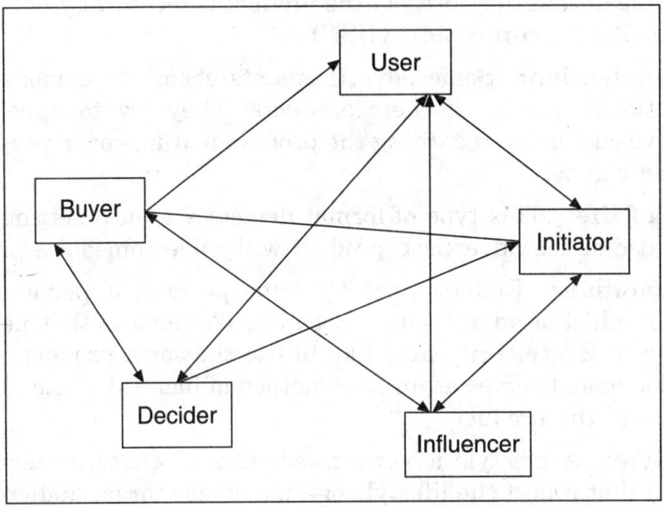

To develop an advertising theme, it is essential to know the profile of the target market, in terms of different broad characteristics like demographics, psychographics (i.e. consumer's values, attitudes and life styles) and geographic (i.e. where precisely the consumer can be found). The advertising theme as such conveys to the potential buyers what the product offers and why the product is suitable to them. For example, if a television brand wants to convey good performance, it must appeal to the consumers' need for good picture and sound quality. On the other hand, if another brand wants to project exclusive appeal, it might emphasise upon how the brand fits into the target customer's life style. Thus, advertising themes can be diverse but each theme tries to convey, what is the **distinctive quality of the offering,** especially from the point of view of the target market. Thus, the core of all creative advertising themes is to **offer newness and relevance to the target market.** Success depends on the advertisement's ability to occupy the target audience's mind with the proper selection of phrases, symbols, sounds and visuals.

How to Say It—The Execution Format

A good appeal may not achieve its results if it is not presented in a proper manner. There are, however, many different ways to convey an appeal. The major formats used are: Product uses and benefits, demonstration, slice of life, testimonials, lifestyle, association, comparative advertising etc.

1. **Product uses and benefits:** On many occasions, an advertiser decides to present the product's uses, benefits or attributes and availability. As an extension rule, such advertisements sometimes highlight certain distinct aspects or special qualities of the product. Such highlighting of the superiority of the product is technically referred to as **unique selling proposition (USP).**

2. **Demonstration:** Some advertisements choose to demonstrate the key functional quality of their products. They try to appeal to the prospective customers regarding the product features or to prove certain advertised claims.

3. **Slice of life:** This type of format depicts a typical setting showing how the use of the advertised product will solve someone's problem.

4. **Testimonials:** Endorsement by some prominent personality is a common method of advertising a product. The idea is that people who identify with the celebrity may like to use the same product. At times, such endorsement serves as an easy method of increasing the consumer's awareness of the product.

5. **Lifestyle:** A lifestyle advertisement shows scenes or sequences of situations that reflect the lifestyle of a particular target audience. Many impulse or routine consumer products like soft drinks, cigarettes and fashion goods, and high priced durables frequently use this method of advertising. For example, the advertisement of *Hero-Honda* motorcycle says: *"What is life without a little passion? Let the passion overtake you"*. This advertisement campaign tries to attract the younger age group of consumers and accordingly uses many props.

6. **Association:** This format concentrates on drawing some analogy to convey the product's .message. Generally, psychological benefits of the product are highlighted by this method. The purpose is to create some emotional attachment. That is, the advertised product becomes exciting, exotic or symbolic in some way.

7. **Comparative advertising:** Here, one brand of a product is directly compared with the brand being advertised. Generally, in this type of advertisement, the sponsor's brand is shown to be superior to some leading brand(s) with respect to certain key functional attribute(s) or, if not, cheaper in price. For example, in India, for a brief spell of time HCL photocopier had run such campaigns against Modi Xerox, where it highlighted the price disadvantage and lack of range of Modi Xerox's copier machines. Similarly, TVS Suzuki made a direct comparison with Hero Honda 100 cc motorcycle on seven product specific counts, including price.

Some realities about Marketing Communication are briefly outlined in Exhibit 9.11.

EXHIBIT 9.11

Realities about Marketing Communication

- Customers are continuously bombarded with so many messages and promotional stimuli that few are registered. Even if they see or read some messages, they are often misunderstood or retained in a distorted fashion.
- To overcome the noise in communication clutter, the message needs to be exceptional in delivery or creativity.
- Messages must match the interest of the target audience.
- Communication works in different ways for different types of buying decisions.
- Type of communication mixes will vary with the type of purchase (involvement in the buying process).
- Communications are more effective in creating brand awareness or preference rather than generating actual sales.

DEVELOPMENT OF CREATIVE STRATEGY

Intuition, judgement and market research or psychographic data are used in the creative process. Generally, these can offer useful suggestions about the setting, appearance of characters, nature of music, choice of fantasy and so on. The results help in framing the basic appeal or theme to be used in the advertising campaign to be projected in different ways. Success will depend on the creative team's ability to conceive a feeling through the right combination of phrases, symbols and jingles.

To understand how creative advertising appeals are developed, let us cite some specific advertisements and discuss what are the underlying unique elements noticed in each case.

1. **Example of Surf Excel: "Daag achche hain" Advertisement**

Headline: *Daag masti hain/Daag achche hain.*

Subhead: When kids go out get dirty, they don't just get dirty. They experience life, they make friends, they learn, they get stronger, they get ready for the world outside. So dirt is an experience for kids and hence, getting dirty is a natural phenomenon.

Baseline: *Daag achche hain.*

Relevant cues: A new idea is being proposed—a radically different way of looking at dirt. As it is targeted at the homemaker, the ad tries to get her to see the positive side of dirt, as long as surf excel is there to take care of the negative effects.

Entertainment: The picture of two children having fun will catch the eye of both kids and their parents. The ad projects a fun experience for the kids—so that Surf excel is able to access the target segment, i.e. the homemakers.

New approach: This campaign focuses on its target, i.e. the homemakers and her needs for taking care of her kids. Surf tries to identify with the homemakers' desire to see their kids experience life fully.

2. **Example of Lux: Chocolate Seduction Advertisement**

Headline: Skindulgence.

Subhead: Indulgence your skin with New Lux Chocolate Seduction Soap. Rich with real cocoa and strawberry vitamins, it nourishes your skin and leaves it looking deliciously gorgeous. Chocolate Seduction is a special offering from Lux, a part of our Celebration Range to mark 75 years of stardom.

Baseline: 75 years of stardom.

Relevant cues: The presence of a new solution with new ingredients—cocoa—would catch people's interest and induce trials. Also, the unique never-heard-of association of chocolate with personal care products is definite to arouse curiosity in the public. Attaching Lux's 75-year anniversary celebrations to it also sparked interest.

Entertainment: Using Kareena Kapoor, a popular artist from Bollywood plus the wordings "Chocolate Seduction" are guaranteed to draw attention to the advertisements. These factors also ensured retention in the consumer mindspace, along with generating excitement about the brand/product.

Brand reinforcement: Lux stuck to its core brand promise of beautiful skin—reinforcing Lux's brand image in the market.

Negatives: The advertisement might be more attractive to the wrong target segment, i.e. the male viewers because of the strong sexual undertones—which might also subdue the main message which is beautiful skin.

3. **Example of Orange: "Whenever you go, our network follows"** The TV commercial orange, Hutch cellular service, is about this cute little dog that keeps following its master (a little boy) wherever he goes. Irrespective of what the boy is doing or where he is going, the mutt sticks to his heels, doing its best the keep up with its master. And even though the boy seems rather unmindful of his pet, the dog loyally tails him... in a ways only dogs can tail their masters. 'Wherever you go, out network follows. Hutch,' is all that the explanatory super says.

It is also the most uninspiring way of advertising 'quality of network'. And all it took is one delightful little ad from Hutch to demonstrate how awfully pedestrian that class of cellular service advertising can be.

Delightful ad; that is how this particular Hutch commercial is generally viewed. Delightful because of the excellent use of a warm human metaphor to communicate how the Hutch network sticks to the cellular consumer like a shadow. Delightful because the ad does not follow the usual I-am-the-answer-to-your-problem sort of hard sell. Delightful because the ad does not resemble our regular ad in the first place, and, in fact, keeps us guessing about the nature of the product being advertised till the very end.

Not a single shot of a handset anywhere in the ad. No talk of people staying in touch with loved ones. All the ad does is tell an endearing tale that establishes the concepts of 'roaming' and '24 × 7 connectivity' by mirroring the relationship that a cellular service provider should have with its consumers.

The average Indian has started traveling a lot more, be it intra-city, within the country. So a cellular network that keeps the consumer connected, wherever he goes has become a fundamental need—and a strong reason-to-choose a cell phone service.

The campaign is, in the process, aimed at reinforcing Hutch as a superior network. Due credit has to be given to the agency for creating such a charming metaphor for network availability. They have not tried to talk technology in Hutch/Orange advertising and have attempted to simplify and humanize the advertising idea, minus all the jargon.

The beauty of this ad lies in its execution. The sight of the poor mutt running slavishly behind the boy, stumbling to keep pace, sitting dutifully by its master... your heart goes out for the dog in every frame. All in all, the ad campaign was done wonderfully well and instantly struck a chord with the target audience.

STAGES OF ADVERTISING PLANNING

A stage-wise summary of advertising planning is now outlined.

Stage 1: Situational analysis. Communicate to whom? Selection of target market, especially, to define the key demographic and psychographic characteristics of the target market.

Stage 2: Media selection and scheduling. Which media to depend on? Choose a combination of media that will get the message across to the targeted market. Also, determine the scheduling of these media that will achieve the optimum exposure.

Stage 3: Message formation. What to say? To determine the advertising appeal/theme (major claims) for the campaign.

Stage 4: Creative strategy. How to say it? To develop and choose a creative strategy (art of presentation) for the advertising campaign.

Stage 5: Advertisement evaluation. How to assess the impact? To measure the effectiveness of an advertisement, one should conduct market research to find out brand recognition and message recalls, unaided and aided, among a representative sample of consumers.

Examine what impact it has made on the consumer's attitudes towards the advertised product/brand.

Assess the generation of enquiry for durable and trial purchase or redemption rate of coupons in case of non-durables.

Ascertain the sales changes that are possibly the direct consequence of advertising. That is, eliminate the effect of other marketing variables affecting sales by the proper choice of control measures. Though sales may not increase within a short span of time, an effective advertisement is likely to influence the buyers both psychologically and at the time of purchase.

Exhibit 9.12 Outlines ten commandments of successful Advertising.

EXHIBIT 9.12

Ten Commandments of Successful Advertising

- Attract attention
- Visual clarity
- Concentration on central benefits
- Comprehension and credibility
- Positive emotions
- Unity of Style (functional benefits vis-a-vis emotional images should be properly reflected)
- Consistency of style
- Match the audiences' level of knowledge
- Differential advantage
- Images rather than words

CHAPTER 10

Pricing Concepts and Strategies

Pricing is one of the important elements of the marketing strategy for a product. Generally, managers remain tight-lipped when they are asked to discuss their company's pricing strategies. They invariably feel that price formulation is their secret weapon to fight the battle of market share and achieve organisational objectives. This sensitivity carries over to marketing literature as well, where pricing remains one of the least dealt with topics of research. This veil of secrecy on the part of managers and the paucity of standard literature on pricing, cannot however, deter us from dealing with such an important topic. Pricing enables a marketer to achieve his financial and marketing objectives. Moreover, it acts as a strong tool to influence market demand and react to competitive moves. To the consumer, it expresses the symbolic value of the product, in particular where product quality cannot be easily judged, price generally assumes the key factor in evaluating the underlying quality.

Pricing has also received the attention of politicians and government regulators as they virtually control the supply and demand of every product. Through various enactments and fiscal measures, the government tries to protect the interest of consumers and channelise the country's resources in a planned manner. This high visibility and vulnerability of price has led to the emergence of non-price competition to avoid price wars and public scrutiny. Nevertheless, the importance of pricing decisions has increased in recent years.

The process of arriving at a specific price level for any product is, however, a difficult one. There are no clear cut rules that may ensure a "correct price". Consequently, the price of a product is often said to follow from experience. The reasons behind this perfunctory treatment of pricing are partly because of the in-numerable number of internal and external variables involved at the firm level. But, focussing on any single aspect result in a shallow insight into the area as a whole.

Another complexity arises due to the intricate interconnection of price with the other marketing mix variables, which must all be synchronised finely to achieve the desired synergistic impact. This leads to the "chicken and egg story". That is, should the product quality and attributes be decided first, and then the price? Or should the product quality be dictated by the prevalent price structure for products in the same category. It is not possible to give a definite answer. However, recent changes such as greater competition, deregulation, inflation, changes in technology etc. have made price a more active strategic instrument. This has created a greater need to evolve sound pricing strategies in general, and to build up a repertoire of tactical pricing for managing various products.

We shall here discuss the various pricing concepts and strategies, based on intuition and logical reasoning. Although the exact choice of price level will depend on various factors, in this chapter we shall highlight different conceptual issues and practical considerations in developing a pricing strategy. Certain myths about pricing are enumerated in Exhibit 10.1.

EXHIBIT 10.1

Five Pricing Fallacies

1. Consumer acts rationally in buying decisions.
2. Quality determines the price.
3. It is wise to price relative to the competition.
4. If you are not the market leader, you cannot control the price.
5. Price low initially; increase it once you get a firm footing in the market.

We begin this discussion by enumerating the various types of objectives that a pricing programme may serve. Subsequently, we make a strategic analysis of different factors that have a major bearing on pricing decisions. Then, we discuss some of the popular pricing strategies. Finally, we shall examine some of the practices followed in Indian companies.

PRICING OBJECTIVES

These should be derived from an organisation's overall objectives. These are essentially some tasks to be achieved. Quite often a product has a multiple number of pricing objectives, with some implicit understanding of priorities. Generally, they provide guidelines to the operating manager. The probable pricing objectives are to

- earn a certain return on investment in the subsequent period;
- achieve a certain amount of market share in the foreseeable future;
- attain a certain amount of growth in sales;
- stabilize the market, i.e. to restore order in a fluctuating market;
- undermine the efforts of new entrants to gain footholds;
- prevent competitors from entering into one's territories;
- make competitors accept one as the price leader;
- avoid government investigation and control;
- maintain the loyalty of middlemen and get their sales support;

- augment the sale of weak items in the product line;
- enhance the image of one's products and firm;
- recover the investment made within a set period of time; and
- to set the price at a level that will maintain the employment level.

In general, pricing objectives are meant to serve certain profitability criteria like returns on investment, turnover, cash flow, survival during extreme economic crisis; or to achieve some sales objective in the form of market share, sales growth; or to enable a company attain a competitive position like maintaining leadership, creating potential barriers, or matching competition; finally, the proper selection of pricing objectives may allow an organisation to achieve some social objectives (i.e. employment generation, discouragement of conspicuous or wasteful consumption).

STRATEGIC ANALYSIS OF A PRICING DECISION

Price planning requires a strategic analysis of various factors that have a major bearing on pricing decisions. As such, there are many external and internal factors that a marketer must consider in his pricing decisions. The former emanates due to the environment in which a company operates, while the latter stems from within the domain of the company which is marketing the product. Let us take a brief look at these internal and external factors.

Strategic Factors in Pricing

Internal	External
Costs	Demand
Company objectives	Competition
Other marketing mix elements	Legal restraints

Internal Factors

1. **Costs:** Marketers often choose the simple method of adding the various costs related to a product, plus a suitable markup. This method runs into difficulty, as there is no accommodation of external factors like demand, competition etc., and the problem of estimating future costs is quite tricky in practice. Nevertheless, this suits one-time-sale situations, like contract bidding, where the supplier has to add a reasonable margin to cover the selling expenses and profit.

2. **Company objectives:** Many companies have competitive pricing objectives clearly specified, with which price plays its role. As stated earlier, these objectives could be to maintain price leadership, a follow-the-leader strategy, market share, maintenance of growth, undercutting competition or discouraging the entry of new companies to the business. Firms try to exploit their respective positions (i.e. dominant or weak).

Depending on their own assessment, they set short-term objectives, like achieving certain market share and long term objectives, price leader or follower etc. Managers can use their knowledge of competitive strengths and weaknesses in predicting competitors pricing responses.

3. **Other marketing mix elements:** Proper pricing facilitates many other marketing-mix activities. For example, when a product is priced high it must be followed by superior quality, and the brand supported by effective advertising to establish an image of prestige. Similarly, when a company sets its price low in order to gain entry into the market or to increase its existing market share, it must accordingly choose the level of promotion and distribution programmes. Pricing strategy also influences channel arrangement. The use of intermediaries requires that sufficient margins are provided to pay for the agents' commissions and incentives. When a line of products is to be priced, the composition and inter-relationships between products must be carefully assessed. The pricing issue becomes particularly intricate when a company markets a portfolio of products consisting of substitutes as well as complementary products. Price bears a special relationship to the success of a new product. In other words, pricing decisions must support the firm's other marketing strategies and vice-versa. The ability to achieve several financial and marketing objectives in the face of stiff competition certainly indicates an excellent pricing mechanism of a company.

External Factors

1. **Demand:** Marketers not only require to know how many people will buy their product (i.e. what the consumer demand is) but they also need other information like rate of growth, potential market share, consumer characteristics, price, elasticity of demand and the effects of substitute and complementary products. Market research and demand forecasting are valuable tools to collect and analyse this information. Pricing, then, will depend upon the market demand and its related dimensions mentioned above.

2. **Competition:** Apart from studying the costs of one's own products, a marketer should evaluate each competitor's pricing strategy to determine:

(a) how competing firms are strategically positioned in terms of cost structures, capacity utilization, market position, etc. on a relative basis, and the extent to which price forms an active part of this strategy;
(b) which firms represent the most direct competition (actual and potential) for the target market under consideration;
(c) how successful each firm's past pricing strategy has been; and
(d) the competitors probable reaction to the alternative pricing strategies being considered.

It is also important to note that competition in today's market ranges from direct substitutes to remote substitutes. To avoid competitive pricing, product differentiation or distinct market-segments, good personal relationships with customers have to be created by the marketer.

3. **Legal restraints:** Pricing strategies should also take into account the series of acts and laws that are in existence to prevent monopolistic, restrictive and collusive trade practices. Therefore, the legal environment and the constraints imposed by it influence a marketer's strategies.

PRICING STRATEGIES

How does one go about selecting a pricing strategy? Exhibit 10.2 offers a schematic flow chart of different steps involved in developing a pricing strategy. Based on the preceding discussion, it will be noticed that a wide range of pricing strategies can be adopted. Let us enumerate some of these.

EXHIBIT 10.2

Developing a Pricing Strategy

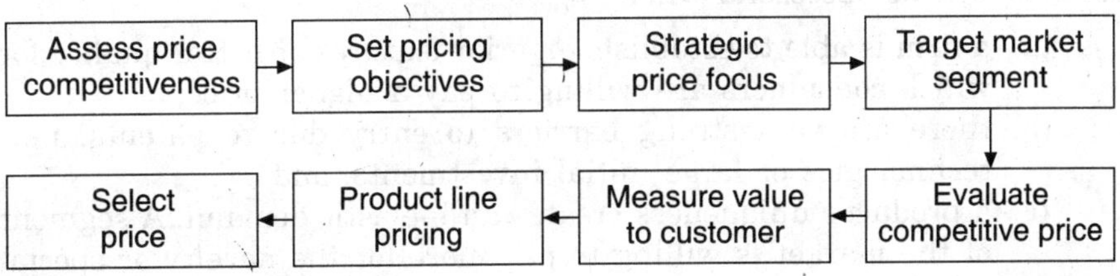

Cost-Plus Pricing

This strategy adds a mark-up to the cost of the product and is generally used when

(a) the product is quoted in a competitive bidding situation or government contract; and
(b) a new product is launched.

Target Return Pricing

Here a target return as a percentage of investment is chosen to arrive at the selling price. This method initially partitions total costs into fixed and variable[1] costs. Then, the manager calculates the price assuming the units to be sold. Also, one might use break-even analysis to calculate the minimum amount of production (or sales) where the company can completely recover the fixed costs.

---

[1]The variable cost varies with the volume of production.

Penetration Pricing

This strategy deliberately chooses a low price for a product in order to gain a higher market share, or to attract new customers who are price-conscious, or to gain entry into a new market. Penetration pricing is more often used to reduce the attractiveness of a market to prospective new entrants. Conditions favouring penetration pricing are:

(a) An extremely price-conscious market.
(b) Competitors unable to match the lower price level.
(c) Establishing an initial market hold.
(d) The capacity of a company to derive the advantage of greater economies of scale from higher volume.
(e) The ability of a company to sell higher-margin complementary products.
(f) Preventing the entry of new competitors.

Skim Pricing

Premium or skim pricing involves setting such a high price for a product so as to be able to take the "cream" of the profits from the market. This method will be successful when

(a) a firm is able to establish superior features or better quality for which consumers are willing to pay a higher price;
(b) there are very strong barriers to entry due to patents, new technologies or large initial investments; and
(c) a product's uniqueness creates an inelastic demand. A segment of the market is willing to pay more for the novelty or special service.

The comparison between Penetration and Skim Pricing is shown in Exhibit 10.3.

EXHIBIT 10.3

Choosing between Penetration and Skim Pricing

Determinant	Penetration	Skimming
Objective	Long-run market share	Short-run profit
	Risk-taking	Risk aversion
Demand	Price elastic	Price elastic
	Few market segments	Multiple market segments
Competition	Deter new competitors	Accept new competitors
	Few barriers to entry	High barriers to entry
Product	Image seen as unimportant	Seeks prestige image
	Long product life cycle	Short product life cycle
Price	Pressure for prices to fall	Prices can be sustained
	Need to move fast	Fewer pressures in market

(Contd.)

Exhibit 10.3: Choosing between Penetration and Skim Pricing *(Contd.)*

Determinant	Penetration	Skimming
Promotion	Customers understand product	Unfamiliar product
Distribution	Existing system	Unfamiliar channels
Production	High scale economies	Few economies of scale
	Experience curve effects	Few experience effects
Finance	High investment	Low investment
	Slow payback	Fast payback

Competitive Pricing

There are a number of competitive pricing strategies pursued by dominant and weak companies in a business. These may be:

1. **Price leadership strategies:** They are generally pursued by organic-stations having a larger amount of resources. The price leader typically tries to set a price level for its product.

2. **Pre-emptive pricing:** This strategy is used as an early line of defence to protect a dominant market position. One might undercut competition by setting the price level lower with the aim of achieving a higher volume of business. Conversely, it may allow a firm to carve out a niche in a particular segment of buyers.

3. **Follow-the-leader pricing strategy:** Companies with weaker competitive strengths adopt a follow-the-leader pricing strategy. This method will ultimately allow a company to capture the price-sensitive customers.

4. **Negotiated pricing:** For many custom-made products, the buyer asks for a proposal indicating the exact nature of specifications and services that will be offered in the contract. In such situations, price is often the outcome of buyer-seller negotiations.

Perceived Value and Psychological Pricing

In setting prices, one may assess how the product is perceived by the customer. For example, for an industrial product one may ascertain consumer feedback on different aspects of the product, such as the following:

- Performance
- Service level
- Product innovation
- Maintenance costs
- Delivery schedule

A customer's response to each of these dimensions and the evaluation of various competitive offerings on the same dimensions on a suitable scale may generate a subjective evaluation of different competitive offerings as given in Exhibit 10.4.

EXHIBIT 10.4

Consumer Perception Evaluation

Attribute	Importance/Weightage	Companies		
		A	*B*	*C*
Performance	40	4	7	5
Maintenance cost	20	5	3	6
Service level	15	6	3	4
Delivery schedule	15	4	3	6
Product innovation	10	4	6	5
	100	4.6	4.4	5.2

Here, three companies have been judged on a seven-point scale, where the higher value of the scale indicates superior offering. The consumer assigns some weightage to various factors of importance and rates all the companies on these same dimensions and ultimately combines these two in some manner to arrive at an overall picture. (*Note:* such evaluations take place in an implicit manner in a low involvement purchase decision.)

In this situation, company C can presumably set a higher price for its product because it is perceived to be better, according to the weighted average of consumer perception. A strategy of setting prices on the basis of consumer perception is an effective tool to derive competitive advantage.

EXHIBIT 10.5

Alternative Pricing Strategies and Value Implications

Price / Quality	Low	Medium	High
High	Rip-off strategy	Overcharging strategy	Premium strategy
Medium	Poor-value strategy	Medium-value strategy	High-value strategy
Low	Economy strategy	Good-value strategy	Superb-value strategy

Image or Premium Pricing

When it is difficult to determine the quality of a consumer product by inspection, consumers have been found to use price levels to determine quality. Thus, marketers often try to build up a product's image by charging a high price. Alternative pricing strategies for a specific quality perception are outlined in Exhiblit 10.5. Let us also highlight a check list of issues that determine premium pricing through Exhibit 10.6.

EXHIBIT 10.6

Premium Pricing

• What?	• Why?
— Quality	— Exclusivity
— Perceived value	— Clutter avoidance
— Price	— Differentiation
— Scarcity	— Branding
— Uniqueness	— Image
— Transiency	— Product category
— Benefits	— Competition

Odd Pricing

When marketers deal with relatively inexpensive items, they resort to pricing their products at some odd or round-off figure like Rs 2.75 and Rs 5. Incidentally, Bata has the distinction of pricing their shoes, say at Rs 359.95, 199.95, 276.95, a clever psychological method that has since been copied by other companies.

Base Point Pricing

This pricing system involves the selection of one or more locations to serve as base points. Customers are charged prices as if their orders are distributed from these points regardless of where the booking is made. This system is more common in the case of steel, coal and other core sector products.

F.O.B.

Freight on board is followed by the name of a specific place, e.g. F.O.B. factory or F.O.B. Calcutta. The name of the place indicates to the buyer the point up to which the seller will be responsible for shipping. At this point the buyer takes charge of the products and assumes the responsibility for further transportation.

Economic or Low Pricing

Ever since Nirma created history by introducing a detergent brand at nearly third of the prevailing price and offering a threshold quality level, low pricing has become a potent weapon not only to win competitive battle but also to create new market segments or expansion of the existing consumer base, as value for money is a strong customer priority. Understanding consumer's price perception based behaviour and elasticity of response vis-a-vis competitive offering are important determinants of marketing success in the new environment. Failure to choose right price has led to failure of new brands.

Price Discrimination

Price discrimination refers to the practice of charging different prices to non-competing customers through the granting of trade discounts, commissions, allowances or rebates because of volume, payment term or quality demand. The following conditions must hold good to sell products and services at varying prices:

(a) Customers are separated—geographically or by trade status.
(b) Customers demands are of different magnitudes and price elasticities.
(c) Reselling by one customer to another is not possible.

A market segmentation strategy implies differential pricing in different market segments. However, at times a price differential policy may result in unfair practices.

PRICING PRACTICES

Pricing in Indian companies is part of the total portfolio, and has not yet been accorded its due status as a variable that cuts across many diverse corporate functions. Most of the pricing decisions in Indian companies are based on a combination of cost, demand and competitive factors, along with non-price factors and managerial judgement. Each firm has evolved its own pricing philosophy keeping in mind its corporate and pricing objectives.

1. Companies generally pursue a policy of profit maximisation as their primary objective, sometimes translated in the form of ROI and gross profit terms. In some cases, particularly those of larger firms or market leaders, product quality leadership (Johnson & Johnson) or market share leadership (Ponds, HLL etc.) are also pursued.

2. Other factors like an oligopolistic (e.g. baby products) versus a competitive market such as soaps, detergents, etc. Price sensitivity to demand and price-quality relationship also affects the pricing decision. As far as costs go, it is probably the most crucial variable for setting and modifying prices; consequently 'mark-up' or 'cost plus' pricing is one of the popular methods of pricing.

EXHIBIT 10.7

Initiating Price Changes

Methods used for reducing customer's sensitivity to price are:

- **Quality improvement:** Offer distinct quality against Competition.
- **Line extensions:** New features are added
- **Unbundling:** Puts extra charge for elements which were previously supplied free (e.g. delivery, installation, extended warranties)
- **Opportunistic pricing:** e.g. rise in petrol price enhances the value of a fuel efficient engine.
- **Repositioning**
- **Reduction in discount:** Withdraw discounts for early payment, trade or volume discount and other allowances for promotion or trading.
- **Cost plus formulas:** Enhanced products can be attractive to new customer needs

3. Competition always affects pricing strategies. To avoid price wars, companies often utilise non-price factors like corporate image, product distinctiveness, distribution strength, promotional backup etc. to maintain their supremacy.

4. The excise duty on products is a crucial factor in the pricing decision. For example, cosmetics, tobacco, all luxury items are particularly vulnerable industries so far as excise imposition is concerned. Any change in the excise policy has a tremendous impact on the cost of all luxury products. Combined with inflation, the increase in excise duty has resulted in the frequent hikes in product prices.

5. As far as the degree of sophistication is concerned, pricing decisions are based more on qualitative than quantitative techniques. There are, however, a few exceptions of companies that conduct market surveys on a continuous basis and use quantitative tools to incorporate demand factor in the pricing decision.

Broadly speaking companies do consider the various inter-related factors discussed here, but ultimately the management applies its 'judgement' to arrive at the pricing strategy.

CHAPTER 11

Sales Management

Product manager's tasks include planning and organising personal selling efforts, deciding sales promotion methods and analysing market feedback to assess market potential and sales forecasts. This gamut of activities is collectively known as sales management. The ultimate objective of sales management is to influence the consumers of the target market or members of the distribution channel and to utilise sales forecasting and other mechanisms to aid the decision making process.

In this chapter, we shall briefly deal with specific activities involved with personal selling and discuss a few popular promotional tactics as well as highlight some of the methods used in estimating market potential and sales forecasting.

PERSONAL SELLING

Personal selling is the means by which firms directly communicate with their customers or distribution channel. The sales person's job is to inform, remind or persuade customers to buy the company's products. Personal selling is utilised to take orders from the intermediary or the customer. Generally, personal selling is the most effective means of promotion for expensive, technical, innovative or complex products. However, personal selling is also used to call on the large buyers. Good personal selling ensures a two-way flow of communication, allows the organisation to concentrate on the best sales prospects, offers the flexibility of negotiation with customers, updates information about competitive products and customers' changing needs as it involves face-to-face communication. Though it is comparatively expensive, the advantages of personal selling have made it almost indispensable and pharmaceutical companies have invariably taken recourse to it on a regular basis.

Organising the Sales Force

Sales personnel are usually assigned to particular sales territories. Considerable attention is given to the formation of the sales territories. In general, a number of factors are considered, such as the physical size of the territory; location; transportation links within the territory; the number of current and prospective customers within it; their general purchasing power; and its sales potential. Sometimes territories are developed according to the type of customer. For example, a sales force may cover a particular type of industry or business group or may be organised by product lines. This is common in multiproduct companies. As market conditions vary substantially from product to product, the ultimate choice of forming sales territories depends on the specific situation. As a result, the sales force is deployed according to geographical location and product or customer type. For all these various types of deployment, however, the guiding principles remain the cost and efficiency.

Managing a Sales Force

Companies need to devote considerable effort to training and developing a sales force after the selection of the sales personnel. Companies use formal training programmes or on-the-job training to educate the sales force about company policies, sharing key product information as well as developing diverse selling skills. This is an on-going process. As selling jobs tend to become routine, it is necessary to constantly reward and encourage sales people to keep them actively engaged and interested in the job. The rationale for motivating them springs from two major factors. First, it is not possible to completely monitor them in the field. Second, the pressure and strain of the job requires to be compensated in some manner. Companies generally conduct periodic sales meetings and sales contests, and offer monetary and other incentives to motivate the sales force. Finally, it is imperative to assess the performance of the sales force on a regular basis. Ideally, one should set a precise, quantifiable statement of sales objectives to be achieved within a time frame. Nevertheless, it must' be reasonable, taking into consideration the company's resources, its overall marketing strategy and the competitive environment in which it operates. To minimise ambiguity, many sales people are simply assigned a sales target for a given period of time. Ultimately, one compares the actual sales with the target.

SALES PROMOTION

Sales promotions are those activities other than advertising, personal selling, and publicity that are intended to induce buyers or trader channel to purchase a product in a specified time period. Generally, it involves non-routine, temporary efforts designed to stimulate the chance of purchase. It is mostly used in marketing where some special incentives or sales or create gift offers are made to the consumers and traders to generate additional demand during the lean periods or festival seasons. In other words, the main purpose of sales promotion is to achieve short-term objectives. The prime target of a sales promotion drive may be either the ultimate consumer or a member of the trade channel. Using this as a basis for creating demand, the basic strategies of "push" and "pull" have developed. Under the *'pull strategy'* the manufacturer attempts to stimulate demand for the product by promotional efforts directed at the ultimate consumers. This is done in the belief that such a demand will encourage the distribution channel to stock the product. In other words, demand at the buyer's end pulls the product through the channels of distribution. The *'push strategy'*, on the other hand, tries to induce the consumers of channel members by offering them various incentives. The difference between push and pull strategies is illustrated in Exhibit 11.1. Generally, a marketer could choose a combination of push and pull strategies.

EXHIBIT 11.1

Difference between Push and Pull Marketing

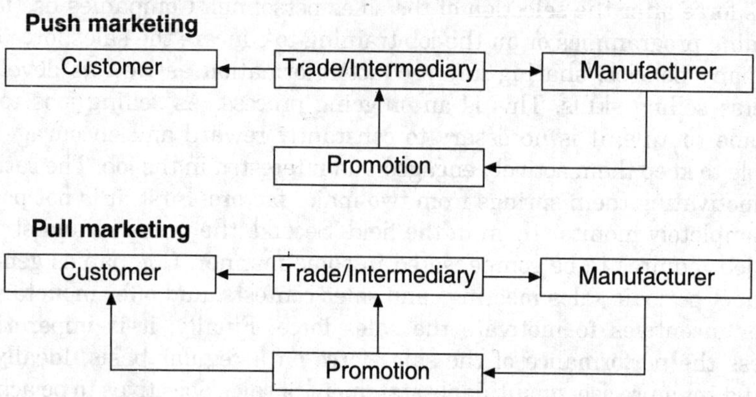

Different types of sales promotion techniques are used to achieve short term sales. Some of the popular forms of such sales promotion are:

- Price discount
- Price-packs (bonus-packs)
- Refunds
- Coupons
- Contests and sweepstakes
- Premiums
  - — On-packs, large packs
  - — Free-in-mail premiums
  - — Self-liquidating premiums
- Sampling
- Continuity plans
- Point of sale displays
- Loyalty reward programs
- Free-standing insert (FSI)

Price discount are the most commonly used promotional technique, and it means a reduction in the price of the promoted product or service for a fixed period of time. These deals are used to stimulate customers to try a new product, to encourage new users to try an existing product, or to encourage customers to continue purchase. It also helps to increase quantity of consumption, make people to purchase multiple units, and accelerate replacement rate. Such price deals are suitable when brand loyalty is low, and price is the primary consideration for customers. But if used too often, it tends to downgrade the brand. These are often used by consumer durables to attract early replacement of existing models. Newly launched goods or products with declining sales also use this kind of promotions. This is known as a pull strategy, because the saving acts as an incentive for the consumer. During the festive season, many stores offer special sales promotion compaigns to increase more footfalls in their shops or to clear out their previous season's stocks, domestic appliance and electronics showrooms announce a reduced price to increase traffic into their stores.

Volume discount, also known as value packs, take the form of bonus packs. Here an additional quantity of the same product is offered free, when the product is purchased at the regular price. This sort of volume is used for promotion products such as soft drinks, toilet soaps, talcum powders and shampoos. It is way of rewarding regular consumers, and it may even persuade non-users to try the product.

Bundled packs are when two or more units of the product are sold at a reduced rate as compared to purchasing individual units. This is usually used for soaps, toothpastes etc. Close up *toothpaste* offers a price deal where two 150 gm *toothpastes will give a saving of Rs 30 to the consumer*. Similarly, razors and blades could also be banded together. This sort of bundling of two packs are common to induce trial of a newly launched product.

Refunds are when the entire purchase price is repaid, and also when a partial amount of the original price is returned to the consumer. At times, refunds are applicable for use on particular products, which, in turn, helps to increase sales and encourages trials of certain items which could eventually turn into regular purchase items. This can be used for consumer durables, as with car companies. *Maruti had announced a cheque of Rs 30,000 on the purchase of an Esteem if the family already owned another Maruti car.*

Coupons are offered either by the retailers or manufacturers that entail the owner to some price savings or a claim of a specified object. *A paints company a few years back, carried an innovative promotion, where at the bottom of each can there was a five rupee coin*. They launched this special promotion campaign to counter the complaint that the paint at the bottom of the can was getting hardened and it was usually too thick to be used. The coin worked as an incentive to counter the complaints, and pushed the painters to use up the entire can at one go instead of letting it dry and harden. Coupons can also be used for consumer durables as with high-end electronic items or car purchases during the festive season. The retailer usually has a scratch-off coupon that entails the buyer to either a discount or a free gift.

Contests and sweepstakes generate interest as well as produce excitement and enthusiasm in consumers. But in early phase consumers in used to shy away from participating in it because of the confusing rules. But now-a-days *a lot of FMCG companies run it, where the winners walk away with many prizes*. It is usually common with consumer goods, to boost sales during off-seasons during lean season or month end. But they are not effective in generating trial of a new product. Consumer durable companies are also adopting such contests during the festive season. The purchase of a certain minimum amount or certain goods leads to scratching of a coupon that could carry a gift item or one of the main prizes.

A **premium** is a reward that is given to the consumer for purchasing a particular product or service. It could be given for free, or by paying a fraction of the market price. This is mostly used by consumer durable companies. For instance, the consumer was given a free colour printer with the purchase of a Compaq laptop, and such offers are given for a limited time period only. **In-pack premiums** are enclosed inside the product pack, as with the free collectors' taazo inside the packs of Cheetos. **On-pack premiums** are attached to the outside of the product package. The new range of Palmolive shower gels come banded with a free loofah. **Near-pack premiums** are when the premium is too bulky to be put on the rack with the product itself. In early eighties detergent powder companies used to give free buckets with the purchase of a large pack of the product. Container premiums are when the product itself is packed inside the gift. *This is often practiced by a lot of snack manufacturing companies, where they give away a bowl or a bottle.*

Product sampling is used by low priced consumer products, specially goods such as perfumes and soft drinks. In large supermarkets there are special counters where they hand out new product samples of food and drink items. As with specialty goods like perfumes, 5 ml vials of new launches are given out with product purchases. *For example, Lotus sun screen lotion was sold free with the cosmopolitan.* They can also be attached on the pack or inside a pack of an already present product. Many companies have promotional compaigns in which the location matters more than anything else. *For example, Tata Telecom had given free handsets and connections to faculty members of IIM Calcutta. Sunsilk has shampoo parlours placed in many of the malls in the city.*

Continuity plans or redemption coupons encourage repeat purchases, such as travelling by a particular airline, collecting bottle caps etc. that later on can be redeemed. *Many years back, Nestle had come out with a similar promotion offer where three empty packs of Maggi noodles could be redeemed for one new pack, hence increasing* *sales.* Such promotion offers are often announced by consumer goods companies and airlines *(frequent fliers)* to retain their existing customers.

Promotion schemes by types of products: Consumer goods, specialty goods and durable goods differ in the type of promotion or deals that can be offered in order to attract consumers. Consumer goods are usually low involvement while durable goods are generally high value purchase and specialty goods have a snob value inherent in them. Promotions have a significant effect in attracting and retaining customers.

The types of promotions or that are effective in case of consumers products are discussed below:

- **Sampling:** This is the most simple form of consumer promotion where the consumer is urged to try the brand and judge the effect. Initially Harpic resorted to this kind of promotional strategy where trials were conducted in people's home by urging them to try using Harpic in their toilets. The whole trial process was meant to create an level of awareness and satisfied customers are likely to become the user of the brand.
- **Educational sales promotion:** Applicable for products like toothpaste and sanitary napkins. *Colgate* uses free dental check-up workshops to increase awareness about tooth decay and therefore increasing usage of toothpaste twice in a day. Such promotion schemes are targeted at children who, in turn, attract parents to these camps, thus instigating usage of the product. Products like sanitary napkins also use the educational promotion programs effectively in India. *Whisper* built a great brand for itself based on its educational promotion programs in schools and colleges. In demonstrational targeted towards young girls reaching puberty, knowledge about sanitary napkins was dispensed along with a tastefully designed free pack of *Whisper* sanitary napkins. The trust created by the brand in the minds of young consumers instigated purchase in later years.
- **Direct selling:** This technique is followed by many brands in India. HUL launched this concept successfully close to a decade back in India when saleswomen were appointed to interact with the woman shopper and understand her FMCG buying habits. In response to the advertisement, she was given trial packs of HUL products like washing powder, toothpaste or soaps. After the initial usage, she was asked to collect the wrapper of the product to claim a 10–20% discount on her next purchase of the same product.
- **Retailer promotion:** HUL launched the Super Value stores, both as a trade promotion scheme and sales promotion technique to attract shoppers. It is a win-win situation for both the company and the shops. By refashioning *kirana* stores, the company

balances out its margin levels by additional sales volume. As for the *kirana* stores, there is growth in profits and a rectified ambience.

- **Co-branding initiatives:** Association with movies, TV soaps, both by in-program placement and co-advertising, is a successful promotion technique. The Colgate Gel MTV VJ Hunt is one specific example of this promotional compaign. The *Krish-Lifebuoy* is another co-branding of the same nature. Brand associations with films provide a great opportunity to stand out of the clutter. The important variables—firstly the fit between the movie and the brand, and secondly the genre, cast and scale of the movie. In execution terms, companies look for association, which goes beyond mere product placement. Apart from HUL's Lifebuoy brand, there were other brands such as Pidilite's Rangeela Acron and Wills Lifestyle brand of John Players, which used co-branded communication to ride on the film *Krish*.
- **Freebies (buy one get one free):** This is an oft-used strategy for promotion of consumer goods. *Himani* tried this strategy with its *Boro Plus Talcum Powder*, giving one pack free with the other. HUL used this strategy to market its *Lux* range of soaps. The launch of the multiple colours and aroma in a toilet soap range of *Lux* was followed by a promotional campaign in which a pack of 4 soaps of different types of soaps were sold by *Lux* at a Rs 2 discount to the aggregate price. The drawback of such a promotional scheme is that it erodes brand value from the customer's mind.
- **Trade promotions:** Discount stores like Food Bazaar, Big Bazaar and Subhiksha have become proponents of this promotional strategy. Discount stores claim to give big discount on bulk purchases. In order to give these discounts, these retail stores need to achieve bulk discounts by getting trade promotions from FMCG giants.

Durable goods: Products like refrigerators, washing machines, automobiles, televisions, air conditioners, mobile phone etc. are referred as durable. These products are usually high priced, bought less frequently and therefore the purchase decision is much more involved as compared to the typical FMCG goods.

- **Co-branding:** This is a new trend in the consumer durables sector. Durables like automobiles are using other brands celebrities and movies etc. to co-brand and co-promote themselves. Sometime back, *Clinic All Clear* shampoo and *Yamaha* motorcycle announced the Clinic All Clear Cool Baal Cool Bike contest with the purchase of Clinic All Clear shampoo in India. In keeping with the trendy, youthful image of the brand, *Clinic All Clear* launched this promotional campaign in conjunction with Yamaha Motor India Ltd., a brand with whom they share their brand ambassador, John Abraham. It is for the first time in India that a co-promotion strategy involving two big brands has been implemented and this is what makes the contest unique. *Hero Honda* and MTV Roadies is another example of this kind of co-branding strategy. Roadies is a TV show in which bikers travel the length of the country with their bikes and experience a true realty show. *Hero Honda* has associated itself with this TV show and is part of the promotion compaign.

- **Festival offers:** In India, festivals like Diwali, Holi, Durgapuja etc. are shopping times for people. Goods like televisions, refrigerator and air conditioners are bought or replaced mostly during festival times. Manufacturers tend to capitalize on this habit by giving large discounts during this period. These discounts can either be in the form of price cuts, freebies or some exchange offers. *LG* introduced a scheme during this Diwali where all its white goods range was slashed in price by 10% and guaranteed gifts were offered with each purchase. Similarly, prices of televisions are reduced by 20% during festivals and a toaster was offered with every purchase. Low end buyers also wait for these kind of festival discounts to make their purchases when easy loan with 0% financing schemes are available.
- **Trade promotion:** For durable goods such as automobiles, manufacturers provide special incentives to dealers for exceeding specific sales targets. In case of mobile phones also, trade promotions include special incentives, revamp of outlet and priority dealer status.

Specialty products: As the name suggests, the specialty goods have particularly unique characteristics where a significant number of buyers is willing to make a special purchasing effort. Examples include specific brands of fancy products, luxury cars, professional photographic equipment, and high-fashion clothing.

- **Opportunity to sample:** Luxury cars use the promotion scheme of offering a test drive at showrooms. Highly priced perfumes use testing kiosks as promotional tactics to attract customers who are given a free whiff of the perfume and are thus urged to buy the product. In case of goods like ultra highly priced sound systems and home theaters like Bose, a live demo is organized for customers so that they can experience live the differentiated offering of the product. In case of SLR cameras, special shops like the Sony World are created where customers can walk in to touch, feel and use the product first hand before making a buying decision.
- **Sweepstakes and contests:** The product gets associated with a contest in which the first prize is the product itself or a chance

at getting the product in a lucky draw. Specialty goods like I-Pod music players were given as a free gift.

Sales promotion: In general sales promotion techniques are supposed to have an immediate impact on sales of a product. They are employed for a limited period to stimulate consumer demand. Sales promotions can be directed at consumers as well as at trade to induce them to make more purchase.

While deciding a promotional strategy the following factors may be considered:

1. **Customer profile:** This consists of the demographic, psycographic profile of customers to decide what sort of a promotion scheme will suit him most.
2. **Attitude and buying behaviour:** Through conducting proper marketing research (survey) one may establish which sort of brands attract what types of customers and how their buying decisions are made.
3. **Competitive strategy:** This is based on collecting proper market intelligence on the competitors' actions.
4. **Brand strategy:** The market share and current brand perception of the product helps in short listing promotional strategies. Care should be taken so that a particular promotional strategy does not erode or dilute a brand's image.
5. **Advertising:** Which media can help in promotion and what sort of promotions complements the current advertising campaign.

TRADE PROMOTION

Like consumers promotions, marketers offer different form of incentives to trade so that they will stock their product. They may take the following forms:

- Volume discount or quantity discount
- Some extra items given along with bulk purchase
- Special discount to display the product
- Count and recount discount—some reward is given if a certain amount is sold in a stipulated time period
- Bill discount—additional time given to pay for the invoice
- Reward in cash, kind or intangible form, e.g. a free trip abroad

The associated problems of promoting products in this manner are:

- Displacement effect, i.e. sales drop after the promotion period,
- Per unit price of the product increases as variable cost increases, and
- Misuse, i.e. traders can quickly judge how good a promotion offer is from their profit angle.

Factors in Choice of Sales Promotion

The ultimate choice of sales promotional strategies will depend upon a number of factors:

EXHIBIT 11.2

Comparative Effectiveness of Advertising, Consumer Promotion and Trade Promotion

Advertising	Consumer promotion	Trade promotion
Franchise building	←→	Non-franchise building
Brand benefit emphasis	←→	Price emphasis
Higher marketer control	←→	Low marketer control
End-consumer is primary target	←→	Trade is primary target
Pull strategy	←→	Push strategy
Long-term impact	←→	Short-term impact
Fixed cost	←→	Variable cost

Source: Adapted from John A. Quelch, Teaching Note for 'Chesebrough-Pond's: Vaseline Petroleum Jelly', Harvard Business School: Boston, Mass.

1. **Objective of the promotion:** The task of introducing a new product requires a promotional campaign considerably different from that intended to increase the sales of an established or widely recognised product. It must also be viewed against competitive activities.

2. **Nature of target market/or Distribution channel:** The choice of promotional strategy will greatly depend on the buying behaviour of the target market and role of the distribution channel.

3. **Support facility:** Display opportunity, point of purchase and sales force support.

4. **Timing of the sales promotion:** The choice of timing will have an impact on its effectiveness.

5. **Reward offered:** The nature of incentives to be offered will have to be carefully assessed.

6. **Cost vs. benefit of promotion:** Regardless of the promotional tool employed, the marketer must determine how much cost is likely to be incurred as well as roughly estimate the sales level to be achieved. Thus, a manager will require to apply judgement while choosing the combination of sales promotion techniques.

MARKET POTENTIAL AND SALES FORECASTING

Market Potential

While managing's product, managers are generally interested in obtaining an estimate of the market size at an aggregate level (i.e. for all competitive brands) under certain assumed business conditions. The market potential may change depending on market factors such as average category price or general economic conditions. In particular, sales potential refers to the maximum possible sales opportunity of the product marketed by a company. When applied to geographical areas, it means the maximum sales volume which could be generated by buyers in the area for some stated period. Area potential can be expressed both in absolute terms or as a percentage of the total market. Generally, the sales forecast is lower than the market potential, because a company may be constrained by resources or other priorities.

Consumers often engage in considerable substitution within a broad product category. Therefore, the degree of substitution as well as the conditions under which it takes place must be considered in the development of the potential. The decisions on whether to include or exclude closely related substitutes which often have a pronounced effect on estimated sales potential depends on this degree of substitution. For example, in estimating the market potential for a low priced toothpaste, a company had to consider the possible sales of toothpowder and other traditional mouth washing items such as neem twigs. Here, the objective was to convert some of the consumers of the other closely substitutable product users to a low priced toothpaste. Similar notions will prevail in estimating market potential for products like two-wheeler, music system, etc., where the consumers generic need can be met by a large combination of items.

Methods of Measuring Market Potential

Different methods are used for estimating market potential. They are known as the direct method and the correlation method.

1. **Direct method:** In the direct method, data on the actual product for which one wishes to estimate the potential is used. The correlation method makes use of data related to, but different from the product at hand. For example, in the direct method, a company used the total industry sales figure to estimate the market potential of a consumer non-durable. Data may be collected from different sales territories. Percentage distribution are used as a measure of the relative potential that existed in each of the territories. These percentage figures are then used to estimate the potential for each territory. Exhibit 11.3 shows the resulting potential.

The principal advantage of using total industry sales to measure market potential is that the actual sales data is used, which makes the method easy to operate.

Often, it is difficult to obtain correct sales figures for an industry. This method will fail to offer reliable estimates when the market undergoes frequent changes. Here, past sales are used to indicate market potential, which tacitly assume certain sales efforts. If these sales efforts are changed, the sales figures are also likely to change. Thus, this method may suggest subjective predictions based on some assumption about business conditions and competitive activities.

EXHIBIT 11.3

Sales Potential Estimation by Direct Method

Sales territory	**Total industry sales volume** (Rs. '000)	**Per cent**	**Company potential*** (Rs)
A	312	9.38	90.8
B	208	6.25	60.5
C	156	4.69	45.4
D	104	3.13	30.3
E	52	1.56	15.1
			242.1

*Figures obtained by applying per cent of industry sales to firm's total sales forecast (Rs 242.1 thousands).

2. **Correlation method:** This method of measuring market potential is based on the idea that there is some association between sales and another variable called a 'factor'. For example, population size is a good general factor that helps in estimating the sales potential for numerous products. As such, many statistical techniques are now available to measure the degree of association between sales and the market factor. For instance, an automobile company was interested in finding out the market potential of spare parts for its vehicles marketed in different regions. It is reasonable to assume that the demand in any area is closely related to the number of vehicles in the area. Exhibit 11.4 shows the application of this method based on hypothetical data.

EXHIBIT 11.4

Sales Potential Estimation by Single Factor Index

Sales region	**Number of vehicles registered** ('000)	**Per cent**	**Potential for vehicle parts** (Rs '000)
North-East	331	2.91	58.2
South	873	7.68	153.6
East	741	6.52	130.4
North	529	4.66	93.2
West	587	5.17	103.4

3. **Multiple factor index:** When a number of important factors associated with the sales of a product are combined, they are referred to as a *'multiple factor index'*. Such an index has the advantage of taking into account several factors which influence the sales of the given product. This combined factor is also known as the *'market index'*. The widely used market index of this type is the buying power index, which is constructed by combining three factors, namely, income, retail sales and population. However, many environment changes, the entry of new competitors and that of new products may influence the estimation of the market potential for a product.

SALES FORECASTING

Forecast refers to amount of sales expected to be achieved under a set of market conditions within a specified period of time. Sales forecasting attempts to predict a company's sales volume for a product in a particular region or market segment during a specific time period. Sales forecasts are important because they serve as basic guides for planning within the company. A good sales forecast helps in the planning and control of production, working capital, distribution, and promotional activities. Sales forecasting in most companies is confined to short term prediction, largely because of a lack of accuracy or reliability of long term projections. It is the pivot of many market planning and control operations. It is the basis for all budgets and future deployment of marketing resources. Sales forecasting leads to a set of sales volume goals which strongly affect many corporate decisions.

Method of Sales Forecasting

Several methods are used to forecast sales. These can be broadly classified as the subjective and the objective methods.

1. Subjective methods

(a) Jury of experts' opinion. Sometimes, forecasts are made by soliciting the opinions of a jury of experts. Here, each expert makes an independent forecast of sales for the next period, usually a year. These estimates are mostly subjective and based on rational thinking. Once different experts have made their estimates, some sort of reconciliation is done, if opinions vary too widely.

(b) Sales force composite. Sales representatives are asked to state the probabilities of selling various quantities of each product to the customers in their territories. The individual forecasts can then be aggregate to arrive at an overall sales forecast for the product or product line. The basis for this technique lies in the assumption that the sales representative is more familiar with the market area, especially about consumer behaviour and competitive activity. For short term forecasts,

sales representatives are found to do a better job than can be done using more sophisticated methods. Generally, industrial product companies base their sales forecast for the following period in this manner.

2. **Objective methods:** These methods generally use some statistical tools, which vary in complexity from relatively simple trend extrapolations, to the use of more sophisticated models.

(a) Trend analysis. A simple objective method of forecasting is the extrapolation of past sales trends. In this method, the underlying assumption is that the future sales will be somewhat like the past. This is more applicable for short term forecast.

(b) Regression analysis. It can be used in sales forecasting to measure the relationship between a company's sales and other factors. For example, a company may find that sales is related to personal income. A regression model to predict sales of motor cycles might be the following:

Sales = $a + b$ (Disposable Income) + c (Average Price) + d (Population size between 20–40)

With historical data on sales, all variables on the right hand side, the coefficients could be estimated and used to develop a forecast for sales.

This technique will enable the manager to estimate the relationship between changes in income and changes in sales. Regression analysis has the advantage of being more objective than trend analysis. Nowadays, several user-friendly computer packages are available for regression techniques.

(c) Survey of consumers. Market surveys could be undertaken for sales forecasting. This involves selecting a representative sample and securing information about the buyer's need, choice criteria, level of competition, and the customer feedback on competitive products. Using appropriate statistical tool set of appropriate leading indicators and one may make an accurate sales forecast.

This method is appropriate for an established product where consumers can relate buying intentions with expectations.

(d) Analysis of market factors. In this method, the principal factors that affect the future demand of the given product should be determined. Their relationship to sales is to be measured and then after studying the behaviour of these factors the forecast should be made. The following example will explain how this method is used.

A television company interested in a sales forecast for colour TVs in India. Before investing in this business they could choose a number of factors that apparently influence demand. Each factor could be measured on a time scale.

(e) Projection of past sales. This method consists of applying a flat percentage of increase to the previous year's sales volume or some average value of sales trends based on the past years data. The rate of increase in sales can be changed according to the nature of the product, and the past rate of growth of the market.

(f) *Exponential smoothing.* This is a type of moving average, which represents the sum of all past sales data, with maximum consideration given to the most recent data. A weighted average of this year's sales is combined with the forecast of this year sales to arrive at the forecast for the next year sales. Thus the equation is

$$\text{Next year's sales} = ay + (1 - a)z$$

where

a = smoothing constant

y = sales for this year

z = forecast for this year

EXAMPLE 11.1. A paints company was interested in forecasting its sales for the next year. The company had the past sales data. The marketing manager used the exponential smoothing technique as a research tool for this purpose.

Data: z = Rs 3.5 crores

y = Rs 3.1 crores

The data file showed that the series of sales data changed slowly and hence the value of a[1] was taken as small. On matching the earlier sales trends the iteration process gave a = 0.6.

Next year's sales forecast = Rs 3.26 crores

(g) *Time series analysis.* The underlying logic is that past data is an expression of causal relations that can be uncovered through quantitative analysis. They can be used to forecast sales.

Four major components of time series data are:

T = trend

C = cycle

S = seasonality
(it refers to the pattern of movements within the year)

E = erratic events
(such as strikes, fire any hazards or disturbances)
and random error.

With the assumption of additive model, we have

$$Y = \text{sales} = T + C + S + E$$

If we assume that these factors interact multiplicatively, then

$$Y = T \times C \times S \times E$$

Here T is in absolute value: C, S, E are in percentages.

---

[1]If the sales data had changed rapidly, then the value of a would be closer to 1.0.

A New Product Forecasting Model

Marketers are often interested in forecasting the total market demand. The model below highlights some of the characteristics that may be incorporated in actually constructing a forecasting model.

1. **Purpose**
   (a) Forecasting of aggregate market demand vs. repeat purchase forecast
   (b) First purchase models vs. repeat purchase models
   (c) Forecasting of total sales vs. weekly/annual sales.

2. **Type of products**
   (a) Frequently purchased vs. infrequently purchased
   (b) New product vs. new brand
   (c) Consumer vs. industrial products.

3. **Units/Level of analysis**
   Unit : Individual vs. household
   Value vs. units brought
   Level : Market segments vs. total market

4. **Format of model**
   Diffusion vs. adoption
   Deterministic vs. stochastic

5. **The dependent variables**
   Type : Brand choice vs. frequency of purchase vs. quantity purchased
   Brand sales vs. brand share
   No. of variables: Single vs. two or more variables
   Type of scale: Nominal, ordinal or interval

6. **The independent variable**
   Type : Time
   Marketing: Price, deals, advertising, etc.
   Customer: Situation specific vs. general customer choice

7. **The required data**
   Type : Primary data vs. historical data on similar products
   Consumer response vs. sales data
   Test market vs. pre-test market
   Representative of number of samples

8. **Analytical procedure**
   Simulation vs. analytical procedure
   Parameter estimation across product classes vs. a product class.

A mathematical model can be developed considering the above or similar characteristics. Generally, computer routines use different multivariate techniques to forecast the demand for the given product. The output of the package will show the estimates either in volume or value terms.

Limitation of Sales Forecasting

Forecasting by any method is rarely an accurate one. This is because there are so many limiting factors which impede the accuracy of the sales forecasts.

1. **Fashions:** Unlike in the past, nowadays, fashion and styles in India change as rapidly as in the West, not just in terms of clothes and accessories but also in decoration, furnishing and other areas. Therefore, while introducing new-styles it is very difficult to predict customer behaviour.

2. **Lack of sales history:** Generally, all the sales forecasting methods are based on what the customer has said or some past sales data. In the case of new products, some guess work is necessary. Thus, it is difficult to obtain accurate forecasts anticipating growth elements.

Accurate calculations of the anticipated growth rate from the existing situation is very difficult in sales forecasting. It is very hard to say whether the present rate of growth will continue, decline or increase. In preparing sales forecasts, a manager estimates a rate of growth which at time may not tally with reality.

3. **Psychology:** The psychological factors play a vital role in sales. A marketing manager cannot predict accurately the future psychological behaviour of the customer. At times, customer's attitudes change suddenly. For example, any political change will create uncertainty in the market.

Because of the above factors, there is a need for the marketing manager to be more cautious and to apply intuition while taking decisions on sales forecasts figures.

CHAPTER 12

Marketing Research

A thorough understanding of the consumer's motivation and behaviour often means difference between success and failure of a marketing programme. In this competitive environment, managers need to gather information to evolve a proper strategy and to assess the effectiveness of various marketing programmes. It is in this sphere that market research aids managers, by providing data collected in a systematic manner. Of course, even without formal research, a manager may have a fair amount of information based on intuition.

In today's marketing environment, a lot of changes are taking place because of government policies, competition or consumer tastes and preferences. For instance, entry of foreign companies or liberal import policy has compelled companies to make a proper assessment of the emerging opportunities and threats. Companies are continuously affected by these policy changes, and are consequently looking for avenues in the form of new product launches, market expansion and diversification. Similarly, competitive threats have forced companies to reposition their offerings. Monitoring consumer tastes and preferences has remained an ongoing area of interest for any marketer. In all these activities, marketing research assumes the key role of providing data collected and analysed in an objective manner, to aid in the decision making process. With formal market research, a manager is able to obtain a clear picture of changing trends thus helping managers arrive at a decision.

As a matter of fact, when a manager acts on intuition, it is also a form of 'soft' market information. Here the manager is collecting and processing the data in an informal manner to make a decision. But as the intricacies of the market dynamics become complex, simple intuitive reasoning fails to grasp the totality of the problem. It is here that market research provides pertinent and timely information and the proper method of analysing data to generate alternative courses of action. For example, in an industrial product, the alternatives before a manager may be either to offer good performance, low operating costs, a low initial price, or good after-sales service. Familiarity with the end users' awareness helps a manager by indicating the likely reaction to each of these options.

Market research aids the manager by presenting the different perspectives from which he/she may choose the best alternative using his/her judgement.

MR FOR MARKETING DECISION MAKING

In this section, we shall highlight some of the marketing decision areas where market research is commonly used. Generally speaking, the marketing decisions can be classified as of operational, tactical or strategic nature.

"Operational decisions" are mainly confined to the management of sales. Here market research helps in ascertaining the impact of various promotions, distribution, advertising and pricing programmes planned by a company. For instance, market research is used to assess the recognition, recall, attitude and sales effect of an advertising campaign. To aid in operational decision making, research is often undertaken to analyse the market share of brands, commission structure of distribution channels, consumer off-take and usage patterns, stores audit and competitive performance.

Tactical decisions pertain to issues having medium term implications.

(a) Research is called for to form market segments.
(b) Consumer perception of brands or positioning.
(c) Consumer attitudes and behaviour analysis studies are widely undertaken to understand the factors influencing the demand; or the important purchase criteria; or the process of decision making.
(d) The impact of promotional measures such as discounts and incentives to trade channels.
(e) Growth of markets and shifts in consumer profile.

Marketing research is also used to aid numerous "strategic decisions" which have long term implications. Generally, such areas are:

(a) Assessment of new product opportunities and concept testing.
(b) Test marketing of new product(s) concepts or ideas.
(c) Product modifications or deletions.
(d) Diversification opportunities.
(e) Socio-economic and cultural trends.

Stages in the Research Process

Marketing research consists of a series of inter-connected stages. Broadly speaking, it is divided into several stages:

Stage one : Problem formulation
Stage two : Planning the research design
Stage three : Mode of data collection

Stage four : Data analysis
Stage five : Communicating research findings

The stages enumerated above are merely an ordered sequence of activities. However, sometimes a stage may be skipped or a stage may overlap with another, and hence these should not be treated as rigid boundaries. The depth or the intensity with which one deals with each of these stages will greatly depend upon the availability of time and resources. In any case, any market research study must carry practical implications on certain identified decision problems. In this sense, it is different from an economic survey. The above stages of the research process are briefly described below[1].

1. **Problem formulation:** Generally, most market research studies are carried out on the basis of some formal briefing on the problems/ symptoms of the market place. The researcher(s) develop a clear-cut statement of the objectives of the research to be undertaken in consultation with the line managers. As the old adage goes, "a problem well formulated is half solved". In fact, it is necessary to judge the various problems before initiating the act of data collection. The best way to express the purpose of a study is by making a formal and precise statement of marketing objective(s) and research objectives. At times, this is also followed by a set of hypotheses based on the research brief. It is in this process that several nascent ideas stated as hypotheses are tested by empirical data.

2. **Research design:** The research design essentially states the procedure of data collection and analysis of information relevant to the problem. Quite naturally, time and resources have a definite bearing on the research design. The researcher(s), during the study, define(s) the sources and mode of collection of data. As such, it is advisable to scan various secondary sources of data before beginning any primary data collection. Duplication and costs can be saved by efficient scanning of secondary data.

While deciding on the mode of primary data collection, several alternatives are faced. These are observations, experiments or surveys. In each of these modes, the exact manner of data collection will have to be defined, and suitable instruments designed. For example, observation techniques may require forming small groups while surveys may require appropriate questionnaires, and experiments will require specifications of settings, manipulation or the control of variables.

3. **Mode of data collection:** The manner in which the data and the sample of respondents will be selected falls under this stage. Depending on the nature of the problem, one may choose qualitative techniques like

---

[1]For detailed treatment of this subject the reader may refer to author's book titled, "*Marketing Research: Text, Applications and Case Studies*", Wiley Eastern, New Delhi, 1991.

in-depth interviews, focus group discussions, experts' opinions or *delphi techniques.* Also, in the questionnaire formulation, one would require to specify explicitly the wording of the questions, choice of rating scales and their measurements. This stage also shows in advance the kind of analysis to be performed. Decisions about sample size and method of sample selection is most important. The process of actual data collection begins after this.

4. **Data analysis:** After the data has been collected and edited, it is subjected to different methods of analysis. The type of analysis is somewhat dictated by the nature of the data collected. Data analysis may range from simple tabulations like graphs, averages or percentages to more sophisticated statistical or psychometric analysis. For obtaining a greater insight into appropriate choice of statistical test in a given problem, one may consult Majumdar (1991)[1].

5. **Communicating research findings:** Finally, a market research study must show its findings to the sponsors/users of the research. Typically, research findings are the translation of data analysis into lucid and usable expressions in marketing language. Here, it is imperative to match the findings with the original decision problem.

In Retrospect

Research enables line managers to generate alternative scenarios of their decisions. In this sense, it is an aid to decision making. Research in test marketing, for example, would provide an objective assessment of the market, but the ultimate decision of whether to launch the product or not is the prerogative of the line manager(s), and finally, rests on their judgement. Thus, while research may be an extremely useful instrument in taking decisions, it should not be considered a substitute to the judgement of users.

---

[1]*Ibid.,* Chapters 8-10.

Part III
PRODUCT MARKET ANALYSIS

INTRODUCTION

In this part, we have made an indepth analysis of 20 products, in Chapters 13–32. The various products covered are namely, commodities such as packaged drinking water, tea, soft drinks, chocolates, malted beverages; toiletries and cosmetics such as toothpaste, toilet soaps, detergents, shampoo, fairness creams; personal use durables such as wrist watches, footwears, mobile phones, digital cameras, motor cycles; home appliances like refrigerators, air conditioners, decorative paints, family possession such as television, and passenger car.

In each product situation, we have discussed the marketing trends, consumer behaviour, and major marketing strategies adopted by the leading companies operating in those product businesses. The objective is to explain the various strategic moves undertaken by the important participants. We have consciously avoided giving exhaustive lists of all companies in the business, thus limiting the discussion to companies from whose activities major lessons can be derived. In this process, the reader will comprehend various issues affecting each product. Thus, the reader can enrich his or her vision and at the same time develop analytical skills. Eventually, it is hoped that this process will enable the reader to adopt the underlying concepts in his or her respective corporate situation.

Chapter 33 offers a note on new challenges for marketers in India, which draws analogies from the various conceptual and empirical issues discussed earlier.

Finally, the book ends with an epilogue in the light of contemporary developments in Indian market.

CHAPTER 13

Packaged Drinking Water

In India packaged drinking water was once upon a time known more as a mineral water. In those days, drinking water was packaged in glass bottles and market was confined mainly to posh hotels and restaurants, consumed mainly by foreign tourists. However, the composition of the market has of late undergone a major change. Today, packaged drinking water bottles are consumed by the entire country, because of increasing suspicion about the quality of source of drinking water. As a matter of fact during the 1990s, the packaged drinking water market expanded drastically. This popularity is evident from the fact that a drinking water bottle is found even in many convenience stores across the country. Consequently, the market composition changed drastically and today 60% of packaged drinking water sales comes from the street corner shops and retail stores.

The packaged drinking water industry in India is reported to have grown by 25% in the last decade. In 2004–05 and 05–06, it grew by an unbelievable rate of 40%. India has already become the 10th largest market for packaged water. In 2006–07, Indian market size was estimated to be Rs 100 billion and is projected to become Rs 200 billion by 2010.

SOME BELIEFS AND MYTHS

There are many interesting age-old beliefs and myths about water in India as listed down below:

- In Veda (one of the oldest spiritual scripts of Hindu religion in India), water is considered as one of the five vital elements of life.
- Water of many rivers like the Ganga, Godavari, Kaveri and Narmada etc. is regarded as the purest water. Many people in India still believe that bathing in those rivers washes away the past sins of their life, though, in reality, water of many such rivers is quite polluted.
- In urban locations, 90% of drinking water is supplied through municipal taps and the remaining 10% of demand is met through

hand pumps and wells. In rural areas, 85% of drinking water is obtained through the river or local tank and 15% through hand pumps and wells. Water purifying methods are boiling cloth filtering and electronic purification. Generally, there is no attempt to purify most of the water used for drinking purpose.

- There is still low level of consciousness about hygiene, and awareness about health issues arising from consuming any drinking water. As more and more water-born pollution cases are coming into limelight, people in India are realizing the importance of packaged drinking water. That is why, it offers a great opportunity for packaged water brands.

CONSUMER BEHAVIOUR AND CHOICE CRITERION

Some generic behavioural patterns observed among consumers of this product are discussed below:

- **Importance of purity and safe:** The consumers, by and large, perceive packaged water to be pure and safe, and hence they are ready to pay a premium price for the levels of purity and safety aspect.
- **Brand and company image:** To get consumer acceptance, a packaged drinking water brand has to develop trust or a consistent image. Thus, the promotional campaigns of major brands in this industry invariably aim at assuring the target consumers about the purity and safety and building an image of their respective brands.
- **Low brand loyalty:** Till now this market is characterised by low level of brand loyalty, as the basic selection criteria of the consumer has remained easy *availability*. Hence, better is the distribution system of a company, better is the chance of its choice. This sort of behavioural pattern is because of highly commoditised nature of the product here. As brands try to establish their image and create some differentiation through heavy promotional campaigns, consumers are then likely to develop a strong preference for specific brand.
- **Price sensitiveness:** As expected, consumers in this market are highly price sensitive. This stems from the overwhelming belief that water, especially drinking water, should be free, as has been the case for years in India. Hence, charging a high price for such a product often gives a negative signal to consumers,

who are reluctant to pay for water in the first place. The example of Nestle, which tried to enter the popular segment with its 1 litre bottle priced at Rs 2 more than the other players and subsequently withdrawn, amply illustrates this fact.

- **Packaging and convenience:** One of the secondary but important aspects of this product is the convenience of use of water bottles and its packaging. As consumers pay for the assurance of purity of water, tamper-proof packaging goes a long way in establishing this trust. Also, with more number of consumers tend to stay long hours out of their home, these class of consumers readily go in for packaged water for the convenience of availability. These classes of consumers who pay for convenience have been one of the major factors of growth of this industry in major cities.
- As discussed earlier, there are many prevalent beliefs that consumers attach to water. In fact, some quarters have consistently protested the growth of this industry on moral and ethical grounds with questions like should water be priced, and should we be forced to buy water just to ensure purity because of the very nature of the product.

MAJOR GROWTH DRIVERS

Let us now discuss what are the major growth drivers for this industry in the following section.

- **Scarcity of water:** The problem of water scarcity is a big threat and according to some surveys, by 2020 the demand for water is going to exceed the supply due to rapid ground-water erosion, growing water pollution, wastage, and also due to the growing population. This evidently shows that there is going to be a huge opportunity for the packaged water industry.
- **Hygiene concerns:** With a rapidly growing middle income class in India, more and more people are becoming health conscious. This class of consumers is the target for all leading brands of drinking water. Moreover, as this consumer group is likely to grow in number, it will be one of the major growth drivers for this industry.
- **Better lifestyles:** Better living standards and its affordability itself induce consumers to pay for purity and thereby giving an automatic fillip to the industry.
- Closely related factor is the rise in per capita disposable incomes. With higher buying power, consumers are getting more concerned about personal health. This in itself makes packaged drinking water a viable concept.
- PVC packaging and later the PET bottles in the mid-1980s gave the real boost to bottled water.

- **Innovative marketing:** Innovative marketing techniques are going to be another major growth drivers for this product. This has been amply demonstrated by Bisleri who opened the floodgates in mid-1990, with re-positioning packaged water as mass-market product, changing its image of exclusivity. Another case in point is the introduction of the bulk segment by Bisleri again in 2000, which reduced the per litre cost of water from Rs 10 to as low as Rs 2, and made a great impact on its sales. Today, the bulk segment leads the profitability margins with growth rates as high as 40% in the last 2 years. By lower pricing of the packages and proper promotions, consumers can be influenced and convinced about the intrinsic value-for-money of this product.

MARKET POTENTIAL AND TRENDS

As seen from earlier discussion, the market potential for packaged drinking water is evidently huge. The potential consumer here could be the entire country and thus, great opportunities can be seized. As some ad said, there is "*boond boond mein paisa*" (Money in every drop) in this industry.

- It is one of the fastest growing industries that outstripped the growth of other beverages in the last few years. There has been a phenomenal increase (i.e. 400% growth) in demand from 1999 to 2006. Despite that, the per capita consumption of packaged water is very low (less than 5 litres) as compared to the global average of about 24 litres.
- In spite of such huge potential of this industry, not everything is rosy. The major concern today is the high inefficiency in the distribution system across India. Today, 60% of the packaged water is consumed in the North and Western India, whereas 80% of the packaging and purifying plants are located in South India (with nearly half of the supply is from Tamil Nadu). This puts serious constraints on efficient distribution and adds to costs of transportation.
- There are also major concerns expressed over purity of packaged drinking water. Most notable of which were the reports of traces of bacteria and pesticides in water-purification process found in Chennai in 2003–04. Such cases have reoccurred time and again which calls for stricter regulations and stringent quality norms by government and regulators. Also, with rapid erosion of ground water adds to the accelerating scarcity of safe drinking water, which could pose real supply problems for the industry.
- At present, there exist numerous set of small to mid sized companies making water purification and packaging. This makes it almost a cottage industry. In future there is high possibility of major consolidation in this industry.

Market Segmentation

The market of packaged drinking water can be divided in three segments: the popular segment with bottles for daily consumption, the bulk segment with bigger containers, and the premium segment with more expensive brands.

The popular segment is basically represented by the four main brands, such as Bisleri, Bailey, Kinley and Aquafina. In this segment the major sizes of bottles range from 250 ml to 2 litres.

In the bulk segment (i.e. 5–20 litres), the two main players are Bisleri and Kinley. These bulk sizes are very convenient for daily consumption in large households or in businesses. These containers are at present marketed at a price of Rs 25–75.

The last segment, the premium one, is basically represented by the two companies Nestlé and Danone with their respective brands Perrier and Evian. This particular segment is characterized by higher price of their water. For example, while Bailey 300 ml bottle costs Rs 3, Perrier sells its bottle of 330 ml at the price of Rs 50.

THE MAJOR PLAYERS AND THEIR BRANDS

There are more than 200 brands of bottled water with 90% of them locally sold. The major national players brands in the packaged drinking water market are shown in Exhibit 13.1.

EXHIBIT 13.1

Segmentation in Packaged Drinking Water

Segment	Company	Brand	Pack sizes	Price
Popular	Parle Bisleri	Bisleri	250 ml, 500 ml, 1.2 & 2 litres	Rs 3–18
	Parle Agro	Bailey	300 ml, 500 ml, 1 & 2 litres	Rs 3–18
	Coca Cola	Kinley	300 ml, 500 ml, 1 & 2 litres	Rs 4–18
	Pepsi	AquaFina	750 ml, 1 & 2 litres	Rs 8–18
Bulk	Parle	Bisleri	5 litres, 20 litres	Rs 25–60
	Coca Cola	Kinley	20 litres	Rs 75
Premium	Nestle	Perrier	330 ml, 750 ml	Rs 50–90
	Danone	Evian	1 litres	Rs 85

Four brands together account for about 77% market share and the remaining 23% market is occupied by numerous number of players. Among them brands like Neer (IRCTC), Perrier (Nestlé), Evian (from Danone), Kingfisher (UB Group) etc. also appear.

The market shares of major brands: In the packaged water market, Bisleri is the leader with 40% of market share. Then, Kinley had 25% share, Aquafina had a share of 12%.

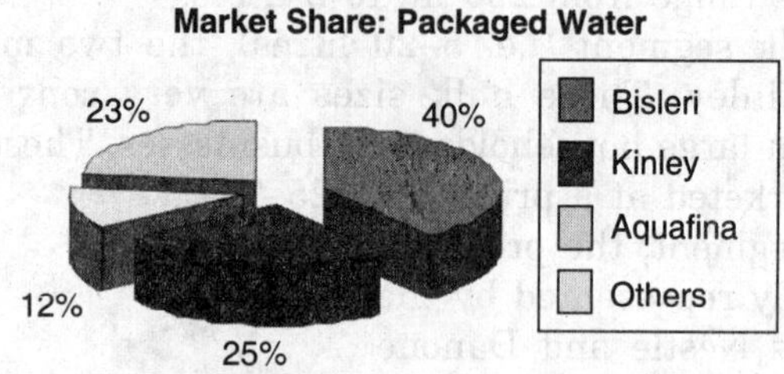

POSITIONING STRATEGY OF LEADING BRANDS

Brand: Kinley

Parent company: Coco Cola India

- 2000: Kinley water launched nationally in India
- 2003: Kinley water becomes the largest selling retail pack in India (35% market share)
- Assurance of safety
- Seven steps of purification (reverse osmosis)
- SKU's: 500 ml, 1 lit, 2 lit, 20 litres
- Key success factor: getting the product within reach of target market
- Kinley reaches 500,000 retail outlets (2003)

Customer targeted

- Urban consumers more exposed to western lifestyles
- Customer who understands the importance of Pure and Safe water
- Consumers seeking convenience

Positioning

- Belief that right to pure, safe drinking water is fundamental.
- **"Purity in each drop"**

Growth strategy

- Inorganic growth: Taking over local players through M&A
- Operational efficiency improvement: Through effective distribution, i.e. making product available everywhere
- Packaging and pricing issue for convenience
- Strategic marketing:
  - Tie-up with institutions like railways, hotels, airlines, hospitals etc.

- — Frequent promotional campaign with retailers
- — Bundling with other service providers like McDonalds, Dominoes or some restaurants
- — Kinley is expanding through take over of local players
- Societal marketing:
  - — Working in collaboration with Government of India for safety message through pure water campaign
  - — Rain water harvesting approach

Brand: Aquafina

- Parent company: Pepsi Co. India
- Launched in 1998
- Market share by the end of 2003 is 10%
- 7-step purification steps
- Assurance of quality and safe water
- SKU's: 1 litre, 2 litre, 25 litre
- Key success factor: Reaching out to the customers
- Aquafina reaches 2,50,000 outlets

Customers targeted

- Urban consumers more exposed to western lifestyles
- Customers who understand the importance of safe water
- Customers seeking convenience to carry bottle with them

Positioning

"World-class quality and convenience to consumers"

Growth strategy

Aquafina has a strategy of growth through the franchise model. Jaipuriya Group of Industries is one of the major franchise of Pepsi for beverages. Other strategies of Aquafina are similar to Kinley.

Brand: Bisleri

- Parent company: Parle Products Ltd.
- Bisleri was first launched in 1969. But it was withdrawn due to lack of demand for colourless, tasteless and odourless drinking water at that time
- Re-launched in 1993. This time brand building efforts focused on Bisleri being healthy packaged water with adequate minerals
- Transparency through PET bottles—sparkling clear water to the consumers

- Created market for packaged drinking water in India and took first movers advantage
- Increased market share through introduction of 500 ml bottles at Rs 5 per bottle (1995)—400% growth achieved
- 1998: Introduced a tamper-proof and tamper-evident seal
- 2000: Introduced 1.2 litre Pet bottle at Rs 10 per bottle
- 2000: Introduced the 20-litre container to bring prices down from Rs 10 a litre to Rs 2 a litre

Positioning

"Sparkling clear water"

Parle does not have the ability to compete against the multinationals on distribution or advertising. So it concentrated on the 20 litre bulk water segment, which constituted 40% of its sales. It is targeted at institutional channels such as railway stations, canteens and hotels. These are tender-driven supply deals, which guarantee a certain volume of off-take but not necessarily deliver high profit to the company.

Bisleri shifted from its initial "Pure and Safe" positioning to a new "Play Safe" positioning following the entry of numerous "me-too" brands that are looking to take advantage of Bisleri's success.

Growth strategy: Bisleri adopted three strategies to counter the erosion of its share. They are strengthening distribution in semi urban areas, competitive pricing to align itself with its rivals and innovative packaging in the form of new sizes and formats.

- Company plans to increase manufacturing facility and widen its distribution network. Bottling capacity will be doubled to 200 million cases per day 10-lakh retail outlets backed by a fleet over 5,000 vehicles
- Plans to procure recycling plants from Japan for its PET bottles
- Recently forayed into the premium segment with the launch of "Bisleri Natural Mountain Water"
- Plans to offer water which will contain vitamin and flavour

New Brands

In 2004, bottled water saw the launch of several new brands including Kingfisher from United Breweries Ltd. whose main business is beer. Another entry was McDowell's No. 1 from McDowell & Co Ltd. whose main business is spirit. Because of the ban on advertising of liquor brands, UB and McDowell entered the packaged water market in 2004, seemingly to keep their brand names alive. Likewise, in 2004, the Indian Railway Catering and Tourism Corporation (IRCTC), a division of Indian railways, expanded the network of its own brand of bottled water, Rail Neer, in many North and East based railway platforms in India. The potential for Rail Neer is tremendous because of the huge networks and passenger traffic of Indian Railways.

FUTURE TRENDS

India, with its 1 billion population size, offer a huge market opportunity. Even if assuming 10% penetration i.e. 100 million, it shows a staggering 36.5–73 billion litres a year. In money terms, at Rs 10 a litre, the potential market is between Rs 36,500–73,000 crores.

The branded bottled water is the fastest growing industry in the beverage sector. As a result, more new companies are likely to enter this market. However, with shrinking margins as well as stiff competition already faced, the future situation will not so smooth. There is a new tendency of shift towards the premium quality segment. Competition in this segment is at present not much. For instance, Bisleri introduced its mountain variant and Coca-Cola is likely to launch some mineral water brand in India.

Innovative Tactics

The development of innovative marketing strategy will be one of the key success factors in this market. For instance, two new categories of drinking water products likely to emerge are: one, the flavoured water and another, the water enriched with vitamins or minerals like fluoride or calcium etc. Such new products will highlight its true benefits of health. Regarding packaging innovations, the companies went for different sizes of bottles. They are also shifting from the PVC bottles to PET, which is stronger and safer and does not smell when burnt. Now they try to invent new design and new types of bottles (corks designed for sportive, etc.), especially on the premium segment.

Arbindo Beverages Ltd. of Nagpur launched a 300 ml pouch pack of water and priced it at Rs 2 per pouch. The pouch was sold at bus stand, railway station, pan shops and kirana stores. This brand is reported to have achieved an average sales level of Rs 1 lakh per day. The idea here is to make water affordable to low end or ordinary customers and be present at common places, like bus stand and railway stations. Customers do not hesitate to spend Rs 2 when they are thirsty and waiting at some bus stop or at some railway stations.

Similarly, Bailey introduced a plastic handle to its 2 litre bottle, which provided lots of convenience to the customer to carry such bottle. The sale of Bailey 2 litre has recently gone up considerably as compared to Kinley or Bisleri's similar 2 litre pack.

Outlook for the Future

The packaged drinking water industry has seen significant growth and changes over the past few years, driven by changing trends in market. The trends, like changing demographics, growing population size and rapid urbanization, are expected to continue in future and it will shape the demand for packaged drinking water industry in India. The Government of India's focus towards making drinking water as a priority sector is likely to ensure more favourable policies to attract more FDI to India.

The packaged drinking water industry uses a lot of plastic material that is really polluting the environment. They will create the biggest constraints for the industry. Indiscriminate re-use of the plastic bottles (when not recycled properly) leads to another menace. In 2002, there was a big hue and cry when 400 illegal water packaging units were found near Chennai.

After the scandal involving the pesticides being found in some of the major soft drinks of Coca-Cola or Pepsi, there is a need of changing the water management practices with more stringent quality checks and regulation. The government of India adopted E.U. standards for bottled water at 0.1 ppb for single residues and 0.5 ppb for multiple residues. Some companies claimed that those new regulations are extremely difficult to put them into practice.

Notwithstanding several challenges to face, market growth will continue because of mounting lack of confidence in public water supplies, a shift in consumer life styles, and greater concern for safe water.

CHAPTER 14

Tea

Tea plays a vital role in the lives of millions of Indians. They take it as a refreshing drink as part of daily ritual. Tea offers livelihood to millions of people who are associated with this industry.

India produces some of the world's finest quality and also the largest variety of tea. Among the famous specialty flavours are Darjeeling tea, Assam tea, and Nilgiri tea, which are grown in the Bengal, Assam, and Tamil Nadu.

Tea is normally classified based on the processing, leaf size and grade. Fermentation creates two major classifications, black and green tea. Black tea is further classified into CTC (cut, tear and curl) and orthodox tea.

INDIAN TEA INDUSTRY AT A GLANCE

- India is the largest producer and consumer of tea in the world.
- Tea production, since Independence has grown by over 250%.
- Tea trading in the domestic market is done in two ways—auction and private selling.
- Tea is currently the second biggest in beverage category after the Rs 7000 crores carbonated soft drinks market.
- Total turnover of package tea was approximately Rs 6500 crores in 2005.
- In the packaged tea category, the unorganized sector accounted for over Rs 1,500 crore.

Market Trends

The tea market in India is witnessing a sea change in recent times. Changes in the life style of Indians have influenced tea consumption pattern. In particular, it has caused the growth of the so-called branded or packaged tea category.

Earlier, tea was mostly sold in a commodity form. However, now-a-days the branded form has gained popularity and led to the entry of packaged tea and tea bags. Out of the 750 million kg of tea consumed in India, around 300 million kg (40%) was sold in the branded form. The branded tea is now estimated to account for 60% of the annual turnover of the tea industry, valued at Rs 6400 crores. In the last two years, the branded tea has grown between 6 and 8%. And it is now projected to register 10% growth in the coming years.

Hive-off the Plantation Business

Of late, the major players in the branded tea business have been undergoing a restructuring process. Not long back, 80% of *Tata Tea's* income used to come from its plantations, but now the emphasis has almost reversed. After *Tata Tea* sold its tea plantations to its wholly owned subsidiaries, plantations contributed just 14% to the company's turnover. It is also making efforts to strengthen its brands, and its acquisition of Tetley in 2000 has helped a lot in this regard. Following a similar step, *HUL* had quit plantations business and concentrated on the branded segment alone. After the sell of Tea Estates India Ltd, *HUL* has totally withdrawn from the plantation activity. Unlike *Tata Tea* and *HUL* who sold off their plantations, smaller players like Warren Tea, Khaitans etc. are still holding their plantations business.

Assam Company Limited (ACL), which had stopped producing branded tea in 2000, is now again planning to enter the branded tea business.

SEGMENTATION

The segmentation of India's tea market by different bases is shown below (Exhibit 14.1)

EXHIBIT 14.1

Segmentation of India's Tea Market

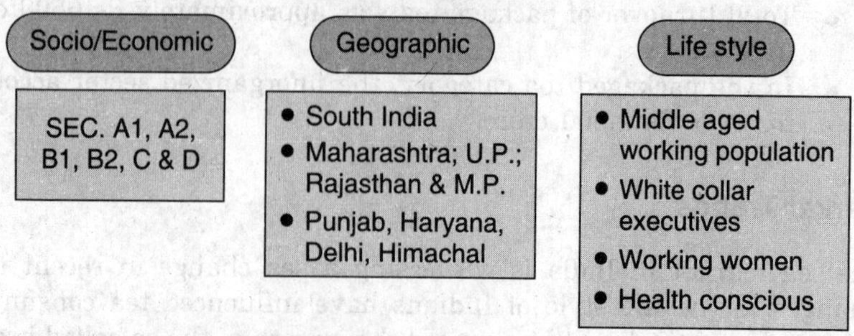

Examples:

- Taj Mahal focuses purely on SEC A & A+ categories.

- Kannan Devan Tea is mode only for Kerala, while Wagh Bakri for Gujarat region.
- Taaza focuses at mainly on working women, while Red Label on families.

COMPETITIVE STRUCTURE

Major players and their market shares: Tea industry is highly fragmented with a large number of small companies.

The branded tea market in India is dominated by two major players. In 2006, these two companies used to command more than 50% share of the market. *Hindustan Unilever Ltd.* (HUL) led this segment with a market share of 30%, followed by *Tata Tea*, with a market share of 21.1%. *Duncans Tea* was the number three player in the branded tea market with a share of 7%, and *Goodricke* followed with a market share of 4%. There are also some well-known regional players like *Jivaraj* and *Wagh Bakri*.

Major Brands

HUL and Tata Tea have offered a family of brands to cater to the different segments of the tea market.

EXHIBIT 14.2

Some of the Major Players and their Brands

Sl. no.	Company	Brands
1.	Hindustan Unilever Ltd.	Brooke Bond–Red Label, Taj Mahal, Taaza and 3 Roses, Lipton's Green Label.
2.	Tata Tea	Agni, Tata Tea, Kanan Devan, Chakra Gold, Tata Tetley and Gemini
3.	Duncans Group	Sargam, Double Diamond, Shakti, Runglee, Rungliot and No. 1
4.	Goodricke	Goodricke, Zabardast, Castleton Caddy etc.

The structure of their brands are as follows:

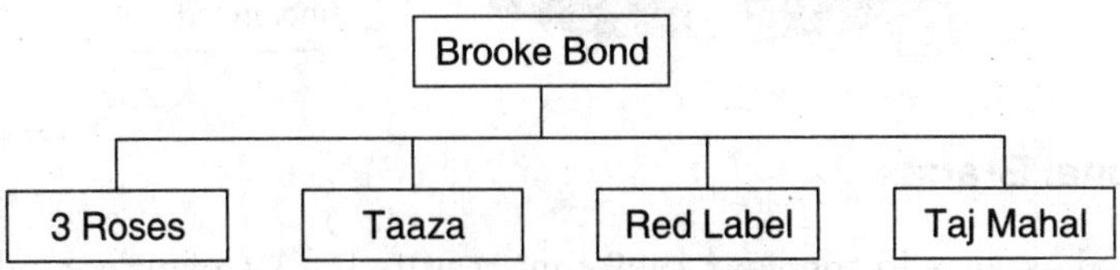

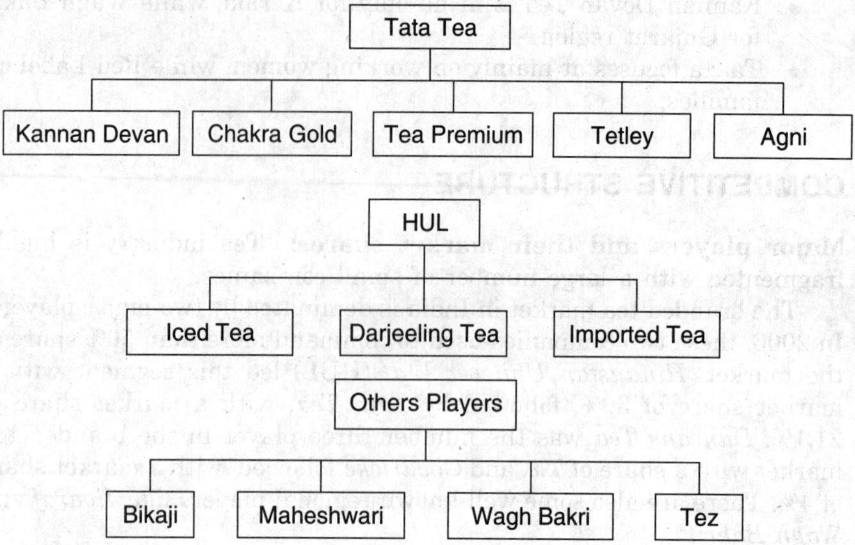

For HUL the Brooke Bond Family consists of in-house tea brands, while Lipton brands focus on the out of home segment. Tata Tea has matching competing brands with the Brooke Bond. For example, Tetley has the same positioning as BB Taj Mahal and Tata Agni has the same positioning as BB Taaza.

Smaller players are divided into 2 types—one group which consists of very powerful packaged local tea brands—e.g. Lal Ghoda in Rajasthan and Wagh Bakri in Gujarat—most of these brands harp on the functionality of the product, i.e. the strength, flavor and smell of tea.

Local loose tea makers usually position their products based on the price factor only and are therefore not a competition. The packaged tea market in India is Rs 6500 crore in size. The market share is as shown below (Exhibit 14.3).

EXHIBIT 14.3

Packaged Tea Market Share (Market Size Rs 6500 crore)

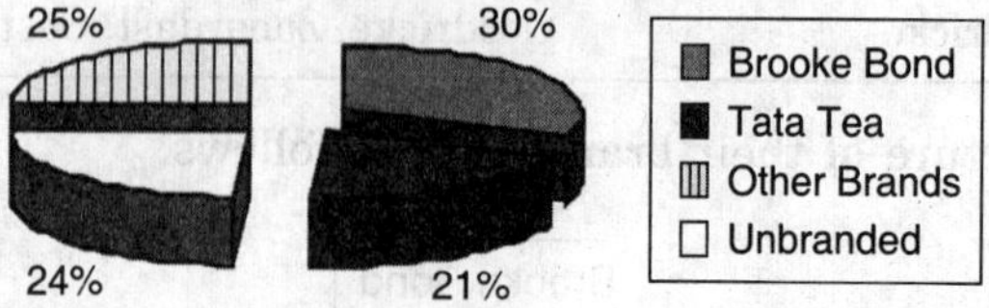

Regional Brands

Reduced exports in the year 1999 that resulted in lower price realizations for Indian tea, led to the entry of many new regional brands, which targeted at the domestic market to keep their business on. The big players who had not witnessed competition from such exporters till then found themselves on the losing side of the battle. Some of the small regional brands, which posed a major threat to the majors, were Lasa, Isaphani, Manmouji, Sugandh, Marvel, Mohani, Tulsi, Mansook etc. During the year 2004, their market share in the branded tea segment grew to around 35%. The major brands faced this competition by adopting newer strategies in the form of value addition.

Value Additions

Changes are inevitable to keep a sector growing and ahead of competition. Following this, the branded tea market has been witnessing various remodeling processes. In order to improve domestic consumption, it is accelerating penetration into top-end segment. The players are bringing in value added products into its basket. *Tata Tea* has usually followed this strategy. *HUL* has introduced new products to target at the health conscious consumers. *HUL* has launched the Red Label Nature Care, which contains the natural flavours of ginger, *ashwaghanda*, *adhimadhirum*, cardamom and *tulsi*.

Meeting Regional Taste Variations

India, generally well known as a country with a vast array of cultures and traditions, has diversified tastes also. In order to cater to the needs of the consumers in the different parts of our country, the tea companies are introducing new brands. *Goodricke*, an active brand in North India, has launched a new brand, which would suit the taste preferences of South Indian consumers. The companies are keeping in touch with the consumers in order to get their regular feedback. Brands like *Dilmah Tea* are focusing on consumer contact programmes. They have set up regional tea parlours and retail outlets not only to improve their sales but also to have a direct rapport with the consumers. In many of the tea parlours, the details about the views and taste preference of the consumers visiting the parlours and retail outlets are collected and compiled in an attempt to come out with products that would suit the palate of the consumers. *HUL* is also into branded tea retailing. It has launched a tea parlour in Bangalore and aims to increase the number of parlours to 100 soon. The Assam Company Ltd., Apeejay Surrendra Group and Infinitea are the other tea companies who have set up special form of ready to drink tea selling outlets.

POSITIONING

The positioning of the leading tea brands is shown in Exhibit 14.4 on functional, symbolic and experiential platforms.

EXHIBIT 14.4

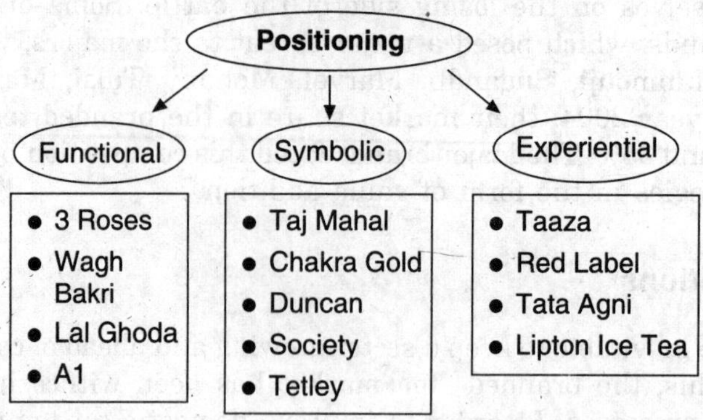

POSITIONING OF SOME LEADING TEA BRANDS

Exhibit 14.5 below shows the Brand Identity Pyramid.

EXHIBIT 14.5

Brand Identity Pyramid

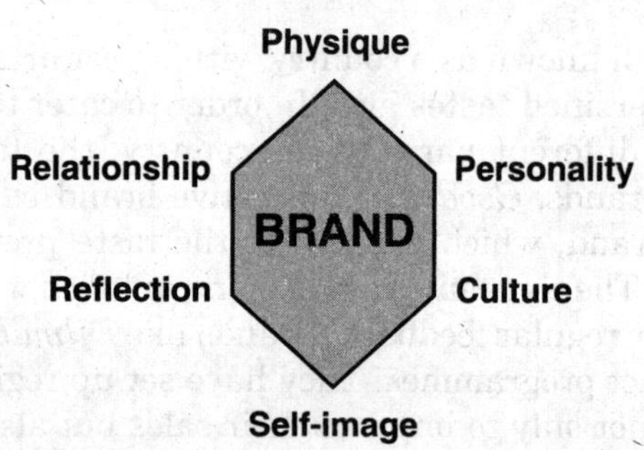

Tata Chakra Gold

Chakra Gold is one of the oldest tea brands in the country and is very popular in South India. It is a brand that is functionally positioned—on the basis of aroma and taste of the product. Tata Chakra Gold harps on Symbolic benefits in its brand of tea, which is better than any other rival brand.

The brand depends a lot on symbolisms—the pack design and symbols have remained the same for decades.

The consumers of Chakra Gold possibly seek the following:

- A satisfying aroma
- Great flavour and savouring true aroma of tea
- A thick liquor.

Exhibit 14.6 shows a possible positioning strategy of Tata Chakra Gold using Brand Identity Pyramid.

EXHIBIT 14.6

The Positioning Strategy for Chakra Gold using Brand Identity Pyramid

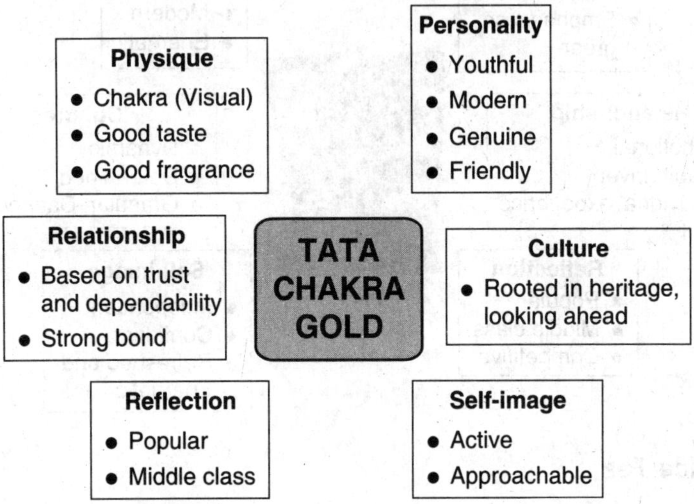

Brooke Bond Taaza

Taaza tea initially belonged to former tea company Lipton. Its purpose was to generate growth by entering low end tea market. The brand name Taaza signaled freshness attribute.

It was the first national brand that provided regional variants to cater to differing tastes—Taaza Dust, Leaf variants were released for different regions. The pouch packaging was viewed as modern and that retained freshness. The consumer benefit of 'amazing refreshment' was supported by the "selection story"—in its advertisement.

In 2003, Taaza was re-launched as Brooke Bond Taaza. The theme communication was changed "*kamaal ki taazgi*" and "*taazgi chan-chana-chan*" was replaced with "*subah se lekar shaam tak taaza*". By the end of 2003, BB Taaza had a new look and was present across pan India.

The target consumer for Taaza is the working woman who has to go through the different roles in daily life.

Unlike emphasizing on the product quality, Taaza talks of the emotional feeling of exhilaration or '*Umang*' all day through.

Until recently, the brand also had a mascot of the Taaza Woman. The colour of green was also permanently in the Taaza pack.

Exhibit 14.7 presents the positioning strategy of Taaza using popular brand identity pyramid.

EXHIBIT 14.7

The Positioning Strategy for Brooke Bond Taaza using Brand Identity Pyramid

Physique
- Image of the Taaza Woman
- Emphasis on green

Personality
- Modern
- Energetic

Relationship
- Emotional
- Habit driven
- Individual experience

Culture
- Dynamic
- Determined
- Granular–Daanedar

Reflection
- Popular
- Middle class
- Competitive

Self-image
- Independent
- Confident
- Refreshed and Energetic

Lipton Ice Tea

Exhibit 14.8 shows the positioning pyramid of Lipton Ice Tea, a new format of black tea with additives such as lemon and peach flavours. The drink is served chilled and comes in bottle, can and fountain formats.

EXHIBIT 14.8

The Positioning Strategy for Lipton Ice Tea using Brand Identity Pyramid

Physique
- Out of home tea
- Ready to drink
- Chilled

Personality
- Modern
- Natural
- Chilled out

Relationship
- More of a physical, less emotional
- Impulse driven
- More in the soft drink category

Culture
- Dynamic
- Determined

Reflection
- Upper class
- Niche

Self-image
- Sexy
- Natural edge
- Confident

Lipton Ice Tea has taken a very niche branding strategy of "Nature's Edge". It is targeted at the urban youth in SEC A+, A categories who would like to have natural refreshment.

Positioning strategy: The underlying idea of this new Lipton Ice Tea brand as a healthy energy drink is to compete with the ready to drink cold beverage. The brand associates with health, youth, adventure and banks on the sensory pleasures of awakening, health and physical simulation.

Changing Image of Tea to Compete with Other Beverages

Tea is perceived to be good for in home and habitual consumption while soft drinks are perceived to be preference of young generation.

- Energy drinks are evolving market with huge market opportunity to tap the young generation of consumers to drink tea.

Therefore, if a young image of tea is developed which is convenient to consume, it will not only be useful for the health conscious individuals but will also be a cool product to consume.

In that case the various marketing programmes shall highlight on the following aspects.

Product

- The product will be available in can (330 ml) and perhaps in cold form
- Packaging to be modern and ready to drink

Value chain

- Production to be outsourced to third party packaging units
- Initial supply will be through Category A retail outlets, restaurants, pubs, health clubs, movie halls and malls

Pricing

- The product will probably be priced at a premium—between Rs 15 to Rs 20 based on the cost structure and other competitive beverage price
- The purpose is to price it at a premium above soft drinks but preferably be lower than Rs 25 price point which currently exists for other energy drinks

Promotion

- Associate with adventure sports, health shows and health clubs
- Promotions to coincide with major sporting tournaments
- Focus also on POP displays
- Marketing channels
  - — Sports and music TV channels
  - — FM Radio
  - — Ads on youth websites
- Explore option of celebrity endorsements

THE ROAD AHEAD

The branded tea market has witnessed a sluggish growth in the past two decades. Despite its performance being below expectation, the market condition is expected to improve in future. This may be because Indian consumers are now passing through a changing phase of lifestyle. With the entry of new players and international brands like *Dilmah*, the tea market is expected to face more intense competition in the near future. Analysts project the growth to be 10% per annum. Moreover, at present most of the tea exported from India is in bulk form. If it is exported in branded form and in the form of tea bags, it would benefit Indian tea sales in markets like UK and USA. If proper marketing initiatives are taken by the Indian companies to penetrate into foreign markets tea business is likely to see a rapid phase of growth.

CHAPTER 15

Soft Drinks

The soft drinks market in India generally consists of different forms of products, such as carbonates, fruit flavour based juices, concentrates in liquid and powder form, speciality drinks like lemon and coconut water. Traditionally, Indians were used to consume plain water and fresh fruit juice at home. And during the summer season, consumption of curd based *lassi*, lemon and cold water outside home were common sights. Generally, the habit of drinking bottled soft drinks at road side retail shops is noticed mainly among the youth.

Despite heavy promotion by Coca-Cola and PepsiCo, in India per capita consumption of soft drinks is abysmally low. Exhibit 15.1 shows a picture of soft drinks sales by volume and value during 2001–2004.

EXHIBIT 15.1

Sales of Soft Drinks by Volume (2001–2004)

	(Million litres)			
	2001	2002	2003	2004
Carbonates	1,080.0	1,193.9	1,263.8	1,390.8
Fruit/vegetable juice	81.8	87.5	95.5	106.0
Concentrates	15.3	15.8	16.4	16.9

Sales of Soft Drinks by Value (2001–2004)

	(Rs million)			
	2001	2002	2003	2004
Carbonates	33,809.8	36,689.0	33,713.7	37,541.7
Fruit/vegetable juice	4,196.0	4,498.0	4,884.6	5,336.0
Concentrates	2,109.3	2,207.4	2,307.3	2,395.3

Branded soft drinks are predominantly (80%) sold in urban areas. Pepsi & Coke—the top two soft drink companies are trying to enter the vast untapped rural areas of India. They were very happy to notice the fact that rural off-take volume grew by 14% to 548 million litres in 2004.

MARKET TRENDS

Growth back on track: Soft drinks emerged stronger after the famous pesticides contamination controversy in 2003. Coca-Cola India and PepsiCo India shrugged off the controversy by bringing out effective counter arguments in their advertisements that reposed trust in their brands. Moreover, a series of initiatives, such as reduction in pack sizes, introduction of new flavours, and taking the advantage of growing number of children and their natural preference for carbonated drinks, the total quantum of soft drinks sales registered a growth of 16% in 2003–04.

Carbonates still dominate soft drinks sales: The introduction of very large pack size, superior advertising campaigns and intensification of distribution ensured carbonated form of soft drinks like Thums Up, Pepsi, Coke etc. to occupy the largest category among various soft drinks.

Fruit juice companies improve share: The trend towards consuming fresh fruit drinks benefited *Parle* with its brand of Frooti, *Dabur* with the Real range, and *Tropicana* with its Tropicana brand. These three companies, though together hold less than 5% volumes share of soft drinks, have gained gradual market acceptance.

As health and wellness have emerged as new elements of focus in Indian society, some soft drinks products also capitalized on this trend. Fresh fruit and vegetable juices started on the purity and health aspect as their positioning platforms. They gained sharply in both total volume and value, at the cost of carbonates and artificially flavoured drinks. Increased disposable income, higher pocket money among youth, imitation of western lifestyles, and aggressive promotion enabled sale of branded fruit and vegetable juices to reach over 100 million litres in volume.

Concentrates sale is falling: The consumption for liquid concentrates is coming down as consumers are increasingly looking for convenience and upgradation. People find it easier to consume prepared fruit juices or carbonates than spending efforts in preparing a drink from concentrates. So concentrates are trying to enter into rural areas, with the slogan of affordability of the small sachet packs.

Ready to drink (RTD) drinks: Beverage and functional drinks such as Lipton or Tata's iced tea, Nestle's instant coffee are available in many urban retail stores, but they have failed to capture a sizeable market base. There is still negligible size of demand for such convenient drinks in India, as there is a general lack of product awareness and appreciation. Similarly, PepsiCo India in October 2004 launched a sports drink called Gatorade and an energy drink such as Red Bull; they are yet to become a popular ready to drink (RTD) beverage. It seems high price is the major deterrent for consumers' acceptance. For instance, Red Bull at Rs 75 for a 250 ml can is still beyond the affordability level of many Indian consumers.

Supermarkets/hypermarkets have boosted soft drinks sales: Supermarkets/hypermarkets outlets are the biggest winners from the distribution of soft drinks. Newly opened supermarkets in the metropolitan areas are adopting a strategy of lowering the retail prices of soft drinks shown on the packaging, as well as engaging in cross-promotions to attract shoppers. These stores that are usually visited by upper economic strata of the Indian populations are used to launch high-value fresh juices and expensive soft drinks.

Volumes grow on small pack sizes: Coca-Cola India aggressively expanded rural distribution through launch of small pack sizes in soft drinks, which enabled the company to sell higher volumes. However, this heavily publicized small pack strategy was not found sustainable for long. In fact, prices for the 200 ml bottle were raised to Rs 6 in the latter half of 2004 as margins began to shrink and bottom lines began to take a beating. Nevertheless, the smaller pack size strategy has not proven successful but for inducing trails.

Tourism led growth: Tourism boom with respect to domestic as well as overseas visitors in India has always led to the growth of soft drinks market. In recent times the size of domestic tourists has grown significantly in states like Uttaranchal, Kerala, Rajasthan, Tamil Nadu and Goa. Similarly, the number of foreign tourists in India in 2004 went up to 3 million from 2.5 million in 2003.

New age businesses make their impact felt: The emergence of a number of new age businesses like call centres, business process outsourcing centres, software, retail and telecom, led to higher disposable income in the hands of younger people who are willing to spend more sum of money on items like soft drinks. Moreover, the rapid spread of supermarkets and multiplexes increased points of sale, combining ambience with affordability. These new age businesses and shopping pattern resulted in greater tendency to spend on soft drinks.

Strong growth forecast in soft drinks: With increase expected in tourism, distribution and a changing lifestyle, total volume of soft drinks is forecast to grow by a compounded average of 11% in the near future.

PERFORMANCE OF DIFFERENT FORMS OF SOFT DRINKS

Carbonates

Standard cola sets the standards: Standard cola carbonate products dominated sales of carbonates with close to 74% of total volume sales and more than 74% of total value sales in 2005. Following cola carbonates is orange carbonates and lemonade/lime with sales of 167 million and 132 million litres respectively in 2005. Brand shares of leading soft drinks brands are shown in Exhibit 15.2.

EXHIBIT 15.2

Brand Shares (%) of Carbonates by Volume (2001–2004)

Brand	Company	2001	2002	2003	2004
Pepsi	PepsiCo	29.5	30.4	30.2	29.6
Thums Up	Coca-Cola	25.2	24.1	24.1	24.5
Coca-Cola	Coca-Cola	16.5	17.0	17.3	17.6
Mirinda	PepsiCo	8.7	8.7	8.4	8.1
Fanta	Coca-Cola	6.1	5.8	5.8	5.6
Limca	Coca-Cola	4.0	3.7	3.6	3.3
Sprite	Coca-Cola	1.9	1.8	1.9	2.0
Everest	PepsiCo	1.9	1.8	1.8	1.8
Kinley	Coca-Cola	1.6	1.5	1.5	1.5
7-Up	PepsiCo	1.2	1.3	1.3	1.3
Duke's	PepsiCo	1.2	1.2	1.2	1.1
Vanila Coke	Coca-Cola India Pvt Ltd	—	—	—	0.6
Others		2.1	2.8	2.8	2.8
Total		**100.0**	**100.0**	**100.0**	**100.0**

Coca-Cola India and PepsiCo, who together have over 96% of the volume in carbonates in India, have since inception pushed cola carbonates ahead of orange and lemonade carbonates. By offering trade or consumer promotions, cola carbonates have always been given priority. While the cola flavour is accepted nationally, preference for orange and lemonade/lime varies from state to state.

Orange ahead of lime carbonates: At the end of 2005, orange carbonates with sales of 167 million litres was ahead of lime carbonates with sales of 132 million litres. The orange and lime carbonates varieties sold in India are non-juice based, as the pricing of juice-based carbonates at a premium is unlikely to attract consumers.

With hardly any difference between the unit price of the two, value sales of orange carbonates were Rs 4.6 billion, lime carbonates stood close to Rs 3.8 billion. Lime carbonates grew at the faster pace of 8% volume growth compared to the less than 7% growth seen in orange carbonates. Even within lime carbonates, growth was driven by the clear varieties like Sprite and 7-Up, while Limca variety showed a decrease.

The preference for orange and lemon carbonates varies from state to state. While orange flavour garners the majority of its sales from the South Indian state of Tamil Nadu, the cloudy lemon drink Limca is popular in the Northern parts of the country.

Mixers not very popular: Mixers continued to whither away in the face of competition from their flavoured counterparts. The retail volume growth rate for mixers was slow at just under 6% in 2005. Branded mixers also faced competition from the unorganised counterparts, which are popular due to their lower prices. While the price of branded mixers hovers around Rs 20 per litre, unbranded mixers come as cheap as Rs 8 per litre. The unbranded players use the bottles of companies like Coca-Cola India and PepsiCo and hence have very little costs involved. Nevertheless, consumers were increasingly shifting towards more advertised, more colourful flavoured carbonate variants, slowing down the growth of the mixers.

Flavours

Standard cola dominates cola flavours: Standard cola carbonates lead the sales of cola carbonates. The only other flavoured cola, Vanilla, has failed to make any substantial impact. In 2003, PepsiCo tried to create some ripples with the launch of its lemon flavoured variant Pepsi Aha! This move also backfired as consumers failed to see any perceptible change in taste from the original cola. The efforts of both Coca-Cola India and PepsiCo to introduce new cola flavours met with little success as some consumers tried out the taste of the new variants but returned to standard cola.

Low calorie cola carbonates: Low calorie cola carbonates are not as popular in India as the more illustrious standard cola. The consumption of low calories items is confined to consumers who are compelled to purchase them for health ground. The reduced preference for low calorie cola carbonates becomes clearer when one looks at the packaging type. Unlike regular carbonates, which are available in returnable glass bottles, low calorie cola carbonates are available mainly in cans, and to a much lesser extent in plastic bottles. The packaging type is also a clear indicator of the target consumers—the niche consumers who are not perturbed by spending a little extra on the cans and plastic bottles for the sake of consuming fewer calories.

Carbonates Distribution

Independent food stores, the biggest channel: With grocers and independent food stores found in every nook and cranny in India and outnumbering other distribution channels, 84% of total sales of carbonates were made through this channel. The smaller pack size of 200 ml and 300 ml glass bottles are the most common pack sizes available in such stores. Even though the channel does stock the bigger 500 ml and 1 litre packs, sales are low.

However, the percentage share of sales through independent food stores is on the decline as more and more supermarkets/hypermarkets and other channels of distribution are on the rise. Unlike independent food stores where sales are targeted at individuals, supermarkets/hypermarkets target the family for take home consumption. The others category comprises mainly street vendors for whom sales of carbonates are a major source of income.

Emphasis on rural areas: Coca-Cola India and PepsiCo are both now giving more attention to rural areas as they have realized the potential for their products, especially for the 200 ml packs with lower pricing. The companies made a major foray into the rural regions when they introduced 200 ml packs. They are now using localised promotions, which would enable them to swell their consumer base. However, difficulties in distribution would remain, as some of the regions in the country will continue to be inaccessible by road and dependence on other forms of transport such as bullock carts is likely to balloon the costs per litre. This is coupled with the fact that retailers in rural areas do not have as much financial muscle as their urban counterparts, and hence producers have to double up on the frequency of making supplies to such outlets so that they are able to collect cash and avoid supplying on credit.

Concentrates

Performance

- Growth in concentrates have slowed down
- Powder concentrates value growth reached Rs 1 billion mark
- Pioma dominated concentrates sales with over 70% volume sales
- Orange remained the most preferred flavour for concentrates

Exhibit 15.3 shows share of major concentrates during 2001–04.

EXHIBIT 15.3

Brand Shares of Liquid Concentrates by Volume (2001–2004)

Brand	Company	% off-trade volume			
		2001	2002	2003	2004
Rasna Utsav	Pioma Industries Ltd.	73.0	70.0	70.0	70.5
Kissan Fruit Kick	Hindustan Unilever Ltd.	8.0	8.0	7.0	6.0
Rooh Afza	Hamdard (Wakf) Laboratories	6.0	6.0	6.0	6.0
Ohm's Orange Squash	Ohm's Food Products Pvt. Ltd.	1.0	1.0	1.0	1.0
Others		12.0	15.0	16.0	16.5
Total		**100.0**	**100.0**	**100.0**	**100.0**
Liquid Concentrate (million litres)		**77.8**	**80.6**	**83.5**	**86.0**
Rasna Rozana	Pioma Industries Ltd.	86.0	84.0	85.0	86.0
Sunfill	Coca-Cola India Pvt. Ltd.	1.0	6.0	6.0	7.0
Tang	Kraft Jacobs Suchard India Pvt. Ltd.	8.0	4.0	2.0	1.0
Others		5.0	6.0	7.0	6.0
Total		**100.0**	**100.0**	**100.0**	**100.0**
Power Concentrate (million litres)		**50.9**	**54.5**	**58.5**	**62.8**

Marginal growth in concentrates: Concentrates grew by less than 5% to just under 149 million litres in 2005, perhaps due to increasing availability of health-positioned drinks such as fruit/vegetable juice, not to mention the presence of carbonates. There was no significant improvement in the sales of concentrates.

Powder concentrates reached the Rs 1 billion mark: Concentrates products comprise both liquid and powder concentrates, with the former holding high value and volume. Liquid concentrates with just under Rs 1.4 billion in off-trade value sales grew by 3%, while powder concentrates off-trade value grew faster, by 5%, to break the Rs 1 billion mark.

There is a clear preference for powder concentrates, because these are more easily available than liquid concentrates across the country and are consumed at home since they are perceived as grocery, not impulse purchases. *Rasna* from Pioma Industries, for example, has become a household name in the country.

Rasna Utsav retains clear leadership in liquid concentrates: Pioma Industries' *Rasna Utsav* was the clear leader in liquid concentrates, with over a 70% volume share in 2005. *Rasna Utsav* is targeted at lower and middle-class rural and semi-urban segments of the population.

Kissan Fruit Kick from Hindustan Unilever has not picked up volume in spite of a series of active promotions. The main reason for the decline in volume sales was its margin and positioning. Regional players provide margins at least double that of Hindustan Unilever. Besides, Hindustan Lever depends on the pull to drive sales, while the business of liquid concentrates, because of its sheer fragmented nature, depends on push by margins. Hindustan Lever also had to contend with the strong brand recall of *Rasna*.

Regional brands ubiquitous in liquid concentrates: Of late host of regional brands have improved their share in volume. The regional companies are able to provide proper supply and better margins, and since the cost of entry is very low, there are a lot of players in the industry. There are several brands that could sell higher volumes if their focus was not so local and seasonal. For instance, Mapro based in Maharashtra sells only in metro cities nationally and sales are completely urban. Moreover, prices of Mapro products start at Rs 63, which is high, and there is no variety of pack sizes and so trial and purchase remains low.

There is also the question of product range. Most of the regional players are niche players who are known for a particular nature of liquid concentrate. Mapro is the only company to have the entire range of syrups, squashes and crushes; Haldirams, predominant in North India, does not pay attention to different flavours of syrups. Kissan has no crushes. Syrups can be used with both water and milk, whereas squashes are usually added to water to make the drink. Crushes are mostly made with fresh fruit extracts and are therefore more expensive.

Guruji, another local brand in Delhi and Mumbai, sells only syrups. Such limited range prevents economies of scale or greater sales share. Almost every local brand sells its greatest volumes during the Indian festivals, where serving traditional drinks is still the norm among the middle end lower-middle-class, which are these companies' target consumers.

Hamdard Laboratories with its *Rooh Afza* brand and Ohms Food Products Pvt. Ltd. with its *Ohm's* brand, maintained their retail volume sales shares at 6% and 1% respectively in 2004. *Rooh Afza* is still strongly associated with seasons and festivals, and this prevents its sales picking up during the rest of the year. A consequence of such linking is that *Rooh Afza* is found predominantly in dry fruit and convenience stores, rather than the foods supermarket stores where chances of sales are higher.

Rasna Rozana the clear leader in powder concentrates: Rozana's main plank is affordability, the company claiming that its cost is lower than Rs 2 per glass. The competition, whatever little bit exists in powder concentrates, is essentially between *Rasna Rozana* and *Sunfill* from Coca-Cola India which held a 7% volume sales share in 2005. *Tang*, from Kraft Jacobs Suchard India Pvt Ltd, with its series of readjustments in positioning, packaging into smaller quantities and price cuts all failed to drive up sales.

Distribution remains urban: Distribution of liquid and powder concentrates remains largely urban, though rural penetration is steadily increasing. In 2005, 21% of liquid concentrates was sold in rural India, less than four million litres, compared to just 8% of rural sales in powder concentrates.

In terms of formats, nearly 90% of concentrates are sold through independent food stores taking a lion's share of 80% of volumes sales. However, organised Western-style supermarkets are beginning to make their mark. From just 7% of off-trade volume sales in 1997, supermarkets/hypermarkets accounted for less than three million litres or 15% of all off-trade volumes in 2005. Some of the other channels that are being used by the companies are street vendors and pharmacy stores in order to ensure that every channel is tapped.

Flavours

Orange the preferred flavour for liquid and powder concentrates: Orange retained its top spot among the preferred flavours in liquid concentrates, with off-trade volume sales of under seven million litres in 2005, a very marginal rise from 6.6 million litres in 2003. Mango held 15% of retail volume sales at more than two million litres, while grape and cola accounted for 10% and 5% respectively. A host of other flavours, including rose in particular, accounted for 30%, or just over five million litres.

In powder concentrates, orange is again the leader, accounting for 85% of all volume sales, followed by lemon and pineapple which together held just 5% of volume in 2005. Pioma Industries promoted *Rasna* with its orange flavour from the outset, and it still continued to hold sway in 2005.

Refer Exhibit 15.4 to have a look at leading flavours of liquid and powder concentrates in 2003 and 2004.

EXHIBIT 15.4

Leading Flavours or Liquid Concentrates: % Volume (2003–2004)

	% retail volume	
	2003	2004
Cola	5.0	5.0
Grape	10.0	10.0
Mango	15.0	15.0
Orange	40.0	40.0
Other flavours	30.0	30.0
Total	**100.0**	**100.0**

Leading Flavours for Powder Concentrates: % Volume (2003–2004)

	% retail volume	
	2003	2004
Lemon	3.0	3.0
Orange	85.0	85.0
Pineapple	2.0	2.0
Other flavours	10.0	10.0
Total	**100.0**	**100.0**

Slow growth in concentrates forecast: Concentrates are the domain of in-home consumption. Any growth will be generated mainly from the retail channel as concentrates will remain a good choice when entertaining guests during festive occasions due to its ease of preparation and low unit costs. Away from home consumption of concentrates is extremely negligible due to the overwhelming preference for other drinks such as the emerging coffee culture, carbonates for the younger population and fresh juices for the health conscious.

Fruit/Vegetable Juice

The growth in total volume sales of fruit/vegetable juice was the fastest among soft drinks sales. This category constituted of two variants. One is the 100% reconstituted juice and the other is juice drinks (up to 24% juice). The two main companies selling reconstituted 100% juice, Dabur Foods Ltd. and Tropicana Beverage Co. pushed their *Dabur Real* and *Tropicana* juice as a healthy alternative to carbonates, equating their juice to the goodness of consuming fresh fruit. The promotional efforts paid off as Indians hitherto sceptical about consuming juice stored in cartons on retail shelves tried out the various flavours available. The growth in reconstituted 100% juice is also aided by the rise in double-income families with less time to spare who are increasingly looking for convenience.

Given the returnable glass bottle packaging adopted by Coca-Cola India and PepsiCo for their juice drinks brands *Maaza* and *Slice* respectively, Indians tend to perceive juice drinks on a par with carbonates.

The trend towards healthy drinks benefited Parle Agro Pvt. Ltd. with its brand of *Frooti*, Dabur Food Ltd. with the *Real* range of 100% fruit/vegetable juice, and Tropicana Beverages Co. with its *Tropicana* brand. Hindustan Lever Ltd.'s share dropped to a negligible off-trade volume share in 2004, as its brand *Fruit Kick* did not take off.

The rise in juice market can also be attributed to the spread of organised retail chains in the metros. The new food and grocery supermarkets have the latest range of equipment to stock juices in an attractive and highly visible manner, which spurs impulse purchases, especially when families shop. Coupled with prices at a discount of at least 2% off maximum retail prices in the nationwide supermarket chains such as Food Bazaar and Giant, juices are becoming attractive purchases for consumers.

Speciality Drinks

Coconut water remained the only speciality drink that continues to have consumer preference. Fresh coconut water is easily available in most regions (except North and N-E region) and cities of India. In this nich market, only a few companies operate. For instance, Cocojal, from Jain Agro Products Pvt. Ltd., is found in North, South and West India, for Rs 12 for 200 ml, or Rs 60 per litre. Sakthi Coco Products have launched Tender Coco Natural Coconut Health Drink in South India, for Rs 12 in a pouch. Apart from these players, there are a host of local players who typically sell Asian juices such as *Jal Jeera*, considered very beneficial in summer because it prevents dehydration, and *Nimbu pani* (lemon juice) from a host of outlets like street kiosks. No organized large players like Coca-Cola India have so far come up with a coconut water manufacturing unit in India.

MAJOR PLAYERS AND THEIR KEY MARKETING STRATEGIES

Coca-Cola India Pvt. Ltd.

Coca-Cola India is a wholly-owned subsidiary of The Coca-Cola Co. USA. Since its re-entry into the country in 1993, Coca-Cola India has transformed itself from a carbonates oriented company into one that is beverage-oriented. This explains its increasing focus on *Kinley* (bottled water), *Sunfill* (concentrates) and *Georgia* (coffee and tea).

Coca-Cola India grew to occupy a leading position in soft drinks with 43% of volume sales in 2004. *Thums Up* became Coca-Cola India's leading brand in terms of carbonate sales, with a volume share of 24%.

Competitive strategy: Although Coca-Cola India owns 70% of its bottlers, many of them have outdated operations inherited from its acquisition of Parle Agro Pvt. Ltd. Coca-Cola India saves on the operational costs such as import duties by using more local raw materials and by upgrading its bottling technology. Coke's primary positioning is a drink for any occassion (e.g. Always Coca Cola)

Coca-Cola is following a strategy of low capital investment game in India. Its vision for the future is on repositioning and repackaging to reinforce affordability for the highly price-conscious population. The company's aim is to increase per capita consumption of soft drinks in rural communities and capture a larger share in urban areas while increasing consumption frequency.

PepsiCo India Holdings Pvt. Ltd.

PepsiCo India Holdings Pvt. Ltd. is a wholly-owned subsidiary of PepsiCo USA, operating in India since 1990.

Competitive strategy: Pepsi is India's highest selling brand of carbonates, with a volume share of nearly 30% in 2004. Worldwide Pepsi has always concentrated on the youth segment. For metro areas it launched "cool zone" scheme (initially in Mumbai) in order to raise off-take. Pepsi has been encouraging bottlers to form joint venture partners and supports them with best practices from their own bottling operations. Pepsi has been strongly identified with sports events. For instance, all its promotion strategies have been geared towards attracting youth with sponsorship of world cup cricket, contemporary advertising campaigns in places such as college fairs and festivals. PepsiCo is found to prefer endorsements by sports stars in contrast to Coca-Cola which typically makes use of film celebrities. Being a 100 year old brand it is trying to convey an image of contemporary and "Generation Next."

Dabur Foods Ltd.

Dabur India Ltd. is one of the leading consumer goods companies in India, with interests in healthcare, personal care products and food. A century old company, it is an Rs 10 billion conglomerate, well-known for medicinal products, especially herbal and ayurvedic medicines. Dabur has consistently followed its platform of health and quality, with the launch of several variants of its Real brand in Cranberry, Respberry, and fortified juices for children, among other products.

Real consolidated its strong position in fruit/vegetable juice with the launch of *Real Active*, a range of unsweetened juice, in 2001. Available in orange and apple, *Real Active* appeals to the young and health-conscious. Ever since its relaunch in 2002, with new packaging having developed to keep the product fresh for longer and give it a better taste, Real has picked up in volume sales.

Competitive strategy: Dabur Foods has consistently stuck to its positioning of healthy drinks for the entire family. This along with the strategy to cater to the taste preferences of Indians at an affordable price has been successful for the company.

Although Dabur Foods is today the third largest company in fruit/vegetable juice, its volume share has grown from 8% in 2000 to 13% in 2004, much faster than its arch rival Tropicana Beverages Co.

Pioma Industries Ltd.

The Ahmedabad-based Pioma Industries Ltd. is another leading company in soft drinks concentrates. Pioma occupied the number one position in concentrates with over 70% volume share in 2004. Pioma extended its range to include other processed food products, beverages and confectionary. The company has planned to enter the vending machine business to market its soft drinks.

Competitive strategy: Pioma Industries saw steady erosion in its volume and value sales in concentrates since 2000. This is partly due to shift in the consumer preference towards ready-made 100% juice as a good health alternative, and also because of entry of small packs of carbonates Rasna Utsav, its liquid concentrate best seller, dropped from a 57% volume sales share in 2001 to 55% in 2004.

Pioma continues to use the company's new brand identity, "Relish a Gain", which is symbolized by a leaf. Pioma launched Rasna Vanilla, a non-carbonated cola drink, in June 2004. The company positions it as 'A healthy drink for kids without any caffeine and phosphorous content in it'. The main plank of this launch for Pioma remained the low cost per glass.

Parle Agro Pvt. Ltd.

Parle Agro Pvt. Ltd. is the maker of Frooti juice. It has more than 17 franchisees in the country across major towns. With increasing competition, Parle Agro embarked on product expansion in its various business segments to sustain growth. Parle's *Frooti* enjoyed a brand share of 40% in 2004. The company introduced 250 ml PET bottles of *Frooti* drinks to encourage impulse purchases, and the 500 ml and 1 litre packs for home consumption.

CHAPTER 16

Chocolates

Chocolate was introduced in the world by Spanish explorers about 400 years ago. Some of the most famous names in chocolate makers are Rowntree, Fry, Cadbury and Terry's. The Swiss then took over the market with their technical and commercial expertise, with Nestle, Lindt, Tobler and Sechaud etc. and perfected the art of chocolate-making on a large scale.

GLOBAL MARKET SCENARIO

Globally, appetite for chocolates shows no signs of abating, but a shift in consumption pattern is increasingly evident. In mature western markets, chocolate consumption is on slight decline due to falling birth rates, market saturation and recent consumer trend towards low-fat diet and increasing nutritional concern.

Swiss-based Nestle is today the world's leading chocolate manufacturer, followed by the US-based Mars Inc. However, different players hold dominant position in different markets. For instance, Hershey holds the top spot in the US.

In 2006, the global confectionery market was estimated to be $120 billion, having risen by almost 19% in value terms compared to level in 2001. During this period of time, in volume terms, the market growth was nearly 13% and it reached a level of 15.7 million tonnes. In value terms, chocolate confectionery is the largest category, accounting for almost 60% of the total sales.

EXHIBIT 16.1

Regional Cocoa Consumption

Europe	43%
Americas	26%
Africa	14%
Asia & Oceania	17%

Source: ICCO quarterly bulletin of cocoa statistics

The emerging markets in Asia, South America and Eastern Europe offer the greatest growth prospects for the chocolate makers. India, despite its humidity and limitation of inadequate refrigeration, is nevertheless seen as a major growth market due to its sheer size.

CONSUMPTION IN INDIA

Compared to western countries, chocolate consumption in India is pretty low, e.g. while per capita chocolate consumption in the UK is a buoyant 8 kilograms, it stands at 165 grams in urban India. Not withstanding low consumption, the total value of the chocolates market is estimated to be of the order of Rs 8.0 billion.

Demand: Past and Future

Demand projections for the chocolate market show a steady growth. Exhibit 16.2 below points out the growth rate will be 6% and the demand level will reach 67.2 MT in 2014–2015.

EXHIBIT 16.2

Market Growth

Period	Growth Rate
1990–91 to 1996–97	6.9%
1996–97 to 2001–02	8.9%
2001–02 to 2006–07	11.5%
2006–07 to 2009–10	7.2%
2009–10 to 2014–15	6.0%

Demand: Past & Future

Year	MT
2002–03	30
2003–04	32.7
2004–05	35.5
2005–06	38.4
2006–07	41.3
2009–10	50.2
2014–15	67.2

India's chocolate market by age group of its consumers and different geographic regions is depicted in Exhibit 16.3.

EXHIBIT 16.3

Market Segmentation

Age Group	Share(%)
2 to 8 years	16
8 to 25 years	53
25 to 54 years	22
Over 55 years	7
Region	
North	35
East	12
West	33
South	20

MARKET STRUCTURE

Leading Players and their Brands

Cadbury has become the generic name for chocolates in India. *Cadbury*, with its Dairy Milk, Five Star, Milk Treat, Eclairs, Golden, is the most popular chocolate brand in India.

Nestle, Amul and Campco have also managed to remain significant players in India. In the near future, Global offerings like Flake, Timeout, Wispa, Caramel, Fuse and Cherry Ripe, etc. one likely to enter the Indian market.

Market Share

Exhibit 16.4 shows the market share of leading players in 2005–06.

EXHIBIT 16.4

Market Share[1] of Leading Players

Company	Share (%)
Cadbury's	68
Nestle	22
Amul	8
Lotus	2

[1]Excludes unbranded chocolates.

Cadbury

Cadbury dominates the chocolate segment with a share of around 68%. Cadbury India's market share in cocoa-based products is 35%, with Dairy

Milk brand alone accounting for 29%. Perk and Five Star account for another 20%.

Nestle

Nestle India holds the second position with a market share of 22%.

BRAND PORTFOLIO

Cadbury

Cadbury's Dairy Milk (CDM): It is the flagship brand of Cadbury's and one of the largest selling and most-recognised brands worldwide. CDM constitutes about 30% of Cadbury India's turnover, with a volume share of 26.3% in the urban market and a value share of 30.7%. Today, CDM is the largest chocolate brand in India.

- **Crackle:** Crackle has a nutty feel to the chocolate which makes it favourite choice to a large number of the consumers in India.
- **5 Star:** 5 Star bars are perennial childhood favourites in India with the soft and messy feel that the copious amounts of caramel impart to the consumer.

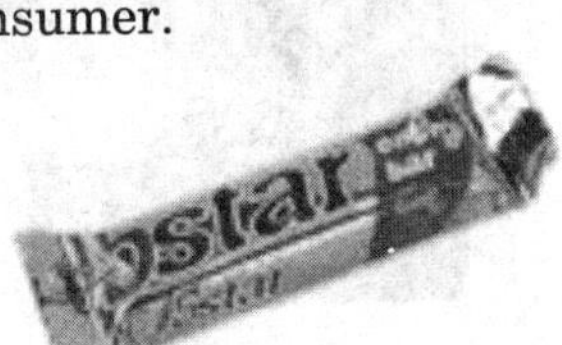

- **Whole Nut:** Whole Nut is another brand combining Dairy Milk's richness with a nutty flavour in order to reach out to a sub-segment in the market.
- **Perk:** Perk attempts to make inroads into the young adult segment by communicating its key brand values of zing, perkiness and fun, also espoused by its choice of Bollywood star Preity Zinta as its brand ambassador.
- **Fruits and Nuts:** This melting chocolate with crunchy pieces of almonds and cashew nuts! makes our mouth water everytime someone bites a Cadbury Fruits and Nuts chocolate.

- **Dark Orange:** Intended to appeal to a different set of taste buds, in the Cadbury's portfolio in India.

Temptation: For lovers of dark chocolate. "Too good to share" tagline.

Bournville: Bournville has an unapologetic bittersweet flavour that lingers on your taste buds long after you have taken a bite. It is named after the headquarters of Cadbury's in Central England.

Nestle

Nestle India

- **Kit Kat:** It is one of the most successful brands in the world and every year nearly 12 billion kit kats are consumed around the globe. It is a crisp wafer fingers covered with chocolayer. It has a unique finger format with a 'breaking' ritual attached to it. Available in pack of 2 fingers and four fingers. Another variant is Kit Kat Chunky which does not have the fingers.

- **New Nestle' Munch:** It is a wafer layer covered with delicious choco layer. It is crisp and light and the largest selling SKU in the category.

- **Milky Bar:** It is a delicious milky treat which kids love. Re-launched in January 2006 with a Calcium Rich recipe.

- **Milky Bar Choo:** It is a soft chewy fudge with white chocolayer that kids love to 'choo'. It is also available in strawberry flavour that promises the fun of a strawberry shake in a MILKYBAR CHOO!
- **Bar One:** It constantly reminds one of 'time for action'.

- **Eclairs:** They are rich milky caramel Eclairs that have a soft center. Nestle Eclairs are consumed by billions of consumers around the globe. Nestle coconut éclairs are available in Andhra Pradesh only.
- **Crunch:** They are crunchy chocolates.

COMPETITIVE STRATEGIES OF LEADING PLAYERS

Cadbury India

Cadbury began its Indian operations as a trading company in 1947. With brands like Dairy Milk, Gems, 5 Star, Bournvita and Perk and subsequently added brands such as Celebrations, Bytes, Chocki, Delite and Temptations Cadbury has, in the last six decades, become one with the word 'chocolate' in India, no wonder it commands 68% of the market share.

For kids across India, the word 'Cadbury' is synonymous with chocolates. It is another classic example of a brand coming to symbolise a product category. For over a half century, Cadbury Dairy Milk has been the preferred gift for children.

Product strategy: The company plans to leverage on the equity of the CDM brand across its entire moulded chocolates portfolio, under a strategy.

Brands like Fruit and Nut, Crackle, Roasted Almond, Caramello, Double Deck and Chunky have already been brought under the CDM fold as part of this initiative. CDM is now available in new 'Purity Seal' packaging which includes aluminium foil enclosed in a sealed poly-flow pack. Larger CDMs are available in poly-coated, heat-sealed aluminium foil wrapped in the branded outer package. These steps are the 'first ever' in chocolate packaging in India.

Growth and expansion: CDM has taken the task of universalising consumption from the smallest town in India to the largest metro, and from the youngest child to the oldest adult. CDM has strategically deployed 'master-branding' strategy on the packaging to bring the entire moulded range under the CDM umbrella, and at the same time it has enhanced child connect to compete more effectively with the increased range in sugar confectionery and other impulse products like branded potato chips.

Advertising campaigns: CDM advertising has always depicted a rich tapestry of human emotions and relationships. In the 1980s, it was positioned as 'the perfect expression of love', captured in memorable copy: '*sometimes Cadbury can say it better than words*'. During the early 1990s, CDM emphasised its international identity, communicating that it was the 'real taste of chocolate'. In 1994 came the path-breaking 'real taste of life' campaign. This campaign created a dramatic shift in the way chocolates were perceived. CDM has increasingly become trapped as a reward for children and this campaign unshackled the brand by re-positioning it to the 'free-child' in every adult. CDM redefined itself as the perfect expression of spontaneous, shared good feelings, providing the 'real taste of life' experience. The strategy paid off: Brand Cadbury grew by over 50% in sales volumes. Then in 1998, the next stage of growth for the brand dealt with popularising consumption in a social context, especially in more traditional settings like weddings. With the campaign '*Khaanein waallon ko khaanein ka bahana chahiye*' featuring Cyrus Broacha, CDM aimed to substantially increase penetration levels. The campaign was launched in tandem with the award winning '*Kuchh khaas hai...*' campaign, and the media strategy was to let the two co-exist towards a common vision: 'A Cadbury in every pocket'. The brand penetrated into smaller towns and sales volumes grew by 40%.

More recently, Cadbury signed on Amitabh Bachchan to endorse the brand. The latest TVC featuring Bachchan and a kid is fittingly titled 'charm'. Charm, very clearly, is what Cadbury is carefully reworking into CDM communications; that and what the company terms 'the joy of consuming chocolate'. The company's repackaging exercise, which used a combination of packaging technologies, was unprecedented in the category. With the redesigned packaging in place, the company decided to communicate the measures it had taken to safeguard quality standards. To add credibility to its pitch, Cadbury took recourse to Bachchan's deep baritone. The commercial has done wonders to consumer confidence.

Brand values: Cadbury Dairy Milk stands for purity: purity of emotions, feelings and expressions. Research has shown that not only is the colour purple strongly associated with Cadbury's, but the Cadbury logo itself has the highest recognition of any logo among popular consumer brands. The 'glass and a half' emblem, the corporate purple and the flowing script have all become synonymous with this outstanding and wonderful brand.

Nestle

Nestlé started operating in India way back in 1912, when it began importing and selling chocolates in the Indian market under the name of The Nestlé Anglo-Swiss Condensed Milk Company (Export) Limited.

After India's Independence in 1947, Nestlé set up its company in India and started its first factory at Moga, Punjab in 1961. The Government wanted Nestlé to develop the milk economy and instill, amongst the community, a confidence in the dairy business. Progress involved the creation of prosperity on an on-going and sustainable basis that has resulted in the transformation of Moga into a prosperous and vibrant milk district today.

Nestlé India manufactures products of truly international quality of famous brand such as Nescafe, Milkybar, Milo, Kit Kat, Barone.

The culture of innovation within the company and access to the Nestlé Group's proprietary technology/brands expertise and the extensive centralized research and development facilities, gives it a distinct advantage in these efforts. It has been offering consumers a wide variety of high quality, safe food products at affordable prices.

FUTURE OUTLOOK

- With the entry of more international players in India, more new brands of chocolates will be soon launched in India.
- Promotion of brands carrying mass franchise without compromise on quality or margins.
- Increasing the market depth including rural India's coverage (so far in case of chocolates, rural areas are not covered).
- Better product quality and packaging.
- Launching sugar free product lines for the health conscious segment.
- To carve niche segments, due to growth in disposable incomes and booming economy.

CHAPTER 17

Malted Beverages

Malted beverages are popularly known as the health drinks in India. Historically, malted beverages have had a strong association with milk. Such drinks used to be consumed in the southern and eastern regions of the country which were having a perennial shortage of milk supply. So, malted beverages positioned themselves as substitutes for milk. However, Operation Flood, undertaken by the National Dairy Development Board (NDDB) in the 1980s, changed the scenario. NDDB could supply sufficient amount of milk in small pouch packets or through its vending machines all over the country, and hence the demand for health drinks was affected. With a view to revive the market, malted beverages were repositioned as an energy drinks with a nutritional thrust. And this positioning still remains.

MARKET SIZE

Malted beverages are usually marketed in white and brown colour forms, where white beverages constitute about 65 per cent of the market. The malted beverages market is estimated to be 82,000 tonnes per annum which in value terms is estimated at Rs 1300 crores and is growing at the rate of 12–14 per cent per annum.

Penetration and Growth

The penetration of malted beverages in India was found to be only 6.1 per cent in 2005. However, there have been clear indications of growth due to several positive trends. More variety of tastes, and flavours, and awareness building efforts by the MNCs increased acceptability of health drink products. Other factors of growth are due to better standard of living, increased health consciousness amongst affluent people, and affordability of the price. This trend is in keeping with the patterns observed across international markets where the growth of the middle-class has driven the uptrend in food industry in general and health beverages in particular. In view of the tremendous growth potential in

India, there have been more efforts put to expand the size of the health drinks business over the last few years.

Consumer Behaviour

Health drinks, specially the brown colour form, have primarily been used in upper and middle-class families. In contrast, the white beverages are consumed more for their therapeutic values. Consumers, by and large, perceive the brown coloured malted drinks as mere taste additives. Energy drinks are generally perceived as a luxury. This explains the slow off-take. Brand loyalties are not very strong as the key target, children, are always looking for new products. Promotion campaigns such as freebies and contests also play an important role in influencing brand choice. These campaigns are mainly targeted at children who force their parents to buy those promoted brands. Free gifts like crystal jars, pet jars and sippers have also been used to attract consumers.

The Competition

The major players in the health beverages market are GlaxoSmithKline, Cadbury, Nestle and Heinz. The market is dominated by GlaxoSmithKline with about 70 per cent share. Cadbury and Heinz have about 12 per cent each, and Nestle only 3 per cent.

The Leading Brands

Malted beverages include *Horlicks*, *Boost*, *Viva* and *Maltova* from GlaxoSmithKline, *Bournvita* from Cadbury, *Milo* from Nestle and *Complan* from Heinz.

Exhibit 17.1 shows the market share of the leading brands.

EXHIBIT 17.1

Market Share

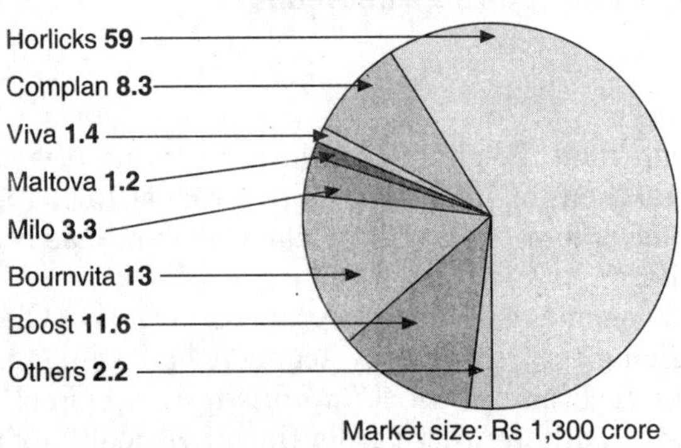

GlaxoSmithKline's *Horlicks* is the leader. The competition is amongst the others for the number two slot.

BRAND POSITIONING AND STRATEGY

Let us analyze the marketing strategy of the major players in the malted health drinks.

Complan

Complan is a health drink marketed by Heinz in India. Earlier marketed by Glaxo, the brand was sold to Heinz.

Brand positioning: Complan is a **complete planned food** drink enriched with 23 vital nutrients in right quantity and proportion essential for healthy growth. It is promoted as having ideal combination of nutrients for driving children's growth. *Complan* has claimed to offer 100 per cent milk protein, one of the best quality proteins in the right quantity, to provide healthy physical growth.

Complan for whom? Complan is positioned as being a brand for growing children. This has been the communication of the brand in all its advertisements, and even on its packaging. However, the brand has also tried to attract the busy executives, pregnant women, lactating mothers, aged and convalescent persons. The advertisement message of *Complan* has always emphasised on the growing children segments.

Packaging: An important aspect about *Complan* is its association with growing children. Every SKU of Complan has the 'Complan Boy' and 'Complan Girl' printed on it.

Competitive positioning: *Complan* is targeted primarily at children to augment their growth potential. This is communicated through sponsoring many events in cricket, tennis and squash, aimed at the budding talent. The sponsorships were for events like Complan Under-15 National Cricket Talent Search, squash under 19 tournaments—something meant for growing children.

Boost

Boost is positioned on the energy platform in India. It was developed by the Indian R&D team in 1974, and launched first in 1975–76 in Kerala. Boost was launched nationally in the early 80s and has been targeted at the young children.

Boost has been one of the fastest growing brands of Glaxo's consumer portfolio. Realising that the energy segment had a huge potential, GSK India launched the brand as the *'Vitaminised Energy Fuel'* with a unique choco-malt taste, a differentiator from the other health drinks. The main advertising line of *Boost "Boost is the secret of my energy"* has become a ubiquitous line in every household today.

Re-launch of Boost: The year 2002 saw the re-launch of the *Boost* brand, enriched with **Power Boosters**. The **New Boost** includes copper and Biotin in addition to existing vitamins and minerals, which lead to consistency in performance. Along with the new benefit, it also has a contemporary packaging with new branding. The company, with 10 per cent share, decided to re-launch the product using cricketer Sachin Tendulkar, who has been their brand ambassador for the past decade.

Brand positioning: The position of the brand can be analyzed by answering a few basic questions:

- **Boost for what?** For fitness and health. Physical fitness is the key to success in every activity of life. People who are fit know no bounds and strive for excellence.
- **Boost for whom?** Boost has always been targeted at the young generation, between the age group of 8–14. This section of population is generally most enthusiastic about sports, and also with high-energy needs. Also, this is the age group that seeks role models to imitate in life, and the usage of sportsmen like Kapil Dev, Sachin Tendulkar, Virender Sehwag etc. who have become the icon of success in the field of cricket, has helped to create a healthy perception of the brand in the minds of young the Indian populace.
- **Boost for when?** Whenever and wherever energy is needed; before any physical activity.
- **Boost against whom?** All health drinks meant to be consumed with milk.

Packaging: A tall cylindrical straight jar symbolizes athleticism and fitness containing a brown coloured powder substance. The colour combination and the signage of the jar reflect vibrancy, enthusiasm and vigour.

Brand strategy: Initially the brand *Boost* was limited to the malted health drinks category. Boost tried to capitalize on the image and perception created in the consumers' minds—of a healthy and fitness drink.

Milo

Milo is a low-fat chocolate malt energy drink packed with essential vitamins and rich in flavour. A delicious and convenient nutritional energy drink for all family members—especially for growing children and active people, MILO is fortified with 13 vitamins and minerals and contains five grams of protein per serving. MILO is available both as a powdered milk additive and in convenient Ready to Drink cans.

Packaging: A cylindrical straight jar in green colour that symbolizes taste and energy containing a brown coloured powdery substance that helps in attaining it. The colour combination and the signage of the jar reflect an Energy Drink.

Brand positioning: The position of the brand can be analyzed by answering the following questions.

- **MILO for what?** Nutritious Nestle MILO, with its unique delicious taste, gives the confidence, energy and spirit to succeed in an active life.
- **MILO for whom?** For all family members—especially for growing children and active people.

The advertising line focuses MILO as *"Energy Food Drink"*. MILO is the number one chocolate malt beverage brand in the world.

Brand strategy: MILO has always been targeted at the young generation. This is the section of population most enthusiastic about sports, and also with high-energy needs, in India. MILO emphasizes on tasty way of getting all the essential nutrients.

Bournvita

Bournvita is a malted chocolate nutritional drink made with wholesome ingredients, which is good for both physical and mental health.

Packaging: A tall cylindrical straight jar that symbolizes athleticism and fitness containing a brown coloured powdery substance that can help in attaining it. The appearance and the signage of the jar reflect energy, enthusiasm and vigour.

Brand positioning

- **Bournvita for what?** For nutrition and health. Though it is more based on the nutritional plank, the brand appeals to both the children and their mothers.
- **Bournvita for whom?** Bournvita has always been targeted at the young generation, the specially 8–14 year old boys. Also, at this age many a time the mother makes the health drink purchase decision, so positioning is such that it also appeals to the mother who wants her children to be bright, energetic and successful.

For a growing kid who is healthy, intelligent, energetic and glowing. Also stresses the family factor indirectly suggesting healthy kids are a secret to a happy family.

- **Bournvita for when?** Every day to ensure you are energetic throughout the day.

Brand strategy: Cadburys have had some very successful strategic associations, which have added to the brand equity.

Bournvita Quiz contest was a very successful strategy to associate *Bournvita* with some of the best young brains in the country. It gave the brand a tremendous fillip. Bournvita interschool chess tournament in

Mumbai, which was graced by the presence of V. Anand, was another such successful Brand Association.

Horlicks

Horlicks is a nourishing malted food drink, which combines the wholesome goodness of malted barley, wheat and dairy ingredients. Horlicks was acquired by the Beecham Group in 1969 and is currently a GSK brand.

Packaging: Horlicks is available in cylindrical jars that symbolize strength, retain the goodness of malt in a rough way. The colour combination and the signage of the jar reflect peace and health—both mental and physical.

Brand positioning: The position of the brand can be analyzed by addressing the following questions.

- **Horlicks for what?** For a good night's sleep to stay fresh all day long. The name Horlicks is synonymous with health.
- **Horlicks for whom?** Traditionally, Horlicks has been targeted at the older user.
- **Horlicks for when?** As part of an evening routine, having a hot, milky drink—such as Horlicks—ensures a good night's rest.

Brand strategy: *Horlicks* has come up with a new brand called *Junior Horlicks*. The *Horlicks* brand was re-launched in 2002, with the tag 'Nourishment for Internal resistance'. The re-launched repacked product contains a "combination of nutrients that act as Resistance Builders" and helps "build up the immune system of the child". *Horlicks* aims to give a more spirited and happening drink in interesting flavours, instead of drab nourishment.

FUTURE TRENDS

Product: There is an opportunity to fill up the need gap through products based on the categories like

- Ready to drink health drinks
- Fruit based health drinks.

Price: There will be a need for a health drink which is affordable to the lower middle stratum of the society.

Place: Proliferation of health drinks is bound to have an impact on the supply chain, making it more complex. Generally, supply-chain capabilities would determine the success of competing companies.

Promotion: The promotion strategy will depend on the respective brand. For instance, currently all brands focus on health and fitness plank. However, the prospective fruit based drinks could be promoted on newer elements of health platform; the ready to drink health drinks could be promoted based on the convenience they offer.

CHAPTER 18

Toothpaste

Toothpaste is used for basic maintenance of our teeth. There are other solutions to this need as well, like ayurvedic neem twig and other products. Toothpaste Industry in India is estimated at around Rs 2500 crores in 2006. This size is computed based on the organized sector's sales only. That is, it does not take into consideration the sales turnover of the unorganized sector and other categories of oral care products.

Salient Features

The average per capita consumption of toothpaste in India is approximately 90 gms, and many people in rural India still clean their teeth with traditional products like twigs of the neem tree, salt, ash, and other herbal items. The penetration level of modern oral care products in India is around 49 per cent. In the countryside, there is low oral hygiene consciousness and widespread dental diseases.

According to a survey on the oral care market, less than 15 per cent of Indian toothpaste users brush twice a day. The toothpaste market has been growing at an average rate of around 4–5 per cent in the last few years. With increasing awareness and advertising campaigns, industry sources expect the overall penetration of oral care products in India to rapidly increase to around 65–70 per cent in the next 3–4 years time.

Product differentiation is totally based on branding. With low brand loyalty, major players have consistently increased their advertising budget to build their brand's equity and market share.

Toothpaste is generally classified into gels, whites and herbal (including ayurvedic type) form. While the whites form has made a deep penetration among general users, Gel variety has become popular among youth and herbal form has attracted the therapeutic conscious toothpaste users. However, the rapid expansion of the market was taken place due to a massive transition of market from toothpowder to toothpaste in urban market. As urban markets are becoming more difficult to penetrate further, the fight is now moving into the rural hinterland.

CONSUMER EXPECTATIONS

Consumers of toothpastes want the product to satisfy at least the following needs:

- Healthy, clean teeth
- Prevent tooth decay
- Prevent plaque, tartar and other gum and teeth diseases
- Fresh breath

Customer Segments

From a buying behaviour perspective, three different segments of consumers exist in the toothpaste market.

Habit-driven segment: The buyers belonging to this segment are characterized by low involvement in the buying process. They just go to the store and pick up a fixed brand of their choice. If the current brand fulfills their bare minimum functional needs, they repeat purchase. However, this is not to be confused with brand loyalty. This is just habitual buying that, in the long run, may lead to brand conviction if it is supported with appropriate communication, and timely availability of the product to the consumer. Generally, when the particular brand is not available in the store, then such consumers tend to switch brands without any hitch.

Value-driven, price-conscious segment: A proportion of consumers belong to this category. Their primary concern is price and the value proposition(s) their favourite brand projects.

Variety seeking: Such consumers are fond of making new experiments, so they keep trying new brands out of curiosity and excitement. A case in point is brands that have shifted the appeal from healthy living to a zingy lifestyle.

Buying Behaviour

Because toothpaste is a low cost, frequently purchased item, it is a low involvement buying. Also, among the major brands not much differences are noticed; hence the dominant buying behaviour is habitual. To counter the problems of low-involvement, one of the strategies employed by marketers is that of linking the brand to some involving issue. An example is the emphasis some brands of toothpaste lay on avoiding cavities.

MAJOR PLAYERS AND THEIR BRANDS

The toothpaste market is characterized by the presence of few large multinational companies like Colgate Palmolive India Ltd, Hindustan

Lever Ltd, Procter & Gamble, SmithKline Beecham consumer Healthcare and a handful of Indian companies such as Dabur, Anchor Health & Beauty Products, Vicco Laboratories etc.

Traditionally, Colgate and HUL were the main players in the toothpaste market of white and gels form. Then Procter & Gamble joined the market. Domestic Indian companies like Balsara and Vicco Industries used to produce the ayurvedic range of toothpaste along with their other ayurvedic products. Anchor company, that was more famous for its switching products, made a successful foray into this sector by launching toothpaste and positioning itself as first 100% vegetarian toothpaste. Companies such as Dabur and Baidyanath operated in the toothpowder market.

Colgate introduced *Colgate toothpowder* so as to capture the lower end of the market.

A Macro Analysis of the Toothpaste Industry

Applying Porter's 5 Forces Model in this industry, the following picture emerges.

Rivalry among players: The toothpaste market is dominated by large multinational companies like Colgate Palmolive, Hindustan UniLever Limited & P&G, apart from a handful of Indian companies such as Dabur, Anchor.

Threat from substitute products: The average per capita consumption of toothpaste in India is very low and many people in India still clean their teeth with traditional products like twigs of the neem tree, salt, ash, and other herbal items. Toothpowders are the only substitute to toothpaste.

Entry Barriers: There are possibly substantial entry barriers because of huge investments required to promote any new brand, setting up of distribution networks and existing intense competition. Consequently the business is not experiencing entry new players.

Bargaining power of suppliers: Most of the companies in the industry are integrated backwards, which reduces the supplier's clout. Manufacturing is largely outsourced.

Bargaining power of customers: Intense competition within the industry results in offering promotion packages to allure the consumers (e.g. buy one, get one free concept).

COMPETITIVE STRATEGIES AND BRAND POSITIONING

The marketing strategies of the major players along with their brand positioning are described below.

Colgate

Colgate is a household name in India, with one out of two consumers using *Colgate* toothpaste. Consistently superior quality and value for money, resulting from advanced technology inputs, have enabled Colgate to maintain its undisputed leadership and emerge as India's No. 1 toothpaste brand across all categories for eight out of nine years since 1992.

Currently, Colgate holds 51 per cent share of the toothpaste market. Its flagship brand, *Colgate Dental Cream* (CDC), is the largest selling toothpaste brand in India with a 39 per cent market share. It is indeed a brand which evokes confidence, commands loyalty and guarantees satisfaction.

It made two new brand extensions, namely, *Colgate Herbal*—targeted at traditional consumers who seek natural ingredients and *Colgate Cibaca Top*—a brand catering to the economy segment in the market.

Colgate followed a flanking strategy by launch of brands in all price segments. The constituents of the Colgate portfolio are:

1. **Colgate Dental Cream:** The flagship brand of the company and also the market share leader with 39 per cent market share. This brand is positioned as a quality product, catering to all the needs of consumers. It promises healthy teeth, and prevention of cavities. The positioning is communicated through the use of actors posing as dentists in advertisements. When the "dentists" endorse CDC, it serves to create the perception of credibility and legitimacy in the minds of consumers.
2. **Colgate Gel:** This is presented as a lifestyle product, promising fresh breath and an energetic lifestyle. Again, the advertisements show Colgate Gel as being popular with the youth, as a product that enhances energy levels and keeps you fresh all day long.
3. **Colgate Total:** The main feature of this is tartar control.
4. **Colgate Herbal:** It targets traditional customers who seek natural ingredients.
5. **Colgate Cibaca Top:** An offering catering to the economy segment. It is low priced and appeals to the low income group. Sales promotions, free offers signify the strategy for this brand.

The company has never been satisfied with the existing line of products and continues to innovate. The company plans to focus on its core competencies. The company is strong in the oral and personal care segment.

HUL

Hindustan Unilever Ltd (HUL) has garnered a market share of over 33 per cent in the toothpaste market in a short span of time. *Pepsodent* has a 17.6 per cent market share and *Close-up* has a market share of 15.3 per cent. HLL has the following brands:

1. **Close-up:** It is targeted towards youthful mindset. *Close-up* is externally oriented brand. Fresh breath, strong teeth are the areas in which *Close-up* operates.
2. **Pepsodent:** It is focused on providing extended protection from germs, which cause damage to teeth. It gives protection almost throughout the day. HLL pitched the brand to take care of the anxiety of mothers.

Hindustan Lever has come up with a number of innovations and is reinventing its distribution system. It has created a 3-way convergence of product availability, brand communication, brand experience. Some of these innovations are:

- **New channels:** The company is creating new touch points for its brands to make the most of opportunity offered by Indian markets.
- **Network:** The UniLever Network business opportunity will focus on building male and female entrepreneurs by actively partnering them to success. This would be achieved by providing them an earning and self-development opportunity that is both competitive and unique.
- **Out-of-home opportunity:** HUL is also aggressively responding to the rapidly growing trend of out-of-home consumption.

Dabur

Dabur, post acquisition of Balsara, has gained significant presence in the oral care market with a range of products in almost all segments within the category. The company today has a strong range of products—*Lal Dant Manjan* (toothpowder), *Red Tooth Paste, Babool, Promise* and the premium *Meswak*—with approx 30 per cent market share in the toothpowder category and about 8 per cent share in the toothpaste category.

Dabur has the following brands:

(i) **Promise** has a unique clove oil positioning.

(ii) **Babool** (5 per cent market share): This brand from Balsara has a dual positioning. It emphasizes value, by being slightly low on the price and also highlights its natural ingredients—appealing to traditional Indian consumers.

(iii) **Meswak** toothpaste is in the premium segment.

(iv) **Dabur Red toothpaste** is extending the success of herbal position of *Lal Dant Manjan*.

To boost its sales, Dabur has been coming up with innovative ideas such as:

- New campaign has been launched to drive market share in fast growing economy segment of toothpaste.
- New packaging with logo and celebrity: The company had signed Vivek Oberoi for endorsing its Oral Care and Healthcare range of products, and this is the first new campaign being launched with the celebrity for its Oral care product—*Babool*.
- Acquisition of Balsara, which was the pioneer in herbal oral care products.

FUTURE OPPORTUNITY

The toothpaste market is currently appears to be in the maturity stage as far as urban market is concerned. But, there are possibilities of further penetration to increase the sales volume. Overall consumption of toothpaste in India is quite low (only 82 gms), as compared to 262 gms of Thailand and 518 gms of USA. The urban per capita consumption is 153 gms whereas rural consumption is just 38 gms. There is huge untapped market potential in the rural sector. Currently, only a small portion (about 15 per cent–20 per cent) of region has been tapped.

CHAPTER 19

Toilet Soaps

The Personal Care category generally consists of toilet soaps, skin and hair care items, cosmetics and fragrance products. Till the mid-seventies these products witnessed a slow growth as even consumers who could afford perceived them harmful because of chemical composition. Indian women continued to apply natural therapies for their beautification.

Since the eighties many of these personal care items gained greater awareness and importance of purchase among young generation. Secondly, with more purchasing power among working women, personal care products are now more affordable. Moreover, influx of media and western influence have also played a significant role in expanding the demand for personal care products.

TOILET SOAPS BUSINESS

One of the most fiercely competitive markets in India is the personal wash or soap category. There are scores of brands—national, regional, local made soaps—that are vying for the attention of India's 1,100 million users.

According to industry estimate, toilet soap market was about Rs 110 billion in 2004–05 (Exhibit 19.1).

EXHIBIT 19.1

Toilet Soap Market
Total Size: Rs 110 billion
(per annum 2004–05)

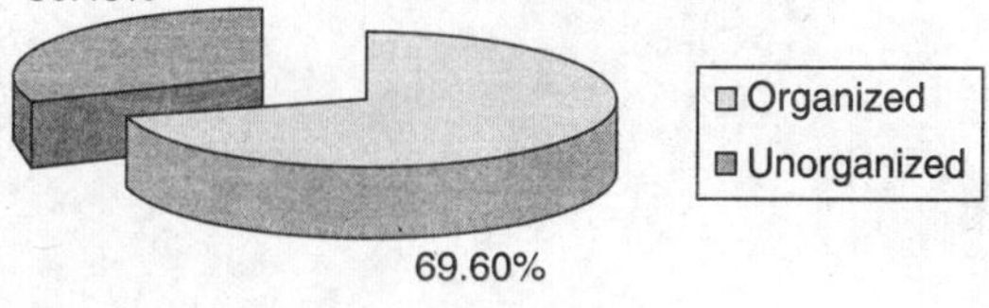

Market Penetration

- Toilet soaps have penetrated into 96.5 per cent of households in the urban market, whereas in rural areas penetration level is about 85.5 per cent. However, liquid soaps which are very popular among developed countries, and their presence is restricted to upper class in large arc still non-starter in India and their presence is restricted to upper class in large metros. Toilet soap brands are not having strong differentiation in the eyes of the consumers. In other words, the market is very fragmented.

Market Trends

Branding: With less number of players after the mid-1990s, brand building exercise gained momentum with more choices.

Down trading: The soap industry went through a difficult phase during 2003–05 when the market experienced the phenomenon of **'down-trading' which** essentially means *substituting a high-value brand with some low-value one*. To combat this problem, Godrej Soap priced most of its soap brands in the price range of Rs 10–15. On the other hand, HLL continued to concentrate on the premium segment to reverse the down-trading problem.

Focus on rural market: Recognizing the fact that use of branded soaps in the rural market is low, some of the leading soap marketers have of late started focusing on the rural segment. In this process companies attempted to shift the consumer's preference from unbranded soaps to branded ones in lower categories and also to encourage trials of premium brands. This tactics has been quite successful and resulted in higher demand for nationally marketed branded toilet soaps.

Fragmentation to consolidation: In the past, many smaller players from the unorganized sector used to operate in the soap industry. However, necessity to reduce cost of operations, need to acquire superior technology to handle unconventional oils, high capital intensity and strong brand equity of some of the larger players have restricted further entry of smaller players.

Continuous new launch: Assuming more growth potential with rising income, in recent times the market has experienced a deluge of new product launches, e.g., *Fairglow*, *Nikhar*, *Lux Sunscreen*, *Lux Moisturizing* and *Savlon*.

Market Segmentation

Price segments: To succeed in the toilet soap market, it is important to make careful choice of pricing. In India, consumers, by and large, are not very affluent and many are very sensitive to prices. Household budgets are tightly balanced and most of them constantly look for better value from FMCG products like soaps.

Going by the price, toilet soap market consists of segments—the super premium, premium, popular, and carbolic segment. Generally, the premium and super premium soaps are priced at Rs 20–40, popular soaps at Rs 10–15 for a 75 gm cake, carbolic segment soaps are priced at Rs 8–10, besides unbranded soaps which are priced at Rs 5–7 per unit.

EXHIBIT 19.2

Soap Price (per 75 gram cake)

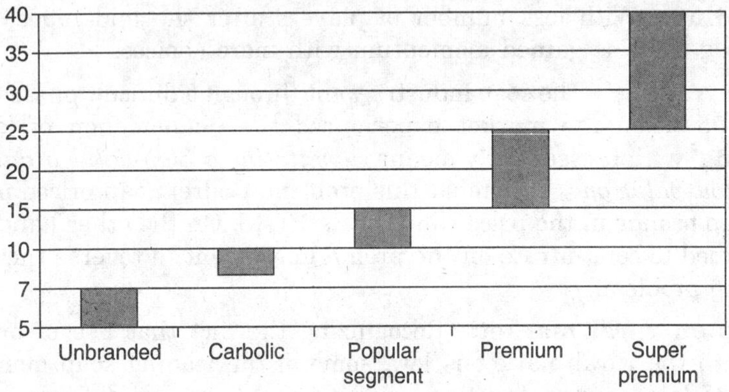

Consumer Behaviour

Consumer habits: In the urban areas, people use municipal supply of water, rural India people usually bathe in well water, river bank or village ponds. *In Kerala,* most homes have wells; they bathe in to bathroom (specially room) or room to well. As winter is severe in north and hot water is not easily available, bathing frequency drops in winter. Again during summer, there is acute scarcity of water in many areas. In coastal areas of south and west India, due to high perspiration/sweat people have regular bathing habit. Generally, consumers do not use soap daily due to lack of habit or desire to economize on the usage. Consumption of soap in India is reported to be at western countries USA, Europe, around 400 gm in India.

Consumer practices: Many Indian families still make use of a common soap for the entire family. This is in contrast to the advanced countries, where an individual prefers to have his/her own personal soap. Till recently penetration of shampoo was significantly low in India, some people were found to be using a bathing soap for washing hair. Liquid soap market is in the nascent stage and usage is restricted to upper middle class urbanites.

Critical Factors of Success

- **Distribution:** It is a most important aspect of this business. A strong distribution network is one of the prime reasons for domination of HLL, which has over 10 million retail outlets.
- **Advertising:** This too plays an important role. The recession in the economy brought down the growth in volumes for most segments. This has made it necessary for firms to increase their advertising efforts in order to increase awareness and in the process generate higher volumes.
- **Brand positioning:** It will depend on the value proposition offered and the consumer perception about specific benefits and image of the particular brand.

Competitive Structure

Players & their brands

- The toilet soap market has a number of leading national and global companies, besides a large number of small players which have strong local presence. The popular and premium brands of toilet soaps include *Lifebuoy, Lux, Cinthol, Liril, Rexona, Shikakai, Nirma, Ganga, Vigil* and *Dettol*. The global brands are *Pears, Camay* and *Dove*.

Market share: The **organized** sector dominates the popular and premium segments with a share of over 95 per cent. The main players in this business are HLL (60% market share), Nirma (15%), Procter & Gamble (11%), and Godrej Soaps (7–8%). The toilet soaps market recorded a dismal growth of 3–4 per cent in the last three years, mainly due to stagnation in the popular segment that accounts for almost 85 per cent of the market. The major brands in this segment are *Lux, Lifebuoy, Cinthol, Dettol,* and *Ganga*.

EXHIBIT 19.3

Market Shares of Leading Players

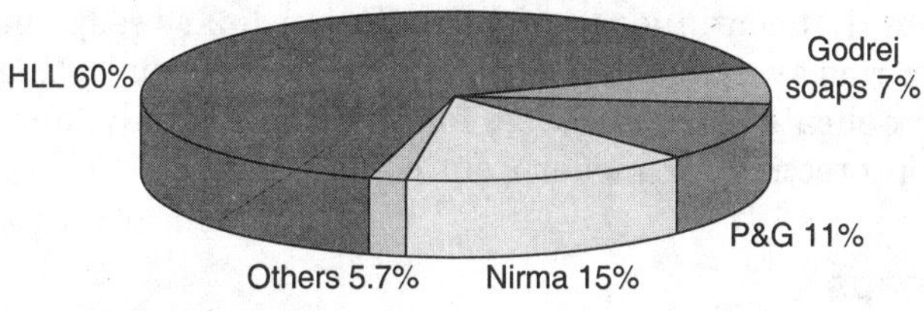

BRAND POSITIONING

This section shall examine the value proposition of leading brands and their consequent distinct positioning in different categories.

Health /Anti-Bacteria

Lifebuoy: Making a billion Indians feel safe and secure by meeting their health and hygiene needs is the mission of *Lifebuoy*. The world's largest selling soap brand offers a compelling health benefit to the entire family. Launched in 1895, Lifebuoy is synonymous with health and remained low priced. The brick red soap, with its perfume and popular Lifebuoy jingle, has carried the Lifebuoy message of health across the length and breadth of the country.

During 2002 to 2004 Lifebuoy experimented with a number of new formulations and repositioning exercises to make it more relevant to be new generation of consumers. *Lifebuoy* is nowadays marketed with a new fragrance and a contemporary shape. The new formulation offers a significantly superior bathing experience and a softer feeling on the skin. The new *Lifebuoy* is targeted at today's discerning housewife with a more inclusive "family health protection for my family and me" positioning. *Lifebuoy* has made a deliberate shift from the male, victorious concept of health to a warmer, more versatile, and direct protection from bacteria etc. for the entire family. At the upper end of the market, *Lifebuoy* offers specific health benefits through *Lifebuoy Gold*. This brand *Lifebuoy Gold* (also called *Care*) helps protect against germs which cause skin blemishes, whereas *Lifebuoy Plus* offers protection against germs which cause body odour.

Dettol soap: Dettol soap was launched in 1981 by Rockitt and Coleman India Ltd and positioned as a 'love and care soap'. Following initial poor response, the company after a few years re-launched the brand in a green wrapper, as a germicidal soap on the '100 per cent bath' platform. In the Rs. 950-crore premium category, Dettol is the leader in the antiseptic category. Subsequently RCI launched Dettol Liquid handwash soap which also created a distinct mark. Various variants of Dettol soap together command 18 per cent of the market.

Protex: This international brand launched by Colgate has not been very successful in India. Protex soap is an antibacterial soap. Protex had a moisturizing formula that enabled skin to retain more moisture, meant for soft and healthy skin. Protex soap claimed that it would eliminate 99 per cent of the bacteria commonly found on skin and create a barrier of protection that continues to protect when ordinary soaps no longer do. Protex soap was available in 4 varieties: *Fresh*, for long lasting freshness, *Gentle*, for delicate skin, *Balance*, for the whole family, and *Active*, for maximum protection for modern outlook seekers.

Beauty Soaps

Lux: *Lux* stands for the promise of beauty and glamour as one of India's most trusted personal care brands. Lux continues to be a favourite with generations of users for the experience of a sensuous and luxurious bath. Since its launch in India in the year 1929, *Lux* has offered a range of soaps in different sensuous colours and fragrances. Lux is available in four different variants—Exotic flower petals and Jojoba Oil, Almond Oil and Milk Cream, Fruit Extracts and Honey in Milk Cream and Sandal Saffron in Milk Cream.

The year 2003 saw one of the biggest milestones in the history of Lux. From being just a beauty soap of film stars, Lux recognized the need for a compelling message about beauty that would resonate with women of today.

Nirma: Nirma promised to offer "Better Value, Better Living." It introduced 'Nirma Beauty Soap' in the year 1992. It is having three different variants and pack sizes. Due to its admirable perfume, Nirma, within a short span of five years, achieved the status of the third largest selling toilet soap brand in India.

Fragrance Soaps

Breeze: *Breeze Scent Magic* is the soap which fulfills the aspirations of rural India. *Breeze* has been targeted at the women segment with the advertisement, saying 'beauty at an affordable price', look and feel beautiful.

Research and consumer visits have shown that the desire for great fragrance featured highest in the daily beauty regime of discount-soap users. Breeze explores this through the proposition of "scent in a soap *Scent ka kamaal, ab sabun mein*" and explicitly propagates the brand promise of the *"Hameshaa kuchh extra"*. It delivers all this and still matches the consumer's needs in terms of price and quantity offered.

Nima Rose: The phenomenal market response received by Nima Rose soap within just two months of its launch is due to its superior product benefits, Nirma's ability to attract low end consumers who saw the brand in television advertisement. Nima Rose soap has got an exceptionally soft rose fragrance—which remains around body for a long time even after bath. This brand had carved a niche in its segment by achieving leadership position. It is available in 100 g and 150 g pack sizes.

Nima Sandal: Indian toilet soap market has seen the emergence of many floral fragrance such as Sandal, Rose, Jasmine, etc. *Nima Sandal* soap has rich and exotic fragrance. It promises benefits of sandal oil and turmeric powder. It is a premium product and is available in 100 g and 150 g packs.

Lime/Freshness Soaps

Nirma Lime Fresh: This brand created a sensational marketing history in the Indian Toilet soaps market, when it was launched in 1997.

Seventeen million packs of Nirma Lime Fresh soap were sold in the very first month of its soft launch. Packed in a poly coated 75 gm carton, this soap is available in green colour.

Cinthol: Today, despite the presence of global corporations, the *Cinthol* brand has carved out a space in the toilet soap market. Cinthol commands a market share of 2.5 per cent by value. In its earliest years when the entire world was using soaps made from animal fats, Godrej bucked the trend by formulating a soap manufactured from vegetable oils.

Today, *Cinthol* has three distinct variants, borne out of market needs and consumer studies. *Cinthol Deodorant* and *Complexion* soap continues emphasis on the 'healthy skin' plank. The soap offers numerous 'do-good' benefits such as total and complete skin protection.

Cinthol Lime Fresh is a strong player in the 'freshness' category. The lime extract provides deep cleansing properties and the excellent long-lasting lime fragrance keeps one feeling fresh.

Cinthol Deodorant soap is the latest offering from Godrej. This new soap-on-the-block is aimed at satisfying a latent problem: hesitation to get close because of body odour. It has a unique long-lasting deo formula that prevents body odour all day long. It comes in two exciting fragrances: Cologne and Spice that keep the user feeling fresh all day.

Liril: According to HLL, the spirit of *Liril*, since its launch in 1975, has remained unchanged. It is symbolic of the energy and exuberance of youth. Liril is not just a soap but an expression of freedom and freshness. It encourages you "to let your hair down and be your most uninhibited self". This is the positioning the soap has taken.

In the early 80's it devised an advertisement compaign in which the LIRIL girl was shown drenched under the falls wearing only bikini. The ad was all about waterfalls, abundant water and the girl splashing about in total abandon singing "*la...la la la laaa..*".

Liril's growth was sparked by the new addition—*Liril Icy Cool Mint.* This new variant refreshed the 25 year old brand's equity of freshness and exuberance of youth.

Liril has of case changed its colour from lime green to orange. The new offering—*Liril Orange Fresh*—was pegged on par with its existing Lime Fresh variant at Rs 16 for 75 gms.

Skin Care Soaps

Pears: It is a transparent amber colour and 100 per cent pure toilet soap. Most soaps with a transparent base use animal fat, *Pears* soap has none when it comes to particularly oily or sensitive skin. What is unique about *Pears* is that it is a glycerine-based soap and also contains natural oils which make *Pears* ideal for dry skin too.

Introduced in India in 1902, *Pears* is manufactured like any other soap, but unlike in conventional soaps, the glycerine is retained within the soap. That is the cause of its unique transparency. After manufacturing, the soap is mellowed under controlled conditions over weeks. At the end of this maturing process, it is individually polished and packed in cartons.

Today, *Pears* is available in three variants—the traditional amber variant, a green variant for oil control and a blue variant for germ protection.

Extending the equity of its glycerine-based winter care brand—*Pears* chose to attract the kids segment. In January 2006 HLL launched a new variant—*Pears Junior*.

Dove: *Dove* soap, which was launched in the USA and European countries by Unilever in 1957, has been marketed in India since 1995. It projected a refreshingly real alternative for women who recognise that beauty is not simply about how you look, it is about how you feel.

Family Soaps

Hamam: Traditionally, *Hamam* has positioned itself as a family soap and provides for all kinds of skin care needs—purification, nourishment and moisturising. Based on this, the new *Hamam* was developed with the perfect balance of *neem* that protects, *tulsi* that purifies and Aloe vera (a new ingredient) that nourishes.

For the first time since its launch in 1934, *Hamam* moved on to a very modern and trendy look. The new *Hamam* now comes in an attractive oval shape. It also offers fragrance that provides a longer-lasting freshness. The packaging too has been modernized and made very attractive. The new *Hamam* is offered at the same prices as old version.

Baby Soaps

Johnson's baby soaps: Johnson's baby soaps are available in three variants, namely, *Johnson's Baby Moisturising Soap, Johnson's Baby Soap Blossoms*, and *Johnson's Baby Milk Soap*. Johnson's baby soaps are enriched with one-fourth baby lotion. All these brands cater to the needs of upper class income group in India.

Wipro Baby Soaps: Using ingredients like almonds and saffron, this brand of baby soap offers therapeutic value by being antispasmodic; the soap also contains vitamins A, D and B2. With a balanced Ph, this is a gentle soap, which moisturizes and nourishes the baby's skin.

Wipro Baby Soft Tulsi and Almond Oil Soap is another variant where *tulsi* and *almond oil* are its main ingredients. The ingredient *tulsi* has anti-bacterial property, which prevents the baby from skin infection. Olive oil helps the skin to balance its loss and absorption of moisture. Moreover, almond oil helps to relieve irritation, inflammation and itching, and is greatly lubricating.

Speciality Soaps

Mysore sandal soap: The mysore *sandal soap* of KS&DL still commands a niche in the soap market. This soap is made from pure vegetable ingredients and contains natural sandal wood oil, which has excellent antiseptic properties, soothes prickly heat and other skin rashes too.

The brand over the years has found market worldwide for its nourishing and softening quality of skin care.

Mysore sandal soaps are today sold in 17 gms, 75 gms, 125 gms, 150 gms pack sizes.

Santoor soap: Wipro, the giant personal computer and software company, launched this soap in 1986. Like Mysore soap *Santoor* has got sandalwood and turmeric. This soap is specially formulated to cool, smooth and soften skin while controlling formulation of skin darkening pigments (melanin). All these skin care methods result in glowing skin of users. Amongst the first brands in the country to launch an offering with the twin ingredient benefits of sandal and turmeric, *Santoor* has of late moved from a purely natural ingredient based appeal, to one of the most preferred beauty soaps of the day. It comes in three variants—*Santoor (sandal and turmeric)*, *Santoor White (sandal and almond milk)* and *Santoor Chandan*.

Moti soap: *Moti Luxury Bath Soap* is a refreshing, soothing and replenishing soap. It comes in two fragrances, sandalwood and rose and has weight of 150 gms. The product is high priced to project it as a premium quality.

Herbal Soap

Margo: All New *Margo*, one of the fastest growing premium soaps in India, promises a complexion aglow with the goodness of *neem*. Vested with antiseptic properties, the neem in Margo cleanses from deep down, removing germs, grime and blemishes—but without removing any vital body oils. This helps the complexion to maintain its delicate sheen and enhances beauty naturally. It comes in a pack size of 75 gms.

FUTURE PROSPECTS

The buoyant Indian economy should ensure higher volumes growth of the **personal care industry**. Because of the sheer size of the rural population, higher share of the revenue pie of companies is expected from the rural areas. Companies in future would largely start sharing the distribution channel of other players in order to expand their market more effectively (like P&G is currently using Marico's distribution channel for its products).

Given the low per capita consumption of personal care products in India, there is a vast scope of growth in most of the categories. However, with the narrowing of the product differentiation, only the efficient companies would survive in the long run. Mergers and acquisitions will help players to consolidate business. Logistics would be the key value driver in the future.

In this industry, it is also important for firms to have a presence in most of the segments or at least across different categories in each segment in order to reap economies of scale with respect to distribution and advertising.

CHAPTER 20

Detergents

The Indian fabric wash products market was a highly fragmented one. There was a sizeable unorganized sector, however since the last decade a lot of consolidation has taken place and now a few major players are dominating this market. Historically, HLL and swastik were the first companies to manufacture detergents in India. HLL test marketed its brand *Surf* between 1956 to 1958 and began manufacturing it from 1959. Swastik launched *Det*, a white detergent powder, in 1957.

India is the third largest detergent market in the world. In the 2004–05, the turnover was about Rs 6000 crore in size and 23 lakh tonnes in volume. The detergent industry has shown a steady growth of 6–8 per cent over the last two decades. See Exhibit 20.1 to observe the demand growth since 1990–91. In the coming future the growth rate is expected to reach 8–10 per cent mark.

EXHIBIT 20.1

Detergent Demand in India (metric tonnes)

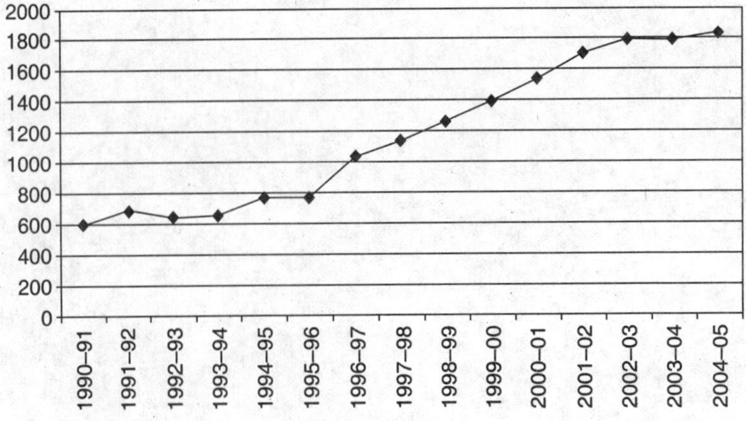

In India, detergents usually come under two categories: detergent bars and detergent powders. According to estimates for ......, detergent bars constituted 40 per cent and detergent powders 55 per cent of the total market. The remaining 5 per cent was taken up by synthetic detergents in liquid form.

MARKET SEGMENTATION

Geographic Segmentation

Nationally, the Northern part of the country is the largest user of detergents (38%), followed by the west (28%), south (18%) and the east (16%). Within urban and rural, the split is 60–40 in favour of urban India.

Price Segmentation

The Indian detergent market can be segmented on the basis of price as Popular, Economy, Premium and Compacts. Popular detergents are priced at Rs 18 to Rs 22 per kg and Economy segment at Rs 35 to Rs 50 per kg. Premium powders are sold at Rs 75 per kg whereas Compacts are sold in the price range of Rs 120–180 per kg. In India, 84 per cent of the total detergent market segment is in the popular price segment while the economy and premium brands constitute 14 per cent and 2 per cent, respectively (see Exhibit 20.2). India produces approx. 2500 KTA of detergents, the market growth being in the region of 6–8 per cent. The per capita consumption of detergents in India is around 3.2 kgs which is very low compared to that in the developed countries like USA and Germany where it is about 25 kg.

EXHIBIT 20.2

Break-up of three Price Segments

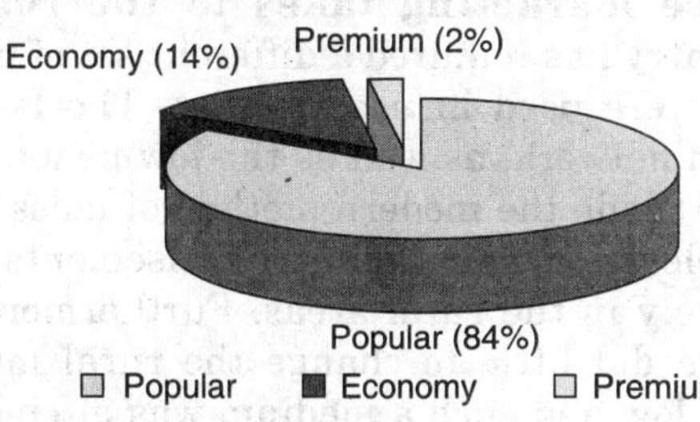

MARKET TRENDS

1. **Saturation hits urban areas:** Large manufacturers are pursuing expansion plans to tap the rural demand across India. However, increased

competition from small companies has forced players to engage in regular price units to maintain their market shares. The near saturation of demand in urban areas has also encouraged smaller players, specially those from the unorganized segment, to confine to particular, pockets of rural areas in order to maintain profit margins. Small packs or sachets are still the best method for large manufacturers to encourage households to switch to branded detergents.

2. **India seen as a "Sleeping Giant":** The rising standards of living in urban areas have seen the purchasing power of the consumer base increase, and more and more consumers trading up to premium detergent products as well as increasing their usage of existing household care products.

3. **Volume over value strategy leads to lower growth across board:** Across the industry both large and small players are pursuing volume over value growth that strategy to allure the new customers. It is generally observed the price sensitive Indian consumers continually demand better price promotions and discounts in order to garner their purchases. Accordingly, manufacturers even the large such as Hindustan Lever and Procter & Gamble have resorted to price cutting measures for their lines of laundry detergents. This strategy was initially applied in the zoom of small sachets and packs that they were meant for irregular users of detergent and for promoting in the rural areas. The price cuts strategy have subsequently been applied to the larger packs (i.e., 1 kg or 500 g) in order to promote brand loyalty and larger volume of consumption.

4. **Nirma Ltd continues to dominate its position on low price segment:** Nirma continues to offer stiff competition to all FMCG giants in detergent business by effectively blocking them out of the mass market. For example, with the excise exemption that it enjoys in Gujarat, the company is able to keep its production costs and final price low as compared to Hindustan Lever, which has high overhead costs due to its stricter quality control.

5. **Laundry care marketing takes to the road:** In detergent business, rural entry has required a different set of marketing strategy from those that were used in urban areas. The lack of electricity, a weak distribution network, as well as the low penetration levels in the rural areas, have made the modern method of mass media advertising ineffective, as television and radio advertisements could not be put across as effectively in the rural areas. Furthermore, the distribution of pamphlets also did little to change the rural mindset, as literacy levels were often low and such a medium was often distrusted if there was no 'live' demonstration of the product. To overcome this problem, Hindustan Lever Ltd embarked on an education-cum-retail campaign through the use of "mobile vans". The purpose of these vans was to penetrate the rural areas by stopping at small towns and villages to

screen movies that were interspersed with the company's advertisements, showing the usage of various products from cosmetics and toiletries to household care products to food products as well. After the movie was shown, a demonstration was often done, after which either free samples were given out or retail sales took place. From a week to a month later, the vans would return to the same location to gather feedback as well as to carry out more retail sales. Once the brand awareness was built, the same brands would be made available at the next nearby *kirana* and/or to the travelling salesman who serviced the rural homes directly. Products that were sold through retail channels also sometimes contained price discount coupons to make the next purchase more attractive and thus develop brand loyalty among the converted users of the brand.

6. **Automatic detergents grow:** The washing machines are gaining rapid entry in urban households over the years urban areas. It is estimated that there are now 75 washing machines for every 1000 households in the urban areas. The growth of washing machines has increased the demand for specially formulated detergent to grow.

7. **Bar detergents losing out to hand wash detergents:** The younger consumers are now more open to trying out the powder detergents, as they are often much easier to use and also more effective. However, the decline in popularity of bar detergents is likely to be a slow process, especially since some people still use bar detergents when travelling, or when hand washing stubborn stains out of their clothes.

CONSUMER BEHAVIOUR

Choice Criterion

The main attributes that consumers look for in a detergent are:

- Functional value (how effective the detergent is in cleaning clothes) vs. affordability (Price).
- Ease of use (must dissolve fast)—this is particularly important to households which do not have washing machines.
- Detergents should also be easy on the skin and must have a fragrance.

Research conducted by P&G on the Indian laundry market indicates that 'fragrance' in detergents is an important factor of delight for the home-maker in her daily laundry chore. Keeping in view about this desire of Indian market, *Ariel Spring Clean* offered a flowery fragrance. Similarly, *Ariel Fresh Clean* contains a fresh fragrance catering to the Indian consumers' special fondness for mogra.

Special Consumer Behaviour at Pattern

Studies have shown that consumers, by and large, find little perceived difference among the existing brands of detergents. They are indifferent among leading brands as long as prices are comparable. This "commoditisation" nature of detergent business has compelled even P&G to lower the price of brands like *Ariel, Tide*.

Consumer Tendency to Downtrade

In recent times, consumers have shown a tendency to downtrade to lower priced brands premium segments. But it all depends on which part of the curve consumers are in and how much they have moved up over the past two years. While consumers in the premium segment are found to downtrade to mid-priced brands, they usually do not go all the way down to the lower-end or economy brands. That is to say, consumers who have with time moved up to premium segment and have got used to a certain level of their performance, the seldon goes back to using really low-priced brands.

Downtrading also happens through a balancing effect on consumption, where consumers reduce consumption of premium brands and supplement them with mid-priced brands. Marketers have addressed that situation by bringing in low unit packs. They have smaller packs, sachets, 200 gm packs of their premium detergents. They also try out promotional offers such as freebies. Finally, through all this, the consumer benefits.

POSITIONING

Perception Map of leading Brands

In Exhibit 20.3 some of the leading detergents available in the Indian market are plotted on two axes such as. Price and Cleanliness/Whiteness. Some strategic groupings emerge here. For instance, *Surf*, *Excel*, *Ariel*, and *Henko Stain Champion* stand out as the premium brands and they are the most powerful detergents in terms of cleansing properties. In contrast brands like *Rin*, *Tide*, and *Mr White* occupy another extreme where the medium price and property of whiteness of clothes are most prevalent. Brands such as *Wheel* and *Nirma* are low priced cater to the basic wash requirements of the customers. Low prices of these brands are the prime reason for their high market share. It is widely acknowledged that Nirma had a very big role in expanding the bottom end of the detergent consumer base.

EXHIBIT 20.3

Perceptual Map of Leading Detergent Boards

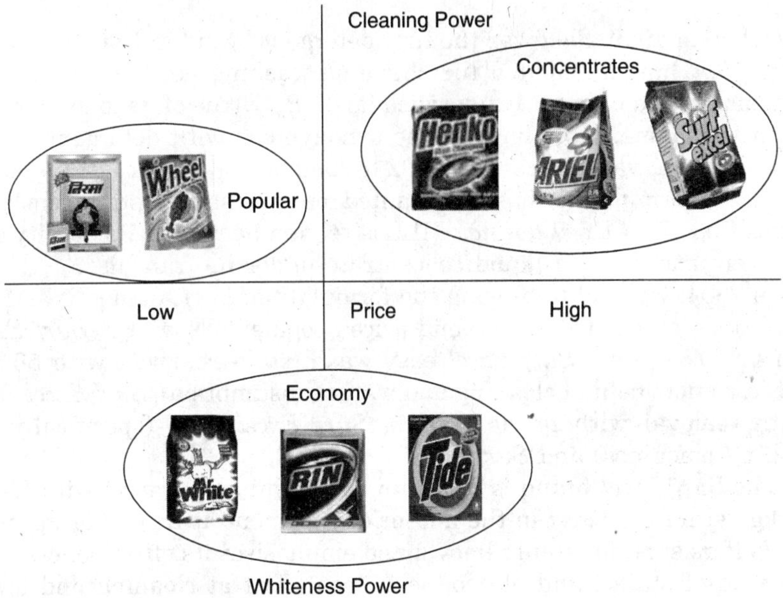

Competitive Structure

HLL, Nirma and P&G are the major players in the detergent market Exhibit 20.4 shows their market share in 2005–06. While HLL dominates the premium segment, Nirma is the leader in the popular segment. Nirma created a revolution in the market by pioneering the concept of no frill low-cost detergents. Currently, the market is highly segmented with the differential between the premium and popular segments at almost seven times.

EXHIBIT 20.4

Market Share of Leading Detergent Players

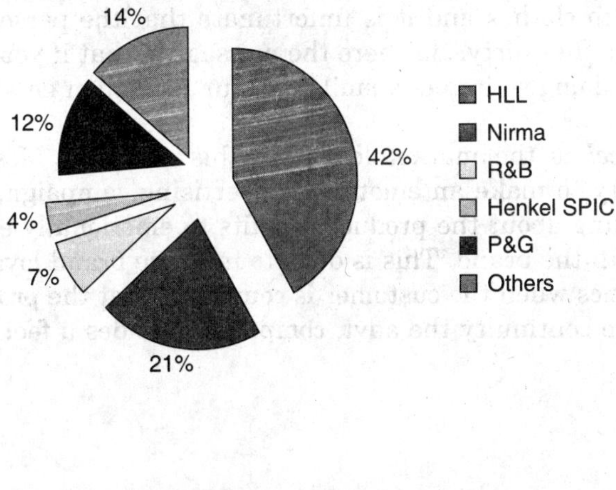

COMPETITIVE ANALYSIS OF MAJOR BRANDS

Surf Excel

Launched in 1959, *Surf* was the first detergent brand in India. Over the years, *Surf* has anticipated the changing washing needs of the Indian homemaker and constantly upgraded itself. By virtue of its long presence this brand name, *Surf*, has become synonymous with detergent.

Surf Excel was launched in 1992 to combat the entry of P&G's *Ariel*. This new formulation has highlighted on the strong stain-removing proposition (*Surf Excel hai na*). HLL is relying heavily in its quality and has even introduced a liquid concentrate under its franchise.

In 2004, HLL, of improving the formulation. *Surf*, named it as *Surf Excel Blue*, and put it in the mid-priced segment. Now, the *Surf Excel* franchise comprises *Surf Excel* easy wash (stain removal, with 50 per cent less effort behind cleaning and water consumption), *Surf Excel Blue* (stain removal with fabric caring), *Surf Excelmatic* (specifically for washing machines) and *Surf Excel Liquid*.

The *Surf Excel* brand is priced in the premium segment with Rs 99 per kg, with *Surf Excel* in the mid-priced segment at Rs 60 per kg. *Surf Excel* offers superior stain removal and emphasises its effectiveness with any kind of stains, and also projects less effort at cleaning and lower water consumption as its benefits.

The *Surf Excel* brand was caught in the middle of the HLL and P&G price war, where P&G drastically reduced the prices of *Tide* and *Ariel* in 2004. Since the price war was unsustainable, in this situation, HLL has chosen to respond by concentrating on its consumers and building their brand loyalty. Their communication has focused on emotionally connecting with the consumers. The idea behind their latest campaign, "*Daag acche hain*", launched after "*Surf Excel hai na*", is to make sure that the existing consumers stay with them and prevent switching to a cheaper brand. They are focussing on building brand loyalty to prevent switching and increase usage by encouraging consumers to go ahead and get dirty.

The *Surf Excel* ad is different from the other creative ads in this category. Most detergents usually say that dirt is the worst thing that can happen to clothes and it is unfortunate that the person concerned got his/her clothes dirty. But here the message is that if you want to get dirty and in doing so it gets a smile on your face, then go ahead and do it.

Surf Excel is the market leader in this category. Most detergent companies try to make an emotional advertising campaign. They move on from talking about the product benefits to emotionally engaging the customer with the brand. This is done to increase brand loyalty. It is an effective tactics when the customer is convinced that the product is good but to ensure continuity the advt. compaign provides a feel good factor.

Contrary to this usual practice of emotion element. *Surf Excel* has positioned itself on the opposite end of the spectrum in this category. The advertising encourages children to dirty, and in an indirect way this act ensures greater usage of the brand, *Surf Excel*.

This entire campaign aims at ensuring customers to continue with this brand and do not switch over to competitive products. The emotional connect is trying to justify the premium.

As we discuss the positive outcome of this campaign, we must also examine if this is creating any form of dissonance in the minds of the consumer. We believe that *Surf Excel* is only building on its brand promise of 'Assurance'. Earlier it was saying that *'Surf Excel hai na'*, and consumers, need not worry as this brand will solve their all dirt related problems. Now they are going one step ahead and saying that get dirty and still there is *Surf Excel* to take it.

The ad campaign is known to have successfully passed on the message to its customers, and HLL was able to arrest the falling market share.

In another campaign, post the "*Daag acche hain*" campaign, *Surf Excel*, in its newest ad, promises to tackle the toughest stains without damaging the colour of the fabric. Smart sensors within the product profess that can differentiate stains from colours, thus tackling the really tough stains, especially on coloured clothes.

The company has introduced a number of variants such as *Surf Excelmatic*. It is meant for front loaded machines with a specially designed low suds formulation that promises a "superlative clean". Another variant is *Surf Excel Liquid* for those preferring the modern and convenient way to wash. The liquid form penetrates deep allowing great wash results. For the really tough stains, the liquid can be applied directly on the body of stain (through a stain treater).

Ariel

Ariel is the Procter & Gamble company's leading detergent board. It epitomizes **'stain removal'**. Introduced in India in 1991, *Ariel* has continuously led other detergents in product innovation. It was the first to bring the 'compact detergent' technology in India; the enzyme technology for superior and safe stain-removing power; the proprietary 'smart eyes' technology which helps detect and remove stains better than any other detergent; and the latest is superior cleaning in a choice of fragrances.

Over the years, the brand has enjoyed endorsement from celebrities such as Shabana Azmi, Begum of Pataudi, successful actress and homemaker of the Pataudi family Sharmila Tagore, TV's most popular 'saas-bahu' duo Smriti Iraani and Apara Mehta, and lakhs of homemakers in India.

Ariel contains safe ingredients for normal fabrics and skin under recommended usage conditions for laundry, and meets stringent human and environmental safety standards. Procter & Gamble has launched *Ariel* in a choice of two fragrances—**Ariel Spring Clean with a floral fragrance, and Ariel Fresh Clean with a refreshing fragrance.**

Ariel in its choice of two fragrances—*Spring Clean* and *Fresh Clean*—is available at all leading general and chemist stores and the price remains unchanged at Rs 145 for 1.5 kg; Rs 99 for 1 kg; Rs 50 for 500 gms; Rs 22 for 200 gms and Rs 2 for a 20 gms sachet.

"A to Z *daag ke liye jo de taaza khushboo*.": Traditionally, all ad-campaigns of *Ariel* have stressed the fact that *Ariel* is a powerful stain remover. Their latest campaign also maintains that trend, but along with it, there is also a stronger emphasis on the new fragrance feature that has been introduced. The description of the ad is given below.

A man cooks dinner for his wife, who is away. He stains his shirt in the process, but uses *Ariel* to remove the stain.

The key emphasis of the commercial is on the following three factors:

- *Ease of use:* By showing the husband as the one who washes the clothes, the ad reiterates the fact that the product is easy to use.
- *Fragrance:* This is the central message of the commercial. In fact, the emphasis on fragrance is more than the emphasis on stain removal.
- *Stain removal:* As has been the case with all earlier commercials of *Ariel*, this one also shows how effective the product is in removing stains.

Henko Stain Champion

Henkel SPIC India Ltd launched this brand in 1994, in South India, focusing on the superior product performance as compared to the existing blue detergent products.

While carving out a brand campaign for *Henko Stain Champion Powder*, the ad agency had to device suitable means to overcome the problem of consumer inertia.

While it was positioned in the premium segment of detergents, *Henko* had the unenviable task of making users, attuned to using the *Surf* brand, to try the new entrant. There was the twin challenges of reducing the chance of attrition by competitive compact detergents and making the current *Surf Wash Booster* user try *Henko* by creating a distint 'premium brand' personality.

In the second phase, when *Henko* was re-launched in 2000 with a new packaging and new advertising, the task in front of the agency was now to build a loyalty base for the brand. This was done by creating a sort of dissonance in the *Surf* user's mind and positioning *Henko* as a better option. Banking on the insight that the usage of *Surf* was more a habit than a conviction oriented action, the brand targeted at today's generation of young women, who want more contemporary solutions for traditional problems. The television commercial developed for *Henko* focused on 25 to 40 year old housewives from SEC A, B and C households—with a young woman who helped her mother drive away clothes stains with *Henko*, rather than the traditional 'blue detergent'.

The media strategy was focused on addressing *Surf* users' media habits through their choice of channels/programmes. 'During the concentrated bursts of *Henko Stain Champion*, the strategy was to outshout *Surf* in those channels/programmes for the first six weeks and then use shorter edits for frequency and top of mind recall.' The result—the brand touched volumes averaging 800 tonnes per month and touched a volume base of 1000 tonnes in October 2001.

The Kerala trick: The agency aimed straight at the local Malayalee's heart with a commercial that used a popular serial actress Rashmi Soman to capitalize on *Henko's* popularity in the state. The scenes showed a grandmother staining her *sari* with betelnut juice, the ad interspersed with a kathakalli sequence and the courtyard of the *tharawad* (ancestral home) to get the brand emotionally closer to the Malayalee through a mix of cable and satellite channels in early 2001. The strategy worked—brand volumes shot up from 83 tons per month to 150 tonnes, coupled with a pride of association that was earlier reserved for the predecessor—*Surf*.

Currently, the brand belongs to the top end premium segment, with a market share of nearly 9 per cent. It has focused on stain removal, which extensive research has shown to be the highest order need for Indian consumer. It also promises to remove the toughest of stains.

The main proposition of this brand is being high-on-quality and low-on-price. As we have seen, earlier campaigns had basically used the idea of positioning *Henko* as a better option. Other ideas that have also been employed are a regional association to strike emotional chord, as we saw in the case of Kerala, freebies from *Henko* (e.g. *Pril* cleaning bar free with every *Henko Stain Champion*) and use of celebrities like Urmila for the north and Laila for the south.

Punchline: *"Iske power pearls kapro mein geheraee tak jaye aur daag ko jar se nikal dein"*

The main focus of its campaigns is on the fact that its product performance is much superior as compared to its rivals. What it really tries to do is to bring out the technological aspect, and the campaign has no social/emotional angle as such.

Tide

This world famous brand of detergent of the P&G was launched in India sometime in 2000. In order to attract the price-conscious consumers to its fold, P&G initiated a price war with HUL brands.

This brand of detergent targets the "superior whiteness" and "whiteness maintenance" laundry needs of a homemaker in India, which have been shown to be externaly important.

The Ad campaigns of *Tide* have an underlying theme: *Chaunk gaye? White ho to Tide ho...* .

One of its earlier ad campaign shows a man chasing a woman across the lawns, with her white *dupatta* in his hand. Suddenly, he comes across a *dupatta* that is whiter, and then the concept of *Tide* is introduced.

The ads showcase the detergent's cleaning power and superior whitening abilities. As such, some of the ads also try to focus on the value proposition that *Tide* offers: high performance at low cost. These campaigns have absolutely no emotional aspect, but bring out the social consciousness of white clothes, that is so prevalent in India.

The different SKUs of *Tide* are Rs 88 for 2 kg; Rs 43 for 1 kg; Rs 20 for 500 gms; Rs 10 for 200 gms and Rs 2 for a 20 gms sachet.

Rin Advanced

Rin Shakti is another detergent brand of the Hindustan Unilever Ltd. (HUL). In 2004, it was re-launched as *Rin Advanced*, in order to counter the growing popularity of *Tide*.

Rin Shakti falls roughly into the mid-price to low-price category, which clearly differentiates it from *Surf Excel*. However, a problem that HUL was facing in recent times was the significant price cuts of Proctor and Gamble's brands: *Ariel* and *Tide*. In order to keep pace with the competition, HUL brought the price of *Surf Excel* down significantly, resulting in the latter having prices comparable with *Rin Shakti*. Since *Surf Excel* has traditionally been the premium brand and *Rin Shakti* the popular one, this move was expected to customer confusion, resulting in cannibalization between HUL's products, and possible shift of HUL's consumers to Proctor and Gamble.

The advertisement campaigns for *Rin Shakti* involve the concept of "*double safedi*". It focuses on the whitening of clothes, which means it directly competes with *Tide*. The differentiating factor is that it stresses on a "Pure Clean Technology": it claims that its formulation does not contain residue-like minerals—which most other formulations do—and thus, it is able to achieve better results.

The campaign concentrates on the social acceptability and attractiveness of white clothes by portraying a man walking along the road, and being greeted and cheered by various groups of people as he walks past them.

The focus of *Rin Shakti* is on whitening, which is intrinsically different from that of *Surf Excel Blue*, which is positioned as a stain remover. Thus, the two brands are clearly targetted at different segments. However, due to the recent similarity in prices, some overlapping of consumers, it has resulted in a phased withdrawal of this brand.

Henko Mr White

Mr White from Henkel SPIC is a Rs 50 crore brand and has a current market share of 14 per cent in the mid range detergents segment. *Mr White* has become the number 2 brand in its category and has been steadily growing over the past 5 years. This is the only eco-friendly detergent in its segment, though this fact has not been sufficiently emphasized in its ad campaigns. The brand promise has been one of superior product performance, and unique dazzling whiteness. This can be clearly gauged from the name of the brand: "Mr White"—personifying the brand as the customer's helper who will do all the work for him.

Henkel India Limited recently re-launched its *Mr White* detergent powder across the country with an enhanced formulation, a fresh new fragrance and in all-new pack.

The brand now promises the "Power of 2—Lime + Blue". Lime removes stains and provides a fresh and lingering fragrance, while blue gives enhanced brightness. This quality combination would simplify the washing process. The re-launch of the *Mr White* brand is expected to add technological superiority in the segment and offer significantly higher order benefits. The packaging wears a completely new and innovative look.

An ad campaign had a little girl stopping her grandfather from playing cricket in the neighbourhood, as his clothes were not "*Sabse white*", and thereby causing turmoil for the mother. The ad goes on to show a scientist recommending Henko *Mr White* as the right detergent to get clean white clothes. The ad ends with: "*Thoda sa green thoda sa blue. Thoda sa jadoo. Mr. White. Sabse white.*"

Similar to *Tide*, this detergent's campaign uses social consciousness that requires ensuring that your clothes are the whitest, as the primary emphasis. Moreover, the ad uses an expert to promote its product—this is based on research which states that voices of authority are extremely important in the consumer's mind, and often drive—him to make a decision.

Henkel SPIC plans to corner a huge chunk of the mid-range segment market by bringing in, for the first time, premium values, thereby enabling the consumers to really experience a good quality product at a reasonable price. This focus is quite evident during the campaign as well.

Nirma

Nirma created a marketing miracle, when introduced in the domestic marketplace. In 1969, when the detergents were priced so exorbitantly, it was a luxury item for most of the Indians. Nirma envisioned the vast Fabric Wash market segment and sensed a tremendous potential therein. This product was priced at almost one-third to that of the competitor brands, resulting into instant trial by the consumers. Owing to its unique environment-friendly, phosphate-free formulation, the consumers became loyal to this brand, helping it to overtake the decade's old brands, in terms of volumes.

Super Nirma washing powder: Exploding the myth that 'better quality always demands higher price", Nirma introduced a spray-dried blue coloured washing powder in the premium segment, in 1996. Available in 25 gms, 500 gms and 1000 gms packs, this brand out-classed all its competitor brands. Though priced almost 40 per cent less, it provided a very attractive 'value-for-money' proposition. This brand, within a short span of two years, had cornered a substantial market share in the premium detergent segment and continues to perform well.

Nirma followed a unique marketing mix strategy:

1. *Price*—Lowest prices in the segment
2. *Product*—Basic product offering as good a cleaning as, say *Surf*
3. *Promotion*—Carried out extensive advertising
4. *Place*—Through local retailers

The communication campaigns of Nirma focused on one aspect, i.e. value for money. All Nirma products were offered a very good value in reference to the price that was charged. For example, *Nirma popular* was a better quality product, but not priced very high from Nirma.

Wheel

Wheel is a detergent brand that caters to the laundry needs of the mass market. It was first launched in the year 1987 in order to combat the threat posed by Nirma. *Wheel Green* is the single largest (No 1 by market share) detergent brand in India by value.

The detergent belongs to the popular segment and caters to the mass market. It is packed with powerful lather (power foam) that cleans even tough dirt stains on collars and cuffs with ease. It, therefore, cleans effectively with lesser effort, making a laborious chore like washing—light and easy. Moreover, *Wheel* does not burn hands or harm clothes like *Nirma*, which contains a high percentage of soda. Thus, *Wheel* was launched with a formulation superior to its competition and has continued to evolve year after year. Since its inception, *Wheel* has stood head and shoulders above every one else. This is reflected not only in the quality of the powder, but also in sensorial issues like the lemon fragrance and the far more gentle effect on hands.

In providing solutions, *Wheel* has always been highly consumer-need led. In the consumer's mind, the product has successfully found a place in the price-value matrix by always striving to provide superior performance at an affordable price.

Moreover, with its latest upgradation in formulation, *Wheel* has become the first mass-market detergent powder, which provides a superior wash with reduced effort. Till *Wheel* introduced them in the mass-market segment, power speckles were a property of only premium segment washing powders. This has further strengthened the consumer's perception of the brand as a high quality detergent powder available at an affordable price.

Brand values: *Wheel* is committed to improving the lives of mass-market consumers by helping them manage their household better on limited resources.

Millions of mass-market housewives have found an ally in *Wheel* to unshackle them from the 'chore' of washing clothes. The brand realises their position and tries to deliver a laundry solution that partly reduces their burden and provides relief in managing the household. *Wheel* not only helps them to earn their family's appreciation for laundry done efficiently, but also as smart home-makers who make a noticeable difference in the way they manage their home. This helps then to earn their family's—and specially their husband's—appreciation which is their utmost desire. The joy of recognition by their family motivates them to carry on uncomplainingly with their tough life.

In short, *Wheel* can be summed up as—'*Mehnat kum, phir bhi dhulai No. 1.*' *Wheel* is, projected as, the by price-conscious housewife's choice.

FUTURE TRENDS

The detergent industry is set to grow at 10 per cent per annum. With penetration already high, growth would come largely from

- Upgradation from bars to powder
- Increasing per capita consumption
- Increasing use of premium powders.

There will be an effort by firms to avoid the commoditization of the product. We have seen how markets had gradually got commoditized and differentiation got reduced in similar categories and at similar price points. Thus, companies will increasingly emphasise on branding and emotional connects in order to reduce their susceptibility to price wars.

Chapter 21

Shampoo

Hair care products consist of hair oil, shampoos, conditioners and hair colour. The size of different hair care products in 2005–06 is shown in Exhibit 21.1. The size of the shampoo market reached Rs 850 crore and 30,000 tonnes in volume terms. The shampoo market is the fastest growing item within personal product category and it has expanded by nearly two-and-a-half times in last few years, though the market is confined mainly to the urban locations in India (see Exhibit 21.2).

EXHIBIT 21.1

Hair Care Constituents

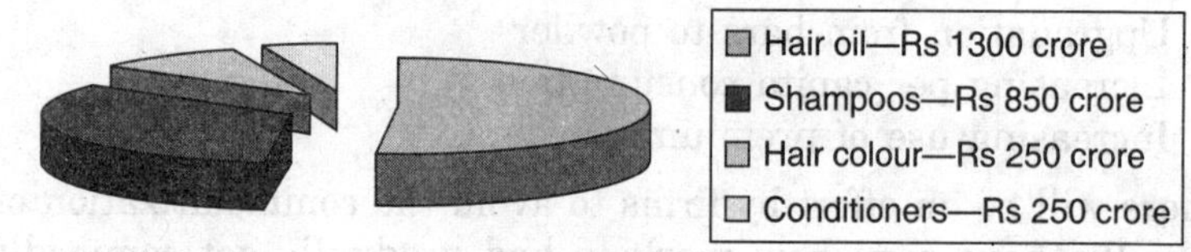

EXHIBIT 21.2

Urban-rural Market share

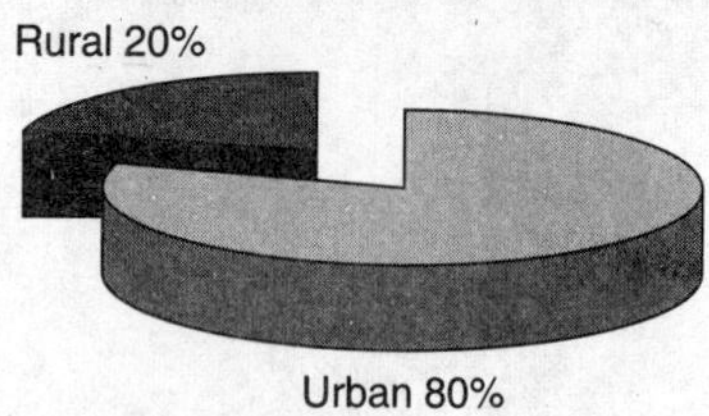

SHAMPOO USAGE IN INDIA

Unlike soaps and detergents, which boast of penetration level of more than 90 per cent, shampoo remains a low penetration category. As per the industry estimates, the urban market penetration of shampoo was about 36 per cent whereas in the rural market, usage was of the order of 12 per cent of the total population. Thus, there is a considerable scope for expansion by converting non-users.

Hindrance to Growth

Major barriers to shampoo use in India were:

- Common beliefs that shampoos contain chemicals and so it could damage hair;
- Shampoo is viewed more as a glamour value and lack of conviction about the functional usefulness of shampoo.
- Until pouch packet was introduced, a large section of the market found even the price quite high and not affordable.

Strategies Adopted to Increase Penetration

Over the last decade or so, marketers have tried different possible experiments to expand their market penetration. Initially major players have tried to create awareness and dispel some of the myths by heavy advertising. Among many innovative strategies like offering of shampoo for particular nature of hair or special formulations, small size packs, especially introduction of sachets etc., shift from the glass bottles to plastic bottle pouch pack lowering of unit price seems to have been most effective. For instance, Cavin Kare introduced a 50 paise sachet of *Chik*, when most other sachets were sold at Rs 2. Such a lower price strategy was instant success, with the *Chik* brand expanding by 40 per cent after its launch. Similarly, a new 50 ml bottle of *Chik* priced at Rs 6 (when most other brands were available in 100 ml bottles and above) has also been well received. HLL has also offered its 50 paise pack for *Lux* shampoo. The company claims the 30 ml bubble pack for *Clinic Plus* (Rs 8), is a cost-effective alternative for sachet users. While sachets are difficult to store and re-use, the bubble pack allows the user to extract just the right quantity for a single wash.

Innovation in Features

Fighting the perception that shampoos are essentially glamour products, marketers have emphasised upon specific functional benefits. The creation of an anti-dandruff shampoos was a step in that direction. *Clinic Plus*, one of the first anti-dandruff brands, is the largest shampoo brand today. *Clinic All Clear*, an anti-dandruff extension targeted at the youth, has also managed to garner a good amount of market share. HLL has also experimented with different versions of *Sunsilk* for dry, normal and oily hairs. Procter & Gamble's *Head & Shoulders, Menthol* and *Pantene Lively Clean* offered distinct functional benefits to their target users. As such, these add-ons enabled brands to command a price premium over the plain shampoos, this strategy enabled those brands to gain volume as well as earn better margin. Exhibit 21.3 shows a spectrum of benefits highlighted by different benefits.

EXHIBIT 21.3

Spectrum of Product Benefits

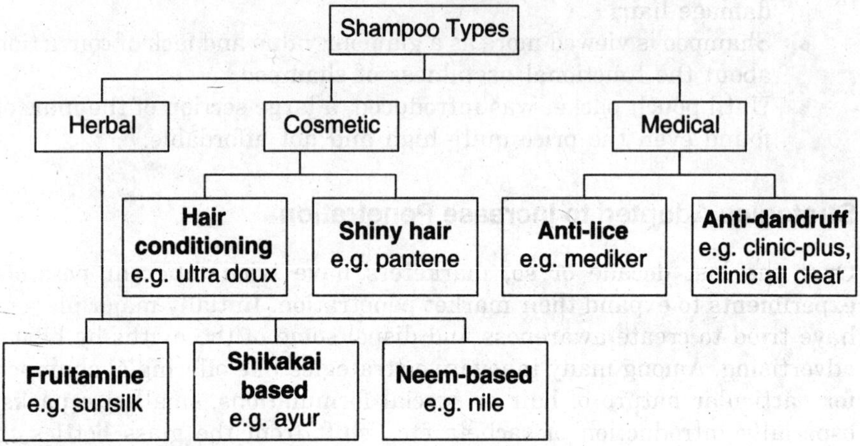

GROWTH STRATEGY

As mentioned earlier, one of the key barriers to shampoo usage is the reluctance to apply a synthetic product on hair. Like in advanced countries, in India also herbal shampoos have become a fast growing category. Shehnaz's beauty parlours, *Ayur* from RDM Traders Private Limited and *Nyle*, a herbal shampoo launched by Cavin Kare, are some of the early herbal base shampoos in the Indian market. All these herbal compositions claim to use traditional Indian herbs such as *shikakai*, soap nuts and *amla* as ingredients and have received good response from the market. Herbal shampoos today account for 10 per cent of the market size. *Nyle Herbal* is among the top five shampoo brands in the country. Even traditional brands such as *Sunsilk* have been emphasising natural ingredients such as 'fruitamins'. However, high price is still a key barrier when it comes to wide acceptance of herbal shampoos. This is why, 90 per cent of the herbal shampoos is still the choice of urban elites.

Already a number of companies have launched many specialized nature of shampoo brands. For example, Dabur has leveraged on Vatika's brand equity to launch *Vatika Herbal shampoo*, Godrej Soaps has leveraged its dominance of the hair colour market to launch *Godrej Colourgloss* shampoo for users with coloured hair. Cosmetic companies such as Biotique and Lotus Herbals are also having herbal shampoos on the shelves. Pharmaceutical companies like Johnson & Johnson have launched medicated antidandruff shampoos. The scope for further value addition in shampoo is getting limited.

It was the packaging innovation, especially sachets in post 1987 which expanded the market. Of late with increasing advertising, the shampoo usage in India has gone up in the urban areas. The thrust has now shifted to value addition, targeting and fine positioning to build brand loyalty in the face of increased competition.

CONSUMER BEHAVIOUR

Traditionally, the Indian woman used oil and shikakai for beauty and health treatment of their hair. The age-old habit was to apply oil on the hair and later on wash it. The nutritional function was thus catered to by oil. This habit continued with the advent of the shampoo when it was used primarily as a cleansing agent after the usage of oil. Shampoos were used only on special occasions like weddings and festivals etc. Shampoos were viewed primarily as a beauty care item. Its usage was restricted because shampoos were considered harmful and a potential cause for hair loss due to their chemical content. Gradually shampoos have gained acceptance as a regular use hair care product for better nourishment, growth of hair and reduction in hair fall.

Factors in the order of importance are:

1. Look and feel of shampoo
2. Benefits offered by shampoo
3. Price of shampoo

Exhibit 21.4 shows the importance of different factors of choice.

EXHIBIT 21.4

Choice Criterion

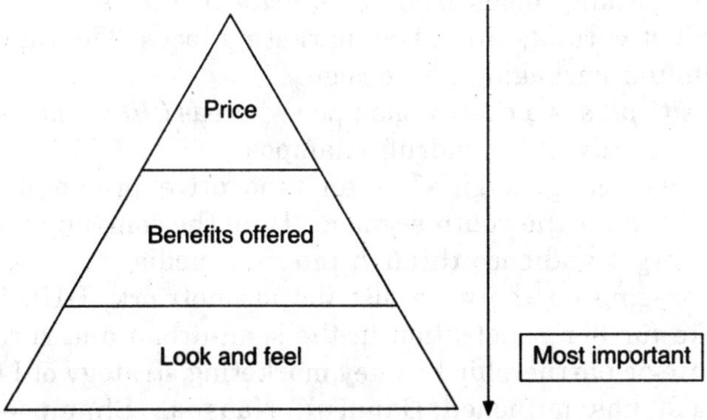

MAJOR PLAYERS AND THEIR STRATEGIES

Although consumers today find a large number of options, but all said and done the shampoo market in India is practically dominated by Hindustan Unilever Ltd (HUL) and P&G. Taking advantage of first mover in this product category, HUL commands 65 per cent of the volume share and 68 per cent share by value. P&G discontinued its shampoo manufacturing operations in India after 2000. Currently, P&G imports the materials required and serves brands like *Pantene Pro-V, Head & Shoulders* in India. Cavin Kare Limited is a late entrant in this business. It was pioneer in focusing on the herbal segment which, subsequently, many small players have entered.

HUL Brands

Sunsilk was launched in 1964. It was the first branded shampoo of HUL. It was positioned as the 'Hair Expert'. *Sunsilk* has identified different hair care needs and offers the consumer the desired benefits of the shampoo. *Sunsilk* comes in a wider range of packaging and designs. *Clinic Plus* is another successful shampoo, launched in India in the year 1987. It claims to offer the five most important hair care benefits such as, strengthens weak hair, prevents hair breakage, softens roughdry hair, shine for thick and healthy hair, and contains anti-dandruff ingredient. The franchise also includes *Clinic All Clear Total*, first introduced in 1996. It is a dual shampoo—that fights the dandruff flake, and enriches lost nutrients to make hair healthy and beautiful. *Clinic All Clear Total* is a dandruff solution for everyday use.

Marketing Strategies of HUL

- The benefits are more compelling and relevant since the variants are harmonised in terms of the product mix—fragrance, colour and ingredients are all well linked to cue the overall synergy. This specially holds true for *Sunsilk Naturals*.
- Product variants are a key marketing focus. The range comes in premium packaging and design.
- *Sunsilk plus* is a beauty shampoo whereas *Clinic plus* is positioned as primarily anti-dandruff shampoo.
- Sunsilk "gang of girls" is an innovative promotion campaign launched for the youth segment. Here the company tries to reach the target audience through internet media.
- Leveraging on the wide distribution network, HUL is trying to make further penetration in the semi-urban and rural markets.
- Strategic partnership is a key marketing strategy of Lever. Lever Ayush has launched Dandruff Naashak Shampoo, which is positioned as herbal and 100 per cent effective in two washes.

Proctor & Gamble Brands

- **Rejoice:** *Rejoice* is the first shampoo which P&G India launched in 1997. The brand offered stiff competitive challenge to HUL's *Clinic Plus* brand. Positioned as "Gives twice as smooth hair at an affordable price", *Rejoice* tried to incorporate the varied needs of Indian shampoo users and offered range at affordable prices.
- **Pantene:** P&G's *Pantene* was similarly positioned in the premium slot of the shampoo market against Hindustan Lever's *Sunsilk*. *Pantene* was relaunched in India in 2004, as *Pantene Amino Pro V* and tried to attract woman's inner beauty, with the help of her outer shine (on using the shampoo). The idea is to bring out the best in women.
- **Head & Shoulders:** Head & Shoulders offers the fine combination of anti-dandruff efficacy and hair conditioning. It was offered in premium segment and comes in a new pack-design and logo in six variants.

Key Marketing Strategies of P&G

- Proctor & Gamble was a late entrant in shampoo segment; hence its marketing strategy was primarily to reduce total dominance of HUL in the shampoo market.
- It indulged in constant price wars with HUL's corresponding brands in the same category.
- Their brands were carefully launched and generally positioned in premium popular, and mass market segment, e.g. *Pantene* was targeted for premium segment of the market for women primarily whereas *Rejoice* was targeted to mass market segment as a shampoo that gives twice as smooth hair at affordable price.
- Packaging was another aspect, as all the products came in multiple SKUs, thus driving the market.

Dabur Brands

- For persistent dandruff problem, *Vatika Anti-Dandruff Shampoo* is the natural choice. The key benefits they convey are:
- This herbal treatment of hair is completely safe and cures dandruff from within.
- Enhancing hair's natural beauty, without damaging or making it dry.
- *Vatika Anti-Dandruff Shampoo* uses the natural strengths of lemon and henna. Cleaning and curing difficult dandruff, while conditioning the hair to give it body and strength.

Vatika Heena Cream Conditioning Shampoo is positioned as a natural shampoo that conditions from deep within, while gently cleansing and nourishing one's hair. The few benefits conveyed are:

- Created by the Vatika Expert with a perfect balance of natural ingredients like henna, green almonds and shikakai.
- Unlike chemical shampoos that are harsh, *Vatika* is mild on one's hair, leaving it soft, silky and radiant, with the gentle and caring touch of nature.

Anmol Natural Shampoo is again positioned as a herbal one. The benefits highlighted by the brand are:

- It is enriched with the goodness of amla, olives and shikakai that gently clean the hair and nourish it from the roots to make the hair shine naturally, giving it that extra sheen.

Anmol Silky Black is again positioned to retain that aspired black colour by Indian masses. The benefits conveyed are:

- The shampoo is enriched with the goodness of almond, amla and shikakai. Available in Re 0.50 and Rs 1 sachet and 25 ml and 100 ml bottle packs.

Key Marketing Strategies of Dabur

- The company has multiple variants or range of shampoos with the same set of positioning, i.e. benefits of herbal ingradients.
- The company has used brand name "Anmol" which Indian masses can easily connect to. "Mustard" and "Amla" are also the traditional hair nourishing ingredients.
- The company has developed a website in Hindi for Anmol, specially to appeal to the total masses of India.
- The wide range of SKU's such as 50 paise and Re 1 sachet and 25 ml and 100 ml bottle packs are primarily meant to attract the budget of all types of customers.

Marketing Strategies of Himalaya

Himalaya anti-dandruff shampoo was positioned as "Herbal anti-dandruff formulation that controls dandruff, nourishes and strengthens hair roots and ensure health scalp". With the growing concern for usage of chemicals in the shampoo, it tried to position itself as a shampoo prepared from herbal and natural extracts with no side effects.

- The Himalaya brand provides a clear differentiation by associating itself with traditional ways of health care.
- Traditionally, natural lifestyle products have been positioned at the premium end of the market. Himalaya positioned its products in mid segment.

- Its market research showed that Ayurveda is perceived as an ancient science that, though respected, is old-fashioned; hence it resorted to extensive promotion, thereby trying to merge the ancient science with modern life.

CavinKare

- *Nyle* was the herbal shampoo launched by CavinKare, which uses natural extracts like heena, shikakai and reetha. It was offered in three variants having characteristics like: reducing hair loss, black, bouncy and shiny hair, and strengthening hair. It was forgetted on the mass market and is available in various SKUs.
- *Chik* shampoo is the second largest selling shampoo in this category, in India. It was positioned in Indian market as "Formulated with Active double conditioners that condition the hair and makes hair soft and helps keep it more manageable than ever."

Key Marketing Strategies of CavinKare

- Its shampoo brands competed directly with market leaders such as HUL, P&G, in mid and mass market segment.
- CavinKare's strategy of outsourcing manufacturing activities was a major reason for its success.
- It targeted the local market and within a few years emerged as a leading regional player in the shampoo market in South India.
- Key focus in distribution and marketing, which enabled it to become Pan Indian Company.
- Innovative pricing strategy of introducing Re 0.50 trial sachet, allured many first time users of to best merits of using shampoo for hair over soaps.

FUTURE TRENDS

Some of the likely future trends of shampoo market in India are as follows:

- There will be a continued emphasis on product development and the increasing sophistication noticed in the area of merchandising.
- There will be a concentrated focus on children's hair products.
- Increased focus on shampoos with natural ingredients.
- Growing demand from the low and lower-middle-income households.
- Rising purchasing power to boost sales in rural India.
- Urban India will spearhead demand for more value-added products.

- Growing strategy of providing premium products at mass market prices.
- Traditional *kirana* stores will remain the central point of purchase of existing shampoo brands, where as modern trade (*i.e.* department stores, in-shop counters and specialist stores will push their own brands) will mostly cater to the elite.
- With low penetration Indian market offers huge growth potential.
- Battling the unorganized channel through packaging innovation.

CHAPTER 22

Fairness Creams

People across tropical countries—"historically have demonstrated a marked preference for skin lightening and glow". They are typical desired attributes among consumers in India, whereas attributes like anti-ageing or blonde hair are looked for in the West. Many Indians seem to be obsessed with white and fair skin. This obsession coupled with the increasing awareness among the Indian women towards skin protection has resulted in the spurt in the usage of cosmetics, in particular fairness cream products.

MARKET SIZE AND GROWTH

The fairness cream has reached the size of Rs 1200 crore. The skin care category is witnessing a galloping growth rate of 25 per cent p.a. Reasons for the rapid growth in demand are:

- Larger access television, and increased amount of advertising by MNCs.
- The Indian women are nowadays much more beauty consciousness and even among more folks, many of them are more keen to look presentable and attractive.

Market Penetration

Within the skin care category, penetration levels vary across different sub-categories. Fairness creams (including cold cream) and vanishing cream are the dominant sub-category accounting for nearly 50 per cent of the total market. The lotion form like moisturizing toners, astringent item till recently a small market, is the new and emerging fairness cosmetics which is slowly replacing the conventional creams.

The factors contributing to market penetration are strong advertising and promotion, expansion in distribution and introduction of a variety of superior quality cosmetics products by new international players.

In recent times many new multinational companies have entered Indian market and they have competed effectively in Specially products such as sun-protection and anti-stress cream, where a higher price has been accepted by the consumer's mind due to their specific. Superior formulation or overall quality.

MARKET SEGMENTATION

The fairness cream market is broadly divided into **premium** and mass segment. Following are their characteristics.

Premium segment

- Niche market, with small base
- Scope for increasing volumes by small pack design
- Growth mainly from upgradation

Mass segment

- Huge volume is sold because of
  - — larger base
  - — low price drives first-time users

Understanding the Consumer

Traditionally, Indian women have used home made emulsions like "*chandan*", "*haldi*" etc. for skin and face care. Fairness cream promotion in the initial phase stressed only on the cosmetic benefits and hence use of the same was restricted to special occasions. Concurrently, there was a reservation against the perceived harmful effects of the chemicals used in creams.

Changing demographics and living standards, more working women and exposure to media influence buyer behaviour, and the fairness cream market has been the fastest growing FMCG category in the past few years.

"Cosmetics" in India is a moderately high involvement product. Consumers generally try to learn what type of emulsion they can expect from a host of fairness creams like, "Cold cream", "Night cream" etc. The consumer makes his or her own judgement on the subjective features, using the manufacturer's functional labels as a guide to assess specific usage and effectiveness.

Research has revealed that Indians usually prefer local models in screen or in print advertising. Ads with foreign models are put off as they perceive those fairness creams products to be catering to the needs of western market conditions. However, surprisingly still Indians attach higher quality to imported cosmetics and facial creams.

The introduction of smaller SKUs with lower entry price has been a very successful strategy as the Indian market is still quite price sensitive and use of cosmetics is seen as a luxury.

It is also found that women who have used fairness cream for several years show a tendency to continue to use it regardless of their age. Moreover, currently it is not only women but also a significant number of men use fairness creams.

Traditionally, Indians have favoured fair skinned complexion and considered it important while judging beauty. This has been a significant cause for the success of *Fair & Lovely*, which has the largest market share among skin care products.

Demographic Effect on Consumer Behaviour

Exhibit 22.1 shows the application of Maslon's model in fairness cream market in India. There is a greater tendency to use fairness creams in the Southern India.

The frequency of application naturally decreases with age. Single working women are seen to use skin care creams more than married non-working women. Younger women are more inclined towards branded cosmetics. Urban women tend to make purchase decisions based on ingredients and company image.

EXHIBIT 22.1

Consumer Needs Hierarchy

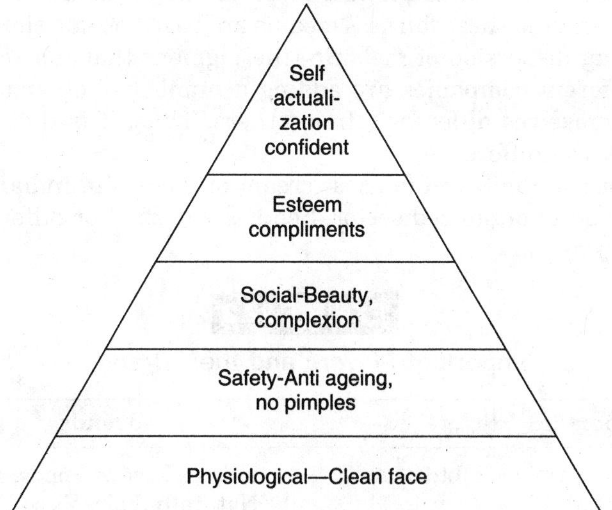

Positioning History of Major Brands

It was in 1975 when HLL launched its first fairness cream under the *Fair and Lovely* (F&L) brand. With the launch of F&L, the market, which was dominated by Ponds and Lakme, started undergoing a change.

The dominance of HLL's F&L continued till 1998 when for the first time CavinCare launched its *Fairever* cream pitted directly against F&L. *Fairever* too proved to be a big success capturing more than 6 per cent of the market share within six months of its launch.

Fair and Lovely targeted the psyche of the Indian women who wanted something more in life, and fair skin was portrayed as a means to that end. This is very clear when the various advertisements of *Fair and Lovely* are studied. They all portray the concept of changing destiny by becoming fairer. The launch of *Fairever* affected the market dominance of F&L, partly because the brand followed nearly the same strategy as F&L. Soon, it became difficult for customers to distinguish between the two brands.

FairGlow offered by Godrej was the first soap to offer the added advantage of fair skin. *Fairglow* was also launched as a cream which was not successful as it did not have any unique feature to offer. Himalaya also launched a fairness cream which became a huge success as it rode on the wave of *going herbal* fad in the cosmetics industry. It offered an *ayurvedic* solution for a fairer skin, and due to its added advantages of no side effects and suitability for all skin types, it managed to gain a loyal customer base.

Sunscreens, though technically not fairness cream, are perceived by many to be one. The properties of anti-tanning are actually misconstrued by many to mean a fairer skin. This is also borne out by the advertisements which show the skin to be glowing after the application of sunscreen.

Though most of these fairness creams are based on one simple formula of controlling dispersion of melanin (the pigment that controls the skin colour), different companies are adding a number of other additives to position themselves differently from others. Thus, it is this positioning that makes the difference.

There are a number of fairness cream producers in India both in the organized and unorganized sector. See Exhibit 22.2 for different brands of leading players.

EXHIBIT 22.2

Important Players and their Brands

Important Players	Brands
Hindustan Unilever Ltd.	Fair & Lovely, Ponds, Lakme
Emami Ltd.	Naturally Fair, Vicco Turmeric
CavinKare Ltd.	
Formerly Beauty Cosmetics Ltd.	Fairever
Paras	Freschia
Godrej Consumer Products Ltd.	Fair Glow
Procter & Gamble Ltd.	Clearasil face cream
Others	Nivea

POSITIONING OF MAJOR BRANDS

Fair and Lovely

Proposition—"*Change your destiny*" transforms a woman in ways, more than just skindeep

Target segment—Women in the age group of 20–50
Packaging—Tubes and soap bars
Market share—53%

Fairever

Proposition—A cream that will help the "*world notice you*"

Target segment—Middle class girls in their early 20s
Packaging—Tubes and sachets
Market share—12%

Fair Glow

Proposition—First fairness soap, blemish free fairness

Target segment—Mass market
Packaging—Bars
Market share—3.5%

Himalaya Fairness Cream

Proposition—Herbal fairness cream—*give ayurveda a modern image*

Target segment—College students
Packaging—Tubes
Market share—2 to 2.5%

Conclusion

Cosmetics is one of the rapidly growing segments where the players have been constantly changing formulations to suit Indian tastes and pockets. New international players are regularly bringing out superior products and evolving innovative strategies to get a foothold in the Indian market and establish a niche market for themselves.

The strong growth in the demand and success of new players in the market has prompted existing players to venture into cross categorization. Ponds first tried cross categorization when it launched its fairness cream under the same brand as its vanishing and cold cream. However it failed to make any significant impact. The fairness cream market still continues to be dominated by the brand *Fair & Lovely*.

CHAPTER 23

Wristwatches

Historically, the wristwatch was a spring-powered mechanical device for time keeping purpose. However, with time it added sophistications in terms of make and styles. By making electronic watch, it was possible to market wristwatches at very low prices. The quartz watch made use of the Piezoelectric property of quartz to keep accurate time. Moreover, by virtue of making elegant looks, quartz models became popular. In the 21st century wristwatches studded with expensive jewels and Pin lever are also able to find a market. Also, with the availability of other electronic devices, specially cell phones, consumers no longer acquire the wristwatch for its primary function. The wristwatch has today become a fashion item, especially among ladies.

CHANGING FOCUS IN WATCH BUSINESS

Traditionally, access to technology used to decide the market standing of a watch company. Consequently, Swiss, American and Japanese companies who used to possess superior technological know- how were famous for watch making. But in today's context, shear advantage in technology is not enough for a watch company. On the contrary, wristwatch makers have to keep in view various fashion aspects. This reflects the changing nature of the watch industry. For example, Tommy Hilfiger who is well known as a premium fashion cloth makers has now entered the watch market.

In India Titan followed this new trend and launched a wide variety of ornamental watches to meet the changing aspirations of the watch market. In contrast, HMT Ltd continued to make high quality mechanical watches and ultimately lost its significant hold on the upper middle class segment, who, in the changed environment, aspired for elegant designs or lower price electronic watches.

Following the WTO agreement and total withdrawal of quantity restrictions, the watch market in India witnessed the entry of low-priced, China-made electronic watches as well as many premium brands like

Rado, Omega, Longines, Tissot, Cartier, Piaget, Rolex, Baume, Mercier etc.

MARKET SIZE

The wristwatch market in India was estimated to be around 27.5 million units in 1995–96. In 2006, it reached the level of 35 million which was valued at Rs 2800 crore. The composition of different price segments is depicted below.

Price Segmentation

On price basis, the watch market is split into four segments (Exhibit 23.1) and popularly referred as low-end, mass market, mid-market, premium.

EXHIBIT 23.1

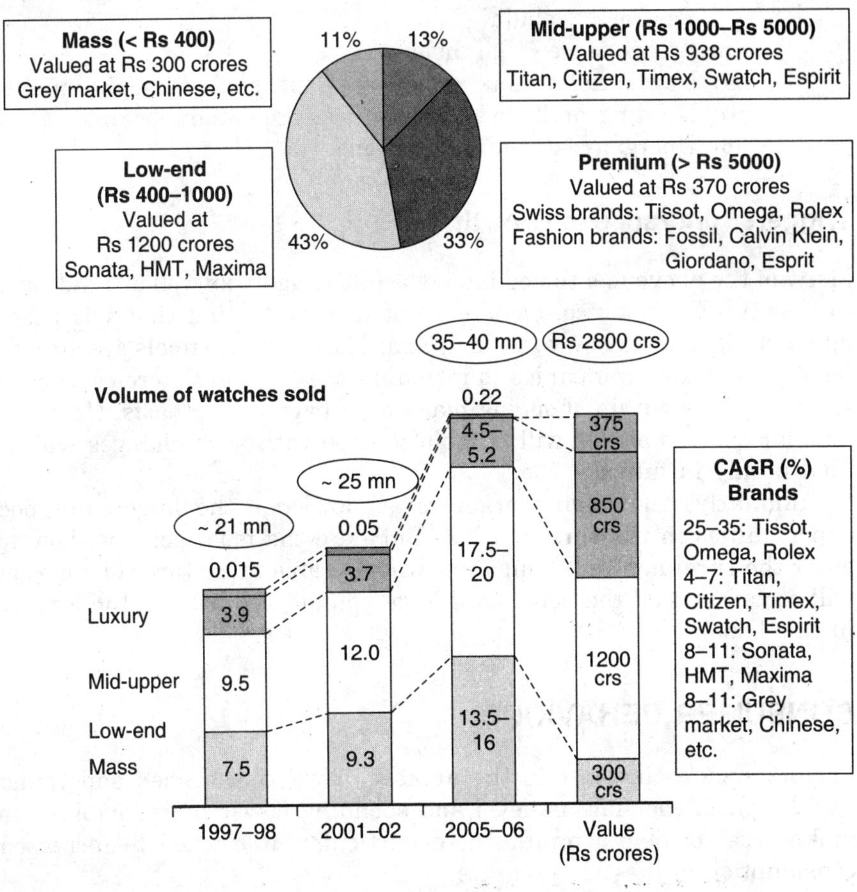

MARKET TRENDS

The wristwatch market in India is experiencing many new trends which are discussed below.

1. Shift in the structure of demand
   - (a) Volume growth driven by the lower-end
   - (b) Value growth driven by premium segment
2. Increase in the number of global as well as local players
   - (a) Significant increase in competition in all segments
     Premium end: Swiss brands
     Mid to upper end: Japanese other global brands
     Low-end: Local/regional Indian Made Foreign Quartz (IMFQ), Chinese made electronic watch
3. Emergence of distinct consumer segments
   - (a) Sharply defined consumer segments with distinct buying patterns
   - (b) More awareness of brands and about global trends among affluent urban consumers; Sub-branding strategy: Raga, Fastrack, Nebula
4. Emergence of new channels
   - (a) New retail outlets emerging (Dept. stores/shopping malls)
   - (b) Existing multi brand outlets getting smart looking
   - (c) Unorganized retail at low-end

Triggers/Hindrance to Growth

Many of the above mentioned factors act as triggers as well as hindrance to growth. For instance, emergence of new marketing channels posed major challenges as how to tackle them. These new channels are already forcing the watch companies to introduce the exclusive store concept or special outlets within shopping malls on a partnership basis. However, how far the companies will be able to cope with such changes will be known only in future.

Similarly, all watch marketers acknowledge the huge untapped opportunities in the rural market. But here the moot point is, how to enter the rural market. Companies who are able to capture this market will certainly read the benefits of huge volume and become the leaders in this business.

CONSUMER BEHAVIOUR

Factors such as increase in the number of working women and young population, higher income level and spending power have combined to make a set of new aspirations. In particular, it has led to increased consumption of lifestyle products.

Specific behavioural trends which can be seen in case of wristwatch purchase are as follows:

- In premium segment, there are watch-collectors and the watch is purchased more as a fashion.
- Of late, among urban consumers watch is purchased mostly for making a gift

Past watch buying practice: Typically urban buyers used to go to any shop dealing with wristwatch, specify a price range to the shopkeeper, and pick up the brand and/or design among those pieces shown.

Current watch buying practice: Some people wear different watches for different occasions. With the increased disposable income and changing aspirations, especially growing fashion consciousness, watch buying patterns are also changing very fast. Customers nowadays go to a shopping mall or company showrooms and ask for a particular brand/make of watch.

When does one buy a new watch? Generally, a customer buys watch either to gift somebody or for self or for a member of his family. Keeping in view this new trend, watch companies are trying to design and position different brands for different occasions and festivals like success in exam, marriage, Rakhi, Onam, Id, X'Mas, Durga Puja, Dewali etc.

How does he choose a specific model? People buy a specific model depending on various factors including looks, price, features etc. Somewhere he tries to find a personality fit. A sporty person will always go for a watch with macho, bigger dial, extra buttons kind of watch. A young executive usually prefers a sober watch so that the watch gives him a feeling of a successful, achievement oriented personality.

Exhibit 23.2 shows the prices of different models.

EXHIBIT 23.2

Price vs Looks of Leading Wristwatch Brands

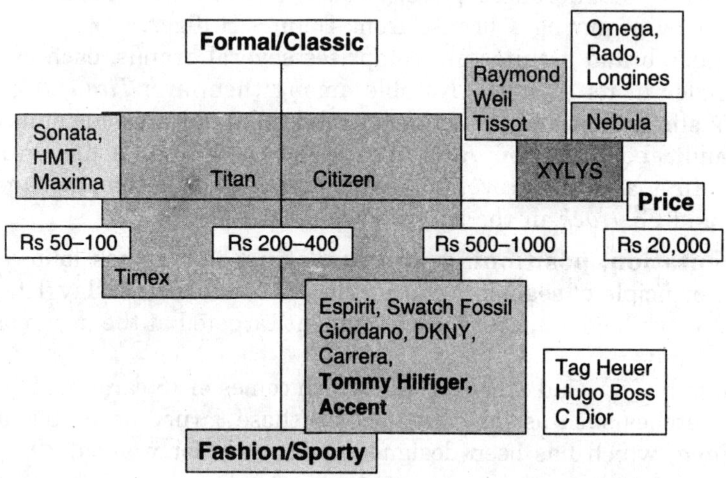

Rural and Urban Market

Watch buying in India is seen to vary among the buyers in urban and rural locations. For instance, in the rural market consumers are more concerned with the price-value propositions. In contrast, urban consumers are more interested in fulfilling their social and psychological needs and found to acquire wristwatch to meet certain life styles. Positioning of some of the existing wristwatches along price and fashion dimension is shown in Exhibit 23.2.

COMPETITIVE SCENARIO

HMT

HMT was the market leader in India before the entry of Titan. It is widely accepted that HMT failed to match the changing aspirations of the Indian watch market. It failed to bring out elegant designs or low priced electronic watch ahead of competition. Thus, HMT, who had a very robust distribution network and a strong loyal customer base, could not leverage on its strengths.

Titan

Titan Industries was established in 1984 as a joint venture between the Tata Group and the Tamil Nadu Industrial Development Corporation. Titan transformed the Indian watch market by offering wristwatches of international styles. In 1995, the company expanded into jewellery business under the brand name of Tanishq.

Leveraging on its understanding of watch market, Titan launched the *Sonata* brands which were targeted at those trying to buy stylish watches at an affordable price. It also entered the premium watch segment by acquiring a license from Tommy Hilfiger.

Titan's brand architecture comprises several brands, each of which is a leader in its segment. Notable among them are: *Titan Edge*—the world's slimmest watch; *Nebula*—in solid gold and precious stones; the Gold and Steel collection; *Raga* 9 to 5—for the woman achiever; *Flip*—India's first and only reversible watch with two movements and dial faces; and *Fastrack* in the sporty casual category.

Segmentation, positioning and targeting: Titan has followed the classic principle of segmentation in the watch market. Today Titan has a wristwatch model in every price segment targeted at the urban as well as rural buyers.

Titan has a brand called *Nebula* which comes in 18-carat gold, besides other watches such as *Insignia*, *PSI* for those turned on by technology and *Raga*, which has been designed exclusively for women.

(a) IBM Linux-Based wristwatch.

(b) Watches will offer advanced features such as automatic time adjustment based on location and access to continually updated content such as news, traffic alerts, weather reports, stock market information and sports scores, instant messaging, etc.—plus, of course, all the capabilities expected of a modern wristwatch such as chronometer, calendar, alarm, and timer functions.

(c) The Times Data Link watch utilizes a revolutionary new communications technology that literally zaps information from a personal computer (PC) to the watch.

Tapping the rural market

(d) The rural market because of its sheer size continues to show a huge amount of untapped potential for the wristwatch in India.

(e) Also, tele-density and internet penetration is on the rise. Launch of *Sonata* range of watches by Titan in the rural market has met with great response from the buyers in rural and semi-urban India.

(f) Indian rural market is displaying a market trend towards consumerism and demand for personal products like wristwatch.

Conclusion

To meet changing lifestyles wrist watch market in India has added an element of fashion in it. Also withdrawal of import restrictions has attracted a large number of foreign watch companies to enter the Indian market. Generally upper middle class people in India are reported to own more than one watch which matches one's attire and occasions. Like in apparel, new styles/models are introduced every season. Large chunky cases with colorful dials are in vogue. The grey market, selling imitations of popular styles and leading brands at half the price, continues to be a menace for the organized sector. The growing popularity of mobile phones is likely to erode the functional importance of a wrist watch.

CHAPTER 24

Footwear

India is the second largest footwear manufacturer in the world, next only to China. Asia and CIS countries are used as an outsourced manufacturing location to take the advantage of lower labour costs compound to developed countries. India is especially strong in the men's footwear segment though worldwide ladies footwear is produced more in number. Indian footwear exporters have recently been focusing on innovative design, state-of-the-art production technology. **In the global market of $160 billion,** leading companies are Nike, Adidas-Salomon, Reebok and Asics.

DOMESTIC MARKET

Exhibit 24.1 below shows the growth of volume of shoes during 2000–04. The Indian market for footwear crossed Rs 100 billion ($2.4 billion) in 2004. In terms of volume, domestic consumption of footwear was approximately 1.8 billion pairs in 2004. Out of these, men's footwear was half of the total market, women's constituted 30 per cent and kids' footwear making up for the remainder. The domestic market is concentrated mainly in the top 20 cities in the country where consumption was 100 million pairs in 2004.

EXHIBIT 24.1

India Footwear Market Volume: $ billion, 2000–2004

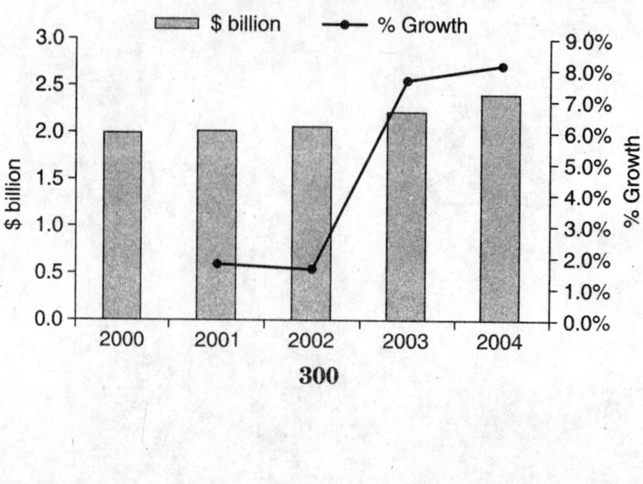

Footwear manufacturing has grown mainly around the traditional leather processing centres such as Chennai, Ranipet and Ambur in Tamil Nadu, Kanpur and Agra in Uttar Pradesh, Jalandhar in Punjab, Kolkata, Mumbai and Delhi.

Market growth: During the period of 2000–04 Indian footwear market grew by 4.8 per cent in value terms. Exhibit 24.2 shows the year-wise growth picture.

EXHIBIT 24.2

India Footwear Market Volume: Pairs billion, 2000–2004

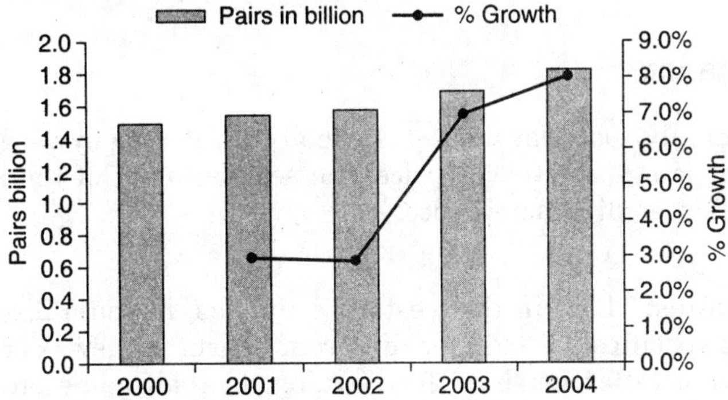

Market volume: During the same period, the Indian footwear market grew by 8 per cent to reach a volume of 1.8 billion pairs. The compound annual growth rate of the market was 5.2 per cent. Exhibit 24.3 projection of market value and volume in 2009.

EXHIBIT 24.3

Indian Footwear Market: Projection for 2009

Market value forecast
In 2009, the market is forecast to *achieve* a value of $3.2 billion, an increase of 31.5% since 2004.

Market volume forecast
In 2009, the market is forecast to *reach* a volume of 2.3 billion pairs, an increase of 29% since 2004.

TRIGGERS TO GROWTH

Prior to the 1990s the size of the domestic market was small. At that time, leading shoe companies were targeting at the 30 million population for their medium-priced shoes or catering to the affluent segment of 2 million population for limited variety of premium shoes.

In the post-liberalisation era, the purchasing power of the Indian middle class population has increased significantly. This has created market opportunities for the premium priced footwear in the price range of Rs 700–1200. Some footwear manufacturers came up with range of sports shoes, like Phoenix's *Power* range, Liberty's *Force 10* and *Geosport*, Action. However, the super premium segment remained in the hands of MNCs who entered the Indian market in the mid-nineties.

Recent massive growth of footwear business in India is attributed to factors like modernisation of the retail outlets, heavy advertising or extensive promotion offered by new players and entry of MNCs. All these generated awareness about branded footwear and made even urban middle-income consumers to look for better in quality shoes.

Segmentation

Internationally, footwear market is usually segmented by usage. Though in India it is still viewed by price, the segmentation of the market by usage is fast goining acceptance.

1. **By usage**

Sports shoes: Like in the western countries, in India also footwear is getting specifically made for different sports in view. For instance, one can find different shoes for running, football game etc. Usually, customers here are found to be loyal, and as of now Adidas, Reebok, Nike, etc. are catering to this small size, but a growing segment of the market.

Party wear shoes: Brands like *Gucci, Red Tape* etc. are specially highlighting on the unique occasions of wearing their footwear. For this class of buyers, the prime consideration is on the looks and decsion of the footwear. Like the wristwatch, here the target customers are persuaded to wear a pair of shoes matching with their own personality. In future, it is likely to have more number of variety in this particular segment.

Professional shoes: Consumers here tend to show strong preference to a particular make or brand and comfort is of primary importance to them. Hence, there is a high amount of loyal customers here.

Casual shoes: As the name suggests, slippers come under this category. Here the ease of wear is often the main driving factor. **Slippers are available for as little as Rs 40 a pair and a maximum of Rs 250 a pair, chiefly made from PVC, rubber or canvas.**

2. **By price**

Super premium segment: This segment includes the expensive brands offering superior quality or design. Usually, the target customers for this segment are upper class people who are willing to pay for quality. Brands like *Gucci* and *Red Tape* cater to this segment who seem to emphasise its exclusivity.

Aspirational premium: This segment typically consists of buyers who generally buy shoes prior to some festivals and particular occasions. Companies like Reebok, Nike etc. are trying to get entry into this segment of the market.

Generally, they have developed a taste for design and looks. The aspiration of possessing a pair of good looking shoes motivates these people. Thus, this premium segment tries to offer a trendy style, both in shoes and sandals.

A few years back, international shoe companies used to release only their basic models of footwear products in India. But of late, they have found growing popularity even for premium quality. India has assumed an important market for them.

Value conscious: This segment includes those buyers who do not have much fascination to possess elegant designs or well-known brand of shoes. They are generally concerned with comfort and looks of the footwear. They typically buy footwear marketed by Bata, Liberty etc.

Popular segment: This segment consists of lower strata of the Indian market who buy footwear as and when it becomes necessary and on festive occasions. In India the size of the popular segment is fairly large. This segment primarily looks for the basic functionality of the footwear and is attracted by promotion offers. Despite being a huge segment, it is still grossly a commodity type market where price is the prime focus. This way most of the unbranded or local made footwear are served to the popular segment.

CONSUMER PREFERENCE

Footwear is one of those personal use items which connote different meanings such as necessity, reliability, luxury, style, comfort etc. for different people.

Consumer Choice Criterion

Factors which help in enhancing the sales of footwear are as follows:

- **Quality:** Traditionally, the majority of the market preferred a reasonable priced footwear. Today, brand like Red Tape is also sold in India to those who acquire such higher priced shoes on account of it being exclusive. This trend indicates that some customers in India have become aware of superior quality in footwear. So, they are buying many trendy styles.
- **Durability:** Shoes are generally durable. But the level of durability desirable depends on specific usage. The sportspersons

and athletic type generally sacrifice stylish accessories, etc. to gain more strength. Durability is the major concern of buyers from the middle income segment.

- **Variety:** At present footwear is made out of all kinds of materials, colours, shapes, sizes. They are used for formal, casual, rugged, running, cycling, trekking purpose. In general, there are numerous options or variety offered to meet specific taste of different nature of customers.
- **Styles:** Customers typically want their shoes to look good. With the increasing westernisation, people are willing to pay more for the looks style and design of a shoe.

With time numerous styles have emerged in the footwear. For examples,

Style	Examples	Brief Description
Boot		Any footwear extending above the ankle. There are numerous designs and types for a variety of uses and made from a number of materials.
Clog		A thick soled wooden shoe sometimes with leather upper.
Lace Up		Any low cut shoe fastened by lacings.
Moccasin		Originally it described a simple one-piece hide, wrapped round the foot and held on with rawhide thongs.
Mule		A backless shoe or slipper with or without a heel.
Sandal		Originally a slab of leather sole attached to the foot by thongs. Today any open shoe whose upper consists of any decorative or functional arrangement of straps. A sandal can be foot low to knee high, or with any heel height, designed for simple utility or casual wear or as a fashion shoe.

(Contd.)...

Style	Examples	Brief Description
Monks		Shoes with a cross over section to fasten the quarters with a side buckle.
Pumps		Heeled shoes with low cut fronts and usually no fastening.

- **Matching footwear pairs:** People who can afford generally keep multiple pairs of footwear of different styles to go with different occasions and sometimes, even dresses, e.g. office shoes and casual shoes are different. Kids have different pairs going with their different dress colours. This western trend has been slowly creeping into the Indian market.
- **Brand name:** Footwear brands have always presented a distinct image, a connection, a trust. Nike is 'Just Do It'—for the generation that likes to do things their own way. They also bank on trendy looks. Woodland is 'leather that weathers'. They are rugged, fit for even a rough usage. Bata is traditional, reasonable and Indian.

Brands are a big attraction today. People want a brand to gain a feeling of recognition. Thus, they associate brands more with style and looks than quality alone.

- **Buying experience:** A big change is occurring in the area of shopping experience, thanks to the emergence of modern retail shops. Traditionally in India, a salesman used to take our footwear size and then suggest specific models of their choice. Today, shoes are displayed on racks in the showrooms and consumers try out their own style. Thus, with the advent of modern trade and awareness of footwear today customers choose their footwear on their own, possibly with minor interference from the salesperson.

MARKET TRENDS

Emergence of New Footwear Companies

In the good old days the name of Bata was synonymous with the Indian footwear market. However, Bata no longer commands such a position. Of late, many new footwear companies gained entry due to their lower price, attractive designs and easy availability. Such footwear caters mainly to the entry level products. They are sold through exclusive showrooms as well as small retail.

Improved Retailing Boosts Growth

As mentioned above, Indian footwear was traditionally synonymous with Bata. It was perceived to be an annual ritual-purchase activity. Generally for rich buyers footwear was a status symbol. As more multinational companies entered the Indian market, footwear retailing was given a major facelift in terms of formats and ambience. In general, footwear stores have become more fashionable places.

In the face of increasing competition from MNCs, erstwhile footwear companies are making efforts to tap the emerging opportunity. For instance, domestic players like Bata and Liberty have also started transforming their retail formats. These companies are trying to position themselves on lifestyle and offering contemporary designs of footwear.

Variety of Casual, Younger Styles

The entry of a host of foreign brands like *Drish*, *Lotto*, *Lotus Bawa*, *Now*, *Oakridge*, *Royal Elastic*, *Sketchers*, *Teenage*, *Teva*, *Timberland*, *Vans*, *Red Tape Allen Cooper*, *Franco Leone*, *Gucci*, *Guess*, *Lee Cooper* etc. has virtually changed the spectrum of fashionable as well as casual styles in footwear. So, every footwear company is making efforts to regularly upgrade their choice of brands to reflect new directions in fashion.

Opportunity in Women's and Kids' Segment

Traditionally, footwear in India remained focused mainly on men. This pattern naturally offered a huge opportunity in the ladies and kids footwear segment. With the rise in the number of working women in urban India who are getting more fashion-conscious, the market for ladies and children's footwear emerged. In fact, many international players entered the Indian market to tap these new opportunities.

International Sportswear Brands

With the entry of specialty sportswear retailers such as Royal Sporting House, Sports, Station and Planet Sports, the organised retailing scenario in the country is undergoing further transformation. For instance, Royal Sporting House has already opened over 40 stores in India, many of which are placed in prime locations within shopping malls. Innovative promotion campaigns, world class merchandising and their elegant looking stores allured rich consumers to go for a pair of sports shoes.

Creation of Exclusive Showroom

In footwear business companies are trying to increase their presence by opening exclusive retail outlets. This strategy was specially adopted to overcome the poor quality ambience of many multi-brand footwear stores, who were typically small, proprietary concerns, with poor displays and catering to a price sensitive consumer base. To boost sales, footwear companies took this bold step to set up their own exclusive retail chains using the franchise route.

Discount Stores and Emergence of Shopping Malls

Of late, many footwear companies have opened discount stores in the urban locations. Consumers are attracted to these retail outlets to avail of the discounted prices and promotion deals.

With shopping malls cropping up across the length and breadth of the country, footwear retailers will enhance their visibility and presence either through exclusive showrooms in malls or as shop-in-shop arrangements with department stores that serve as anchor tenants in these malls.

With the growth of organised retail, especially emergence of modern distribution format, the composition of retail sales of footwear has been undergoing massive change. See Exhibit 24.4 below to observe the rapid growth of speciality showrooms during 1998–2006 and consequent drop in the multi-brand footwear brands.

EXHIBIT 24.4

Retail Sales of Footwear by Distribution Format

	(% value)		
	1998	2003	2006
Speciality showrooms	45.0	55.0	58.0
Multi-brand footwear outlets	50.0	35.0	25.0
Departmental stores	0.0	5.0	7.0
Small rural outlets	5.0	5.0	10.0
Total	**100.0**	**100.0**	**100.0**

COMPETITIVE SCENARIO

Key players in the Indian market as on 2006 is shown in Exhibit 24.5 below.

EXHIBIT 24.5

Competition in Footwear Market in India

Company	Presence as on March 2006
Loft	2 cities
Regal Shoes	7 cities

(Contd.)...

Exhibit 24.5: Competition in Footwear Market in India *(Contd.)*

Company	Presence as on March 2006
Planet Sports	8 cities
Nike	25 cities
Metro	31 cities
Reebok India Ltd	52 cities
Liberty	225 cities
Woodland	All major cities
Royal Sporting House	All major cities
M & B Footwear	All major cities
Adidas	All over India
Action	All over India
Bata	All over India
Khadims	East & South of India
Shree Leather	West Bengal, Orissa, Bihar

MARKETING STRATEGIES OF MAJOR PLAYERS

Bata India Ltd

Bata India Ltd a subsidiary of the Canadian footwear giant, is engaged in the manufacture and retail of all types of footwear. It is India's largest footwear company, selling about 60 million pairs of shoes annually. Bata has five manufacturing units.

Bata makes all types of footwear, such as formal shoes, sandals and sports shoes. Historically, Bata had a very loyal customer base in India. However, the company failed to keep in tune with the changing aspirations of the market. Consequently, many erstwhile customers switched over to other companies because of their superior design, lower price and lifestyle appeal. Bata is trying to reposition itself as a shoemaker for the middle-income people in India.

As a step towards rejuvenating the company, Bata launched many international styles and design to project a trendy and contemporary image to the Indian consumers. It is bringing out more number of lifestyle brands with emphasis on service and quality.

The company has revamped its marketing operations. Bata India has introduced the concepts Flagship, City, Family and Bazaar stores that cater to different segments of the market and to capture the retail boom prevailing in the country.

Bata operates its own retail network of over 1,100 retail stores spread across the country. These outlets are serviced through distribution centres spread out geographically and each catering to a particular region. Bata is trying to take full advantage of its vast retail network to compete with leading global brands like Adidas, Reebok and Nike as well as upcoming regional players.

Bata is trying to increase its volume of business in semi-urban markets in India. As a part of its Market Extension Programme, Bata has created authorised dealers who are exclusively marketing Bata made footwear.

The company is consistently trying to leverage on its established brand names like *Mocassino*, *Super Stride*, *Quo Vadis*, *Jubliee* etc., at the same time creating a niche for its new brands such as *Azaleia*, *Toppers*, *Bubblegummers*, *Weinbrenner* and *Power International*. It has been focusing on specialty products to have better margins. It has been continuously introducing new designs in shoes for men, ladies and children.

Bata was recognised as a household name in India and used to command a high reputation for durability and value for money in its target market. Bata has been trying to regain its old glory or leadership across the country.

Woodland

Launched in 1992–93, Woodland carved a niche for itself in Indian footwear market.

The logo of Woodland projected a status symbol. Woodland targets the upmarket segment and is positioning itself as a "Rugged high quality premium casual shoe". Woodland shoes are today known as a rugged and all-terrain use, by its catchy and tempting ads showing people wearing Woodland shoes for various outdoor activities, which captured the imagination of Indian youth. Woodland delivered its promise on quality which ensured that the company is perceived as a good value for money.

Liberty Shoes Ltd

Liberty Shoes Ltd started operations way back in the early 1950s when it was a small manufacturer-cum-marketer in Northern India. In the 1970s, the company began exporting and until 1983, Liberty was focussed on the export market only.

Today, Liberty is one of the leading shoe companies in the country. It was first to introduce polyurethane soles in India in 1983. At that time, Liberty was a premium brand. However, Liberty has currently re-positioned as a mid-price brand and is often seen as a close competitor of Bata.

Liberty is trying to position itself as a contemporary footwear company. *Force* 10 is its casual brand, while *Fortune* and *Windsor* are its men's formal shoe brands. *Senorita* and *Tip Top* are for ladies. *Gliders* is its largest selling brand by volume, which is an umbrella brand serving children, women and men.

Reebok International Ltd

Reebok International Ltd is headquartered in Canton, Massachusetts USA. It specializes in the design, marketing and distribution of sports and fitness products, including footwear, apparel and accessories.

Reebok entered India through a joint venture with the Phoenix Group in 1995. It is now a wholly-owned subsidiary of Reebok International. It mainly targets at young adult with footwear, sports clothing and other fitness products. Reebok had captured 47 per cent of the premium sports shoe market in India. It has 85 exclusive outlets and markets its product through another 3,000 multi-brand outlets.

In the initial years when Reebok was launched, its footwear products were primarily for the male consumers. It was trying to create a niche among consumers font of sports and fitness. Subsequently, Reebok started attracting women through its range of ladies' footwear. Reebok stores introduced a women's collection. It created a small corner with 20–30 SKUs in apparel and shoes. Within short time, its women's portfolio achieved 15 per cent of the total business.

In 2004, Reebok took a renewed look at women's footwear market. It started promoting the category by opening women's-only stores that would meet the special needs of Indian women. The décor and style of these stores is completely different, sporting a toned-down image. The promotions in the store are laid out keeping in the mind the buying behaviour of women segment of customers. For instance, Reebok has a "Gang up for rewards" promotion for women shopping in groups, when they realised that women do not shop alone!

General strategy: With India not having a sports culture or fitness culture in the mass-market, Reebok had to invest in marketing to develop a fitness culture and currently caters mainly to upper-income urban Indians. Casual apparel, which is now very popular, is also bringing customers to Reebok stores. The company relied heavily on cricket personalities as its prime brand ambassadors.

Reebok India appointed cricketers, like Irfan Pathan, Harbhajan Singh, Rahul Dravid, Yuvraj Singh, as its brand ambassadors, since youths identify cricketers as fitness icons.

Competitive positioning: Reebok is in direct competition with Nike and Adidas in India in sports shoes. Reebok uses its "Wear the Vector. Outperform" marketing campaign in India.

NIKE Inc.

Nike is the largest seller of athletic footwear and athletic apparel in the world. The company is primarily engaged in the design, development, and worldwide marketing of footwear, apparel, equipment, and accessory products. They have now presence in 25 big cities in India.

FUTURE TRENDS

Sports footwear and canvas casual footwear are gradually gaining acceptance in India. The market has also seen intensive price competition from supermarkets and other non-footwear specialists that can offer more value for money footwear, and it is anticipated that their share of the footwear market will increase in the future.

Competition from Non-Specialist Retailers

As experienced in countries like UK, in future footwear companies will face increasing competition from "non-specialist" firms, such as apparel companies who are likely to diversify into footwear and discount hypermarkets or mega retail chains such as Big Bazaar and Vishal Mega Mart etc. These non-specialist retailers are likely to grow their market shares by increasing range of products offered and shopping space allocated to footwear. The footwear companies would then have to respond to this threat by continuing to invest in their efforts to build brands, store environments and product differentiation in order to remain competitive.

CHAPTER 25

Mobile Phones

The mobile phone industry in India has been in a state of rapid progress in the recent years due to the changing dynamics of the market in India. The growth of cell phone market is directly related to the liberal policies adopted in the telecom sector and the price reduction strategy adopted by cellular phone service providers. The liberalization of the telecom sector has changed the face of the industry so much that mobile connection has today penetrated into all walks of people in India. However, it may be relevent to bear in mind that the first mobile service was launched in India in 1996 and since then, the subscriber base has reached 100 million in April 2006. (see Exhibit 25.1 to observe the spectacular growth noticed since 2002 for mobile phone business.

EXHIBIT 25.1

Growth in Mobile Phone Subscribers

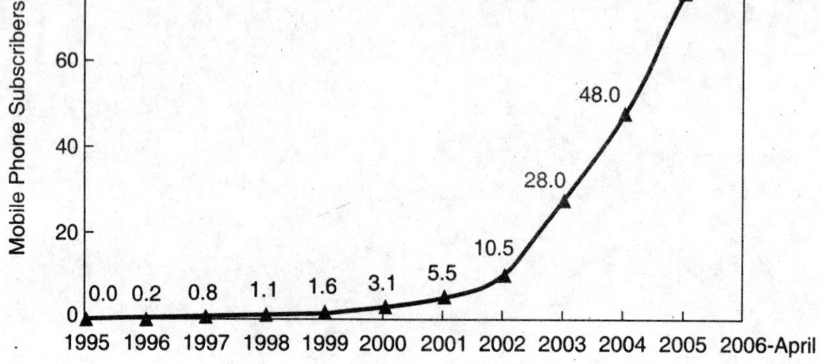

KEY GROWTH DRIVERS

- Ease of regulation, reduction in import duty and in general, supportive government policies helped the cell phone business to achieve ten-fold growth.
- Low cost of cell phone service and handset has spurred the growth at the entry level.
- Fall in cost of mobile phone tariffs and extensive promotion offers allured customers to have personal cell phones.
- Prepaid services created a market environment for the industry to take off—Prepaid dominates postpaid by 3:1 ratio, suiting lifestyle of an average subscriber who is able to maintain a cell phone with an upper limit on her/his telephone bill.
- High disposable income, high level of awareness, compatibility with technology flourishing in the high-end segment regrade and acquire latest model of cell phones.
- Lower cost of mobile telephone tariff and reduced price of cell phone set played important roles in spurring growth of cell phone in India.

Current Scenario

- Initially the growth in mobile phone market was spurred by growth in demand from metropolitan cities, A and B circles.
- India's mobile phone subscriber base grew at a rate of 82.2 per cent. Subscriber base went up from 3 lakh in 1999 to 106 million in June, 06).
- The mobile handset market which was laregely dominated by the grey market till 2003, is now served mostly by large MNCs.
- India's mobile penetration offers huge opportunity for growth.
- Apart from convenience to carry and versatility, as the cost of installing new fixed lines is roughly three times the price of installing a mobile line, people nationally prefer to acquire mobile phone connection.
- There has been an increase in teledensity in all the telecom circles in the mobile segment (Against the world average of 30, India is 13.95 by the end of June 2006).
- In the fixed line segment, teledensity has witnessed a decline in most of the circles.
- Average ARPU in the Indian industry is close to $10.
- Features like integrated digital camera, FM radio and speaker phones are offered at the Price of Rs 5000–8000.
- Upgradation replacement demand is a major driver in metro and class A cities. FM radio, speaker phone, MMS and integrated digital cameras are driving upgradations.
- Mobile music has become a major value-added service and phones with speakers, FM radio and music phones are rapidly becoming popular.

- Leading manufacturers are beginning to set up their handset manufacturing base in India and a few low-priced 'Made in India' models are already in the market.
- The GSM market is seeing increasing bundling between operators and handset vendors.
- Battle for market share is slowly shifting from a price-based front to superior quality where style design and high-end features are the differentiators.
- With the introduction of 3G services, the next wave in mobile upgradation is expected to come from WiFi, bluetooth, high speed internet access and email functionality.

SEGMENTATION

The mobile cell handset market can be segmented by price and user into the following categories:

- **Low end** (<Rs 3500)—Rural India, low stratum of the urban market.
- **Popular** (Rs 3500 to 5000)—(Rs 5000 to 10000)—Urban middle class, specially students, working people, young housewives.
- **Luxury** (Rs 10000 to 25000)—Executives, celebrities, trend conscious people.
- **Super premium or Aspirational** (Rs >25000)—Tech freaks, convergence devices.

By Users and their Expectations

- **Rural or low income urban**—Low price and basic features, larger in size, easy to hold ad operate, and some resale value.
- **Students**—Popular or mid priced sets with some special features. Preferably sleek and small.
- **Young housewives**—Easy to hold and operate. Choice of colours and shapes.
- **Working people**—Special features are must. Fashionable sets are preferred. Sleek design and small size is preferred.
- **Executives**—The features and looks should be fashionable. Newly launched mobile with high brand value.

By Product Benefits

- **Basic**—minimum features of a phone plus SMS, alarm and date facility.
- **Basic multimedia phones**—MMS, FM radio, speakers, polyphonic ring tones and VGA digital cameras.

- **High end multimedia phones**—High resolution cameras, music players, Bluetooth, tri-band and high resolution games.

EXHIBIT 25.2

Market Segmentation

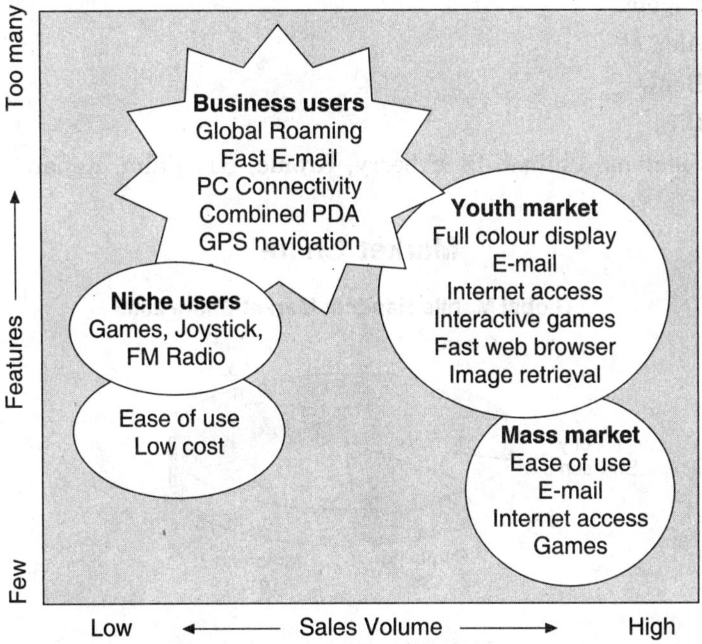

CHOICE CRITERION

- Make/Company name
- Brand image
- Distribution coverage
- After-sales service
- Product range
- Technology
- Battery type
- Product quality—judged by size, weight and aesthetics
- Price
- Resale value/Exchange scheme

MAJOR PLAYERS

As on December 2006, the following companies are already operating or expressed interest to be in the Indian market for mobile handsets.

- Nokia
- Samsung
- Motorola
- LG
- Sony Ericson
- Sagem
- Alcatel
- BenQ
- Bird
- Siemens, Philips, Blackberry, Krome, HP, Palm, Kejian

Market Share

Global Mobile Handset Market Share 2005

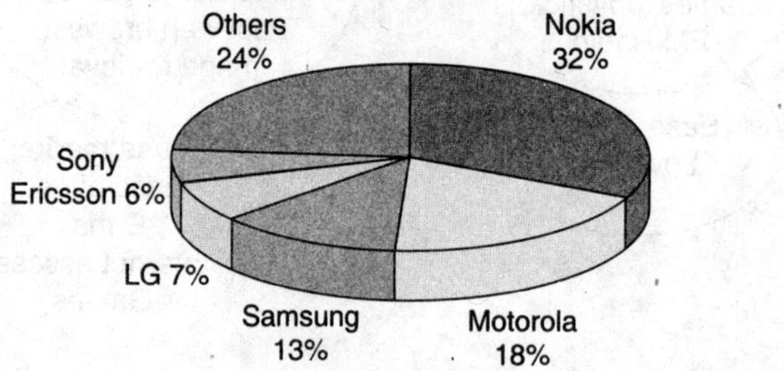

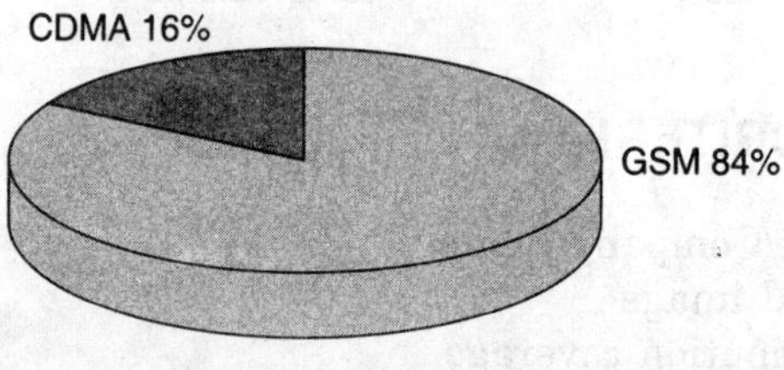

Indian Mobile Handset Market Share 2005

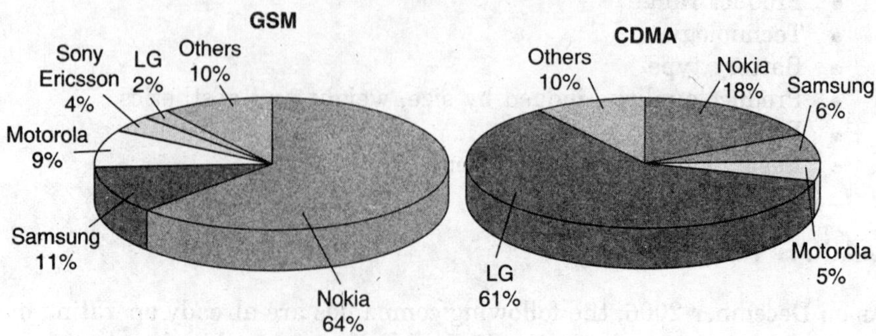

MARKETING STRATEGY ADOPTED

Nokia

A world leader in mobile communications, Nokia has established itself as the dominant or most used mobile telephone set in India by virtue of its vast experience, innovation, and user-friendliness.

Marketing strategies

- Leading edge products; leading technology and design
- Best quality products; best care network
- Variety of choice to meet every price segment
- Good distribution network
- Retail execution
- Strong leadership across major segments
- Co-branding
- Localized manufacturing
  - — Constituted by Nokia manufacturing unit and co-located vendor/supplier units
- Retailing
  - — Nokia priority dealers
  - — Largest organized chain amongst handset manufacturers
  - — Presence across 255+ towns
  - — Superior buying experience to consumers
- Nokia concept store
  - — Destination for evolved replacement consumer
- Nokia VAN operations
  - — A special purpose van—"Showroom on Wheels" operational across the country
  - — Consistent brand experience and full range of products including live demonstration

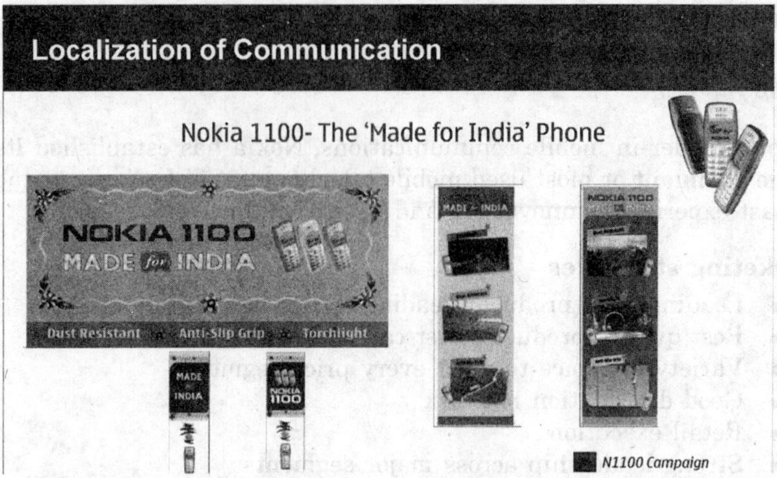

- Glocalization—Maintaining the brand logo, the key message and the underlying philosophy and localizing the brand elements to offer customers an authentic local feel.
- Category creation—Creating and riding growth in mobile convergence
  - — Smart phones
  - — Mobile imaging
  - — Mobile gaming

Distribution

- Strong relationship with channel partners
- Leading player in networks with business relationship with all leading GSM operators
- Nokia care—Delighting the customers
  - — Widest care network
- Presence across 408 cities

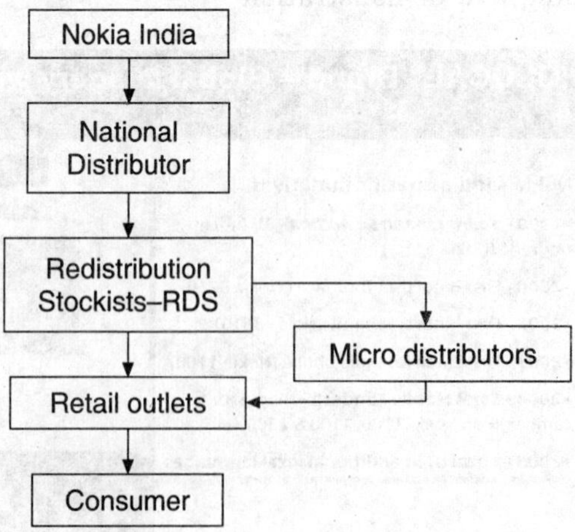

- 560 Nokia care centres with 25 hi-tech facilities
  — 18 × 7 access to Nokia care line
- From 600 + cities with single number
- Multilingual support—6 languages.

The network services

- Widest customers care network
- 408 cities, 560 centres
- 18 × 7 access
- From 600 + cities
- Multilingual support

Strategic tie-up with Bharti Airtel: Bharti Airtel Limited has awarded Nokia an estimated USD 400 million contract to expand its managed GSM/GPRS/EDGE networks in eight Airtel circles and deploy a pan-Indian WAP solution across its networks.

As per the three-year contract, Nokia will provide managed services and expand Airtel networks to cover all towns and cities in the eight telecom circles of Mumbai, Maharashtra and Goa, Gujarat, Bihar (including Jharkhand), Orissa, Kolkata, West Bengal and Madhya Pradesh (including Chhattisgarh). The network monitoring operations will be carried out from Nokia's state-of-the-art Global Networks Solutions Centre in Chennai.

Nokia will deploy the latest radio and core network equipment including Nokia MSC Server System (MSS) mobile softswitch, Nokia Flexi WCDMA and ultrasite base stations, and provide services based on Bharti's capacity requirements, delivering a cost-efficient rollout of on-demand capacity. The contract also has stringent service level agreements and performance metrics for both parties, which are designed to provide consistently high-quality services to subscribers and continuously enhance the user experience.

Samsung

Samsung India is the hub of Samsung's South West Asia Regional operations. The South West Asia Regional Headquarters looks after the Samsung business in Nepal, Sri Lanka, Bangladesh, Maldives and Bhutan, besides India. Samsung India, which commenced its operations in India in December 1995, today enjoys a sales turnover of over US $ 1 billion in just a decade of operations in the country.

- Strategy of selling phones in the medium and high-end segments
- Price range is from Rs 8000–22,000
- Focus on the replacement market, offers phones with advanced features and functionalities
- Poor performance has led to focusing on low-end models

Samsung itself will launch a GSM handset by the middle of 2007 that will integrate Wimax support.

Motorola

Motorola is known around the world for innovation and leadership in wireless and broadband communications inspired by its vision of seamless mobility, Motorola is trying to project itself as a user friendly mobile phone instrument manufacturer. They are highlighting this by designing and delivering "must have" products, "must do" experiences and powerful networks—along with a full complement of support services. Motorola has the following distinction:

- Earliest entrant into the Indian market
- Straddles every price segment—including the sub 2000 with the C 115
- Has wide reach through distributors and initially it had tied up with Airtel telephone.

FUTURE TRENDS

- Mobile phone market in India is projected to hit 250 million by the end of 2008 and 500 million subscribers by 2010.
- Replacement market is expected to increase to 25–30 per cent on account of faster replacement (further induced by exchange scheme).
- In rural markets, the price (cheap and affordable) handsets (new or used) is more important than the brand. Manufacturers should pay attention to bringing the cost down by building voice-only handsets to meet such specific needs of the market.
- Mobile infotainment, gaming and email are going to be in demand.
- Portability (which lets you keep your number if you switch mobile operators) of old cell phone number.
- Increasing preference for colour and camera phones.
- Convergence will be the key word.

CHAPTER 26

Digital Cameras

With the changing lifestyle of the people and increase in the standard of living, the economic value of time has increased exponentially. This has increased the importance of capturing of the moments of life and storing them for appreciation in the leisure time. The digital form of camera makes this sharing of the photographs very easy. Various external factors, specially the price and technological churn in the camera industry, are today bringing about a sea change in the camera market.

CLASSIFICATION OF CAMERAS

On the basis of application technology, cameras can be classified[1] as

- **Conventional cameras:** These use photographic film to record images.
- **Digital cameras:** A digital camera is an electronic device used to capture and store photographs electronically instead of using photographic film like conventional cameras.
- **Mobile phones with cameras:** These are digital cameras that come embedded in some models of mobile phones. It is important to consider this as a separate category since this is the fastest growing camera category in the world today.

MARKET ANALYSIS

Exhibit 26.1 gives an overview of different types of cameras. The demand for digital cameras picked up in India because of rapidly expanding internet population and increasingly large size of young computer literate consumers.

[1]The Annexure provides a more finer classification of different existing camera models.

EXHIBIT 26.1

Comparative Picture of Different Types of Cameras

Parameter	Conventional	Digital	Camera phones
Cost of ownership	Medium	Low-High	Low-Medium
Perceived complexity	Depends upon the model snake	Simple to sophisticated	Simple
Image quality	Medium	High	Low

Size of the Market

In 2003, the market for digital cameras in India amounted to 1 lakh units as against 30 lakh units of conventional cameras. The digital camera market in India will touch around Rs 600 crore by 2008 from Rs 100 crore in 2003. Around 10 lakh digital cameras (excluding camera phones) are expected to be sold by 2008.

CUSTOMER PROFILE

Personal segment: Huge number of urban based consumers

Institutional market: 100,000 photo studios, 750 media houses and 100,000 event and wedding photographers.

Personal Segment

Cameras are very versatile instrument. Historically, it found applications with professionals such as astronomers, physicists, biologists, surveillance agencies, media professionals, documentation companies, and medical imaging experts. But ever since the discovery of low priced, user friendly models, cameras became a personal use item for all. Broadly speaking, in today's context, a typical camera user could be any individual who buys a camera to pursue his hobby, keeping the memories of a tour with family or in general, to capture the invaluable moments of one's life.

In general, camera users can be divided into two categories.

Amateurs: This includes the hobbyist, artists and the individuals who pursue photography for non-commercial purpose. It also includes people who dabble in photography as a social activity, and to increase and preserve social and familial ties, by capturing treasured moments in time to posterity.

Professionals: This includes all the individuals and organizations that make commercial use of photography, and academics and professionals who use photography as part of their scientific research as well as commercial purpose.

Variety of Needs

Depending on the type of the user, the camera satisfies different consumer needs. The basic elements of importance are depicted in Exhibit 26.2 below in the form of a triangle. It shows that three important basic factors are utility, technology and service. The exact weightage attached to each factor depends on the type of the user.

EXHIBIT 26.2

The Triangle of Contentment

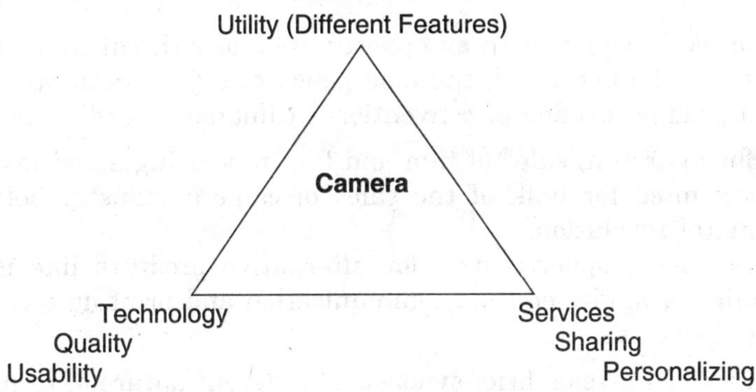

BENEFIT MAPPING

Refer to Exhibit 26.3 to have an idea of different functional benefits desired. The *amateur, professional* classification enables us to better map the functional features that a camera provides to the benefits derived by the user.

EXHIBIT 26.3

Functional Benefits Map

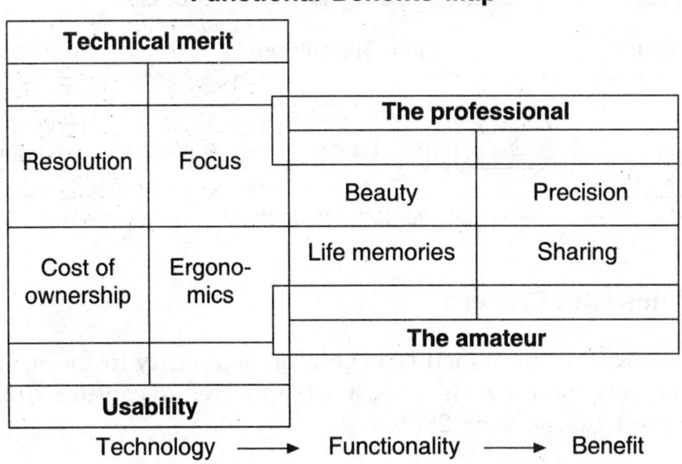

Here is a brief comparison of the different types of cameras, from the point of view of the user.

ADVENT OF NEW TECHNOLOGY

There are two concurrent revolutions happening in the camera industry. They are, firstly, the increasing presence of digital cameras and secondly, of camera phones.

Digital Cameras

Changing technology is both an opportunity and a threat to the camera industry. On the one hand, the emergence of digital cameras and the slow and gradual decline of conventional cameras is leading to

- Sharp drop in sales of film and film processing activities, which accounted for bulk of the sales of camera industry before the digital revolution.
- Increasing opportunities for alternative products like memory chips, graphics editors, communication and printing technology, and so forth.

Exhibit 26.4 gives a brief synopsis of different nature of technology.

EXHIBIT 26.4

Disruptive Technology

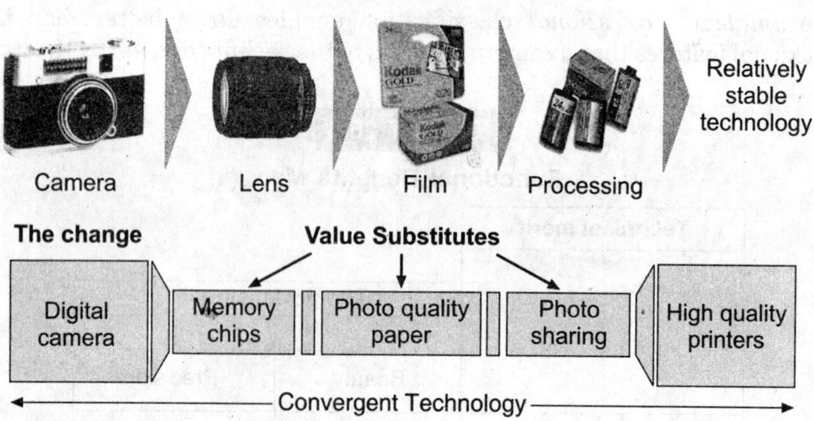

Cell Phones with Camera

Cell phones with camera facility is gaining popularity in India. In terms of volumes, cell phones with camera are projected to capture 70 per cent of the market by the year 2009.

For every one sale of a digital camera, there are four camera phones bought in the world. Consumers buy digital cameras for the express purpose of clicking photos. This is not necessarily the case with camera phones. Generally camera phones serve one of the following:

- An extra facility offered but not always sought for
- A benefit used for fashion or showmanship rather than taking pictures
- A benefit sought out, paid for, but not used for reasons of usability difficulties
- A benefit not used for because of poor photo quality

The strange relationship between camera phones and digital cameras: As mentioned earlier, the number of camera phones is far more than the number of digital cameras, yet the pictures seem to be clicked predominantly on digital cameras.

- Camera phones on an average are less than 1 mega pixel resolution (i.e. they are VGA cameras).
- This makes them comparatively affordable.
- First time users buy camera phones and get their first trial of a digital camera experience through the camera phone.
- But they find the quality inadequate after some sampling.
- After initial experience with camera phones, many of them start using higher resolution digital cameras.

In that sense camera phones act as a transition to adopt some digital cameras, over time.

UNDERSTANDING THE CAMERA MARKET

Consumer Awareness and Habit

- Photography does not rank high on the list of hobbies for any average Indian.
- Pre 1990s, cameras and film were considered luxuries.
- Most Indians rely on studios and professional photographers to take formal pictures.
- Even on travel, use of personal cameras is low. Travellers use the services of small-time commercial photographers in the popular tourist spots, or borrow cameras from acquaintances.
- Since the bulk of Indian families have not actually used a camera, there is a belief that they are complicated gadgets. This attitude is reinforced by the fact that many Indians are only familiar with the ancient and complicated-looking cameras used by studios.

Positive Signs of Growth

- Growing middle class with family values (Lots of "Kodak Moments"!).
- Current penetration level is less than 5 per cent → Implies huge market opportunities.
- Growing urbanization, changing culture, increasing consumer spending on durables and lifestyle products.
- Leisure and travel are increasing among Indians.

Prestige Seeking Behaviour

For a vast majority of Indians, camera is a premium product. In this context, the Prestige Seeking Behaviour Model (explained below in Exhibit 26.5) is used to understand the diverse nature of this premium market.

EXHIBIT 26.5

Prestige Seeking Behaviour Model

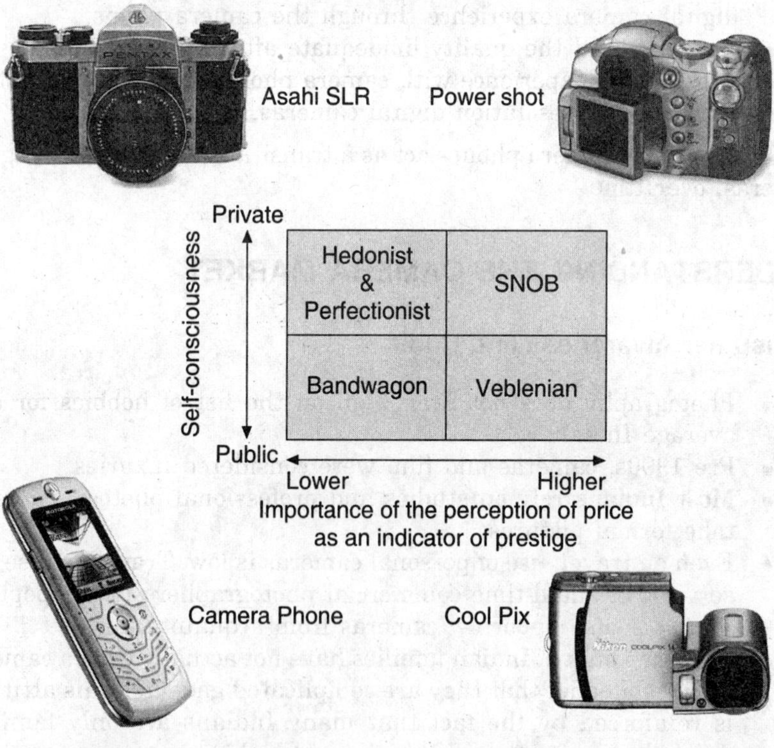

The hedonist: He is highly emotional. Generally, beauty and aesthetic aspect of the camera and the photos appeals to him. He is not concerned with price, rather the artistic and aesthetic value of the photograph is more important.

The perfectionist: He goes for technical perfection. Such consumers will seek out and buy the model of camera they consider to be most technically superior in features in their quest for perfection.

Bandwagon: He buys a camera phone because it is the 'in' thing. He does not really associate price with prestige, rather the ownership of the functional benefits of the camera phone itself that gives him social acceptance in his peer group. Of course, this group may also buy digital cameras and film cameras, but by his nature, he is more susceptible to the new trends and styles and thus the camera phones.

Snob: He will look at price as an indicator of prestige. He seeks exclusivity, but also appreciates the inherent qualities of the product in relation to his own private consciousness.

Veblenian: He seeks prestige by following price, and also seeks social standing within the peer group, by virtue of having been associated with a "premium" product like a high priced branded camera.

COMPETITIVE LANDSCAPE

Exhibit 26.6 shows the global market share captured by leading digital camera marketers.

EXHIBIT 26.6

Global Photographic Products Market Share (% share, by name, in 2005)

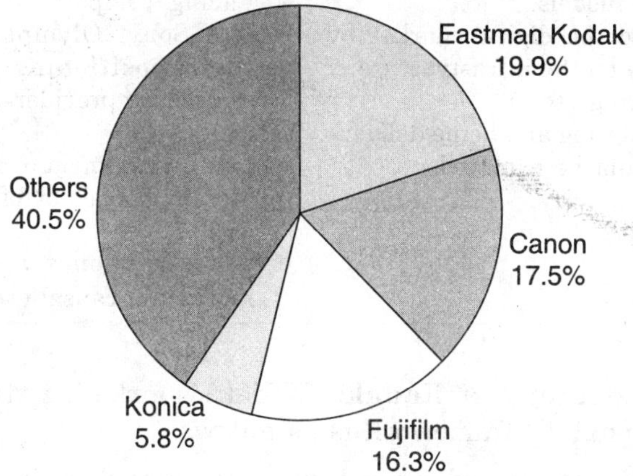

AN ANALYSIS OF TWO LEADING CAMERA COMPANIES

Eastman Kodak

Eastman Kodak India Ltd, a subsidiary of Kodak plc, started operating in India in 1973. It was the first foreign photographic company to set up manufacturing of cameras, films, photo chemicals and other imaging products in India. The traditional camera market of India has largely been given shape by Kodak.

Kodak also has a centralized Call Centre that provides service support and a Wedding Club that offers workflow management to professional laboratories and studios.

SWOT Analysis for Kodak

Stengths	Weaknesses
• Being one of the early movers into Indian market, it has a greater knowledge of Indian camera market. • Deep rooted distribution network, coupled with own outlets and allied infrastructure for digital photo printing etc. • Well-established brand in low-medium price segment for traditional cameras.	• Cannot suddenly withdraw from traditional camera, photo printing and film rolls market. • Low impact in digital camera segment. • High degree of vertical integration, i.e. presence in production, as well as sales and service in conventional cameras might be a hindrance to the digital camera making.
Opportunities	**Threats**
• Leveraging the image of Kodak in capturing the first time camera buyers, a huge market in India today. • Working on upgradation of existing entry level models. • Adapting to the digital market by capitalizing on the infrastructure of photo printing etc. • Internet ordering and home delivery systems could be explored.	• Company's image perceived as low end technology. Product extention to digital camera may take more time to get acceptance among present users. • Facing competition from players like Sony, Olympus, because of their positioning as the best technology providers, in every price range. • Low end segment of digital cameras already flooded by brands like Fuji, Yaschica etc. • Camera phones eating into the market for causal users of cameras.

Marketing strategy of Kodak: Kodak's marketing strategy as per the conventional 4P framework is as follows.

Product: Kodak started out in India with sales of traditional cameras. Some of the popular models are *Kodak K225, Kodak KBZoom, Kodak EC100, Kodak KB12 plus, Kodak KB10* and *Kodak Kroma*. Kodak simultaneously made film rolls and further moved into photo developing and printing services through a franchisee model.

Kodak was a late entrant to the digital camera market. They underestimated Indian market's ability to adopt sophisticated digital cameras. That's why, when they introduced digital cameras, sales picked up fast. In India, Kodak is today selling digital cameras like *Kodak LS743, Kodak LS633, Kodak DX6440, Kodak DX4530* and *Kodak DX7630.*

Price: In the traditional camera market, Kodak extensively focused on the first time camera user market, targeting the middle class Indian families. Their popular basic camera models sell at a price point of Rs 995. Other Kodak camera models are available in higher price brackets in India.

In the digital camera segment, the models are priced in middle segment, while professional cameras are available in the premium segment.

Positioning: Today, in the wake of growing digital camera market, Kodak positions itself as a utilitymid price camera.

The concept of "Kodak-moments" targeting middle class family segment, has practically built a whole new market for all the camera players in India.

Targeting the first time camera buyers, Kodak introduced the basic models at 995, and other ideas like exchange offers.

Kodak offers a unique proposition of complete service, i.e Kodak digital printing, wedding clubs, professional services etc. Kodak is taking up the role of converting traditional camera users to digital cameras, by promising ease of use, and addressing technical anxieties of an amateur user through promotions like KODAK EASY SOLUTIONS.

Place: Kodak has one of the most extensive distribution networks in India. They developed a retail network of more than 30,000 outlets, offering photo development and printing services as well as sales of basic camera models of Kodak. In case of digital camera, Kodak is targeting the outlets selling high end consumer durables. In large cities, Kodak also has exclusive outlets for complete photography solutions.

Nikon

Business: For Nikon Imaging, cameras and digital imaging are a core operational domain. Nikon strives to be innovative, realizing the full value of imaging with uncompromising technologies.

Positioning: Nikon Imaging Company now introduces a new positioning statement, aiming to foster a special sense of affinity with their customers. **"At the heart of the image". That's where the challenge is, and Nikon dares to take it on.**

Nikon tries to appeal to the customer's emotional values through three promises:

- **Be true to the heart:** Nikon will deliver the essence of the image.

- **Ignite the heart:** Nikon will inspire a new passion for life with the image.
- **Invent for the heart:** Nikon will make the world's dreams for the image come true.

Products

- Digital SLR cameras
- Digital compact cameras (COOLPIX series)
- Film cameras
- Lenses and accessories
- Film scanners
- Software

FUTURE TRENDS

Globally, the digital revolution has changed the photographic products business a significant manner. But in India the convensional cameras continue to dominate because of low-cost, simplicity of operation, and lack of digital mini-labs and printing facility. As India develops, more number of consumers are likely to possess a digital camera. Initially it will require more advertisement to convine individual consumers about benefits of having a digital camera. Generally, bulk of the mass market would be using a low priced ordinary camera. They require decent quality of pictures, but more importantly, to many of them a printed photograph is still a hard evidence of their endeavours in the past. Because of low level of literacy and lack of computer facilities a rapid penetration of digital camera is unlikely to happen. Till such time, a large number of consumers may be attracted to buy a conventional camera and some of them may acquire some mobile phone with camera attachment. With passage of time an upgradation to digital camera is likely to happen.

The second category of Indian consumers' in particular, the informed hobbyist who makes an informed choice when buying a camera and does not mind spending extra amount of money for the facilities. This segment of buyers can be targetted because of the technology and superior features a digital camera.

Where should the companies go?

- There is no escape for the companies to shift to digital technology and make it available at affordable prices to the consumers. But like old time when film processing was the major business with widespread usage of camera phones processing these photographs to hard copies will give continuous revenues. Such labs would go a long way in striking the right chord with the emotions of the Indian consumers.

- With convergence trend getting stronger very soon consumers small acquire a superior quality of a digital camera within the mobile phones. It would help in integrating the communication and photography even further.

Conclusion

The camera as a stand alone device would only suffice the needs of expert camera users whose aspirations are that of a perfect photograph and who understand the subtle differences between two comparable quality photographs. As for the ordinary consumer whose wants are just capturing the moments of life, a decent camera phone would be sufficient. With the latest camera phones having superb quality, there is dual purpose is an attraction for the sophisticated consumer. There will be more phones with higher resolution cameras which should give a near independent camera experience to the consumer. This trend is also due to the ease of carrying the mobile phones compared to a separate digital camera. This is also the general trend of convergence in the electronic industry with a single gadget serving many different needs of the consumer.

One great innovation which could turn the individual camera industry could be if a printing facility is provided with the camera itself. This would justify carrying of the camera and would be a great way to instantly capture images. The key is sharing of the photographs and the digital age makes it possible today. This innovation could give more instant gradification to the consumer.

ANNEXURE

Classification of Cameras

On the basis of *funtionality*, cameras currently in use can be classified as following:

Ultra-Compact/Mini

Ultra-compact cameras are super **lightweight** and can easily fit in your palm. Some of the cameras in this range are as small as an ATM card. These cameras offer **portability** since they can fit just about anywhere. A consumer may test them out before making the purchase. There are fewer features offered in this size range, which limits the camera's flexibility of use. Those looking for **style** and incredible portability, **ultra-compact** cameras offer the **best value** for the average user.

Compact/Small

Compact or **small** cameras deliver a good mix of **portability**, **convenience**, and **basic features**. These cameras are a little bigger than the ultra-compact size and offer a little more **flexibility** than ultra-compact cameras. Compact cameras are perfect for the **average user**, for taking great snapshots. Due to its size, compact/small cameras are a top choice for people with an active lifestyle.

Prosumer/Medium

Prosumer cameras feature **high quality lenses** and **advanced features** for both **automatic** and **semi-automatic** control. **Prosumer** cameras are a good choice for an advanced photographer who is not quite at the professional level yet. Converter lenses, external flashes, remote controls, filters, and other accessories can be used with the **prosumer** camera. It gives **great quality images** with automatic and semi-automatic controls.

SLR/Large

SLR (single lens reflex) cameras are the larger of the digital cameras and are **loaded with features** and gimmicks. **SLR** cameras are for **professionals** or at least serious photography enthusiasts. This range offers a wide range of **manual features** for unlimited **creative control**, and also the possibility of using **interchangeable lenses**. Digital **SLRs** give the ease of digital with all of the control of a manual camera. This is a **top of the line** camera, and the creative possibilities are endless.

CHAPTER 27

Motorcycles

India is the largest producer of motorised two wheeler vehicles in the world. In India the motorised two wheelers are usually referred as moped, **scooter** and **motorcycle, depending on the size of the engine.** Annual sales of this industry are expected to grow from 6.68 million vehicles in the year 2006 to 7.58 million vehicles in the year 2007, and it is projected to cross the 10 million mark by 2010. Till the mid-1990s, scooters were the most dominant type of two wheelers in India. However, the market has experienced a significant shift from scooters to motorcycles in recent years. Also within motorcycles the 100 cc capacity engine vehicles used to occupy nearly 94 per cent of the total motorcycle sales in 2001–02. In 2005–06, the 100 cc vehicle segment has shrunk to 67 per cent.

GROWTH IN DIFFERENT CATEGORIES

Motorcycles have registered the highest growth among the three categories of two wheelers (see Exhibit 27.1). While the overall two wheeler market grew by 15.5 per cent during 2006–07 over the last year, motorcycles grew by 18.53 per cent, scooters at 0.12 per cent and moped sales grew at 6.53 per cent.

EXHIBIT 27.1

Two Wheeler Segment Growth (%)

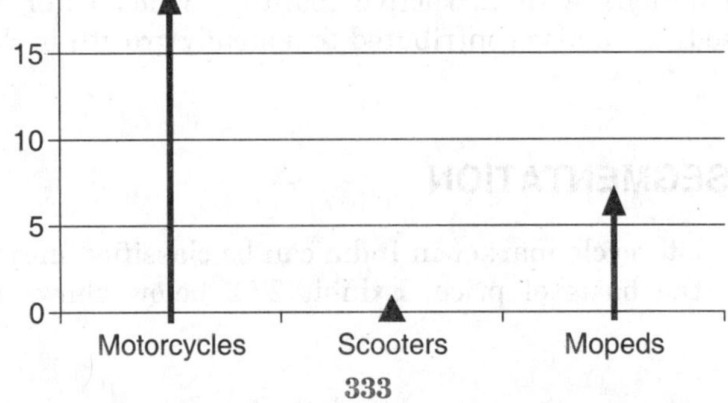

Demand Drivers

Multiple factors have contributed to the growth in demand of two wheelers. The growth is primarily because of the following factors.

Economic development: The Indian economy recorded an impressive growth for the third successive year (GDP growth was 8.4 per cent during 2005–06) despite sleep rise in the international crude-oil price. As overall economy prospers, there is naturally more demand for personal transportation vehicle. This has resulted in increased demand for motorcycles that are now most popular and affordable means of personal transportation.

Improving infrastructure: The impetus given by the Union Government to create a better infrastructure, specially the Golden Quadrilateral Project, the National Highways Program etc., is transforming the economy in a significant manner. This factor has boosted the sale of motorcycles due to better road conditions.

Increasing urbanization and inadequate public transportation system, especially in the semi-urban and rural areas, create a greater need for personal vehicle.

Changing demographic profile: India's demographic picture is, of late, showing a large number of younger age-group people. Also, it is well known that the size of middle class population is also increasing. These trends are leading to increased demand for personal use durables such as two wheeler vehicles, cell phone and camera.

Growth in rural market: Successive good monsoons have increased the purchasing power of the rural market. The rural consumers are today more keen to possess a two wheeler instead of an ordinary bicycle. Moreover, some of the two wheeler companies have taken special initiatives to tap the growing economic power of the rural market in India.

Other favourable conditions: Factors like, expansion in city and higher mobility of the Indian population; Younger generation's increased desire for personal vehicle for intra-city movement; Increased availability and lower rate of interest charged for consumer financing; Availability of more fuel efficient and low maintenance cost models of motorcycles; More choice options with attractive features which cater to diverse consumer needs have also contributed to a steady growth in demand for two wheelers.

MARKET SEGMENTATION

The present motorcycle market in India can be classified into five broad segments on the basis of price. Exhibit 27.2 below shows the major existing brands in each segment. Then we make a detailed description of each segment, target consumers and their expectations.

EXHIBIT 27.2

Market Segmentation of Major Motorcycle Brands in India

Segment	Price	Brand (Make)
Standard	Rs 30,000 to 40,000	**Platina & CT100** (Bajaj), **CD Dawn** (Hero Honda), **Boss & Challenger** (Kinetic), **Star** (TVS), **Crux** (Yamaha), **Heat** (Suzuki)
Executive	Rs 40,000 to 50,000	**Splendor, Passion, Glamour** (Hero), **Discover** (Bajaj), **Victor, Centra** (TVS), **Libero, Gladiator** (Yamaha), **Freedom** (LML), **Velocity** (Kinetic)
Premium	Rs 50,000 to 65,000	**Pulsar** (Bajaj), **CBZ** (Hero Honda), **Unicorn** (Honda), **Apache** & Fiero (TVS), **Zeus** (Suzuki), **Graptor & Beamer** (LML), **GF Series** (Kinetic)
Super Premium	Rs 65,000 to 75,000	**Karizma** (Hero Honda), **Comet & Aquila** (Kinetic)
Cruiser	Above Rs 75,000	**Avenger** (Bajaj), **Enticer** (Yamaha), **Bullet** (Royal Enfield)

Standard Segment

The standard segment is known as the entry-level motorcycles, which contain brands such as Hero Honda's **CD Dawn**, Bajaj Auto's **Platina and Wave**, TVS Motor's **Star** and its variants, Yamaha's **Crux**, Suzuki's **Heat,** and Kinetic's **Boss and Challenger**. These motorcycles are today priced in the range of Rs 30,000 to 40,000.

The typical **profile** of the consumers belonging to this segment is a single, newly employed working professional or newly married people who use the bike to commute small distance. This class of vehicles or segment is most popular in the semi-urban and rural areas. The common consumer's expectations are that of affordability, reliability and low maintenance costs.

Executive Segment

The executive segment is the largest segment of the motorcycle market which is served by Bajaj Auto's **Discover,** Hero Honda's **Splendor Plus, Passion, and Glamour**, TVS Motor's **Victor** and **Centra,** Yamaha's

Libero, Gladiator, and G5, LML's **Freedom,** Kinetic's **Velocity,** and Honda's **Shine**. These bikes are today priced in the range of Rs 40,000 to 50,000.

Hero Honda's **Splendor** (or the new or version called the Splendor Plus) continues to be the market leader in this segment. The Executive segment is witnessing a fierce competition among different players for capturing market share. For instance, the market saw Bajaj's **Caliber,** then an improved model referred as **Hoodibaba,** Bajaj phased out **Wind 125** and replaced it by **Discover**. Hero Honda launched a 2nd bike known as **Ambition** which has now been replaced by **Achiever**.

All these brands of motorcycles are characterized by style, performance, fuel efficiency and affordability. The typical consumer profile is that of a student or a working professional. The consumers expectations are that of comfort, fuel cost, initial price, low maintenance cost, and efficient performance.

Premium Segment

The premium segment really took off in the late 90s when Hero Honda introduced the CBZ. The major brands in this segment are Bajaj Auto's **Pulsar,** Hero Honda's **CBZ** and **Glamour**, TVS Motor's **Apache,** Honda's **Unicorn,** Suzuki's **Zeus,** LML's **Graptor** and **Beamer**, and the Kinetic **GF series.** These bikes are priced in the range of Rs 50,000 to 65,000. The market leader in this segment is Bajaj Auto's Pulsar.

The brands in this segment are characterized by good looks, high power and speed, smooth handling and a certain aspiration-value. The typical owners of these bikes are young men. Their main expectations are superior performance as well as, fuel-efficient motorcycles.

Super Premium Segment

The super premium segment includes bikes such as Hero Honda's **Karizma**, and Kinetic's **Comet** (Kinetics JV with Hyosung of Korea) and **Aquila**. Such motorcycles are generally characterized by sleek sporty looks, high speed, and power. The consumer expectations are that of a fast, elegantly designed motorcycle. These bikes are today priced in the range of Rs 65,000 to 75,000.

Cruiser Segment

The cruiser segment includes motorcycles that are targeted at such consumers who generally seek to own stylish bikes. For these segment owning a motorcycle is a passion. The consumer expectation from a cruiser bike is to provide the rider a comfortable ride, great handling, and the ability to go long distances. Bajaj Auto's **Avenger**, Yamaha **Enticer**, and the **Royal Enfield Bullet** are today priced at above Rs 75,000.

COMPETITIVE STRUCTURE

At present, three major players are controlling 90 per cent of the market shares.

The share of market of leading players in different price segments is shown below in Exhibit 27.3.

EXHIBIT 27.3

Motorcycles: Market Share

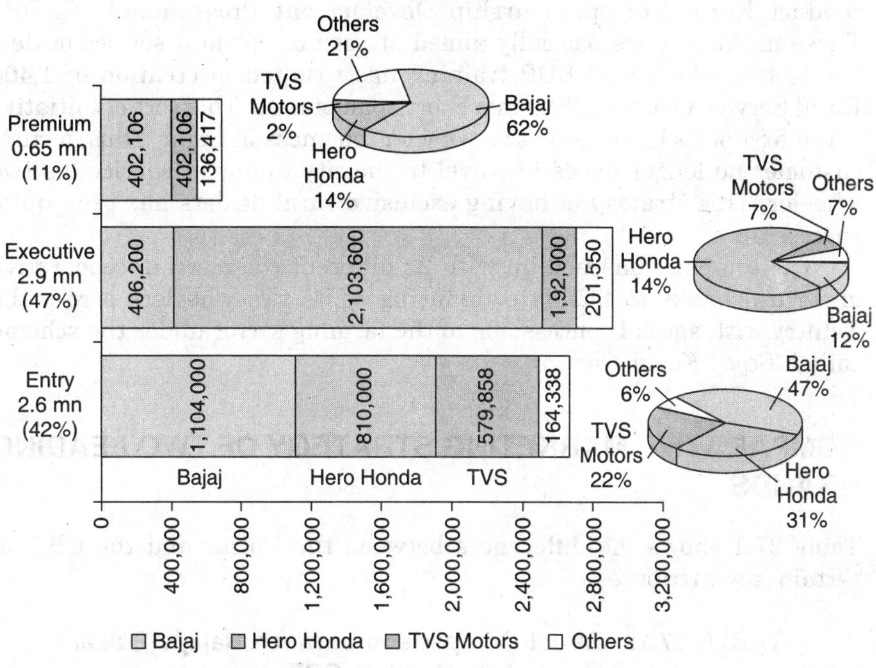

Market expansion strategies: The penetration level of motorised two wheelers in India is just 7 per cent in rural and 24 per cent in the urban market. Because of the enormous opportunities of growth in the rural market two major motor cycle companies (Hero Honda & Bajaj) have been trying to increase their share in rural market. Let us discuss the rural marketing strategy of the two major companies.

Hero Honda's rural expansion strategy: Hero Honda has undertaken a number of social development activities such as Employment Generating Programme, Adult Literacy Program, Rural Health Project, Public Amenities, Road Safety Programme etc., with an indirect mission to create its image in the rural India.

Among other initiatives, Hero Honda has entered into a tie-up with the State Bank of India. The tie-up is aimed at synergising the strengths of the two giants. The deal envisages SBI to help the farmers of Uttar

Pradesh to acquire one of its two wheeler models. Hero Honda has made a similar tie-up with the Punjab State Cooperative Bank.

Bajaj Auto's rural expansion strategy: Bajaj Auto Ltd has taken up an ambitions plan to reach each village with a population size of over 5,000. In the year 2006 Bajaj Auto participated in more than 2,000 rural events like mega or mini *melas*, and village level weekly market called *haats*.

The company has set up specialist dealerships for rural market called 'Rural Dealerships'. As a part of this rural sales initiative, Bajaj Auto has worked with NABARD and a number of NGOs in eight states to conduct Rural Entrepreneurship Development Programmes (REDP). These initiatives are basically aimed at setting up rural service outlets for its two wheelers. REDP training has resulted in creation of 1,400 Rural Service Outlets (RSO) in a short span of time. This sort of initiative is the first of its kind in the two wheeler business in India. Thus, a rural customer no longer needs to travel to the city to buy or service his two wheeler. This strategy of having exclusive rural dealers has been quite successful.

The company has tied up with 22 different commercial, cooperative and rural banks to facilitate financing of its two wheelers across the country with special concessions to the farming sector under the scheme called *'Bajaj Kisan Chakra'*.

COMPARATIVE MARKETING STRATEGY OF TWO LEADING BRANDS

Table 27.1 shows the differences between the Pulsar and the CBZ on certain key attributes.

TABLE 27.1: Direct Comparison between Bajaj's Pulsar vs Hero Honda's CBZ

S. No.	Attribute	Bajaj Pulsar	Hero Honda CBZ
1	Mileage	59.6 km/litre	53 km/litre
2	Price	Rs 56,000–59,000	Rs 54,000–63,000
3	Engine size	150cc/180cc	150cc
4	Styling	Bulky look; sharp lines; flat-seat	Full, but not bulky look; smooth edges; stepped-seat
5	No. of SKUs	2	1
6	Colours	4 (Black, Blue, Red, Silver)	5 (Black, Blue, Red, Silver, Green)
7	Acceleration	0-60 km/h in 6.25 seconds	0-60 km/h in 5.31 seconds
8	Fuel tank size	18 litres	13 litres

Bajaj Pulsar

S. No.	Product	Comments
1	Size/Variety	2 sizes—150 cc & 180 cc
2	Colour	Pulsar is available in 4 colours—black, blue, red, and silver. Each of these comes in the 2 engine sizes.
3	Design	Pulsar pioneered a new look where it incorporated the features such as larger fuel tanks, a bulky look, round headlights and dark colours of cruiser bikes such as Royal Enfield and Bullet.
4	Features	Smooth riding experience; enhanced reinforced chassis; advanced DTSI engine.
5	Brand name	The name Pulsar is supposed to denote the rising pulse and excitement that the rider and the observer feel on riding/observing a Bajaj Pulsar.
6	Services	Bajaj Pulsar comes with Bajaj Autos company-wide policy of 6 service coupons for up to 10,000 kms or 2 years.
7	Warranties	Warranties are available on the various components of the bike parts such as the engine, but not the bike as a whole.
Price		
8	List prices	The 150 cc Bajaj Pulsar has a list price of Rs 56,000, whereas the 180 cc variant has a list price of Rs 59,000.
9	Discount	The discount schemes available on the Pulsar are the company-wide Bajaj schemes offered during the festival season.
10	Allowance	Bajaj Auto does have some large customers such as police departments of cities. These customers get their vehicles at a discounted rate.
11	Finance schemes	Bajaj Pulsar is available under 3 umbrella finance schemes that cover 90 per cent of the cost of the motorcycle. The schemes have payment periods of 12, 24, and 36 months and effective interest rates of 6.6 per cent, 7.7 per cent, and 8.8 per cent, respectively.
Promotion		
12	Sales promotion	Sales are promoted by schemes that give gifts and freebies such as DVD players, mobile phones, and other electronic items. Additionally, a loyalty scheme on servicing and purchase of replacements has also been instituted.

(Contd.)...

Bajaj Pulsar (*Contd.*)

13	Advertising	Bajaj Pulsar was launched with the intention of appealing to the urban, thrill and pleasure seeking young man. The tagline at the time of the launch was "Definitely Male".
14	Public relations	Bajaj Auto has sponsored several events, such as college festivals where Bajaj Pulsar is heavily promoted with test-drives and active sales persons.
Place		
15	Channels	Bajaj Pulsar is distributed mainly through franchisee retail outlets. Additionally, there are some company-owned outlets as well.
16	Coverage	The sales and distribution channels of Bajaj cover the whole country.

Hero Honda CBZ

S. No.	Product	Comments
1	Size/Product variety	Hero Honda CBZ is available in only a single engine size in the 150 cc segment. However, the SKU is differentiated based on whether it has an electric start or not.
2	Colours	Initially, Hero Honda CBZ was available in 5 colours—black, blue, red, silver, and green. The new Hero Honda Extreme is available in red only.
3	Design	Hero Honda CBZ was the first bike to introduce the sporty look bike in India. It was aesthetically different from all other bikes. Its looks were characterized by a smooth curved fuel-tank, stepped-seat, and moulded head-lights.
4	Features	Disc break; first motorcycle in India with 5 gears; Transient Power Fuel Control (TPFC) System; Air Injection System; Adjustable Rear-Shock Absorbers.
5	Brand name	It is not exactly known what the abbreviation CBZ stands for. The new version of CBZ is known as the CBZ Extreme.
6	Services	Hero Honda CBZ comes with the Hero Honda company-wide policy of 6 free and 6 discounted service coupons for up to 10,000 kms or 1 year whichever is earlier.
7	Warranties	Warranties are available on the various components of the bike but not the bike as a whole.

(Contd.)...

Hero Honda CBZ *(Contd.)*

Price		
8	List prices	The non-electronic start CBZ costs Rs 54,000 and electronic start variant comes with a list price of 63,000.
9	Discounts	The Hero Honda CBZ is seldom available on any discounts.
10	Finance schemes	The Hero Honda CBZ is available under the several finance schemes offered by the Hero group in partnership with banks.
Promotion		
11	Sales promotion	The Hero Group promotes its sales by offering some free goods along with the purchase of a bike such as mobile phones. Additionally, the Hero Group also has loyalty scheme called the "Passport Scheme" that allows one to accumulate and redeem points for every part replaced and servicing.
12	Advertising	The CBZ was targeted at the urban youth. The first advertisements of the CBZ focused on how owning a CBZ would help one create a desired impression on a target. For instance, a college going boy wanting to get the attention of a group of girls.
13	Public relations	Hero Honda has been a very prominent sponsor of some of the major sports events in India such as cricket and golf.
Place		
14	Channels	Hero Honda CBZ is distributed mainly through franchisee retail outlets spread throughout the country.
15	Coverage	The sales and distribution channels of Hero Honda cover the whole country.

Bajaj's Pulsar and the Hero Honda CBZ are positioned in the premium segment. Both the brands try to appeal to the young, trendy, and image-conscious consumers. The premium segment of the motorcycle industry took off with the introduction of the Hero Honda CBZ in 1998-99. CBZ completely captured the imagination of the Indian youth who were image and style conscious.

- Seeing its success, other players such as **LML (Graptor), TVS (Apache), and Kinetic (GF170, GF Laser, and Comet)** entered the same segment at various points between 1999 and 2004. However, these bikes were not that successful.

- The CBZ was the dominant bike in the premium segment till 2002 when the Pulsar was launched.
- In 2006 CBZ has been re-launched in the name of CBZ Extreme.
- The most apparent reason as to why the Pulsar emerged as the leader in the premium segment seems to be its price. The 4 Ps **(Product, Price, Promotion, Place)** framework for Bajaj Pulsar and the Hero Honda CBZ is outlined below.

Conclusion

The motorcycle market is heading for a more competitive environment in the near future as the foreign partners (e.g. Honda, Suzuki and Yamaha) of the existing joint ventures are planning to put up their own units in India.

CHAPTER 28

Refrigerators

Generally, refrigerators, washing machines, and air conditioners are known as home appliances. These products have common characteristics such as durability, tangibility, and normally require more personal selling effort, promotion, and services to induce purchase.

Penetration Level

Exhibit 28.1 shows low penetration level of refrigerator compared to television. The penetration of refrigerators remains confined largely to the high-income group across the urban and rural market. The penetration levels in the low-income groups indicate the low utility perception of the product as compared with its cost of ownership. Moreover, there is also a significant difference between the penetration rates of refrigerators in the urban and rural segments. (see Exhibit 28.2)

EXHIBIT 28.1

Growth in Penetration Level of Refrigerators vis-a-vis CTVs

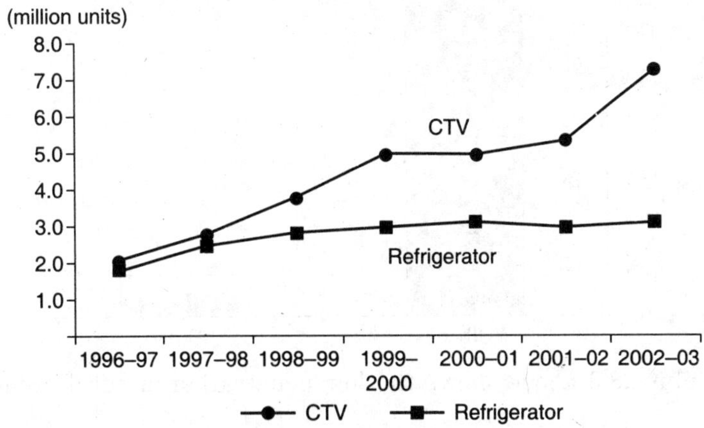

EXHIBIT 28.2

Penetration of Refrigerator in Rural/Urban Market and Income Brackets

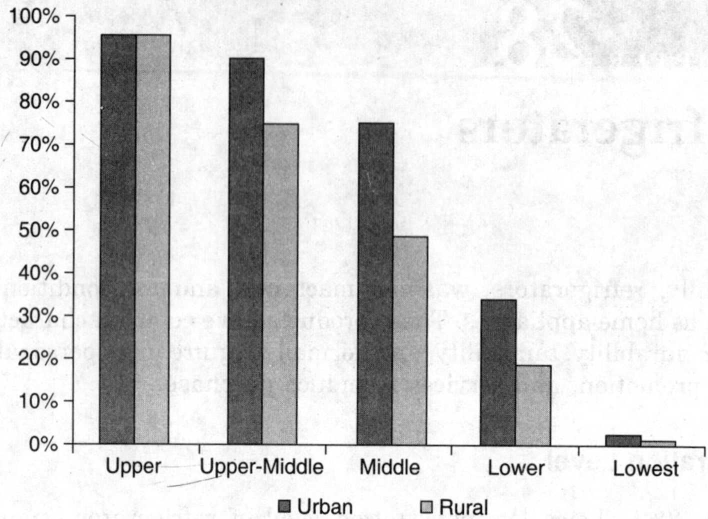

The penetration of refrigerators is generally low among lowest income group and in the rural market (see Exhibit 28.3).

EXHIBIT 28.3

Urban vs Rural Penetration Level

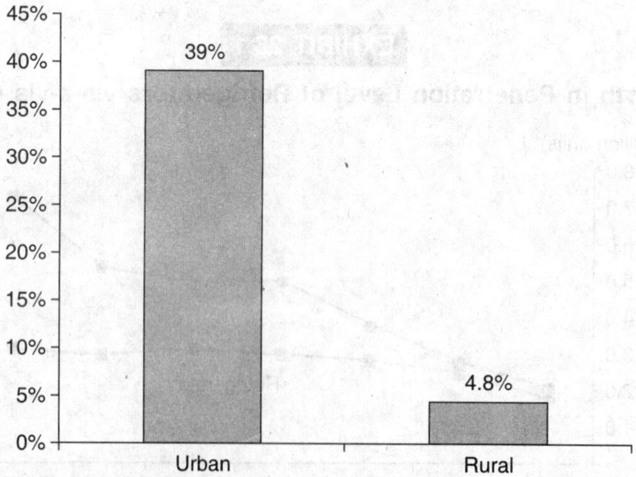

Exhibit 28.3 above shows the low penetration in rural areas.

Moreover, refrigerators are seen to be useful only to the homemaker as compared with a CTV, which is seen as a product relevant to all the members of the household.

MARKET SIZE AND GROWTH

Refrigerator demand has been estimated at 3 million units (around Rs 32 billion by value) in 2001–02. In recent years, the refrigerator market has been experiencing slow growth, despite intensive promotion or deals offered by many players from time to time and even direct price reduction. In terms of value, a moderate level of growth is likely as many urban consumers are of late upgrading to higher-ended frost-free models.

Why Refrigerator Market is Sluggish?

Refrigerator demand in India has exhibited low growth rate in recent years. Several factors seem to contribute to this phenomenon: For instance, the penetration level of refrigerator in the urban market is already high; unfortunately rural consumers see the cost of ownership as disproportionately higher than its utility. Further, CTVs are higher up the aspiration chain for consumers; and mobile phones are also rising in the durable goods purchase hierarchy. As a result, the penetration of refrigerators is confined mainly among the high-income groups and that too, in the urban locations.

Growth in Demand for Similar Consumer Durables

Growth rates for four major consumer durables are shown below in Exhibit 28.4. It shows refrigerators and washing machines followed a similar growth pattern. In volume terms the refrigerator market is more than twice the washing machine market. However, colour television is on a higher priority list of consumers in India.

EXHIBIT 28.4

Consumer Durables: Growth in Demand for Some Home used Durables

(%)	WMs	CTVs	Refrigerators	Acs
1998–99	17.9	35.7	14.0	17.5
1999–2000	5.4	31.6	5.3	15.7
2000–01	1.7	1.2	5.0	18.4
2001–02	3.3	6.7	– 4.8	10.2
2002–03	– 0.4	34.4	5.0	14.6
2003–04	2.8	– 8.2	0.1	15.3

Note: Based on Y-o-Y growth in volumes.

EXHIBIT 28.5

Utilisation Levels Remain Sub-optimal

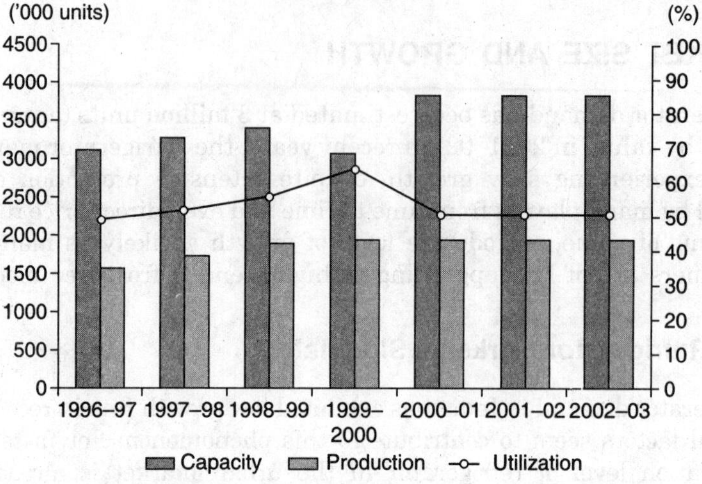

Notes: 1. Based on capacities of key players; 2. Capacity and production are in '000 units; Utilisation levels are given in percentage.

Market characteristics

Seasonality of demand: Demand for refrigerators is generally more in the summer months between March and June and festival seasons. Sales during the seasons are found to be nearly three-fourths of the annual demand.

Industry suffers from excess capacity: In spite of a moderate recovery in demand in 2002–03, the industry remains bogged down by excess capacity. Even in 2005–06, the utilisation of capacity was just 50 per cent of the installed capacity. Exhibit 28.5 below shows sub-optional utilisation of capacity ever since the late 1990s, when players set up capacities in anticipation of high demand.

MARKET SEGMENTATION

Functional Segmentation

Refrigerators are broadly classified into direct cool and frost-free refrigerators, on the basis of the functions performed by them.

Direct cool refrigerators: Direct cool refrigerators are conventional refrigerators. The frost formed in a direct cool refrigerator has to be manually defrosted. Since direct cool refrigerators consume less energy and are less costly than frost-free refrigerators, they are very popular in the Indian market. In the developed countries, on the other hand, they have been completely phased out.

Frost-free refrigerators: In 1992, Videocon first introduced its frost-free range of refrigerators in India. A frost-free refrigerator does away with the inconvenience of manually defrosting the refrigerator. Frost-free technology has been widely adopted by the players in India. However, heating the coils at regular intervals consumes energy and hence, more expensive in terms of operating cost.

Capacity-wise Segmentation

The capacity of a refrigerator usually consists of the freezer and the cabinet.

- Freezer—35 litres
- Cabinet capacity—130 litres

The typical break-up of the capacity for the most commonly used refrigerator is 165 L:

Capacity-wise segmentation are the following:

- less than 165 L
- 165 L to 185 L
- 185 L to 225 L
- 225 L to 270 L
- 270 L to 310 L
- greater than 310 L

CONSUMPTION TRENDS

Direct cool refrigerators dominate the market. Direct cool refrigerators constitute the largest share of refrigerator sales, accounting for almost 87 per cent of the total demand. The low share of frost-free refrigerators is attributed to the price sensitivity of the Indian market and the differential between the price and the perceived value from a frost-free refrigerator. Currently, the price differential between the average price of a direct cool and frost-free refrigerator is Rs 7,000–8,000. The mix of direct cool to frost-free has remained relatively unchanged over the last four years.

Lower capacities dominate the direct cool segment; higher capacities preferred in frost-free. In the direct cool segment, where purchases mostly come from the first-time or entry-level consumers, 80 per cent of sales are in the <185 litres capacity models. This trend is likely to continue, as consumers who are willing to spend larger sums tend to acquire frost-free refrigerators, instead of direct cool refrigerators.

In the frost-free segment, models with a capacity of above 225 litres account for 80 per cent of sales. Further, the demand for models with a capacity of above 300 litres has been growing at a higher rate than the overall segment.

Replacement demand drives growth in the frost-free segment. Demand is expected to remain largely confined to the direct cool segment, as it is the entry-level product for the first time buyers, who account for a significant share of annual demand. However, players such as LG, Samsung and Whirlpool are trying to enlarge the frost-free segment through competitive prices and value-added product features. Demand for the frost-free models would accrue primarily from the replacement segment.

Share of 165 L on the decline; rising preference for higher capacity models. Although the 165 L models account for the largest share of refrigerator sales, there has been a slow and visible shift in demand to larger capacity models, in the past two years. The contribution of the 165 L models declined from around 80 per cent in 1998–99 to around 70 per cent in 2001–02. This is because of the rising preference for higher capacity models arising from the declining price differential between the 165–184 L models and the 185–270 L models.

North India is the largest market for direct cool refrigerators. North India is the major refrigerator market in India, constituting around 40 per cent of the total refrigerator demand in 2001–02. North Indian market is largely dominated by the direct cool refrigerator segment. Around 43 per cent of the direct cool refrigerator sales come from the northern region.

Frost-free leads in the West and South. South (main market is Kerala) and West (main market is Mumbai) together account for around 60 per cent of the total frost-free refrigerator market. This is mainly because consumers in this region value technology, and are comparatively less price-sensitive.

COMPETITIVE ANALYSIS

Key Players

The key players in the refrigerator industry are Whirlpool, Godrej, Electrolux, LG, Samsung, BPL and Daewoo.

Competition intensified with the entry of MNCs. Till the early 1990s the refrigerator industry was confined to few domestic players like Kelvinator, Godrej, Voltas, BPL and Videocon. However, competition intensified from the mid-1990s onwards, after the entry of many foreign players in the Indian refrigerator market. Intense competition brought refrigerator prices down, and provided a wider choice of brands to the consumers. The refrigerator market, which was earlier dominated by BPL, Godrej and Videocon, has recently undergone major changes as the

MNCs like Whirlpool, LG, Samsung, Electrolux etc. have steadily gained control of the Indian market.

EXHIBIT 28.6

Refrigerators: Market Share of Key Players

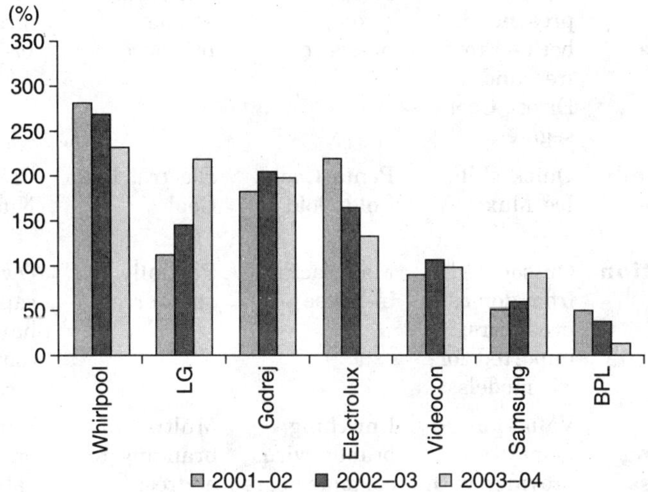

LG moves up to become the market leader. In 2004–05, LG became the market leader. Samsung is also estimated to have gained market share and climbed up to the fourth position. Both LG and Samsung continued to record strong volume growth, while the overall industry growth has been meager. In the race for market share, the two companies were supported by their aggressive promotion strategies and well-diversified distribution network. The combined market share of LG and Samsung is approx 40 per cent in 2004–05. See Exhibit 28.6 to have a look at the market share of key players.

Samsung

Samsung India Electronics Ltd is operating in India since 1995. It is today a leading consumer electronics, home appliance makers in India.

Samsung has projected itself as a high end technology driven player. The urban market is its focus area.

Market Share %	5.9
Segment-wise presence	Moderate presence in frost-free; small presence in direct cool.
Key brands and sub-brands	Samsung BioFresh.
Key marketing strategies	Focused on technological innovations.

A comparative analysis of competitors of Samsung is given below.

	Whirlpool	Godrej	Electrolux	LG
Market share	26.7%	20.4%	16.3%	5%
Segment-wise presence	Strong presence in both—Frost free and Direct Cool segment	Moderate strong presence	Marginal strong presence	Moderate strong presence
Key Brands and Sub-brands	Quick chill, Ice Max	Penta Cool, Cold Gold	Electra, Insta Cool	Preserve Nutrition
Integration levels	Outsourced from domestic producers; imported for FF models	Manufactured in-house	Partially outsourced	Own capacities have been commissioned recently
Key marketing strategies	Value-for-money provider with reasonable priced models with utility features	Enriching brands with customer care and eco-friendliness	Multi-branding to address different price segments simultaneously	Enriching brands with values such as health consciousness

A swot analysis of Samsung is given below.

Strengths	Weakness
• Technological competitiveness • Worldwide R&D facilities • Vast and extensive channel network • Strong brand recall and pull among end-customers	• Currently low market share • Limited range of models being produced in India

Opportunities	Threats
• The direct cool refrigerators segment is growing at the rate of 6 per cent to 7 per cent and the frost-free refrigerators segment at a much faster pace of 20 per cent • Leverage the Brand Samsung to promote the refrigerators along with other white goods • Their manufacturing facility will help cut down lead times in introducing new models	• Lower priced Chinese models • Perception as a high-end technological product and not a basic utility product

Promotion: Samsung India Electronics Ltd has been organizing 'Samsung Dream Home Road' shows to promote the brand Samsung.

Since the refrigerator vies with other consumer durables like CTVs and mobiles for a share of the consumer's wallet, Samsung has used a bundling strategy. They were offering the Refrigerator-AC bundles, or phones as free on purchase of refrigerators etc., thus wooing the consumer.

Haier

Globally, Haier is a premium brand, priced on a par or very close to the most premium brands. It is a very strategic positioning decision that they have taken, because consumers may not have a very high opinion of Chinese made goods. Haier believes that once a customer sees their products, the value comes out on its own. As their products find acceptability, they would take them to the mass market. The main driver is going to be acceptability in the mid- and high-segment.

A swot analysis of Haier is analysis presented below.

Strengths	Opportunities
• World number 2 company • Superior technology—Very low power and water consumption • Large product range	• The rapidly changing industry structure. • Position in the industry depends upon consumer focus, technology adoption • The local rivals can be reduced to contract manufacturers
Weaknesses	**Threats**
• The image of poor quality associated with Chinese made products. • Entering a market where there are well entrenched players • No manufacturing facilities of their own.	• Brand building takes a long time • Not investing in facilities till a strong brand is created

Means to Compete

Ways to compete in the Indian refrigerator market:

- Establish strong brands
- Develop extensive distribution network and continuous after-sales support
- Continuous product innovation and maintain technological superiority
- Product offerings at various price points
- Ability to manage costs and offer competitive prices

Conclusion

Refrigerator industry in India has gone through a turbulent time. In recent years, the market has experienced slow growth, despite many players cutting their prices to a moderate extent. The industry saw low capacity utilization, lower margins. It seems to have lost heavily to other durable products like CTVs, mobiles, ACs etc.

The market is likely to grow by 5–8 per cent in volumes over the medium term, driven by the rising per capita income levels, declining prices, consumer finance, increasing urbanization.

Refrigerators have found more relevance in the urban India, where the need for food preservation is high due to the growing number of working women population. Whereas in the eyes of rural consumers the utility for refrigerators is somewhat low, given their minimal food preservation requirement. Thus, the future growth will depend on improving the relevance of the product, particularly in rural areas, and on cutting the price of the entry-level model significantly.

ANNEXURE

Product Range of Leading Refrigerators Companies as on March 2006

Samsung

Capacity	Price	Features	Models
170–195 litres	Rs 7250–10,000	Deodorizing, moisture control	5
200–300 litres	Rs 10,500–18,500	Deodorizing, moisture control	6
300–360 litres	Rs 20,500–29,000	Twist ice tray	4
400, 440 litres	Rs 29,500–36,500	Bio-ceramic vegetable rack, twistable ice trays	6
520, 570, 640, 680 litres	Rs 42,000–116,000	2 door, water dispenser, door open alarm etc. Separate temperature controls	9

Godrej

Category	Capacity	Models
Penta cool	200–410 L	8
Cold gold infiniti	180–250 L	3
Cold gold deluxe	300 L	1
Superstar	180 and 215 L	2
Champion	100, 170 and 205 L	3
No. 1	170 L	1

Electrolux

Refrigerator	Technology	Capacity	Models
Direct cool	Oxy Aqua technology	170, 190, 230 and 320 L	6
Ozone frost free	DFF44	415 and 445 L	2
		>400 L	2
		275 L	6

LG

Refrigerator	Technology	Price	Models
Direct cool	SFF technology	Rs 11,100–14,600	4
	A one cooling	Rs 7,600–10,300	11
Frost free	Door cooling	Rs 12,500–16,00	8
	Ice beam door cooling	Rs 13,500–40,500	6
	Green ion door cooling	Rs 41,000–58,000	2

CHAPTER 29

Air Conditioners

Despite tropical climate or extreme summer condition faced in most parts of India, the penetration of air conditioners (ACs) was very low until recently because the AC was perceived as an extreme luxury possession among the household sector. Generally, AC sales used to depend primarily on the institutional buyers. The situation seems to be changing fast. Increased disposable income, reductions in price and broadly speaking, its affordability over the past few years led to buoyancy in the AC market. In 2005–06, 1.5 million units of ACs were sold in India, which was valued at Rs 47 billion.

PRODUCT DIFFERENTIATION

Taking into account the cooling capacity and the nature of cooling application, the generic product, air conditioner, is divided into the following types.

Room ACs

Room Air Conditioners (RACs) generally cater to low cooling requirements, range from 0.75 tonne to 4 tonnes. They are used in households and small offices. RACs are referred as **window and split ACs** depending on the mounting principle.

Windows ACs are compact units mounted on the windows. Because of ease in assembling, traditionally in India window ACs were made mostly by small, local companies. However, in recent years large players have increased their presence in window AC by significant reduction in cost through higher scale of operations.

In split ACs, the condenser and the compressor are mounted separately and it is connected to each other through a coil. In the process, the noise level in split ACs is reduced. Split ACs are typically used in rooms which do not have any windows and by users looking for greater aesthetics, especially in small one-room offices and in larger shops and commercial establishments. Because of the higher level of technology involved in making split ACs (compared to window ACs for the same tonnage requirements), the prices of split ACs are higher.

Packaged ACs

Packaged ACs cater to higher cooling requirements of 5T–15T, and are generally used in offices, hotels and restaurants, cinema theatres. As the manufacturing process of packaged ACs involves more technical expertise, packaged ACs are produced by large players in the organised sector.

Central ACs

Unlike room or packaged ACs, which are unitary systems, central air conditioning involves a central cooling plant. Central ACs handle refrigeration requirements ranging from 10T to a high of 1,650T.

Market Size

According to the Refrigeration and Air-conditioning Manufacturers' Association (RAMA), the market size for room air-conditioning in India was estimated at Rs 46.79 billion in 2006. The RAC market has grown from a level of .25 million units in 1993 to an estimated 1.5 million units in 2006.

EXHIBIT 29.1

Segmentation of AC Market in India

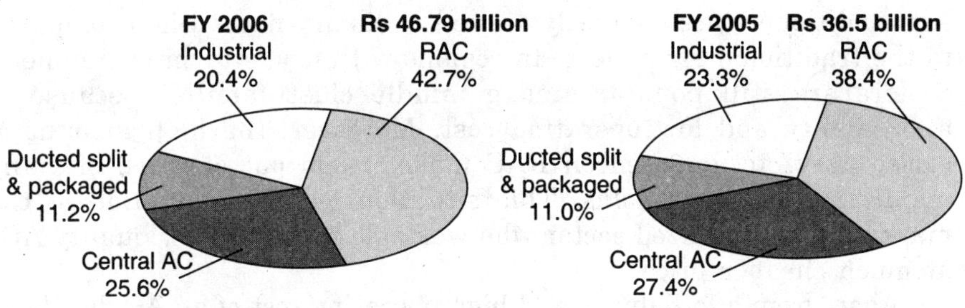

Region-wise Market Size

Among the four regions, North India consumed the largest amount of RAC, followed by the West. While North India accounted for 37.1 per cent of RAC sales during 2006, West India accounted for 27.1 per cent.

MARKET TRENDS

Customer Segmentation

The RAC segment is dominated by the household segment, which accounted for 60 per cent of total demand in 2006 whereas the share of the household segment was 55 per cent of the total demand in 2002.

The commercial segment, comprising offices and business establishments, accounted for 40 per cent of the total RAC sales in 2006, as compared with 43.5 per cent of the total RAC sales during 2002.

Household segment's demand for a RAC is generally found to depend on a number of factors as depicted in Exhibit 29.2 below.

EXHIBIT 29.2

Factors Affecting Demand

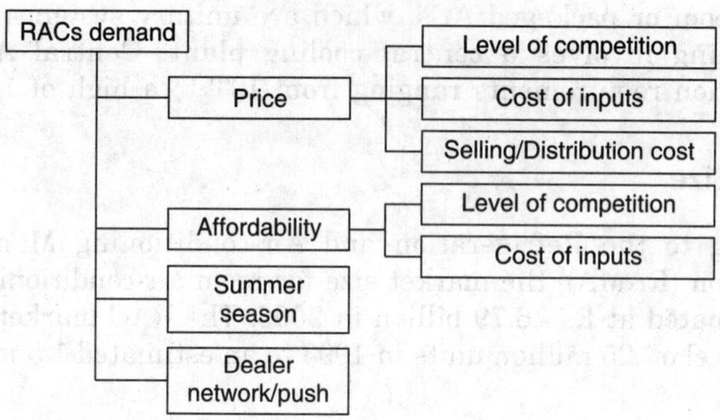

Characteristics of RAC Market

Air conditioners are generally viewed as luxury items when compared to the traditional air coolers. In regions with dry, scorching summers, coolers are still popular among middle class families because of affordability and low operating cost. Moreover, the high amount of excise duty etc. imposed on RAC makes them out of reach of many middle income households. This situation led to domination of the market by unorganized sector who was able to supply low quality ACs at much cheaper price.

Apart from affordability and high operating cost of an AC, low level of penetration of ACs is also because of lack of continuous supply of electricity in many parts of India and frequent voltage fluctuations faced in the country side.

Nonetheless, the situation seems to be changing fast. Increased disposable income and reduction in price led to continued buoyancy in the AC market. Presently, upper-middle income families in India are found to be favourably disposed to install at least one AC in their home. Such a change in attitude had major impact on sales growth and that is why, AC market in India registered a 18.5 per cent growth Exhibit 29.3 below shows actual sales from 2002–03 to 2005–06 and a projection of expected sales till 2007–08.

EXHIBIT 29.3

Sales Volume

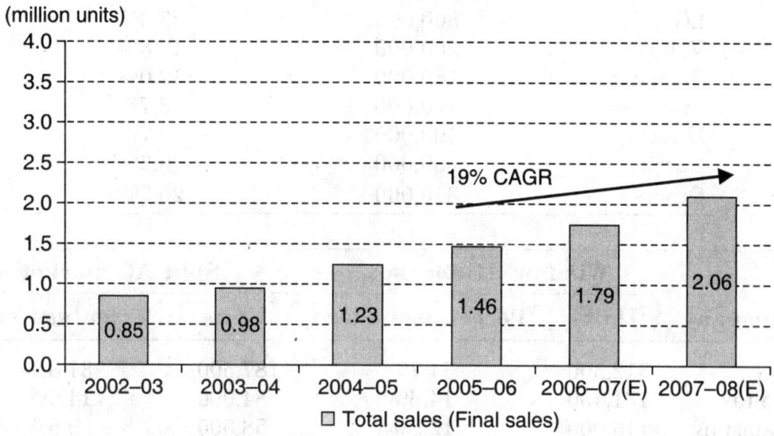

Split AC accounts for 30 per cent of demand for RACs in India. Declining prices and lower cost of operations is resulting in faster growth for the split RAC than the window ACs. Generally, software companies, restaurants, commercial complexes, and shopping malls, etc. are increasingly going for split ACs. Because of increased sales growth in the split AC segment during recent years, the share of window ACs in total RAC sales has declined from 81 per cent in 2000 to 70 per cent during 2004.

COMPETITIVE STRUCTURE

Historically, the RAC industry in India had a predominance of the unorganized sector. At that time, Carrier used to command a large amount of the Indian market among the organized players. It was encashing on its global image of pioneer in AC technology and differentiated itself on the basis of cooling efficiency of its compressors. However, with entry of Korean companies such as LG and Samsung during the 1990s, the older established players like Carrier and Fedders have substantially lost their market share. Table 29.1 and Exhibit 29.4 below show the market share of leading AC makers in the year 2006.

TABLE 29.1: Total Air Conditioner Market

Company	Units	Percentage Share
LG	500,000	33.3%
Voltas	200,000	13.3%
Samsung	180,000	12.0%
Videocon	130,000	8.7%
Hitachi	100,000	6.7%
Carrier	80,000	5.3%
Others	310,000	20.7%

	Window AC market		Split AC market	
Company	Units	Percentage share	Units	Percentage share
LG	312,500	34.7%	187,500	31.3%
Voltas	131,400	14.6%	84,000	14.0%
Samsung	116,000	12.9%	58,500	9.8%
Videocon	71,500	7.9%	48,600	8.1%
Hitachi	60,000	6.7%	40,000	6.7%
Carrier	48,000	5.3%	32,000	5.3%
Others	160,600	17.8%	149,400	24.9%

EXHIBIT 29.4

Market Share of Industry Players in 2005–06

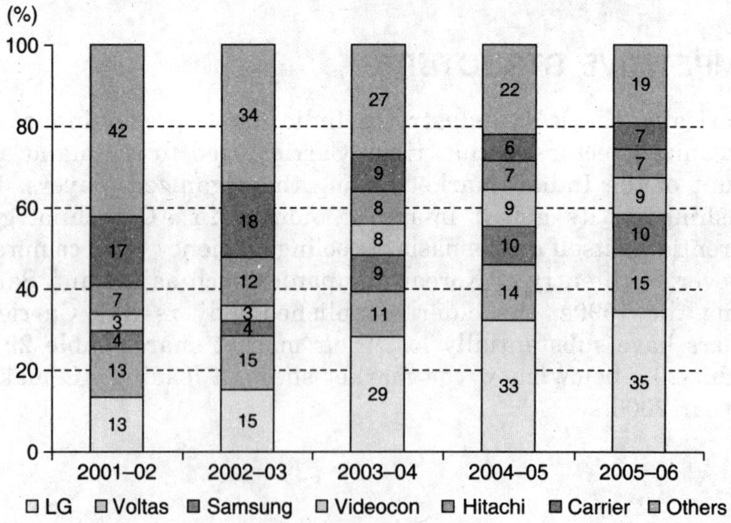

Positioning of Key Players in the Industry

Exhibit 29.5 shows a positioning map on capacity and price of the key RAC players operating in India.

EXHIBIT 29.5

Price-Capacity Mapping for Window AC Models on Offer in India

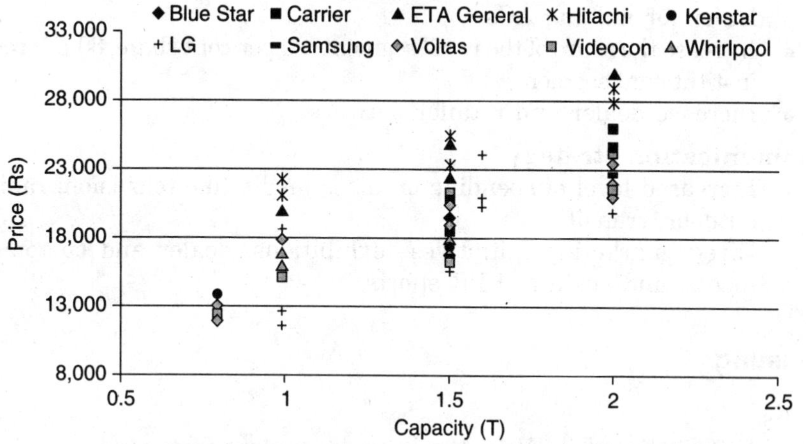

MARKETING STRATEGIES OF TOP THREE PLAYERS

LG

Focus

- product development
- aggressive promotion has been the cornerstone of LG's strategy

Positioning

- Health Air system as a USP

New initiative

Recenly launched a range of commercial ACs targeted at the corporate segment.

Communication strategy

- Communication strategy focus on the benefits derived from its technology.
- Communication tries to connect with women who are of late assuming leading role in such delicate products.

Voltas

Focus

- More on engineering excellence

Positioning

- As an original equipment manufacturer for global brands like LG and Electrolux

New initiatives

- Launched new models targeted at the household segment
- Voltas has entered into a contract manufacturing agreement with Haier for making ACs
- Increase the share of the retail segment (20 per cent share, 80 per cent institutional segment)
- Increase dealer and retailer network

Communication strategy

- Increased level of spending on mass media like television, radio, outdoor, transit
- Direct marketing initiatives—exhibitions, dealer and customer meets, and sustained PR efforts

Samsung

Focus

- Differentiated itself on the basis of product features

Positioning

- Targeted at the higher-value commercial market segment

New initiative

- Plans to invest US$5 million to manufacture heat exchange components for ACs

Distribution

- Increase in total number of retail points, expansion by 35 per cent
- Distribution network is also strengthened

Future Prospects

The air conditioner market in India has been experiencing a rapid growth over the last few years. The demand for aesthetically superior models, especially split ACs, is expected to rise. Generally speaking, penetration of RAC is likely to increase because of a number of favourable market conditions. For example,

- With higher disposable income and larger number of families in the upper and upper-middle income categories, the market demand will certainly go up
- At the same time many AC companies choose to reduce price in order to have more rapid expansion of the market
- Wider choice of brands the market will face intense competition

STRATEGIES FOR GROWTH

Facilitate Growth in the Domestic Market

- Position the AC as a productivity enhancer to deepen penetration in offices
- Educating consumer on running cost of AC and ways to reduce it
- Tie-up with contractors, architects to optimally design rooms for least AC running cost

Facilitate Growth in Exports

- Benchmark Indian plants to the best in the world
- Understand best practices in operations and educate Indian players
- Participate in tradeshows, conferences in target markets

Work with the Government to Shape Policies

- Ensure implementation of safety standards
- Ensure national level quality/performance standards
- Define clear procedures/paperwork for imports/exports

CHAPTER 30

Paints

The Indian paint industry traces its origin to 1902, when Shalimar Paints Company was set up near Calcutta. Today the industry is highly fragmented. While the large or organised sector has only 14 players, there are over 2000 units in the small scale or unorganised sector.

The Indian paint industry is estimated to have reached Rs 50 billion in value terms and the demand was around 6,50,000 tonnes per annum in 2006. The per capita consumption of paints in India stands at 0.5 kg per annum as compared to 1.6 kg in China, 8.8 kg/annum in Malaysia, 26.9 kg in Singapore and 22 kg in the developed countries. India's share in the World paint market is just 0.6 per cent.

PRODUCT CLASSIFICATION

Paints are generally classified into two major types.

1. **Decorative or architectural paints:** It consists of paints such as acrylic, oil-bound distempers, enamels, plastic emulsions, cement paints, wood finishes. The demand for decorative paints arises from household painting, architectural and for other display purposes. The composition of various decorative paints in 2006 was as follows.

Composition of Decorative Paints

Enamel	50%
Distemper	19%
Emulsion	17%
Exterior coatings	12%
Wood finishes	2%

2. **Industrial paints:** Industrial paints are made up of automotive paints, powder coatings, marine paints, high-performance coatings and special purpose finishes. The composition of industrial paints in 2006 was as follows.

Composition of Industrial Paints

Automotive paints	50%
High-performance coatings	30%
Powder coatings	10%
Oil coatings	5%
Marine paints	5%

The industrial paints are used in automobile, engineering and consumer durables. Margins are comparatively lower in the industrial paints as compared to the decorative paints. Being technology intensive, here the unorganized sector does not operate. To bag an order from an automobile manufacturer, collaboration with a well-known foreign paint company is a must. In the industrial segment, many of the players have tie-ups with foreign majors or are owned by them.

MARKET SEGMENTATION

As explained above, the market is broadly classified as decorative and industrial paints.

Decorative/architectural paints market can be further segmented on the basis of the following:

- **Customer types:** Household market; Institutional use
- **Product categories:** Distempers, enamels, emulsions etc.
- **Price:** Premium, popular or economy

Industrial paints market can be further subdivided into the following categories depending on the end users.

- **Automotive paints:** Products in this category are used for OEM and replacement purposes in automotive industry. It includes rust protectors, finishes, glosses etc.
- **Marine paints:** These points include a variety of products for fouling control, ballast tanks, cargo tanks, cargo holds etc.
- **Powder coatings:** These paints include coatings for automotives, furniture, appliances, personal computers and peripherals.
- **High-performance coatings:** Used in automotive, aviation and firearms industries.
- **Other general industrial finishes:** It includes various thinners, enamels, clears and finishes required in paint applications.

CONSUMER BEHAVIOUR

In household sector decorative paint is still viewed as a luxury. Generally households undertake a painting exercise once in 4–5 years. It assumes a high involvement purchase decision as the painting cost is fairly expensive. Most often, the company choice is made on the recommendation of the retailers and painters.

In the industrial paints category, product characteristic is of utmost importance. Other parameters of consideration are issues such as credit terms, logistics service and relationship with the paint company. Of late, paint companies are trying to customize their products as per the specific industrial applications. Though this customization involves a cost, it is fast becoming a differentiator in terms of developing long-term contracts with the customer.

SENSITIVITY OF THE INDIAN PAINT INDUSTRY

1. **Price of raw materials:** Various factors that have influenced the operations of paint industry are discussed below.

The raw materials cost make a whopping 70 per cent of total cost. Any increase in the prices of the raw materials adversely affects paint prices. Of the 300-odd raw materials, nearly half of them are imported petroleum products. Thus, change in global oil price and import policy affects the bottom-line of the players.

The Indian government used to levy hefty amount of excise duty on paints. Recently excise duty was slashed across the board from the level as high as 60 per cent to around 20 per cent.

2. **Working capital:** The paint industry is highly working capital intensive because of the following factors:

(a) Paint is produced in batches. Moreover, to maintain a wide range of shades, if requires high quantities of raw material and finished goods.
(b) Sales in low volume lead to higher unit cost of storage and packaging costs.
(c) A wide dealer network implies high inventory turnover period.
(d) A decorative paint company had to manage hundreds of Stock Keeping Units (SKUs), depending on the pack sizes, shades etc. Now, with the installation of computer aided designs, it is required to have only some base colour combinations.

3. **Distribution:** Generally, most of the decorative paints sales happen through retailers, who are either exclusive stockists or multibrand outlets. The retail outlets vary in terms of quantity of paints stocked, location, breadth and depth of range. In general, it requires huge investment to develop dealer networks, especially in urban and semi-urban markets and industrial zones.

4. **Plant location:** New plants are located in places near the markets to achieve logistic efficiency and moreover, because transporting paint is a cumbersome process. Generally, the location of new plant is chosen to minimize the transportation cost.

5. **Technology:** The paint industry is technology driven. As customers demand better performance in terms of appearance, finish, protection etc., the selection of foreign collaborators and technology assumes an important strategic issue.

MARKET TRENDS

The key trends noticed in the Indian Market are as follows:

1. **Reduction in excise duty and infrastructural boom:** Till the early nineties, paints were seen as a luxury product, and the government used to levy exorbitant amount of tax. With over 50 per cent taxation, the growth of the paints industry was severely restricted. The government's policy has changed considerably in the post liberalization era. The excise duty on paints has been brought down from 35 per cent in 1993 to 20 per cent in 1996. Following this, the paints industry has experienced a rapid growth. Paints demand has further surged due to general economic prosperity and added emphasis on housing and infrastructure sector. Similarly, the industrial paints have grown by over 15 per cent per annum as the automobile industry went through a good phase.

2. **Move towards customization—"Instacolour"/"Colour world":** Changing customer preferences and increasing customers involvement in choice of exact shades have led to mass customization of paints. Leading paint companies now allow the customers to choose the shade of paint. Asian Paints has launched a concept called "Colour World" where a customer can select shades of his choice from among hundreds of shades. Similarly, Jenson and Nicholson launched "Jensomatic" machines for the same purpose.

3. **Move towards more use of industrial paints:** Generally, industrial paints market is less price sensitive than the decorative paints. Also, the demand pattern is not seasonal. Moreover, serving the industrial market does not involve much of distribution costs compared to the retail market and thus, it offers higher margin.

In developed countries, the industrial paint usage is 60 per cent and the balance 40 per cent is used in decorative segment. But in India decorative paints still command 70 per cent of the market. This is primarily because industrial applications of paints, except for automobiles and white goods, are mainly out of statutory compulsions. With growth in economy and growing awareness about anti-corrosive and protective properties of paints, demand for industrial paints is likely to increase.

4. **Concentration on premium decorative paints:** Construction boom in India has its impact on the decorative paints. In recent times interior emulsion paints is reported to be growing by over 25 per cent. Further, these products are priced at a premium and sold mostly through exclusive outlets in urban locations and offer higher profit margin. Thus, top paint manufacturers are naturally fighting for more share in this segment.

5. **Segment domination:** Asian Paints and Goodlass Nerolac dominate the decorative and industrial segment respectively. Wall "finishes" have assumed new rage with many urban households. They want to put a stamp of distinctive artistic taste on their interiors. Consequently, decorative paints choices have begun to multiply. Asian Paints has launched "Royal Play", a special effects paint. As per the industry reports, sales of "Royal Play" is doubling every year. Nerolac launched 'Impressions', a range of wall finishes. It tied up with Disney to launch a range of custom made stencils of around a dozen cartoon characters. Berger is also trying to attract kids with its Galaxy (part of its Illusions range), which has "magic paint" and a set of stencils with which walls/ceilings can be painted with stars, moons, comets and other heavenly bodies that glow in the night.

SUPPLY CHAIN

Any decorative paint flows through various stages with special focus on the ownership pattern and the terms of trade.

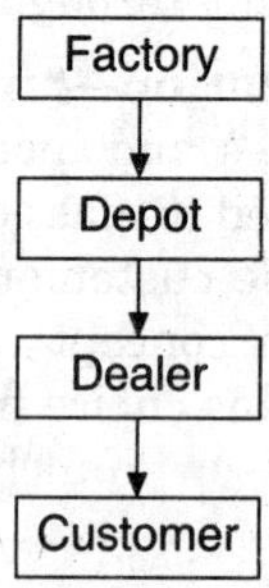

The first link in the chain is the factory. It has to be emphasized that the efficiency in obtaining the raw material in terms of time and cost. The speed of the production processes is also very important, particularly since inventory turnover periods are significantly high. The backward integration more of many players, specially to hedge against price uncertainty, has reduced cycle time for procurement of raw material of paints.

Another important aspect of the supply chain of the paints industry is the preference for small multi-location plants as opposed to large centrally located plants. Though larger plants enjoy economies of scale in production, multi-location plants are preferred because of lower freight cost incurred for smaller volume of operation. As the packaging size gets larger, it takes a larger capacity of freight container which is today costlier than small one.

The second stage of the supply chain is the depot. Given the nature of paints as a product, storage requirements and strict quality control in the depots are essential to prevent loss of inventory due to product deterioration or not meeting the product specifications. In order to maintain the rigorous and strict standards, depots are normally owned by companies themselves.

The next link in the product flow chain represents the primary sale where the ownership of the product is transferred out of the company. This link of the chain is called the dealer. Dealers can be of two types:

(a) **Dedicated dealers:** They stock products of single company only. Whilst they are independent of the company in terms of ownership, they are loosely integrated with the parent company. The terms of trade are naturally more favourable for dedicated dealers as opposed to independent dealers. This translates to higher margins, exclusivity of distribution, and greater variety of product lines stocked, technical support to make procurement more efficient etc.

(b) **Independent dealers:** With independent dealers firms face competing pressures while on the one hand, they need to offer greater margins to give more shelf space on the other, they need to keep margins down to increase company profitability. While terms of trade are not as favourable as those of dedicated dealers, it is necessary to note that, given the nature of the paints industry where a wide dealer and distribution network is the primary critical success factor, the terms of trade are much more skewed in terms of dealer than that in any other consumer product industry. Given the fact that higher margins can be charged from industrial paints, companies try to maintain a larger proportion of industrial paints in the product portfolio offered to dealers. Also, the move to customization has made it necessary for companies to invest in information channels which carry data on consumer preferences back from the dealers to the company.

The last and most important link of this chain is the consumer. Some major characteristics of the household as well as industrial buyers were discussed in the section on consumer behaviour.

COMPETITIVE STRUCTURE

In India, in the organised sectors leading players in the paint industry are Asian Paints (India) Ltd (APIL), Goodlass Nerolac Paints Ltd (GNPL), Berger Paints, Jenson & Nicholson Ltd (J&N), Shalimar Paints and ICI (India) Ltd. The size of the organised paints industry is estimated at around Rs 3,500 crore and they hold 70 per cent of the total market. Over the last decade, the industry has been going through a consolidation. The major players have developed a vast dealership network.

Market Share

The market shares of the leading players in the decorative segments in the year 2004–05 are shown below.

APIL dominates the decorative segment with a 38 per cent market share. The company has more than 15,000 retail outlets and its major brands are *Tractor*, *Apcolite*, *Utsav*, *Apex* and *Ace*. GNPL, the number two in the decorative segment, with a 14 per cent market share, has its distribution network to about 10,700 outlets.

Company	Market Share
Asian Paints	38%
Goodlass Nerolac	14%
Berger Paints	9%
ICI	8%
Shalimar Paints	6%
Jenson and Nicholson	1%

The share of industrial paints in the total paint consumption is very low compared to global standards. It accounts for 30 per cent of the paint market whereas in most developed countries industrial use of paints is about 50 per cent.

The market share of leading players in industrial segment in the year 2005–06 is as follows.

Company	Market Share
Goodlass Nerolac	41%
Asian Paints	15%
Berger Paints	10%
ICI	9%
Shalimar Paints	8%

Goodlass Nerolac dominates the industrial paints segment with 41 per cent market share. It has a lion's share of 70 per cent in the OEM passenger car segment, 40 per cent share of two wheeler OEM market and 20 per cent of commercial vehicle OEM market.

APIL, the leader in decorative paints, ranks second in the industrial segment with a 15 per cent market share. With its joint venture Asian-PPG Industries, the company is aggressively targeting the automobile sector.

MARKETING STRATEGIES OF MAJOR PLAYERS

Asian Paints

Asian Paints started in 1942 is now India's largest paint company with a turnover of Rs 30.2 billion. It has 30 manufacturing facilities and operates in 65 countries in the world. The prime reasons for its success are its strong consumer focus and adoption of innovative marketing strategies.

The customer first approach—key to AP's success: From the beginning, Asian Paints has fostered a customer-centric approach to business. AP adopted the simple marketing concept of "going where the customer is".

Innovative marketing strategies: In the early 90s, for the first time in the paint industry Asian Paints offered the consumer over one thousand shades through Colour World. This concept of Colour World provided a new direction for the paint industry where the consumer could obtain- a service interface, apart from getting a choice of innumerable shades.

Recently Asian Paints introduced a toll free service where consumers call and ask queries related to painting. This service known as Asian Paints Home Solutions is currently available in 10 cities, viz Hyderabad, Bangalore, Kolkata, Delhi, Chennai, Ahmedabad, Mumbai, Pune, Coimbatore and Cochin.

Another innovative marketing program is the launch of Kids World. Under this, the company offers painting designs for Kids rooms and Kids Corners in any household. For the first time it has invited the customer to get into a Do-It-Yourself mode with these designs.

Royale Play is another innovative concept introduced by AP. It is a collection of innovative and ready to use special effect finishes for interior walls, comprising a range of special effects. And each of these effects is available in a shade palette that is fitting for that effect in interesting colour combinations. The revolutionary product gives wall paint a whole new usage.

Supply chain: Asian Paints has harnessed the powers of state-of-the-art supply chain system using cutting edge technology to integrate all its plants, regional distribution centres, outside processing centres and branches in India. All the company's paints plants in India, two chemical plants, 18 processing centres, 350 raw material and intermediate goods suppliers, 140 packing material vendors, 6 regional distribution centres, 72 depots are integrated.

Goodlass Nerolac Paints Limited

Goodlass Nerolac has tied up with the global automotive paint manufacturer Kansai Paints. It is the leader in the Industrial segment with a market share of 41 per cent in industrial paints and 65 per cent of which is in automobile sector. It has a turnover of approximately Rs 1,200 crores. The company has five manufacturing units and a network of over 11500 dealers across the country. The company manufactures a diversified range of products as follows.

Products: GNPL offers products for both industrialized and decorative segments.

In the **industrial** paints segment, it offers the following:

1. **Auto paints:** Nerolac offers a total painting system to the auto makers with a range of products.
2. **Industrial coatings:** Nerolac enjoys a market share of more than 40 per cent in the industrial paints segment.
3. **High performance coatings:** The Ameron Division of Kansai Nerolac services offers high performance coatings and gives customized services to different nature of industrial applications.
4. **Powder Coatings:** Polycoat Powders Ltd, is an associate company of M/s. Kansai Nerolac Paints Ltd, occupying the No. 1 position in the powder coating segment in India, offering products such as Epoxy Powder (6000 series), Epoxy Polyester Powder etc. and a range of Polycoat finishes.

Decorative: The company had around 17 brands under its portfolio. The brands broadly are classified into three categories—premium, popular and economy. 'Nerolac' is the mother brand and the three sub-brands under the mother brand are *Nerolac Excel*—a premium exterior emulsion, *Nerolac Allscapes*—premium interior emulsion and *Nerolac Suraksha*—the popular paint category.

Nerolac has a wide range of exterior paints that cater to different consumer requirements. Nerolac offers an economy pack under the brand name *"Nerocem"* which is a cement paint. It offers a brand called *"Suraksha"* which is a plastic paint. It has a special pattern pack under the brand name of *"Nerotex"* which is a texturised paint. It also offers the premium exterior feature packed under the brand name *"Excel"*, which is an acrylic exterior paint.

Nerolac also offers special paints for wood and metals. While enamels are recommended for metal surfaces, the brand called *Wonderwood* is meant for wooden surfaces.

Marketing strategies: Goodlass Nerolac has followed a totally different marketing strategy. Unlike Asian Paints, GNPL decided to concentrate on the industrial paints segment which is technology driven. Consequently, it has developed collaborations with a number of global paint manufacturers for different nature of paints. It has tie-ups with Kansai Paint for auto coatings, Valspar Corporation for powder coating, Ameron Coatings for high performance coatings, Nihon (Japan) for sealants and underbody compounds. It also has collaboration with Du Pont, USA.

Nerolac serves around 70 per cent of the total paint requirements for Maruti cars. It serves to other leading automobile companies such as Mahindra Ford, Pal-Peugeot, Bajaj Auto, Telco, Ashok Leyland, M&M, TVS Suzuki, Hero Honda and Hindustan Motors. It thus dominates the OEM segment with a 70 per cent share of passenger cars, a 40 per cent share of the two-wheelers and a 20 per cent share of commercial vehicles market. Its major customers in white goods category are Godrej, Voltas and Whirlpool.

Nerolac's industrial paints are marketed under brand names such as *Gossolite, Palm Tree, Soldier* and *Derolite*. In decorative paints, the company launched new brands in *Zola Coat, Satin Emulsion, Guntex* in addition to its already existing brands, *Excel* and *All Scapes*. Goodlass Nerolac Paints recorded a top line growth of 16 per cent to Rs 6.53 billion in 2003–04. The company posted a more impressive growth in net profit by 45 per cent.

ICI Paints

ICI India is a subsidiary of its UK based chemical giant ICI. Paints business in India owes its success to the performance of its well-known brands such as *Dulux*, *Duco*, and *2K*. It has concentrated on decorative paints and auto refinishes. They are present in all categories—Decorative-Dulux-Velvet Touch emulsion, enamel, Weathershield, Wash & Wear.

It has Weathershield, which is an exterior wall finish. Others include Maxilite, Farco, Supercote. The auto sector is marketed under the brand name Duco—which commands a premium in the particular market—where quality is stressed upon. ICI offers *Ducoregent* in the mid priced, range, *Permobel* in the economy segment.

Conclusion

The Indian paints industry is on the verge of a massive growth phase. India's recent drive for infrastructure development and rapid industrialization has pushed the demand for industrial paints, coatings and automotive paints. Moreover, many middle class people are now able to afford decorative paints. Thus the paints industry is already growing at 25–30 per cent and in the foreseeable future both decorative and industrial paints market are expected to maintain this growth level.

Increasing complexity of the supply chain due to mass customization and large number of SKUs and brands, the companies are investing in massive warehouses and distribution centres and are backing themselves up with the latest in SCM and ERP software.

As bulk of the base raw materials come from the petroleum sector, the raw materials are likely to be more costlier in the long run.

Paints industry in India is increasingly taking the shape of a typical FMCG industry. In future paints will be marketed more aggressively. Companies will leverage on long time supply contracts, innovative advertising and distribution strength to gain market share. Customers are likely to benefit from increased competition, better customization, wider choice and better services.

CHAPTER 31

Colour Television

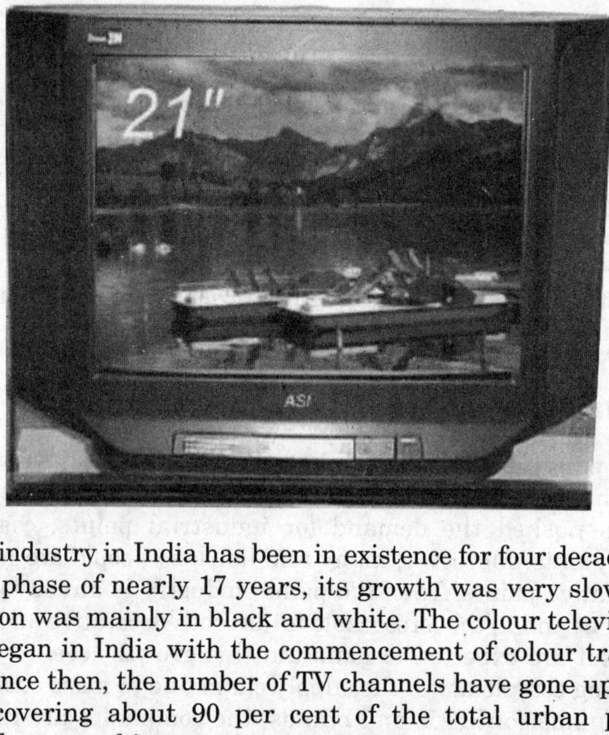

Television industry in India has been in existence for four decades. During the initial phase of nearly 17 years, its growth was very slow when TV transmission was mainly in black and white. The colour television (CTV) industry began in India with the commencement of colour transmission in 1982. Since then, the number of TV channels have gone upto 100 and they are covering about 90 per cent of the total urban population. However, the ownership or penetration level of colour TVs is still confined to urban areas. In 2005–06, CTV household penetration was estimated at around 25 per cent only.

HISTORICAL TREND

1984–85 to 1988–89: Significant demand growth: The introduction of colour transmitters led to an increase in CTV demand in the mid-1980s, and during the 1984–85 to 1988–89 period CTV sales recorded a growth of 46.2 per cent, to 1.3 million units.

1988–89 to 1992–93: Higher duty levels affect demand: During the 1988–89 to 1992–93 period, demand declined 11.6 per cent, due to an increase in CTV prices. (Prices of 21″ CTVs increased from around Rs 14,000 in 1989 to 20,000 in 1992.) The increase in prices was due to a significant increase in the excise duty on CTVs (up to Rs 4,875 per set) and CTV components.

1992–93 to 1996–97: Rise in cable and satellite network and rationalisation of duty structure spurt growth: During the 1992–93 to 1996–97 period, CTV sales grew by 26 per cent, on account of an increase in the number of cable and satellite channels and reduction in the import duty on CPT and other CTV components.

The launch of satellite in 1991 allowed viewers to access the Star channels. In 1992, the launch of the Zee TV channel resulted in the expansion of cable television. Subsequently, the number of channels increased substantially. There was a rapid increase in the number of cable & satellite (C&S) homes in western and northern India during 1992 to 1994. During the 1992 to 1996 period, C&S homes increased from 0.41 million to 11 million. From 1996 onwards, Tamil and Telugu channels accelerated the rate of growth of televisions demand in Tamil Nadu and Andhra Pradesh.

Meanwhile, the duty on CTVs was reduced from 85 per cent in 1993–94 to 52 per cent in 1996–97. This resulted in a decline in CTV prices and demand increased for CTVs.

1997–98 to 2005–06: World cup and increased competition: During the 1997–98 to 2005–06 period, CTV sales grew by 18 per cent, per annum which total sales volume reached to 5.4 million units. It was valued at Rs 70 billion. The increase in sales was due to a number of factors.

- *Decline in prices*: Prices declined as a result of intense competition from players such as Videocon, LG, Samsung, Sansui, Akai and Baron International. These players followed an aggressive marketing strategy and introduced lucrative promotion packages like gifts, exchange offers, and discounts, which resulted in a significant boost in demand.
- *Increase in consumer spending by fixed income segment following implementation of* the fifth pay commission by Government in 1997–98.
- *Increase in rural demand* following successive years of good monsoon and record harvest.
- *CTV purchases* have also picked up, on account of the world cup cricket as well as soccer event held during this period of time. A sizeable portion of the colour TV sales is accounted for by the mid-size segment. However, given their smaller base, the 14-inch and the large-screen segments are growing faster and they have assumed more strategic importance to the various CTV marketers.

DETERMINANTS OF DEMAND

Demand for CTVs depends on a large number of factors. Apart from price and affordability, other factors like promotion package, ageing of CTVs, availability of new models, aspiration for consumer durable purchase and number of nuclear families etc. influence the purchase of a television set. (Refer to Exhibit 31.1 for more details)

EXHIBIT 31.1

CTV Demand Determinants

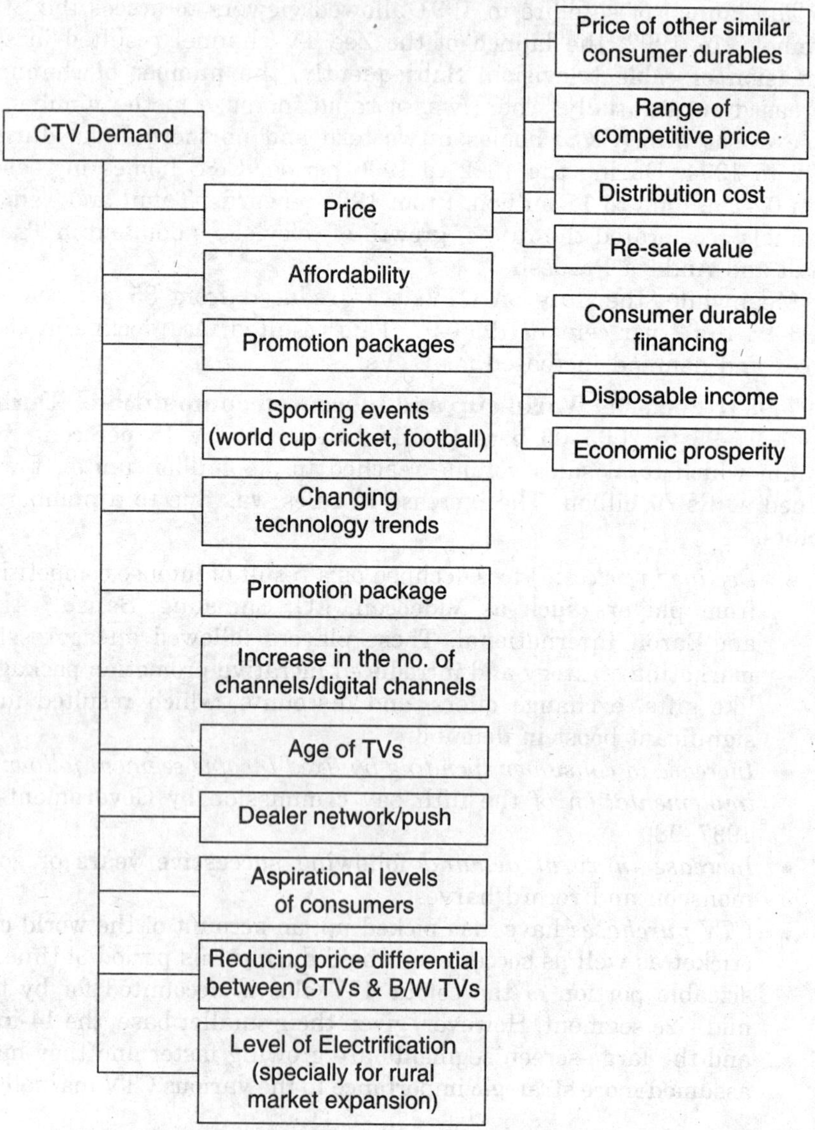

Market Segmentation

In the case of CTV the segmentation can be done on the following basis:

- Size—14″, 20″, 21″, 25″ and 29″ and above
- Price
- Geographic location

MARKET TRENDS

- Huge surplus capacity exists even after meeting domestic and export target.
- Entry of many international companies and exit of many state government owned domestic players (e.g. Uptron, Kellfon, ECIL etc.)
- Low penetration into the rural market.
- Indian market is 'value-for-money' driven and highly price sensitive.
- Technology is increasingly used to add features, superior performance or reduce the cost of product by higher scale of operation.
- Along with a sophisticated product, customers look for better level of services, attractive promotion schemes.
- Colour television (CTV) industry was hit by stagnant demand in the mid 1990s. Subsequent growth in the CTV sales is primarily because of innovative marketing strategies and cost cutting measures adopted by foreign owned TV companies.
- CTV manufacturers like BPL and Videocon have resorted to price cuts while others have lowered production levels in the face of rising inventories. The results are mixed. For instance, demand for 14-inch CTVs was hit by the reduction in the prices of 20-inch CTVs. Demand for larger sets (25 & 29 inch) has also slowed because of the price factor.
- Direct price reduction strategy does not appear to make consumers to acquire new CTVs. This phenomenon shows that the product has attained maturity stage in PLC.

COMPETITIVE STRUCTURE

Existing Players

The existing players can be classified into three types:

1. Low cost players: Videocon, Akai, Sansui, Panasonic
2. Mixed players: Onida, BPL, Samsung, LG, Phillips
3. Premium or quality focussed: Sony

Mirc Electronic most popular brand is Onida. It has revamped its strategy, by spinning off the existing sub-brands—*Igo* and *Candy*—into independent brands. *Igo* will take on the lower-end of the television market while *Candy* is now forgeted at the medium price segment. The strategy is aimed at further broadbasing the product offering of the company, which has largely dominated the top-end of the television market, across multiple market segments.

BPL has used umbrella branding to create a certain image for itself. The corporate name, BPL, has established itself into the credo of building winning competencies, abilities and infrastructure. This has enabled BPL to become a contemporary, yet an Indian entity.

BPL has had a strong presence at the mid-segment of CTV. It now wants to enter the low price line by introducing *Evelux* into small towns and rural markets. This requires strong distribution, deep penetration and service support. This move is primarily to the emerging rural market and take on competition from the Chinese and low priced brands. The company also plans to launch a premium sub-brand Digital BPL that will include high-end convergence product. The mother brand BPL will continue to operate in the middle segment of the CTV market.

Philips is a famous consumer electronics company and it stands at number three in the Asia Pacific region. Philips was somewhat late entrant in the CTV business in India. It changed its pricing policy to establish itself as a leading player in the Indian market. Philips has all along tried to establish its brand to reflect its international image as well as the fact of technology sophistication.

The company has recently launched a number of new colour TV models. It plans to introduce newer models in the price range of Rs 9000–9 lakh across the 14″ to 54″ range. These new models will be promoted under the existing sub-brands—Match Line and Power Vision.

Videocon has adopted a multi-brand strategy where it promotes Akai, Toshiba, Sansui and Kenwood along with the mother brand Videocon. Underlying the importance of having multi-brands, the company is trying to increase its market share. The company wants the customers to perceive Videocon as a product with value and having the latest technology. Videocon has used sub-branding as a marketing tool for its range of CTVs.

LG chalked out three phases of communication strategy:

- During the first phase (till mid–1998), the emphasis was on commu-nicating its global credentials and establishing a strong foothold in India.
- The second phase tried to make higher awareness with focus on the "esteem factor" and differentiation.
- In the third phase, the company tried to build on the relevance and recommendation scores, so as to increase its market shares.

LG's strength lies in a great product at a reasonable price. The company aims at building an image which is beyond the product itself.

Sony, for the first time, is cutting prices and re-defining its premium image. Their business strategy has been transformed to "retain price and increase features in some cases, and retain features and reduce prices in others". The company is putting in place a network of exclusive Sony outlets called Sony World. These outlets display the entire Sony range of top-of-the-line products. This strategy has served twin objectives. Firstly, these swank outlets enabled Sony to retain some resemblance of a premium image without relying too much on price. Secondly, they help the company to compete with the grey market as the entire range is available with an additional promise of efficient after-sales service.

Samsung is a subsidiary of Korean Samsung Electronics. It came to the forefront during its aggressive promotion compaign runs during the 1998 Soccer World Cup. The company conveyed a personality of a sportsman "who is pushing old boundaries by developing new technology and products". Hence its ad-line 'Challenge the limits'. The message that the brand conveys is the one at the edge of latest technology. It is seen as a brand, which is technologically superior. Samsung has achieved good results due to a mixture of aggressive marketing, increasing product portfolio, use of information technology in logistics and customer service, and enhanced productivity.

National Panasonic has entered the market through a dominant 80 per cent stake in the joint venture with Salora international. Its entry brand 'Top Dome' failed to create the image of an economical brand. It has made some headway with distribution and service network though it is still confined to the northern India.

Thomson, though it is the top selling brand in the USA, has not been able to make a significant dent in India. Technologically and financially a very strong company, it has joined with Dynavision of Dynasora TV fame. Thomson has been mainly in the south. It has adopted the policy of parity pricing with the local brands, but at the same time it has not compromised on the technology. It is hoping to create sufficient brand equity and presence before resorting to premium pricing.

MARKET SHARES

In terms of market share the top three companies till 2001 were, BPL, Onida and Videocon. The position, however, changed from 2002–03 onwards, on account of aggressive marketing and increasing popularity of LG and Samsung and in the process they captured the lost market share of BPL and Videocon.

Table 31.1 below shows the shifting market share of various leading companies in October 2002 vs 2003 after the entry of Samsung, LG.

TABLE 31.1: CTVs: Market share (%) of key players

Player	Oct. 2002	Oct. 2003
BPL	9.75	3.98
Philips	6.28	5.39
Sansui	6.72	8.98
Videocon	7.33	9.19
Onida	12.08	11.59
Samsung	13.51	15.84
LG	15.29	20.83
Sony	32.1	20.0

Even in the flat TV markets, LG and Samsung have become the leaders. Exhibit 31.2 shows their share of the leading TV brands/players in October 2003.

EXHIBIT 31.2

Samsung Slips back to the Second Position in the Flat CTV Market

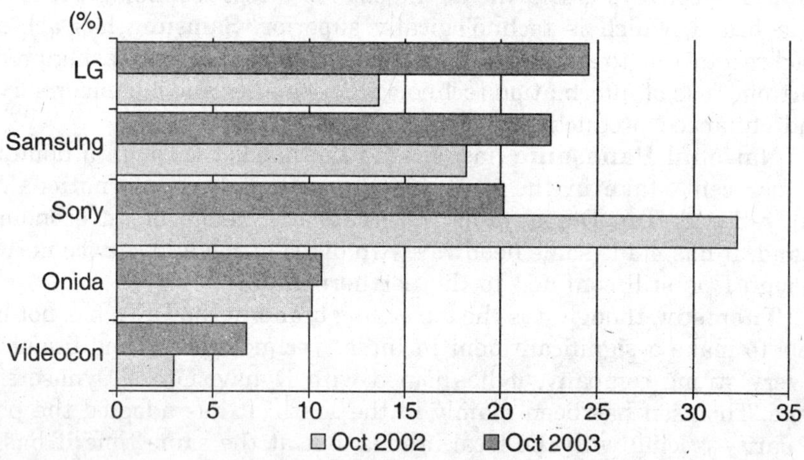

MARKETING STRATEGIES

To achieve the desired target, the companies have formulated various marketing strategies to meet the aspirations of their specific targets. Each player has its unique set of strengths and weaknesses. While some of them concentrated on price, brand building, some have looked at improving distribution, quality perception, etc.

Price Comparison

Table 31.2 below shows the price range of different models of leading players. Through the pricing strategies (i.e. high and low) the companies are trying to position themselves.

TABLE 31.2: CTV: Inter-firm price comparison across CTV segments size of screen

Company	14″	20″	21″ (Rs per set)	21″ Flat	25″	29″
Videocon	6,500–7100	8,250–14,700	12,490–20,490	10,800–17,300	22,990	27,990
BPL	6,750–9,490	8,500	10,200–14,800	13,790–23,990	22,380–24,212	31,190
Onida	7,600–8,990	9,500–11,990	11,000–19,900	18,990–20,990	24,990	29,990
Philips	7,500	9,900–11,990	12,900–20,500	19,990–23,990	—	24,900–28,900
Akai	6,500–9,490	8,330–13,000	9,990–14,990	16,500	—	—
Sony	15,200	—	—	18,490–25,200	—	—
Samsung	7,500–9,650	10,050–11,990	12,140–20,990	19,990–23,990	—	—
Panasonic	9,500	11,590–13,990	14,490–17,290	19,990–22,490	23,990	29,990
Thomson	7,490–10,990	10,000–13,990	14,000–19,490	17,990–21,990	24,990	—
LG	7,600–9,500	9,600–14,990	11,300–17,990	16,990–25,000	21,990–23,690	26,990–41,900

CTV is increasingly getting commoditised, so players are trying to move up the value chain. The mobility barrier for any company would be

- Image
- Access to technology
- Deep pocket

Inter Brand Comparison

In Exhibit 31.3, the circles represent the size of the brand (CTV sales in value terms). The key CTV brands are plotted on the graph based on their value market share and the proportion of the value to volume market share.

Sony, Panasonic, Thomson and Sharp are largely a part of the 2nd quadrant. These companies operate in the premium segment, where realisations are higher and volumes are lower. The image of Sony as a premium player is significantly high as compared with that of other players in the same quadrant (the company has exited the conventional CTV segment and is focusing only on flat CTVs).

EXHIBIT 31.3

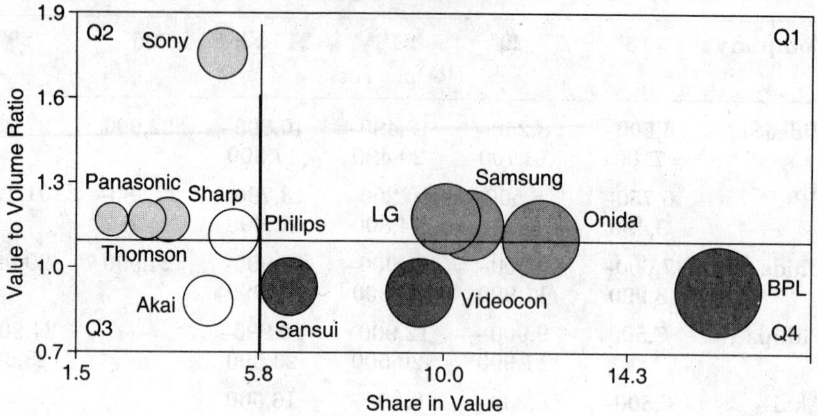

Philips, which is currently a part of the 2nd and the 3rd quadrant, could possibly shift to the 2nd quadrant in the long term, due to a shift in its focus on premium products, particularly in the large size flat CTV category.

LG, Samsung and Onida have been very successful due to the mixed product strategy (models catering to different economic segments) followed by them. These players are in the 1st quadrant where value and share both matter. It can be also observed from the Exhibit 31.3, that BPL and Videocon are largely volume based players (i.e. lying in the 9th quadrant).

NEW MARKETING FOCUS

TV has turned out to be a necessity for middle class houehold and status symbol for lower economic class. However, some distinct changes are already noticed on the marketing front. For instance,

1. **Increased competition: Better quality at lower prices:** With the entry of many global players into the Indian TV market, the initial advantages that the Indian companies enjoyed in terms of a well set distribution network and brand identity have vanished away. In fact, some of the erstwhile, Indian companies have learned from the new players and they have improved their technology to cope with the threat of competition. So, with the initial advantages of long presence Indian market has been offset by superior technology of new players. Thus, the competition among players of matching capabilities has called for new dimensions of success. Such a scenario requires continuous innovation, adaptation and utilization of technological know-how to deliver superior quality at lower prices.

2. **Importance of all segments:** If a CTV player wants to be market leader in terms of market share, then it has to participate in all segments.

In CTVs, for example, Phillips has not been aggressive in the 14, 20 and 21-inch segments where it lies below most other big players. But it continues to be very strong in the upper-end segment and looks forward to maintain that.

On the contrary, Onida, whose most of the sales come from the high end, will need to avoid such a trap in order to remain a top player, specially with the lower and middle strata poised for a growth. To an extent, Onida has been doing it. The company has finally moved beyond its old slogan of "neighbour's envy, owner's pride" and therefore it has now encashed on its pride in developing core competence in sound, through its KY technology, and therefore, re-launched as KY Rock. Some other recent launches include the Onida Wallscape, a flat-screen TV that is only 15 cm thick; Onida Pure Flat, with a 100 per cent flat screen; Onida Twister, with a motorised swivel base that helps rotate the screen to suit the angle of vision.

Onida is trying to position itself on the premium, high-tech plank and even pushing its own models on obsolescence. Here a company introduces a new model of CTV say at Rs 11,000, and gradually brings down its price to Rs 10,000 and finally withdraws the model. Then launch another model at say Rs 11,500, bring the price down and then discontinue it. And so on. So, effectively the company chooses to make its own model redundant almost every year. The underlying idea is to create new value segment. Onida is not ignoring the mid-to-low-end segment, although most of its sales come from higher-end models. As the market at the lower end began expanding exponentially, Onida decided to launch its Igo budgetline series at far more competitive prices.

In the long run, one can expect massive growth in the CTV market as the fundamental drivers for demand growth are all there in the market. The 14 inch segment has grown by 15 per cent. It is expected to continue in the future as well. Therefore, all the players will need to continuously focus on all segments and be amongst the leaders in each to sustain growth.

3. **Flexibility in pricing:** A large section of the consumers of TVs still remain quite price sensitive. Therefore, price will continue to be a major competitive tool in the foreseeable future in almost all the segments except for high end category where technological superiority may be the decisive factor.

4. **Differentiation—more important than ever before:** With the rapid increase in the number of players in the market and consequently an even more rapid increase in the number of models, a comparison of their features and relative advantages has become a complex process. Further, the relative advantages of one over the other may be so miniscule and it may finally be impossible to make a comprehensive and meaningful comparative analysis before making a purchase. In such a scenario, being able to differentiate one's brand is of immense importance.

With the metropolitan markets getting almost saturated, it is the semi-urban towns and rural areas that offer the greatest scope for expansion. Further, the rural-urban divide today is thinning. There is large-scale migration to cities where a distinct class of new consumers is emerging and every TV company wants to cater to this segment. The marketing of durable product like CTV has to keep in mind the lifestyle requirements of Indians and the income constraints.

As the television market becomes more competitive, strategies are going to be constantly under the microscope. Market feedback will be used to fine-tune strategies, and make mid-stream changes. The main battle rages on in the area of positioning of products. It is important for TV makers to straddle the market with products for its various segments. At the same time, market perceptions of quality will be critical. So, even as the market expands at a promising rate, the demand for better quality and service at lower costs will continue to become more pressing.

5. **Focus on the rural market:** Gone are the days when companies used to consider rural sales a bonus to the total sales turnover. Today rural markets are more than shoring up bottom lines. Rural incomes have changed drastically over the last few years, influencing market behaviour. The high income combined with low cost of living in the villages has meant more money to spend. And with the market providing them options, tastes are also changing. The fact remains that the options available to the rural consumer are nowhere near what they are in the urban supermarkets. And for obvious reasons. It is physically impossible for a company to cover all the three million outlets in the country. The quest is for higher volumes to offset marketing costs, be it transaction costs of distributors or low selling price.

Conclusion

The integration of the world TV markets and producers would require changed strategies. This cross-border expansion would be achieved in several ways. Companies would export their products from the home country, buy a foreign company, conclude an international alliance, or setup foreign production facilities. Thus, not only the colour television market but the electronic industry as a whole would see a sea change in the products and services. Indian brands will continue to face tough challenges from the strong foreign players.

CHAPTER 32

Passenger Cars

Until the early 1980, in India owning a car was considered to be a luxury possession. During those days there were only three producers of passenger cars, namely, Hindustan Motors (HM), Premier Automobiles Ltd. (PAL), and Standard Motors Private Ltd (SMPL), and Mahindra & Mahindra (M&M) used to make utility vehicles (jeeps). Initially these producers had obtained licensed technologies from the UK, Italy, and USA then each had a very small output level. During that era car manufacturing was licensed, expansion was restricted; there were quantitative restrictions (QR) on imports.

HISTORICAL TRENDS

In 1982, the Government of India set up the Maruti Udyog Limited (MUL) as a joint-venture with Suzuki Motors Corporation of Japan, where the government owned 80 per cent of its equity. In 1984, MUL manufactured over 12,000 cars mainly from imported completely knocked down (CKD) kits. In 1990, MUL produced over 50 per cent of all passenger vehicles produced in India.

Economic liberalization, started in July 1991, led to the delicensing of the passenger car segment in 1993. Quantitative restrictions (QR) on imports continued. The 90s witnessed the emergence of Maruti Udyog as the market leader in the passenger car segment. Between 1995 and 2000, several international players—Daewoo, Hyundai, Peugeot, Fiat, Ford, General Motors, Mercedes—entered the passenger car market in India. With the entry of so many foreign car companies passenger cars and utility vehicles both witnessed significant technological advancements. Moreover, because of rise in customer expectations in terms of improved vehicle performance, fuel economy, safety, comfort and convenience, compliance with stringent environmental regulations, the basic characteristics of the Indian car market charged perceptibly.

Automobile companies started investing in service network to support maintenance of on-road vehicles. Starting in 2000, some landmark policy changes such as removal of quantitative restrictions (QR) and 100 per cent

FDI through automatic route were introduced and exports were given a thrust. The market experienced the thrill of intense competition as a number of new cars, models were launched. As such consumers in India found a wide range of car models to choose from. In other words, the passenger car market in India changed into a buyer's market.

Current Scenario

- India is 11th largest passenger car market in the world.
- India is the second-biggest market for small cars after Japan. It accounts for 60 per cent of the domestic market.
- India is the fastest growing car market in the world, growth rate of 20 per cent.
- Domestic sales of cars crossed the mark of 1 million in 2004–05.
- 2/3rd of auto component production is consumed directly by OEMs.
- Growth of domestic sales and exports of automobiles during 2001–02 to 2005–06 are shown below (Exhibit 32.1).

EXHIBIT 32.1

Domestic Sales Trends

Category	2001–02	2002–03	2003–04	2004–05	2005–06
Passenger cars	509088	541491	696153	820179	882094
Utility vehicles	104253	113620	146388	176360	194577
MPVs*	61775	52087	59555	65033	66366
Total	**675116**	**707198**	**902096**	**1061572**	**1143037**

***MPV:** Multi-purpose vehicles.

Automobile Exports Trends

Category	2001–02	2002–03	2003–04	2004–05	2005–06
Passenger cars	49273	70263	125320	160670	170193
Utility vehicles	3077	1177	3049	4505	4486
MPVs	815	565	922	1227	1093
Total	**53165**	**72005**	**129291**	**166402**	**175772**

Source: SIAM

MARKET SEGMENTATION

The passenger car market can be segmented on the basis of car chassis length (as per the International Auto industry norm), retail price and type of ownership and use. Different possible types of segments formed are shown in Exhibits 32.2 and 32.3.

EXHIBIT 32.2

Segmentation by Chassis Length

Segment	Segment's share (%) in total sales in 2005–06	Number/names of players	Remarks
A1: Mini (upto 3400 mm)	8	1 Maruti Udyog Ltd (MUL)	
A2: Compact (3401–4000 mm)	54	5 MUL, Hyundai, Tata Motors, Fiat, General Motors	Tata Motors dominates diesel car model, Hyundai and Maruti dominate petrol version car sales
A3: Mid-sized (4001–4500 mm)	16	8 Maruti, Hyundai, Tata Motors, HM, Ford, GM, Fiat, Honda-SIEL	Intense competition faced due to the large number of players
A4: Executive (4501–4700 mm)	2	5 Skoda, Toyota, Daimler Chrysler, Hyundai, GM	Although dominated by Skoda and Toyota, competition is increasing in this segment
A5: Premium (4701–5000 mm)	—	5 Honda-SIEL, Daimler Chrysler, Toyota, Skoda, Hyundai	This segment is dominated by Honda-SIEL.
A6: Luxury (> 5001 mm)	—	1 Daimler Chrysler	
Utility vehicles	20	10	Dominated by Mahindra, Toyota and Tata Motors

Source: CRIS-INFAC

EXHIBIT 32.3

Price Based Segmentation

Segment	Price range	Car models as on Dec. 2006
A (Economy)	Under Rs 3 lakh	• Maruti 800, Alto, Omni, • Reva
B (Entry Mid-range)	Rs 3–5 lakh	• Ambassador • Fiat Palio • Hyundai Santro, Getz • Chevrolet, Opel, Corsa, • Maruti Zen, WagonR, Versa, Esteem, Gypsy • Ford Icon & Fiesta • Tata Indica, Indigo • Mahindra Bolero
C (Upper Mid range & Premium)	Rs 5–10 lakh	• Chevrolet Swing, Optra, Tavera • Hyundai Accent, Elantra • Mahindra Scorpio • Maruti Baleno • Toyota Corolla, Innova • Tata Safari • Mitsubishi Lancer, Lancer Cedia • Honda City
D (Luxury)	Rs 10–15 lakh	• Ford Mondeo & Endeavour • Chevrolet Forester • Skoda Octavia Classic & Combi • Honda Civic & CR-V
	Rs 15–30 lakh	• Maruti Suzuki Grand Vitara • Hyundai Sonata Embera, Terracan & Tucson • Mitsubishi Pajero • Audi A4 • Opel Vectra • Honda Accord • Mercedes C Class • Toyota Camry
	Rs 30–90 lakh	• Audi A6, A8 & TT • BMW X5, 5 Series & 7 Series • Mercedes E Class, S Class, SLK, SL & CLS-Class • Porsche Boxster, Cayenne, 911 Carrera & Cayman S • Toyota Prado
	Above Rs 1 crore	• Bentley Arnage, Continental GT & Flying Spur • Rolls Royce Phantom • Maybach

Segmentation by Ownership and Usage

Based on the ownership and usage of the cars in India, there are four key customer segments:

- **Individual customer segment:** This customer group consists mainly of salaried employees.
- **Self employed persons (SEPs) customer segment:** This segment of buyers usually purchase the car in the name of their company—the use could be personal, official or both. SEPs include sole proprietors and professionals such as doctors, lawyers, accountants, architects, engineers etc.
- **Corporate customer segment:** This segment includes any private and public limited companies. The car is registered in the name of the company at the time of purchase.
- **Commercial customer segment:** Commercial buyers include taxi and tourist (TT) segment and the lease/rental segment. The TT category includes the meter taxis and the tourist vehicles (vehicles marked T). The purpose of purchase is commercial.

MARKET TRENDS

Segmentation and the Customer Behaviour

Individual segment: This segment had a share of around 55 per cent in the overall car demand as in 2006 with its share being the highest in the mini and compact category.

The drivers of car demand for individuals are mainly:

- Cost of ownership (price, taxation, running costs, and finance costs)
- Promotional efforts (discounts and schemes, advertising)
- New model launches.

The sensitivity to cost of ownership is highest for this segment. For this reason, individuals have a higher presence in the small car segment, due to its lower prices and higher fuel efficiency.

Self employed segment: This group of buyers in 2006 consumed around 15 per cent the overall car sales, with a relatively large share in the executive and premium category. An SEP buyer usually registers the car in the name of the company and uses the car for official as well as personal use. Since he is able to claim taxation benefit, the effective cost of financing decreases, thereby reducing the sensitivity to prices as compared to an individual.

The drivers of car demand by SEPs are:

- Running cost of the car

- Look for more fuel-efficient models and diesel variants with superior designs (for instance, improved diesel can models and other benefits of technologies).

Corporate customers: In 2006 corporates accounted for 15 per cent of the overall car sales. They contribute 28 per cent of the sales in the mid-size segment with a greater presence in the higher-mid-size segment, as compared to the lower-mid-size segment.

The drivers of car demand by corporate segment are:

- Changes in depreciation and tax rules, which determine whether the corporate chooses to purchase the car in its name, lease it from car leasing service providers or use the services of car rental companies.
- Brand image of the car manufacturer.

Commercial: The commercial segment consumed around 12 pe cent of the overall car sales, with a greater share in the compact and mid-size segment as compared to the 3 per cent share in the premium and executive segment.

Key demand drivers in this segment are:

- Fuel efficiency (km per litre) of the car and cost of fuel (Rs per litre)
- Model preference

Consumer Expectations

Apart from the initial price (which is often taken care of by auto finance arrangement), in India the basic customer expectations have been the following aspects:

- Fuel efficiency
- Comfort and convenience
- Safety
- Additional space and performance

Fuel efficiency: The constant rise in fuel prices has been the key driver for change in customer desire for higher fuel efficiency. Hence, companies in India have started laying emphasis on newer engine technologies like V-TEC, MPFI and CRDi, and developing vehicle using alternative fuels such as compressed natural gas (CNG), liquefied petroleum gas (LPG). These technologies lower the running cost of a vehicle by improving fuel efficiency and reduce the maintenance cost.

Comfort and convenience related factors: Electric power steering (EPS) systems are increasingly being used to reduce effort and fatigue for the driver. The use of improved suspension systems provides increased riding comfort. An increase in the demand for comfort in a vehicle has resulted in the development of technologies like one-touch adjustable steering column, integrated navigation radio, power sliding door, power lift gate and mobile multimedia systems.

Safety-related factors: Technological changes are introduced with the sole objective to provide more safety or reducing the impact of accidents on passengers. Commonly used safety features include advanced safety interiors (such as air bags), collision avoidance systems, anti-lock braking system (ABS), and disc brakes for all wheels. Such safety related features are also slowly introduced in many Indian car models.

Space and performance: Traditionally, there is demand for extra space, and better performance. Notwithstanding varying importance to the above list of factors, fuel efficiency will continue to top the list of customer expectations.

Key Drivers of Growth

Rising income levels: The buying decision of a passenger car is influenced largely by the cost of ownership. As a result of high car prices, car demand is dependent on the growth in income levels, which, in turn, is linked to the growth in the economy. Rise in purchasing power in the country would mean passenger car market will be on a sustained boom. That is why, with present rate of growth the passenger car market which was 1 million in 2004–2005 is likely to cross the 3 million mark by the year 2015.

Car penetration level: There is a potential for much higher growth in the domestic market due to the fact that the current car penetration level in India is just 7 cars per thousand.

Demographic profile: Changing demographic distribution is conducive for growth. India 70 per cent of population below 35 years, (who are the best prospect buyers), of cars nearly 130 million young people the working population group by 2009.

Infrastructure development: With the implementation of National Highways Development Project underway, it is expected that it will provide a big boost in demand for premium and luxury segment cars.

Financing options: Higher disposable income coupled with the availability of easy financing options is likely to boost the demand in passenger car.

Used car and utility vehicles market: The development of a vibrant used car market will drive the growth of new cars and UV sales by:

- Helping owners to dispose of their old cars and utilize the sale proceeds for buying a new car model
- Creating potential market for new cars, as the existing owners of cars are likely to upgrade to new in models
- Alluring a part of two-wheeler owners to buy economic priced cars and thereby, increasing the population size of car owners.

Other favourable conditions: Rapidly growing middle class population, vibrant economy, availability of trained manpower at competitive cost, fairly well-developed credit and financing facilities and local availability of the raw materials and components at a competitive cost have made India one of the favourite destinations for global passenger car makers. With the establishment of production units by major global car companies in India, in the near future there is going to be significant increase in the exports of cars, which will, in turn, help companies achieve lower cost in domestic car prices due to economy of scale, thereby leading to increase in domestic demand.

- **Environmental regulations:** Under the Auto Policy of 2002, the Government of India has announced an environmental policy for automobiles. This policy encourages manufacturers to produce cars and utility vehicles with improved technologies and alternative fuels, which will be lower in price and emission levels. Sales of new cars are also likely to increase, since customers will be deterred from buying older cars due to higher road tax on the same.
- **Replacement rate and scrapage:** The replacement rate of passenger cars depends on the availability of new car models, affordable financing schemes, income levels and tax related incentives. Compared to earlier practice, holding period of passenger cars has considerably reduced. Moreover, with the availability of new models at affordable prices, older vehicles are likely to be replaced much faster.
- **Government policy on tax:** In India the price of a car is heavily dependent on the various nature of tax (e.g. excise duty, sales tax rates) imposed. Of late, the government is pursuing an auto policy with a view to make Indian Automotive Industry more competitive in world arena. This will result in lowering of tax which will lead to reduction in car prices and offering of better value proposition to customer, leading to increased demand.

INDUSTRY SCENARIO

Competitiveness of Indian Companies

The Indian car industry derives its competitive advantage from its large domestic car market potential, abundant low cost skilled manpower and component manufacturing facility. It will continue to attract foreign car companies as long as India will possess these strengths. However, lower productivity of labour and the threat of Chinese exports loom large over car manufacturers in India. According to industry source, as of now the strengths and opportunities still outweigh the weaknesses and threats. Exhibit 32.4 shows SWOT analysis of India's present passenger car industry.

EXHIBIT 32.4

SWOT Analysis of the Passenger Car Industry

Strengths	Weaknesses
• Large domestic market — Provides a spread of larger volumes — Manufacturers derive benefits from low cost of production • Sustainable labour cost advantage • Competitive auto component vendor base — Continuous improvement in productivity and quality standards of Indian vendors — Global companies are increasingly utilizing India as a low cost source base • Government incentives for manufacturing plants — Liberalised investment norms	• Low labour productivity • High interest costs and high overheads make production uncompetitive • Various forms of taxes push up cost of production
Threats	**Opportunities**
• China—Favourite among global manufacturers — Main threat to India's emergence as a manufacturing — Significantly higher domestic mid-size car volumes	• Asia—A bright spot in the global auto industry — Presence in fastest growing automobile market—India to benefit from this growing demand

Competitive structure: The Indian passenger cars and utility vehicles industry comprises 14 players. As on January 2007, they had an aggregate capacity to produce 1.72 million cars. The market is certainly very competitive where the key parameters of success in India depend on many factors that are discussed below.

Key Success Factors

Some important factors that provide key to growth and profitability for a company in the Indian market are as follows.

Presence Across Multiple Segments: In a car manufacturing plant, the press shop, paint shop, engine and transmission assembly, and machine shop are required to manufacture different models. Installation of all these facilities involves high costs. However, a car manufacturer who has a presence across various segments can ensure better capacity utilisation by using all these common manufacturing facilities. This also reduces fixed overheads.

As customers show a tendency to upgrade from an existing segment to a higher one after some years, the company having presence across various segments can hope to retain its existing customers. Keeping in view this, MUL, has added a range of models—Maruti 800 in the mini segment, Zen, WagonR, Alto and Swift in the compact segment, Baleno in the mid-sized segment and the Grand Vitara in the high-end SUVs segment. In the process the company can offer its range to a customer wanting to upgrade to a higher priced car.

At present, companies such as MUL, Hyundai Motor India and Tata Motors score high on this factor, as they cater to all price segments with models in different segments, especially in the high volume mini and compact segments.

Cost-competitive Operation: Having low cost operation is imperative for earning higher profits. In recent times most car manufacturers have taken special drives to lower their cost of production. Increased amount of localisation and reduction in the vendor base have enabled them to bring down cost to some extent. Moreover, an attempt has been made to reduce overhead cost by increasing the use of common components and scale of operation. (e.g. manufacturing a larger number of models on a single platform).

Wide Dealer Network: Having a large service centre network is very important to cater to existing customers since after-sales service and access to original spare parts act as distinct advantages. On this parameter, Maruti Udyog Ltd, Hyundai Motor and Tata Motor are far ahead of their rivals, since they are continuously building up an extensive dealer and service network across the country.

Expansion of market territory: Till recently, passenger car demand in India was concentrated mainly in the urban areas and that too, around 25 per cent of the sales were confined to the country's four metros. Therefore, initially most players had set up dealership in the major cities. But over the past five years, the demand from the smaller cities, semi-urban and even rural areas has been growing. To meet this demand, companies are setting up dealerships in smaller cities and towns. Very soon showrooms may be opened in smaller towns to cater to the demand for high-end passenger cars and utility vehicles.

Easy Availability of Finance: Getting auto finance has become much easier. Car companies are making exclusive tie-ups with banks to offer loans to their customers in various regions. For instance, MUL tied up with the State Bank of India (SBI) to offer finance to its rural and semi-urban customers. This move has increased Maruti's rural reach significantly.

International Tie-ups: Car manufacturers who enjoy strong support from parent companies have an advantage over other companies in terms of the following.

Strong brand: Most multinational companies in India own a strong global brand, by which their products are identified. For instance, Honda owns the Accord and City brands and Toyota owns the Corolla and Camry brands. These are international brands, renowned for their high quality and are, therefore, easily recognised by customers. Consequently, the products of such companies can be easily marketed in India, lowering marketing costs and providing an edge over other competitors in the Indian market.

Strong technological support: Most passenger car companies who have set up manufacturing units in India are global players. Strong parentage ensures access to new models, research and development, and assurance of service support for its existing customers. For instance, Maruti Udyog derives its strength from its parent Suzuki Motors, Japan.

Launching of new models: The Indian subsidiaries of foreign car manufacturers have a comparative advantage over Indian manufacturers since they have access to the model portfolio of their parent companies. As a result, they can launch new models, without making large investments to develop the same for the Indian market.

MAJOR PLAYERS AND THEIR MARKETING STRATEGIES

Maruti Udyog Limited

Maruti continues to be the leader in the Indian market with a 55 per cent overall market share. Maruti's accomplishment has been significant for three reasons:

- First, the run-away hit of the Maruti 800 cc car in India since the mid-1980s convinced international automotive companies like Ford, General Motors, Toyota, Honda, Mitsubishi and Hyundai about the depth and potential of the Indian passenger car market. It also inculcated belief in other Indian auto companies like Tata and Mahindra that they too could diversify into passenger car making venture.
- Equally important point to remember is that the rise of Maruti shaped the growth of the Indian auto component industry.
- Product variants and careful positioning which is discussed below.

Maruti 800

- Launched in 1984 in A-1 segment (mini car).
- Underwent many cosmetic changes and a major change, in the form of MPFI technology.
- The Maruti 800 was until recently the best selling car in India, it is now a close second behind the Alto.

- Changed the market scenario forever, laid the foundations for a future where the importance of the customer is higher, and where a car is affordable by the Indian middle class.
- Offers value propositions in terms of affordability, fuel economy and ease of servicing.

Targeting

- This brand would continue to register strong growth in the A1 segment as long as India's penetration level of motor cars remains low.
- India is the second largest two-wheeler market (estimated size is 50 million). With cheaper credit facilities, any user of two-wheelers, especially in the higher end segment, could be shifted to such cars in the A1 category.
- To penetrate deeper into the Indian market, Maruti has tied up with India's largest bank, the State Bank of India to finance cars. With this tie-up, the company expects to reach parts of the rural market, which have so far not been covered by car financiers.

Omni

- The Omni is available in three variants—5-seater, 8-seater and LPG.
- It is positioned as "A small car that is BIG on space".
- The selling proposition of this vehicle is—utilitarian abilities.

Gypsy

- Launched in 1985 as a vehicle with off-road abilities like rear wheel drive, high ground clearance and a heavy duty clutch.
- The main selling proposition of the jeep is it is "all weather all terrain ability".

Zen

- Launched in 1993.
- Novel features included an all aluminum engine and increased performance.
- Increased performance, better technology and fresher looks were the main selling propositions of this car model.

Esteem

- Launched in 1990 as the Maruti 1000 in 3-box form.
- It is available in three variants—LX, LXi, VXi, with an all aluminum engine.
- The value proposition of the car is that it is a car "Big on Features, Performance", i.e. it offers all the advantages of a big car. *viz.* space, power and handling at a reasonable price.

WagonR

- This car was launched in 1999 in India.
- This car is available in DUO specification with the option of driving in Petrol/LPG.

- The selling proposition of this car model is mainly its unique combination of space, power, convenience and economy.

Alto

- Launched in the year 2000, this car is available in three variants—Alto, LX, LXi.
- Most fuel efficient car in A2 segment (Petrol).
- The value proposition—was that for the same mileage as M800 this car offered higher power, better styling, and overall performance—with a slightly higher price tag.

Baleno

- It was launched in 1999 positioned as a luxury car.
- Some features provided in the car includes—noise reduction, automatic climate control, tilt adjustable power steering, high ground clearance.
- The main selling proposition of the car was performance, luxury and techno savvy, with the tag line "surprising performance" used extensively in the advertisement campaign.

Versa

- Launched in 2001 with a big bang, with the "Big B" Amitabh Bacchan as the brand ambassador.
- This strategy probably was not very effective. So the car was later repositioned as a family vehicle, and the campaign was changed with the tag line "the joy of travelling together".
- It is available in 5-seater and 8-seater version.
- Its main selling proposition was that it was India's first luxury multi-purpose vehicle.

Grand Vitara

- The launch of the Suzuki Grand Vitara in 2003 was one of Maruti's many attempts to bring an international Suzuki brand to India (others being the Alto and WagonR).
- The selling proposition of this car model was composed of an internationally recognized and respected brand, luxury, performance and excellent off-road ability.

Swift

- This car's features consist of Suzuki's latest technologies in the areas like airbags, anti-lock braking systems, digital microprocessor controlled engine management system, funky and attractive styling, and automatic climate control. It is available in three variants—LXi, VXi, ZXi.
- It has been positioned in the high-end B-segment of the Indian car industry and was perceived to counter the entry of Ford Fusion and Hyundai Getz.
- This car also marks a new concept in marketing for Maruti, with separate, dedicated floor space allocated for the Swift in each of

its showrooms across India; it had specially trained service executives whose sole job was to convey to potential customers the unique value offered by the Swift.

- Swift has won "Car of the year 2006" CNBC auto car award.

Hyundai Motor India Limited

Hyundai Motor India Limited (HMIL), a subsidiary of Hyundai Motor Company, South Korea, is the second largest car manufacturer in India, with a 20 per cent share. HMIL presently markets 35 variants of passenger cars in six segments.

Variants of car models and positioning are as follows.

Santro

- Hyundai Santro was launched in India in 1998.
- It is positioned in the B-segment and is among the successful selling cars in the segment.
- Hyundai Santro is powered by the advanced Hyundai Epsilon engine which produces incredible power at a much lower rpm compared to any other car in its category.
- The *positioning* has evolved over the years, conveying mainly the functional benefits of the model to connecting with the consumer on an emotional level. From "a Tall Boy Model" to "Complete Family Car", it now talks of "The Sunshine Car".
- *Positioning* was mainly done with two major objectives:
  — Establishing the credentials of Hyundai as a world-class auto maker in India
  — Projecting Santro as the most technologically advanced car in its class.

Getz

- Getz is a Euro styled premium hatchback positioned in high end B segment.
- It is the most spacious car in its category.
- **Promotion**—highlights interior space "Give yourself your own space"

Accent

- Hyundai Accent has been designed keeping in mind the expectations from a true luxury car.
- It is available in five variants and is positioned in C segment.
- With its blend of design, responsive engine and well decorated interiors, the Accent offers lots of elegance.

Verna

- The Verna with its looks and distinctively sporty style is a car model projecting an image of elegant, practical and safe driving.
- It is positioned in the C-segment.

Elantra

- It is being positioned as India's first "Performance Luxury" car in the D-segment.
- Elantra is available in 2 different 4-cylinder, powerful engine configurations. Other features provided include an ultra smooth all wheel independent suspension, Gas Shock Absorbers and Tubeless Tyres.

Sonata

- It is positioned as a Luxury car in the E-segment.
- It is targeted towards people who consider themselves motivated and energetic, sophisticated and elegant. Sonata looks sharp, strong and modern.

Terracan

- It is positioned as an SUV.
- A dexterous combination of form and function. Rugged yet refined. On and off the road, Terracan is designed to rule.
- It is projected as the last word in diesel technology with unmatched performance, power, refinement and fuel economy.

Tucson

- It is positioned in the SUV segment.
- The performance, strength and frugality of a diesel engine together with quietness and smoothness of petrol is a reality.

Brand Ambassadors

Leading celebrities like Shah Rukh Khan, Sania Mirza, Preity Zinta are the brand ambassadors for the company's products.

Tata Motors

Tata Motors Limited is India's largest automobile company if one includes commercial vehicles. In the passenger car, it makes brands such as Indica, Indigo sedan and the Marina, its station wagon variant, in both petrol and diesel versions. Tata Sumo, Spacio and Tata Safari (the country's first sports utility vehicle) are the company's multi-utility offerings.

Tata Motors is the third largest player in the domestic car market with a market share of 16.4 per cent (April–Dec.2005). The company's domestic market share in utility vehicles segment is 13.4 percent (April–Dec. 2005).

Variants of Car Models and Positioning

Indica

- Indica was launched in December 1998, It captured the imagination of the entire nation as the first indigenously designed and manufactured car.
- The basic concept in the design was to provide interior space like Ambassador and external dimension like Maruti Zen, incorporating

world class standard of safety and design at a price close to Maruti 800.

- This brand of car was positioned in the B-segment where most of the competitive car models were much smaller. So, Indica's positioning statement of 'More Car per Car' highlighted this uniqueness.
- The car was targeted at the middle class customer base who are price conscious and wanted a car that has more space. It also targeted at the two wheeler segment to switch to a four-wheeler.

Indica V2

- An improved version of the original Indica.
- In 2001, the Indica V2 became the fastest-selling automobile in Indian history when it chalked sales of 100,000 in less than 18 months.
- The car had several added features like a SuperDrive Engine, BlockShock Absorbers, a SmoothRide Suspension, Easy Shift Gears and Wide Tread Tyres.It offered the power and comfort of a large car with the easy maneuverability of a small one.
- Taking off on the success of the Indica V2 diesel, the Indica V2 Petrol was launched in September 2001.
- In the year 2004, New Indica V2 was launched which was refreshingly different, with everything from a sporty new look, as well as stylish interiors.
- In November 2005, Indica V2 Turbo was launched. It is the only car in the B segment to offer a Turbo charger.
- Indica V2 is available with four variants: Indica V2 DLX, Indica V2 DLG, the Indica V2 DLS and the Indica V2 DLE.

Indigo

- A premium car developed on the Indica platform in the midsize (C) segment.
- Indigo SX series was launched in 2005 to cater to the premium mid size segment. The variant Indigo SX was rolled out with a number of premium features like leather upholstery, LCD screen, and beige interiors.
- Indigo is available in petrol and diesel versions.
- Indigo petrol is available in three variants: GSX, GLX, and GLS. Indigo diesel is also available in three variants: SX, LX, LS.
- New Indigo V series is also available in petrol and diesel models with two variants each in the respective models.

Indigo Marina

- Provides the luxury of a sedan; it has the utility and convenience of a multi-utility vehicle.
- It is also positioned in the midsize (C) segment.
- It is available in petrol and diesel models with three variants each in the respective models.

- "We like to carry our world with us", which highlights a car that has enough space to carry everyone and everything you have ever loved, right by your side as one drives.

Tata Sumo

- The Sumo incorporates all the features that are comparable to any other MUV in its class.
- The Sumo Victa has five variants including the Victa GX Turbo, Victa GX, Victa EX Turbo, Victa EX and Victa LX.
- It is powered by a 1948 cc, diesel engine.
- "What you drive is who you are" targeting the individual customer by emphasizing that this vehicle reflects one's personality.

Tata Safari Dicor

- The new look Safari Dicor sports a chrome plated front grill, large 16-inch alloy wheel rims and stylish bumpers with integrated fog lamps and crystal clear lights.
- Safari DICOR has a host of technologically advanced safety features like Anti-submarine seats, Anti Lock Braking System (ABS) with Electronic Brake Force Distribution (EBD), 3-stage collapsible steering column, front airbags for both the driver and co-driver.
- "Reclaim your life"! is the tagline of Tata Safari Dicor, a Sports Utility Vehicle (SUV) in the premium range.
- Targeted at the working professional in metros, the brand message is that the car enables users to get out there and reclaim lost ground, no matter how busy one is.

Fiat cars: Tata Motors and Fiat have signed an agreement to cooperate on dealer network sharing, which encompasses the sale of Fiat cars through the Tata Motors outlets in India. Following this agreement, across the country, Tata dealers undertake sales and servicing of all Fiat made cars, i.e. Palio, Petra, Adventure and Uno.

Hindustan Motors Limited

Hindustan Motors Limited (HML) is India's oldest automobile manufacturing company, established in 1942 by Mr. B.M. Birla. Commencing operations in a small assembly plant in Port Okha near Gujarat, the manufacturing facilities later moved to Uttarpara, West Bengal in 1948, where it began the production of—the Ambassador.

At present, it is a one billion turnover company manufacturing passenger cars, utility vehicles and earthmoving equipment. HML has collaboration with Mitsubishi Motors.

Variants of Car Models and Prince Positioning are Outlined below.

Ambassador

- **Features highlighted:** Space, sturdiness, easy availability of spare parts.

- **Major customers:** Taxi segment.
- **Positioning:** Trustworthy and safe car.

Ambassador Grand

- **Features highlighted:** Power steering, power brakes, remote shift gear.
- **Major customers:** Taxi segment–65%, institutional purchase–16%.
- **Product positioning:** Niche segment.

Ambassador Avigo

- **Features highlighted:** Power steering, power brakes, remote shift gear, alloy wheels, leather trimmed seats, chrome trimmings.
- **Positioning:** Luxury.

Mitsubishi Lancer

- **Features highlighted:** Rally proven engine, tried and tested safety mechanism incorporated.
- **Positioning:** Mid-size car segment—"own the road".

Mitsubishi Cedia

- **Features highlighted:** Combination of style, luxury, performance, power.
- **Positioning:** Luxury car.

Pajero

- **Features highlighted:** Unique balance of power, performance and efficiency.
- **Positioning:** SUV.

Montero

- **Features highlighted:** Stylish and luxurious SUV.
- **Positioning:** Reflection of supremacy.

Pushpak

- **Features highlighted:** Easy servicing, economical Ambassador spares, commercial vehicle.
- **Positioning:** MUV.

Trekker

- **Features highlighted:** Ability to carry goods and passenger with ease, Ambassador spares.
- **Positioning:** MUV.

Porter

- **Features highlighted:** Midsize goods carrier. Easy servicing, economical Ambassador spares, available everywhere.
- **Positioning:** MUV.

Mahindra & Mahindra

Mahindra & Mahindra (M&M) is the market leader in the Indian Multi Utility Vehicle (MUV) and tractor segments of the automobile industry.

Over the years, M&M secured significant success with introduction of models like Bolero, and Scorpio. Today, Mahindra & Mahindra made vehicles has come to represent high quality, ruggedness, durability, reliability, and ease in maintenance (a sample list of their existing models are shown in Exhibit 32.5. The company has targetted at varied nature of customers such as individuals, traders, entrepreneurs, contractors, tour operators, taxi owners, car hire companies as well as government departments, institutions and the Indian Army.

EXHIBIT 32.5

Mahindra & Mahindra's Range of Car Models

Types of vehicles	Brand name
Utility vehicles	Commander, Maxx, Bolero, Scorpio
Pickups/Vans	Pick-up, Utility, Bolero Camper
LCV (for JV with ITEC)	Cabking, Tourister Minibus, Loadking
Alternative Fuel Vehicles	Bijlee, Tourister, CNG Minibus

Honda SIEL Cars India Limited

Honda started operating in India in 1995. It was following a JV between Honda cars of Japan and Shriram India Electrical Limited, who are more popular as manufacturer of the 'Shriram Honda' series of portable generator sets in India.

Variants of Car Models and Positioning

Honda city

This car was Honda's first offering in India. Today, it occupies the premium end of the entry level cars in the Indian car market. With its variants priced between 7 lakh to 8.3 lakh, Honda City has established itself as a fuel efficient, long lasting, reliable car.

Positioning: The Honda City has been positioned as the VFM option from Honda. Best-in-class fuel efficiency, high resale value, high reliability and hence low maintenance costs, and lower purchase price through easy financing are cited as factors in its favour. It is also positioned as a Hi-tech car: a positioning that all Honda cars enjoy in India.

Honda Civic

Launched in 2006: This is Honda's latest offering in India. It is referred as Honda's best selling car. Civic carried with it unparalleled image, so much so that despite being less than a year old in India, the Civic already outsells all other cars in its category, which includes such big names as the Toyota Corolla and the Skoda Octavia. The Civic variants are priced between 11 lakh to 12 lakh.

Positioning: Being positioned as a hi-tech car, the Civic advertisements often use terms like 'exhilarating' to position the car as one that is powerful, fast and fun to drive.

Honda Accord

Honda Accord is one of Honda's best known brands across the world. In India it is competing with other world famous brands such as the Toyota Camry and the Hyundai Sonata. Priced between 15 lakh to 17.3 lakh.

Positioning: This car model is positioned as a luxury vehicle. Its advertisements often carry the word 'Unbeatable' or 'Unmatched'. Honda's hi-tech image is an added advantage.

Honda CR-V

CR-V has enjoyed a unique position in the Indian passenger vehicle market for most of its life—until the entry of the Ford Endeavor and the Hyundai Terracan. With all other well-known SUVs priced well over 20 lakh, the CR-V (along with the Endeavor and the Terracan) is the affordable, premium SUV. The Honda badge, however, gives it an edge over its competitors. The CR-V is priced between 15.2 lakh to 16.3 lakh.

Positioning: This vehicle is positioned as a good blend between luxury and adventure.

Ford Motors India

Ford Motors India is a wholly owned subsidiary of Ford Motor Corporation of the USA. It had first launched the Ford Escort—one of its well-known international car brands which is no longer offered in India due to poor sales. Next in line was the Ford Mondeo—a car that has been very successful in the European market in the past—which also had poor sales in India and hence withdrawn.

From these two failures, Ford Motors realized that none of its existing cars designed for the western markets—was suitable to Indian market conditions. Ford, the decided to create entirely new car models for the Indian market, and the Ford Ikon was born. The company's product line up in India today consists of four models, viz. the Ikon, the Fiesta, the Fusion and the Endeavor.

Variants and positioning

Ford Ikon

This car competes in the entry level sedan segment of the Indian car industry. Priced at around 5.4 lakhs, this car is well built, offers good quality, image and affordability.

Positioning: Initially, FordIkon used to focus on the contemporary style, features and performance. As the brand matured, the brand has started focusing more on the price of the car and needless to say the Ikon has cut its price in recent years.

Ford Fiesta

This is Ford's latest offering in the Indian car market. Fiesta is a car that exists as a hatchback in the European market but has been stretched to a 3-box form in India along with the usual "Indianization" that every car undergoes before it gets launched in India. The Fiesta is priced from 6.6 lakh to 8.2 lakh.

Positioning: To stand out from the clutter of launches in the car market in the "emerging" Indian marketplace, Ford appointed Abhishek Bacchan, a rising star in the movie industry, as their brand ambassador. Ford has positioned the car as one that is fun to be with and have used the "Go Fida" (*'fida'* is a Hindi term that means fanatically impressed) tagline to go with the advertising of the car.

Ford Fusion

Ford Fusion has a two box design that looks like a "fusion" of an SUV and a hatchback. Priced between 6.7 lakh and 8.5 lakh across the variants, the Fusion has been viewed as something that is too expensive to experiment and has therefore seen many price revisions in the recent past.

Positioning: Launched initially with the "Go anywhere" tagline to impress upon the prospective buyers the off-road abilities of the vehicle, the Fiesta now comes with a tagline that goes "the no-nonsense car", highlighting its unique features like high ground clearance.

Ford Endeavor

For an SUV that costs 'only' 15 lakh to 17 lakh the Endeavor is huge, spacious and commands on-road presence like no other passenger vehicle in the Indian market.

Positioning: The positioning of this brand has predominantly harped on its size and presence in addition to its off-road capabilities.

General Motors India Private Limited

General Motors entered Indian market in the post-liberalization time with its Opel and Daewoo brands of cars. The Opel Astra and the Daewoo Cielo were a welcome change in the Indian market and did reasonably well when they were launched. However, afterwards both Opel and Cielo were not doing well and hence withdrawn. Subsequently, the company launched Corsa and Vectra from the Opel marquee, but they were also discontinued like Astra and Cielo.

General Motors has now decided to bring in the Chevrolet brand name to India given its recognition and image. Four models now make up the GM's portfolio of passenger cars in India, viz. Aveo, Tavera, Optra and SR-V.

Variants and Positioning

Chevrolet Optra

This was the first car to be launched under the Chevrolet brand name in India. Priced between 9.2 lakh to 13.3 lakh, the Optra is priced slightly on the higher side but offers very many features.

Positioning: This has been positioned as a luxury car with premium quality and features of a high end car.

Chevrolet Tavera

The Tavera is known as the Isuzu panther in some of the markets where it is sold. Priced between 7.1 lakh to 10.2 lakh, this vehicle has seen some success.

Positioning: GM is targeting this car at the typical Indian Joint family and showcased the safety, space and comfort features of the vehicle as its unique selling proposition.

Chevrolet Aveo

This is a car that has been designed specifically for the Indian market for a price of 6.8 lakh to 7.7 lakh. Chevrolet Aveo offers a good looking, spacious car.

Positioning: Saif Ali Khan and Rani Mukherjee are the brand ambassadors for this car that goes with the tagline "Now, that's performance" meaning that the performance of the car is what GM intends will make it and its selling proposition.

Chevrolet SR-V

This is GM's latest offering in the Indian market. Priced between Rs 8–9 lakh. This car model is targeted at high income individuals who are looking for a good car that is spacious and luxurious.

Positioning: GM has highlighted the various features as well as its style.

Skoda Auto India

Skoda Auto is the World's premium luxury car maker, entered Indian market in November 2001. Skoda Auto India until now has introduced 12 luxury models including the flagship model Skoda Superb and the recent Skoda Laura, in India.

Models

SkodaSuperb

- Flagship model, perfect blend of unique design, lavish luxury, great performance and uncompromised safety.

SkodaLaura

- Based on A5 platform, loaded with cutting edge technology.
- Most modern and dynamic design, specially customized and tested under Indian conditions.

SkodaOctavia

- **SkodaL&K**—Top of line most luxurious model.
- **SkodaRS**—4 door sports luxury car for dynamic lifestyle.
- **SkodaOctavia Elegance**—Diesel model.
- **SkodaOctavia Rider—**Most powerful engine demonstrating technological and design expertise.

Toyota Kirloskar Motor Private Limited (TKM)

Toyota Kirloskar Motor Private Limited (TKM) was incorporated as a joint venture between Toyota Motor Corporation, Japan and the Kirloskar Group, India in October 1997. TKM plant is located near Bangalore in Karnataka, where it manufactures the Innova and the Corolla.

TKM has also launched its premium luxury Sedan—**Camry** and the premium SUV—the **Land Cruiser Prado** to cater top end customers.

Positioning of Different Models

Toyota Corolla

- **Features:** Powerful engine, automatic climatic control AC and luxurious interiors.
- Corolla dominates the premium mid-size car segment in India commanding over 27 per cent of the market share.
- **Selling proposition: "World's no.1 best seller"**.
- **Target customers:** Corporate senior and middle level executives.

Toyota Camry

- The car is equipped with Vehicle Stability Control, front and side curtain airbags, ABS, cruise control.
- Premium luxury segment car.
- Developed with a theme of "creating a new standard for premium luxury".

Toyota Innova

- Innova is India's first 3-row seating passenger car.
- Addresses the contrasting needs of customers offering space with style, sophistication with reliability, elegance with sturdiness in one car.
- Available in 5 variants.
- **Target customers:** The new 8 seater version in V Grade is primarily aimed at families who prefer closeness to exclusivity. Tourist taxi operators have also been given a choice, with a new 7-seater version being introduced in the E grade.
- **Brand ambassador:** "Aamir Khan".

Daimler Chrysler India Pvt Ltd

Mercedes-Benz India Ltd was formed in 1995, as a 51:49 joint venture between the erstwhile Daimler Benz and Telco. In 2001, DaimlerChrysler took over 100 per cent ownership and the company was re-named DaimlerChrysler India Private Ltd, a fully owned subsidiary. The company has its assembly facility in Pune, Maharashtra.

Models

The company started with one model—the Mercedes E Class—in 1995. Over the past 7–8 years, it has introduced most of the global range of products in India. While the E, C & S Class passenger cars are assembled in India, other models are imported as completely built units (CBUs) and retailed in India. DaimlerChrysler India has maintained a constant thrust on the quality of its products and customer service.

Positioning: The company caters to the elite layer of customers who are typically widely traveled and have high expectations. Hence it has focused on bringing out products that incorporate the latest technology, with best in class performance and safety features.

FUTURE TRENDS

- Tata's plan to launch a passenger car at a price of Rs 1 lakh will be the major driver of growth in the mini segment. Also, the abolition of special excise duty (SED) of 8 per cent on small cars will help the manufacturers to price their models lower, leading to growth in the segment. A large part of the demand for the mini segment will come from two-wheeler customers upgrading to passenger cars, mostly in the semi-urban and rural areas.
- The **compact segment** is also expected to make a significant contribution to the growth of passenger cars sales in the near future, driven by new entrants and price cuts. The success of Maruti Swift has led to the emergence of a new compact plus segment, priced between mid-size and compact cars. These cars offer greater space than the compact segment models. The possible launch of more models in this segment is likely to drive growth in the compact segment.
- The **mid-size segment** is likely to grow in future, driven by current compact car owners upgrading to mid-sized models. The lowering of prices, launch of new models such as Ford Fiesta, General Motors Aveo, and Hyundai Verna and the expected launch of new models such as Renault Logan, Skoda Fabia will also boost the purchase of mid-sized cars, making it the second-largest segment.
- **Higher price segments**, namely the executive, premium, and luxury segments, are expected to grow at a fast pace (although on

a small base), driven by the availability of internationally renowned brands, better highways and the perceived prestige attached to bigger cars.

- **Exports** are likely to grow, driven by the compact segment which, with a share of around 60 per cent in total domestic car sales, has the advantage of cost-competitiveness. Today, most foreign markets favour small cars because of relatively high fuel efficiency and easy manoeuvrability. With high domestic sales of compact cars and low-cost skilled labour, India is a cost-competitive manufacturing base for these models. As a result, compact cars made in India are increasingly being exported to countries in Europe, South America, South Asia and South Africa, with Hyundai Santro Xing, Maruti Alto and Tata Indica topping the list.
- Comparatively higher price of petrol vis a vis diesel will boost the share of diesel cars models, and hence more diesel car models are likely to be offered in future. Players such as Maruti, Hyundai, General Motors, Volkswagen and Renault are likely to launch diesel cars in the mainstream car segments (compact and mid-sized) Also, the launch of diesel models based on well-accepted technologies like CRDi will improve the perception of customers towards owning a diesel car.
- Given that the regulations governing vehicular emissions are becoming increasingly stringent, automobile manufacturers are experimenting with alternative fuels such as CNG and LPG (CNG has the lowest toxic gas emission levels). Several automobile manufacturers such as Fiat India, Hindustan Motors and Tata Motors, have begun manufacturing cars operating on CNG and LPG and this trend is going to pick up in the near future.
- Share of hybrid vehicle which runs on two sources of power such as gasoline engine and battery-powered electric motor and is estimated to be 1.5–2.0 times fuel efficient than normal petrol cars, is going to increase in near future due to firming up of fuel prices as well as strict environmental norms.

CHAPTER 33

Marketing Challenges

This chapter highlights some of the emerging marketing challenges that marketers will face in the not too distant future and shall discuss the implications of many newer developments, brand building excercise and rural marketing in India.

Marketing in India has been quite different from its practice in the more developed countries. At one time the market was largely dominated by few large players. The market place used to contain a large number of small entrepreneurs and local *kirana* stores. However, all of that is changing at a rapid pace. This change is going to be more in the case of trade channels in the metropolis or urban areas. Some companies are even strategezing on the possibilities of having shopping malls even in semi-urban areas. For example, Reliance is all set to take the concept of hypermarkets to smaller towns.

Such a sharp change in the distribution system is going to affect the entire value chain at various levels. It is very important for companies to identify how the evolving market changes affect them and how they should prepare themselves to adapt to the imminent change. The main impact of this emerging market structure will be in the following areas:

- Sourcing
- Warehousing and supply-chain
- Packaging, promotion schemes, etc.

Let us examine how these will get affected.

Sourcing of agricultural raw materials: More than 60 per cent of Indians directly or indirectly depend on agriculture or agricultural related activities as a means of their livelihood. The sharpest impact would therefore be visible in this area. As of now, farmers realize less than 30 per cent of the value of their products. Most procurement happens through middlemen, to whom the farmers bring their produce and once having come to the *mandi*, the farmers have no choices but to sell on the spot. Many a time they do not realise a commensurate price, which is otherwise known as distress selling.

While initiatives such as institutionalizing commodity exchanges are already on, the groundwork and awareness is, to a large extent, due to initiatives such as *e-chaupal*. Thanks to such initiatives, farmers are aware of the market prices of the commodities and therefore can bargain for better prices for their produce. As a matter of fact, weekly *haats* can be better utilised to serve as venues for creating awareness amongst farmers, educating them about crop rotation, hybrid seeds, etc. and at the same time selling of branded products.

The biggest advantage that changes in retailing formats will bring to this segment of the market will be by cutting down unnecessary cost and even eliminating middlemen. This way both the farmers and the companies gain by getting a larger share in the value pie. Different companies have adopted varied approaches to deal with this. ITC Foods, for instance, has formalized the role of middlemen by bringing them under its fold. Reliance, on the other hand, has planned to eliminate them altogether by setting up their own procurement centres where farmers can directly sell their crops.

Efficiency in the supply chain: Warehousing in India is another area that will be strongly affected by the newer formats of retailing. Currently, losses in transportation, especially of perishables, are as high as 40 per cent. This is quite a gigantic figure compared to the advanced economics. Most of this loss arise because the number of warehouses is less than needed, lack of sufficient cold storage facility and absence of refrigerated logistic support. Modern retailing format requires-efficiency in logistics to be also cost effective. They would therefore need to invest heavily in these areas. As a matter of fact, outsourcing ventures in these areas, like providing refrigerated trucks for transportation, collection and sorting centres have already started to come up and marketers for these service companies need to educate the old hands about the advantages of procuring their services.

Packaging: While these changes are taking place in the background, more pressing challenges will arise that marketers need to confront. Shopping malls and hypermarkets store provide higher visibility to products and spur considerable degree of impulse shopping. While that may sound as good news, it also implies that packaging will have to be addressed more closely. So far, packaging in India was essentially seen as something purely functional but now good marketers can use creative and catchy packages that can attract customer attention while walking down the aisle. Also, packaging can be used to communicate the value proposition of the product or even to educate customers about the product. A very good example of this can be seen in the case of MTR Foods. MTR has hired specialists to redesign a new catchy cover pack for its products that on the back prints useful information on common queries that users generally have.

Coverage of super markets: Another major deviation the marketers will have to confront will be in the domain of delivery. So far the focus of marketers had been on penetration, reach and availability. These three terms summarized in totality what distribution meant to the marketers. With supermarkets and malls coming up, companies now do not have to worry about the last mile and incremental cost of covering one more outlet. However, now it would be mandatory for them to be present in each and every hypermarket.

Power equation between marketer and modern stores retail: Another facet of the same experience is going to be the change in the supplier-retailer power equation. Currently, owing to small size of retailers, large suppliers were able to push through their products at reasonably low margins. However, with hypermarkets coming up, which will have much larger offtakes and centralized procurement, an *a-la* Wal-Mart can happen in India as well. That is to say that suppliers will have to bid aggressively to ensure that leading chains carry their products. Also, they will need to give higher margins to the retailers, now that the latter would command higher power.

Creation of consumer pull: Again with availability out of the equation, sales would largely be determined by strength of respective brands and value for money they offer. This would mean higher advertisement expenses for all firms. Companies can and should venture into providing complementary services necessary with respective products that will help in effectively differentiating their offerings from that of their competitors.

NEW CHALLENGES AND BUILDING EXERCISES

The new challenges in the market will be of following nature:

Brand Identity: The Indian market is full of opportunities but at the same time fraught with many hurdles. Of late the basic characteristics of the market are in a rapid transformation. The products often cater to three distinct purposes like essential or necessity, comfort and luxury status. They meet the demands of the entire cross section of population. Price and elasticity of demand varies across products and consumers. Individual FMCG items are of small value although all FMCG products put together account for a significant part of the consumer's budget. The consumer in the not too distant future will spend little time on the purchase decision of first moving consumer products. Brand loyalties or recommendations of a reliable retailer/dealer drive purchase decisions and brand switching is often induced by heavy advertisement, recommendation of the retailer or word of mouth. All these factors together call for more efforts to create a brand identity before the consumers.

Shift from unorganised to organised retail: The emergence of various forms of modern trade, be it entry of Wal-Mart through the Bharti alliance, or Reliance retail etc. will infuse the retail space with the much awaited competition. Modern trade has finally taken off in this land of *kiranas*, informal markets and *haats*. Supermarkets, Hypermarkets, malls etc. are already seen in the urban landscape. The rural markets will also change when new shopping malls will replace the traditional *mandis*.

New formats of delivery: With the increased consuming power of the Indian middle class and also due to increase in the number of apartments and housing colonies, home delivery has assumed more importance. Moreover, due to time pressure people are no longer interested in shopping for low involvement everyday use products and would as well have them delivered at their doorstep. New delivery models need to be experimented with. For example, a home delivery chain may serve the purpose of a mall or warehouse in the outskirts of the city. In such a case product ordering can be placed through SMS or the net. The products will then be home delivered at regular intervals of time.

Total customisation: The consumer is today flooded with options. He has the liberty to select the product, the mode of payment and even the mode of delivery all leveraging on the use of IT and the internet. Technology has revolutionised the market place taking competition to new heights. It will be a great mystery how to meet the individual taste and preference of a market as diverse as India.

Challenges in new product launch: New products require a large amount of investment in the areas of product development, marketing research, test marketing and national launch. Creating awareness and developing franchises for a new brand requires enormous initial expenditure on launch advertisements, free samples and product promotions. Still a marketer is never sure about success in India!

Media Challenge: The challenge associated with the launch and/sub-sequent brand-building initiatives is due to existence of a very broad range of mass media options. TV reaches 90 per cent of urban consumers and 35 per cent of rural consumers. Alternatives like wall paintings, theatres, video vehicles, special consumer promotions become expensive but they must be carefully chosen to make any new product launch successful.

Distribution challenge: India has six million retail outlets, of which two million are located in 5,160 towns and four million in 627,000 villages. Supermarkets are gradually coming up in India. This makes logistics planning, particularly for new players, extremely difficult. It also makes new product launches difficult since retailers are reluctant to allocate space and resources to new or slow moving products. Critical factors for success are the ability to build, develop, and maintain a robust distribution network.

Challenge of players from the unorganized sector: Factors that enable small, unorganized players with local presence to flourish include the following:

- Basic technology for most consumer products is fairly simple and easily available.

- The small-scale sector in India still enjoys exemption or lower rates of tax, etc. This makes them more price competitive vis-à-vis the organized players.
- A highly scattered market and inadequate transport infrastructure limits the ability of MNCs and national players to reach out to remote areas in small towns and villages.
- Low brand awareness enables local players to market their spurious look-alike brands.
- Lower overheads due to limited geographical boundaries, family management, focused product lines and minimal expenditure on advertising or promotion.

RURAL MARKETING OPPORTUNITIES

"There are a lot more poor people in the world than rich people. To be a global company and to have a global market share, you have to penetrate into the rural segment."

—Keki Dadiseth, Former Chairman, HUL

Gone are the days when a rural consumer went to a nearby city to buy branded FMCG or durables. That was in an era when only a select portion of rural households consumed branded goods, be it tea or toilet soaps. In those days only a handful of large companies flocked to rural markets to establish their brands. Today, rural markets are critical for every marketer—be it for branded toiletry or a two-wheeler. There was a time when marketers thought van operations, cinema commercials and a few wall paintings would suffice to entice rural folks to their folds. Thanks to television, today a customer in a rural area is for more aware about myriad products and specific brands in the market place. In the 21st century an Indian farmer going through his daily chores wearing jeans may sound absurd. It is now a reality for Arvind Mills, though. When it launched the Ruf & Tuf brand of jeans, it created quite a sensation among the rural folk within a few months of their launch.

Trends indicate that the rural markets are coming up in a big way and growing twice as fast as the urban, witnessing a rise in sales of hitherto known as typical urban gadgets like refrigerators, music systems and mobile phones. Studies on ownership of durable goods indicates the same trend. Marketers have to depend on rural India for products like—transistors, wristwatch, two wheelers and TVs for volume growth. Even in lifestyle products, rural India is assuming a significant mass for many marketers.

According to a National Council for Applied Economic Research (NCAER) study, there are as many 'middle income and above' households in the rural areas as there are in the urban India. There are almost twice as many 'lower middle income' households in rural areas as in the urban areas. At the highest income level, there are 1.6 million households in rural areas. As per NCAER projections, the absolute size of rural India is expected to be double that of urban India.

Marketing experiences have echoed that a sound network and a thorough understanding of the village psyche are necessary for making inroads into rural markets.

What is Rural?

As such, there is no uniform definition of the rural market. Indian **Census** has defined rural by multiple criterion, density of population, infrastructure condition, occupation such as, 75 per cent of male population engaged in agricultural activity. The Industry definition is in terms of population size for different class of products. For example,

- FMCG: A market is refered as rural if population is less than 20,000.
- Durables: A market is called rural, where population < 50,000.
- HUL: A market is called rural.

Other generally accepted characteristics of rural markets are:

- Low income; largely non-salaried people or irregular flow of income.
- Low awareness level
- Low literacy
- Poor infrastructure—roads, electricity, telecommunications facility
- Greater sense of community
- Influenced by opinion leaders
- Low media reach
- Large sized dwelling

Some Myths about Rural Marketing

There are certain myths prevalent with respect to this class of consumers. Let us discuss some of them.

Myth 1: Rural is one homogeneous mass: Rural households are classified into four main categories: R1, R2, R3 and R4. This is done based on two parameters—the education of the chief wage earner, and the type of house, *pucca*, *semi-pucca* and *kutcha*. Within the rural segment, there are large differences between these classifications. R1 is the most upmarket rural consumer, with 95 per cent of these homes having electricity. With respect to other facilities like TV, cooler, fridge, etc., their penetration in R1 in quite high. Thus, it is inappropriate to consider the entire mass as homogeneous.

Myth 2: Companies/brands can thrive on urban markets in India: One out of every 7 people in the world is from rural India. The rural market is bigger than the urban market for many product categories.

The estimated annual size of the rural market for certain categories is shown below.

• FMCG	Rs 65,000 crore
• Durables	Rs 5,000 crore
• Agri-inputs (incl. tractors)	Rs 45,000 crore
• 2/4 wheelers	Rs 8,000 crore
• Total	Rs 1,23,000 crore

In general, there are low penetration rates in rural (per 1000 households), and saturation in the urban sector. As a result of this, FMCG companies are turning to the rural segment for growth. Some of the indications that the rural market has finally arrived are:

- In 2001–02, LIC sold 55 per cent of its policies in rural India.
- 50 per cent of BSNL mobile connections in small towns/villages.
- 43 million Kisan Credit Cards (KCC) issued (against 32 million credit plus-debit cards in urban) resulting in tremendous liquidity.

Myth 3: Rural India—a black hole for communication: Media exposure levels in the rural segment are quite high for the more upmarket consumers. For R1, 50 per cent of all viewers are exposed to the press at least once a week, and 75 per cent to TV at least once a week. 70 per cent of R1, R2 and R3 can be reached through mass media, with improving infrastructure. A *"Haat"*, the formal weekly market, 80–90 per cent of consumers can be reached.

Myth 4: Rural GDP is all about agriculture: The sectoral break up of agriculture, industry and services in the rural India shows that services are gaining more importance, though most of such services are related to agriculture. This changes the mindset with which marketers approach this segment.

Myth 5: Rural disposable income is a function of the monsoon and not growing: There has been a growth in the rural disposable incomes despite monsoons failing in recent years. How did this growth take place if agriculture is fully dependent on the monsoons? There are two main reasons for this:

1. **Increase in area under irrigation:** The percentage coverage of the area under irrigation has improved from 27 per cent to 43 per cent over 3 decades, which has been mostly responsible for the independence from the monsoons.
2. **Decreased contribution of agriculture to rural income:** This is now only 50 per cent. The remaining 50 per cent income comes from non-farming activities.
3. **Yield and production up by 50 per cent:** This is as compared to 15 years ago.

Thus, agriculture has become more resilient than before. As more stability in incomes sets in, the propensity to spend would increase dramatically. An NCAER projection shows how the segmentation within this category is going to change, with people moving rapidly to occupy the higher levels. Thus, rural market is definitely seeing growth.

Myth 6: Reach and only reach is the key: The general feeling among marketers is usually that, for a rural market the challenge lies only in getting into the rural market. Once you are there, it is good enough, since there is less competition and people are not that discerning. However, this perception is fast eroding. The reality is just the opposite. There is now severe competition even in this arena. The distribution of population and incomes is skewed, hence 17 per cent of villages actually have 50 per cent of rural population and wealth, and witness significant competition. Typically rural consumers are today more brand loyal and understand symbols better. This also makes it easy to sell look-alikes. The rural audience has matured enough to understand the communication developed for the urban markets, especially with reference to FMCG products. Television has been a major effective communication media for the rural masses, and as a result, companies are gradually adapting their communication to rural phyche and taste. Advertisements touching from the emotions of the rural folk, it is argued, could drive a quantum jump in sales.

Myth 7: Urban trickle down effect works in rural: There is a need to differentiate brand according to regional disparities, and especially from the rural mindset. The differentiation may necessarily begin in terms of the product content. It may also be in terms of packaging, communication or association with the brand. In general, the brand has to be made relevant by understanding rural consumers needs. Even offering the same product in different regions with different brand names could be adopted as a strategy. At times it is difficult to pass on an innovation over an existing product to the rural consumer, unlike his urban counterpart—like increased calcium or herbal content or a germ-control formula in case of toothpaste.

Rural marketing requires proper adaptation of every element of marketing (that of product, pricing, packaging, advertising, and media) planning to focus on the rural customers as their target. And, this becomes only possible when a marketer views a rural market as a separate entity. The urban-like village dweller should be seen as an urbanised person from the districts. The village then becomes a location or a suburb of a district. And the district becomes the basic geographical entity. Since the urban-like populations in the villages are taken as a part of the district, they will represent the dominant part of the market in most of the districts. This will compel the kind of attention that it deserves. A district perspective removes the complexities, heterogeneity, access and targetability that have hindered rural marketing initiatives.

The Coke Ad with Aamir Khan was especially successful since it was targeted at the rural consumer, hence it was actually able to get the message across. Rural consumers view everything from a completely different perspective and marketers need to realize this fact.

Consumer Insights

Marketing research on rural India has shown several unique consumer insights in this regard which are briefly discussed below.

Keep communication simple: To quote statements of some typical villagers. I am eager to learn, but I can do so only if you talk my language and signage.

- It is *great fun* to watch TV, but I cannot understand and relate to it.
- I am *willing to listen* and change, only if you interact and engage with me.
- I am simple—I take things literally especially when it comes to advertisement.
- I cannot read or write, but I can understand *symbols, colours and images*.
- *Talk to me in my language*, in a simple way, that is what I understand.

Thus, rural communication must reach a typical consumer's level of literacy and awareness.

Familiarity breeds comfort: Only if it is familiar, rural market will then trust it. Supporting insights are:

- I have faith in the familiar, *i.e.* brands I have used.
- I am satisfied with my familiar things, so why should I change?
- I am averse to taking risks, particularly if it is new and unfamiliar.
- Security gives me comfort; and familiar things make me feel secure.
- Repetition makes it familiar, so I feel reassured.

Thus, the **propensity to try new things is relatively low**.

Luxuries@ Rs 5: *Jo chahoon woh paoon, lakin panch rupai mei.* (Get whatever you like, but it must priced less than Rs 5)

Supporting insights are:

- I buy low cost products because it fits into my budget, as they give the value I am seeking.
- At any time I have limited amount to spend but I need to buy a number of things, so LUPs (lowest unit prices), are important.
- Rs 5—my laxman rekha—I do not have more than that to spend.
- Rs 5 and Rs 10 are magical price points in rural areas.

Show genuine value–will pay for it: Rural market will pay more only if you show them that they will get commensurate value out of it. Supporting insights are:

- If I see and feel the difference—only then will I believe and act.

- Show me the value—Quality; only then only I buy.
- If I can sense the difference. I do not mind paying a little extra for it.
- If I can not see the difference, I can use the cheaper one.
- Price is important; yet it should meet my expectations.
- Packaging and brand experience are the key.

Haat—meri duniyan: Haats are rural people's window to the world—where they experience new things. Supporting insights are:

- Haat is my outing. I am looking to explore.
- Haat gives me an opportunity to buy products that I wish to buy.
- Haats are a festive outing and lots of fun—where I get to see new things.
- I regularly visit a Haat and where I am open to change.

Thus, keeping in mind some of above consumer insights about the rural markets in India, marketers must take initiatives and evolve strategies for their rural marketing operations.

RURAL MARKETING CHALLENGES

Though the opportunities in rural markets are huge, there are many unresolved issues. One major limitation here is that of micro size—most FMCG players just do not have the critical mass for going all out for rural marketing. That is why most FMCG players are trying to concentrate both on rural and urban marketing. They focus on urban markets for value and focus on rural markets for volumes.

A few *generic* strategies, given the changing dynamics, are:

- Keep a tab on the ever changing realities of the market. The product offerings must match the needs of the market rather than the missions of the marketer. There is going to be a paradigm shift in the retail model once the giant retailers establish their foothold in rural India. Leveraging on their large size they will dictate terms.
- Reducing product costs by streamlining distribution. Organised retail chains have set up systems for inventory management and quick servicing, thereby offering the opportunity for a company/supplier to reduce distribution cost by reducing intermediaries like wholesalers/distributors and supplying directly to the warehouse of a retail chain. Can this business model be implemented in rural areas?
- Understand the new formats and technologies and how they are shaping businesses. The e-chaupal model triggered a small revolution. IT can similarly be leveraged to gain better access to the rural market. Use of technology can bring far reaching changes in the marketplace.
- Improve quality standards. Very soon the consumer will demand higher quality and they will be willing to pay higher prices. The rural consumer is here to stay and his specific aspirations must be met.

Epilogue

India has come a long way from protectionism to a free market. The Indian economy which was heavily protected from global competition is of late experiencing the pressures of a free market. It is witnessing fundamental shifts. The days when the central government used to decide what is good for its citizen are gone. Today in most products customer decides what to buy. Increasingly the customer is getting more choice, better service and convenience, high quality and safe products, and more value for money. Marketers have realized that they have to remain consumer focussed if they want to survive. Thus, marketers are increasingly realizing that the old marketing concepts shall no longer serve their purpose.

CHANGING ENVIRONMENT AND ASPIRATIONS

In the current market scenario the market is offering immense new opportunities and is changing its form rapidly. Marketing is passing through a turbulent phase, where newer concepts and marketing practices are continually evolving. Thus marketers are adopting different principles to remain customer friendly or market focused. They are trying to team up with their supply chain as well as trading partners. All marketing actions are geared towards serving the customers better, faster and at lower cost.

The marketer is giving more attention to the consumer by providing value for money. These forms of increasing attention to the customer are known as Efficient Customer Response (ECR). Let us see how a typical marketer tries to implement the ECR system.

Changes in the Form of Marketing

For a very long time, McCarthy's 4Ps of marketing and the principle of Segmenting, Targeting and Positioning (STP) were dominant. But in the current scenario, the whole marketing form is undergoing a metamorphosis. Marketers are increasingly giving more and more importance to the customer by offering him some distinct value. Marketing is changing its face from segment-based marketing to relationship marketing to one-to-one marketing.

EP.1

Marketing Metamorphosis

1. **Segmentation:** The Indian market is well known for its diversity. A marketer necessarily tries to partition the market in terms of segments. The rationale behind this is that a company cannot serve all customers in the market as the customers are too numerous and diverse in their buying nature. Thus, it becomes inevitable for a company to choose its market segments that it can serve most effectively. Thus after segmenting the market, a marketer invariably targets at specific market segments and develops products and marketing programs tailored to such segments.

2. **Deliver potential product by offering superior customer value:** Marketers have realized the true value of the principles of STP and 4Ps of marketing. Now, it has become imperative for them to provide some extra value to the customer to influence his/her needs ultimately and convert them into effective demand. Marketers have realized that while meeting the aspiration of the customer, it is most vital to keep price in mind. Thus, the basic product offering will have to be augmented with more new features and functions and ultimately the horizon for the

EP.2

Gradual Expansion in the Product Offering

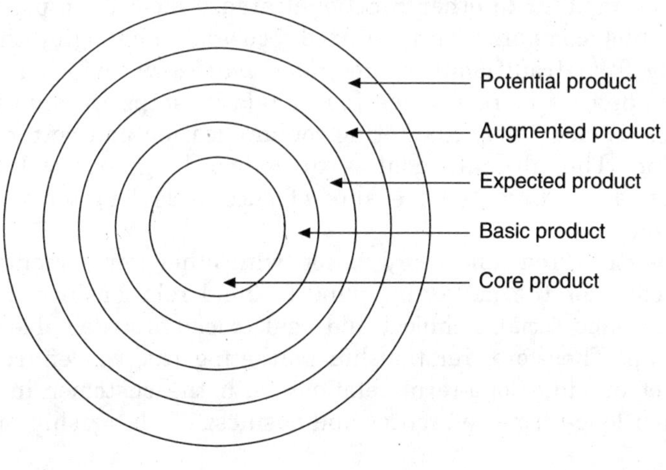

potential product will increasingly widen and the marketer will try to elevate its customer to the highest level and remain competitive in the marketplace. For instance, we may cite the case of a car where all marketers are trying to offer superior design and features. The same story is repeated when we look at any mobile telephone set or any fast moving consumer goods like soap or toiletry.

3. **Relationship marketing:** Alvin Toffler has written in his book *Power Shift:*

EP.3

Long-Term Relationships

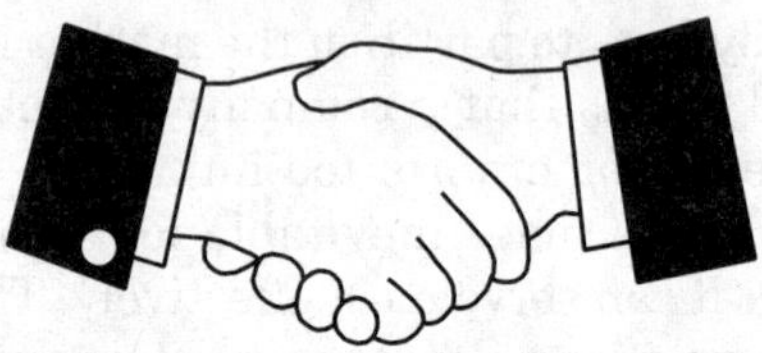

> *"No one buys a share of Apple Computer or IBM stock because of the firm's material assets. What counts are not the company's buildings or machines, but the contacts (relationships) and power of its marketing and sales force, the organizational capacity of its management..."*

This point is amply reinforced by the acquisition or merger of existing companies. In brands these cases marketers spent billions of $ to get access to a market and for a set of relationships and the anticipated support such relationships would provide.

In recent years companies have put their concerted efforts into increasing production, marketing efficiencies mainly through re-engineering and TQM applications to achieve the benefit of economics of scale. On the other hand, if marketing remains "ill-focused and over-indulged" compared to other functional areas, such a company cannot survive. Thus, companies have started focusing on changing the face of marketing from traditional to *integrated marketing*, which is a cross-functional process of re-engineering of relationships through focus on core competencies, lively marketing communication and better forms of networking. The ultimate goal is to deliver long-term value to the customers, and where the measure of success is long-term customer satisfaction.

Cooperation from and coordination with other departments is very much needed for the marketing wing to build relationships at various levels—economic, social, technical, and legal, to lead to sustainable customer relationship. Therefore, relationship marketing can be defined as "the practice of building long-term relations with the customer in order to retain their long-term preferences and business". Relationship marketing results in strong economic and social ties mutually beneficial to both parties, i.e. the marketer and the customer. It cuts down on transaction costs and time. The new focus of attention are shown in EP.4.

EP.4

Changed Focus of Attention

Area	Traditional marketing	Relationship marketing
Segmentation	Demographic	Behavioural
Advertising	Push	Pull
Promotions	Mass	Tailored
Pricing	Set by firm	Set by customers
Sales management	Data from sales	Marketing effort-value and market share
Distribution	Intermediaries	Complimentary
Channel	Constrained	Multi-channel marketing
New product	Share, profit	Expansion
Launch		New metrics

4. **One-on-one marketing:** Because of continuous fragmentation and consolidation of the marketplace it is difficult to sustain relationship marketing and ultimately it will give way to one-on-one marketing. Generally comparative advantage generated by relationship marketing are likely to be soon emulated by the competitors because of easy access to technology and widespread availability of information.

The companies will then have to focus on establishing deeper relationships with the individual customer on a more personal level. Thus, most of the companies will try to build "partnership" in the customer-relationship continuum. At present, relationships of different companies with their customers differ from one company to another. The levels are shown in EP.5.

EP.5

Customer-Relationship Continuum

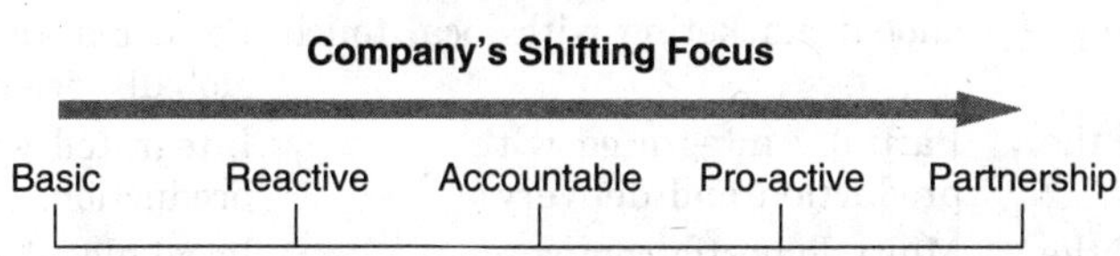

Basic: Once the company sells the product, it does not follow-up in any way.

Reactive: The salesman sells the product and tries to encourage customers call on whenever problems are encountered.

Accountable: The marketer checks with the customers to know whether the product is meeting the customer's expectations and tries to improve the company's offering.

Pro-active: Here the companies regularly check with their customers in search of suitable suggestions to improve the product use or to incorporate them in their new products.

Partnership: The company works continuously with customers to discover ways to deliver better value.

Obviously, a company's one-on-one relationship marketing strategy will depend on how many customers it has and their profitability.

EP.6 shows different focus elements under relationship & one-to-one marketing.

EP.6

Different Approaches under Relationship & One-to-One Marketing

Criteria	Relationship marketing	One-to-one marketing
Orientation	Customer and competition oriented	Individual customer orientation
Product	Value added and customized product/service with price premium	Highest level of variety and keep lost/price relatively low
Knowledge of the customer	Economies of scope	Mass customization
Competition	Comprehensive knowledge to get other products/service of the company sold to the customer	Collect information on future nature of competition
Nature of competition	Ologopolistic competition and niche market	High-tech competition
Features	Customized service	Customization of product plus service
Pricing	Premium price based on special services offered	Assess what the customer could bear
Advertising and promotion	Database marketing communication	Interactive dialogue
Scope of the market	Global marketing with local touch	Local marketing globally oriented
Nature of the marketing	Partially integrated with production and delivery	Integrated with design production, delivery
Nature of the company	Multi-domestic company	Local-global company

Currently the Indian market is undergoing sea change. Marketing function is passing through a turbulent phase, where it is offering both opportunities and challenges. Thus, marketers must adapt respective strategies to retain their customers and remain market focussed.

The changes are taking place in different directions. Interestingly all these transformations are focussed towards the customer. The marketers are trying to give maximum possible attention to the customer and providing the customer highest value for money.

There are several reasons for this transformation. For instance. Indian market is no longer deprived of choice: we are experiencing many changes in the marketing environment. Customer's perception of a product was earlier that of just a commodity, but now the perception is changing with more options, competitive environment, and ever increasing customer demand.

The expectations of customers are increasing, they are asking for superior quality, better service and more value for the same price, and whosoever could provide him increasing value for money, the marketer will be more successful. With increasing access to technological advances, companies shall regularly come up with new or superior products.

As Indian customers are becoming more discerning and they are increasingly looking for a complete product, which calls for superior product management.

Index